Book 1

W9-BTR-573

PhonicsWorks™
Lesson Guide Basic

K12

Book Staff and Contributors

Kristen Kinney   *Senior Content Specialist*
Lenna King, Amy Rauen   *Instructional Designers*
Mary Beck Desmond   *Senior Text Editor*
Jill Tunick   *Text Editor*
Suzanne Montazer   *Creative Director, Print and ePublishing*
Sasha Blanton   *Senior Print Visual Designer*
David Batchelor, Carol Leigh   *Print Visual Designers*
Kim Barcas, Stephanie Williams   *Cover Designers*
Amy Eward   *Senior Manager, Writers*
Susan Raley   *Manager, Editors*
Deanna Lacek   *Project Manager*

Maria Szalay   *Senior Vice President for Product Development*
John Holdren   *Senior Vice President for Content and Curriculum*
David Pelizzari   *Vice President, Content and Curriculum*
Kim Barcas   *Vice President, Creative*
Laura Seuschek   *Vice President, Instructional Design and Evaluation & Research*
Aaron Hall   *Vice President, Program Management*

Lisa Dimaio Iekel   *Production Manager*
John Agnone   *Director of Publications*

Credits

About K12 Inc.

K12 Inc. (NYSE: LRN) drives innovation and advances the quality of education by delivering state-of-the-art digital learning platforms and technology to students and school districts around the world. K12 is a company of educators offering its online and blended curriculum to charter schools, public school districts, private schools, and directly to families. More information can be found at K12.com.

978-1-60153-126-1
Printed by Walsworth, Marceline, MO, USA, July 2020.

Contents

Sounds /ĭ/, /ŭ/, /ch/, and /y/

Sounds /sh/, /aw/, & /kw/ and Syllables

Sounds /oi/, /ū/, & /ks/ and Sound Practice

Sounds Long Double o & /ow/ and Sound Practice

Sounds for Letters *a, m, s, t, b, f, c, h,* and *j*

Sounds for *l, n, p,* & *r,* Sound Review, and Vowels

Sounds for *o, d, g, k,* and *v*

Getting Stronger: Sounds /ă/ and /ŏ/

Sounds for Letters *i*, *qu*, and *z*

Getting Stronger: Sounds /ă/, /ĭ/, and /ŏ/

Sounds for Letters *u*, *w*, and *x*

Sounds /ă/, /ĭ/, /ŏ/, and /ŭ/

Sounds for Letters *e* and *y*

Getting Stronger: Sounds /ă/, /ĕ/, /ĭ/, /ŏ/, and /ŭ/

Introduction

This book provides the following information for K[12] PhonicsWorks:

- ▶ About K[12] PhonicsWorks
- ▶ Lesson Guide
- ▶ Activity Book
- ▶ Assessments Book
- ▶ PhonicsWorks Readers
- ▶ PhonicsWorks Online

The Lesson Guide contains detailed lesson plans for each day and is organized by unit. The lesson plans are placed in the order in which you will use them. Activity Book and Unit Checkpoint Answer Keys are included for you in the lesson plans.

The Activity Book supplements the Lesson Guide and provides an opportunity for students to do some work on their own. While many of the Activity Book pages can be completed independently, we recommend that you provide instruction and guidance (for instance, reviewing the instructions and sample task together) as necessary.

Note that the pages in the Lesson Guide and the Activity Book are also available online in the Materials list. The online version will match the book version unless it has an "update" label.

K¹² PhonicsWorks™ Program Overview

Reading is the most important skill for success in school and society.
— SUSAN L. HALL AND LOUISA C. MOATS, *STRAIGHT TALK ABOUT READING*

Introduction

You *can* teach your child to read!

The K¹² PhonicsWorks™ program is based on the best current research and years of firsthand experience. K¹²'s approach is—

- Explicit; lessons directly address relationships between sounds and letters.
- Systematic; lessons build logically, sequentially, and step by step.
- Multisensory; lessons engage students in a variety of visual, auditory, and tactile activities.

The PhonicsWorks program is organized into two parts—Basic and Advanced—typically completed over the course of two grades. When combined with instruction in literature (such as K¹² Language Arts Literature and Comprehension program for Kindergarten and K¹² Language Arts program for Grade 1), PhonicsWorks offers a comprehensive and balanced approach to help students acquire the critical skills and knowledge required for reading and literacy.

General Objectives

PhonicsWorks is designed to help students achieve these important goals:

- Recognize the relationship between sounds and letters.
- Blend sounds represented by letters into words.
- Read and spell longer, unfamiliar words by breaking them into syllables.
- Read grade-level text with fluency (appropriate speed and accuracy).
- Read "sight words" (high-frequency words such as *said* or *was*; many of these words do not follow the patterns that have been taught).

Before You Begin

Before you get started, familiarize yourself with the PhonicsWorks program.

Standard Curriculum Materials (K¹² Supplied)

PhonicsWorks Basic includes the following materials:

- *K¹² PhonicsWorks* training video
- K¹² PhonicsWorks Basic Kit
- *K¹² PhonicsWorks Readers Basic*
- *K¹² PhonicsWorks Basic Lesson Guide Book 1* and *Book 2*
- *K¹² PhonicsWorks Basic Activity Book*
- *K¹² PhonicsWorks Basic Assessments Book 1* and *Book 2*
- Online activities

PhonicsWorks Advanced includes all of the materials in the Basic course, as well as an Advanced Tile Kit.

Additional Materials (Learning Coach Supplied)

You will need to have the following materials on hand, which are labeled "Also Needed" in offline and online Materials lists:

- 3½ x 5-inch index cards
- Index card file box
- Black, nontoxic marker
- Dictation notebook (either loose-leaf paper in a binder or a spiral-bound notebook)
- Pencils
- Folder with loose-leaf paper (for portfolio materials and notes on student progress)

Prepare in Advance

When it's time to begin instruction, you will be well prepared if you take the time to *watch the video, read the lesson plans, and practice using the Tile Kit.* The *K¹² PhonicsWorks* video introduces the PhonicsWorks program, shows you how to use the Tile Kit, and explains teaching procedures.

Sounds and Letters: Basics of Phonics

Printed words are made up of letters that represent sounds. When we read words, we turn the letters into their corresponding speech sounds.

Consider the word *cat*, which has three letters:

c a t

The word *cat* also has three speech sounds, or phonemes (FO-neemz), which are written as follows:

/k/ /ă/ /t/

You will notice that sounds are written within slashes that we call *sound boxes*. The *K¹² PhonicsWorks* video provides a guide to pronouncing basic phonemes in the English language.

Let's look at one more word. Consider the word *boat*, which has four letters:

b o a t

Although the word *boat* has four letters, it has only three sounds:

/b/ /ō/ /t/

Over the course of the PhonicsWorks program, students will learn the following relationships between sounds and letters:

- Some sounds are represented by only one letter. For example, the sound /m/, as in <u>m</u>ouse, is almost always spelled with the letter *m*.
- Some sounds are represented by a combination of letters. For example, the sound /ch/, as in <u>ch</u>ip, is almost always spelled with the letters *ch*.
- Some sounds can be spelled more than one way. For example, the sound /k/ can be spelled *c*, as in <u>c</u>at; *k*, as in <u>k</u>ite; or *ck*, as in chi<u>ck</u>. The long o sound, /ō/, can be spelled *o*, as in n<u>o</u>; *oa*, as in b<u>oa</u>t; *oe*, as in t<u>oe</u>; *ow*, as in sn<u>ow</u>; and *o-e*, as in h<u>ome</u>.

Course Instruction Guide

Number of Lessons

K¹² PhonicsWorks covers a total of 360 lessons: 180 in the Basic course and 180 in the Advanced course. Lessons are organized into groups of five lessons. Every fifth lesson presents online review activities and an assessment.

Lesson Time

These lesson times are estimates. You and students might take more or less time per lesson. Feel free to split the lessons into smaller segments and provide breaks for students as needed.

- ▶ **Basic:** 180 lessons; 30 minutes offline, 20 minutes online
- ▶ **Advanced:** 180 lessons; 30 minutes offline, 20 minutes online during the first semester and 20 minutes offline, 20 minutes online during the second semester.

Working Offline and Online

In the printed Lesson Guide, you will find step-by-step guidance for the offline portion of each lesson. These direct, explicit, and systematic lessons help students build a strong foundation of letter–sound knowledge. After the offline portion of the lesson is finished, students are ready to work independently online to reinforce, through engaging review and practice, the core lesson content. Some students may benefit from a short break between the offline and online portions of each lesson.

PhonicsWorks Basic Program: Lesson Guide Components

Unit Overview and Lesson Overview

Each new unit begins with a Unit Overview to help you understand the topics to be covered in the unit. A unit covers five days of instruction. Each day, the first page of the lesson plan indicates the materials; objectives; and any advance preparation, keywords, or Big Ideas you will need to be familiar with before you begin teaching.

Sight Words

Typically, students learn three new sight words every other week. Do not worry if students are unable to master all of the words for the week, because later lessons provide many opportunities to review them.

It is recommended that students work on no more than five sight words at a time. For example, if students master two of the three words for a given week, it is fine to add the third word to the following week's list, for a total of four words. However, if students are unable to master all three of the words, do not add all three to the following week's words.

Preparing sight word cards: You will need two sets of sight word cards to complete the Sight Words activities. One set of cards is supplied in your PhonicsWorks Kit. For the second set, you may either create your own using index cards or print a set from the online lesson and cut them into cards. If you create a set using index cards, you will need 3½ x 5-inch index cards and the list of words found in this section of the program overview. Use a bold black marker and print each word in neat, large, lowercase letters. Keep the two sets of cards somewhere convenient. As you work through the Phonics lessons, you will gradually add these cards to the file box (sight words box).

Here are the sight words in the Basic course:

- the, and, is
- on, to, in
- it, he, was
- says, have, with
- where, from, there
- that, of, put
- two, they, both
- you, went, we

- what, their, want
- said, your, so
- who, see, or
- for, she, her
- does, why, one
- were, my, are
- Mr., Mrs., Dr.

Get Ready

These activities help students review previously taught sounds and letters, and reinforce skills and concepts from earlier lessons.

Learn

In this section of the lesson, new concepts are introduced and practiced through a variety of multisensory activities, including the following:

- Listening to sounds in words
- Manipulating letter tiles
- Completing Activity Book pages with fun written activities
- Writing words and sentences that you dictate

In the first eight units, students practice phonological awareness. Phonological awareness is the ability to recognize and distinguish sounds of speech in language. We learn to speak before we learn to read; we learn to hear sounds before we learn which letters represent those sounds. Accordingly, in the first eight units of PhonicsWorks Basic, students focus on phonological awareness activities, distinguishing and manipulating sounds. Activities include Sound Chains; Finger Stretching; and Head, Waist, Toes.

Be patient. Do these activities thoroughly and well. Research has shown that explicit phonological awareness instruction leads to better reading.

Try It

This section of the lesson asks students to apply their new knowledge of a concept in a variety of ways. They may be asked to read from a PhonicsWorks Reader, write words or sentences in a Dictation activity, or complete an Activity Book page.

- **PhonicsWorks Readers:** The K[12] PhonicsWorks Readers are "decodable readers" with a carefully controlled vocabulary almost exclusively made up of letter–sound patterns and sight words students have already studied. Even though these stories are written in words students have studied, most beginning readers still need plenty of time to figure out the words. When students read the stories, you serve as a guide to help them when they have difficulty. The lessons offer detailed suggestions about how to help students read accurately and sound out challenging words.

Monitor progress: As students read, it is very important that you sit next to them and carefully observe their progress. Lesson plans provide instructions for taking notes while you listen to students read. These notes will help you decide which letters and sounds students still need to work on and which sight words are still difficult for them. You may want to keep a small notebook in which you can write the title of the reading assignment, the date, a list of skills students have mastered, and what they need to work on.

▶ **Dictation:** Early in the PhonicsWorks program, students will use letter tiles to create words dictated to them. As students' skills progress, students move to writing words and then sentences. It is important that you follow the instructions for Dictation as outlined in the Lesson Guide. Research indicates that these steps are the most effective for reinforcing students' letter–sound knowledge.

▶ **Activity Book Pages:** Students will complete two to four pages in each unit of PhonicsWorks. In most cases, after you have read the directions to students and observed them complete one or two examples, they may finish the page independently. Be sure to review students' completed work, making note of any letters and sounds they still need to work on and which sight words have yet to be mastered.

Online Overview

The last section of the Lesson Guide provides an overview of what students will accomplish during their online, independent review and practice of concepts taught to date. You may choose to sit with students during this time, but these activities were designed with plenty of audio and engaging animation to help them work independently.

Unit Checkpoint

Every fifth lesson in the PhonicsWorks program provides a Unit Checkpoint to help you determine how well students have learned the skills covered in the unit. On Unit Checkpoint days, students begin by spending time online completing review and practice activities. The activities provide a fun, interactive way to review concepts from the unit.

Unit Checkpoints and Answer Keys: You will find the Unit Checkpoint assessment pages in *K¹² PhonicsWorks Assessments.* You will find Answer Keys in the Lesson Guide. You can also print both the Unit Checkpoint pages and the Answer Key from the online lesson.

Please note: Throughout the PhonicsWorks program, the Lesson Guide for Unit Checkpoints contain test exercises that are not listed on students' Unit Checkpoint pages. This is not an error. The exercises printed only in the Lesson Guide are for you to assess students' listening skills. Please follow the directions and note students' verbal responses on the Unit Checkpoint page to use later when scoring the Checkpoint.

After you have scored the Unit Checkpoint, remember to ***return to the computer and enter the results***.

"Getting Stronger" Units

After the tenth unit of the Basic course, every other unit is called a "Getting Stronger" unit. These units are designed to strengthen students' skills through review and practice. If students are consistently scoring 100 percent on the Unit Checkpoints in prior units, you may choose to skip the Getting Stronger units. Before skipping the unit, have students take the Unit Checkpoint to make sure they have truly mastered the content. ***Please note: If you choose to skip these units, you will need to return to the computer and mark all the lessons in the unit as "completed."***

Should you skip ahead? Each student learns to read at his or her own pace. This variation is natural and is generally not a cause for concern. We have designed PhonicsWorks to meet the needs of a broad range of students, and we believe most students will benefit from working through all lessons in the program.

While some students might be able to skip some of the Getting Stronger lessons, most students will benefit from the review and practice. This practice helps ensure that they have thoroughly mastered early reading skills and that they are making progress toward achieving what cognitive psychologists call "automaticity." That is, they are on their way to becoming skilled readers who can automatically turn printed letters into their corresponding speech sounds without having to linger over individual letters and sounds. It's like reaching the point in math when students can quickly add and subtract mentally without having to count on their fingers, or in music when they can play "Twinkle, Twinkle, Little Star" on the piano without having to search for the notes.

Most students need repeated review and practice to achieve automaticity. When you come to the Getting Stronger lessons, however, you may feel that students have sufficiently mastered the skills taught in prior lessons. If they are consistently achieving perfect or near-perfect scores on the Unit Checkpoints and if you feel that they will not benefit from further review and practice, then you may skip the Getting Stronger lessons and move to the next unit.

Keep a Portfolio

To document students' progress, we recommend that you keep a portfolio of their work. You can compile a comprehensive portfolio by keeping all of the following items:

- The box of sight word cards
- Completed Activity Book pages and Dictation activities
- Your notes from Try It activities
- Completed Unit Checkpoint pages

PhonicsWorks Advanced Program: Lesson Components

In the Advanced course, lessons are presented much like the lessons in the Basic course (see above). The first four units of the Advanced course review the content of PhonicsWorks Basic, and the remaining units provide instruction in more advanced phonics concepts, such as blends, long vowels, and difficult spelling patterns.

Sight Words

The first four units of the Advanced course cover the 45 sight words from the Basic course. During this time, students will work on approximately 12 words per week. As in the Basic course, two sets of sight word cards are required. One set can be found in your PhonicsWorks Kit, and you may either make the second set yourself using index cards or print the second set from the online lesson. Here are the other sight words for the Advanced course:

- too, walk, talk
- again, out, pull
- next, my, friend
- goes, anything, begin
- down, know, after
- mother, father, only
- even, look, gone
- love, very, some
- none, more, held
- would, could, should
- brother, sister, baby
- many, animal, while
- together, people, other
- above, here, move
- these, against, now
- every, neighbor, behind
- once, come, about
- please, follow, saw
- everything, under, whether
- nothing, over, almost
- children, write, number
- because, its, first

The Tile Kit:
Multisensory Instruction

PhonicsWorks lessons incorporate *multisensory* instruction. Lesson activities ask students to look, listen, touch, move, and speak.

The Tile Kit is at the core of this multisensory instruction. The Tile Kit contains letters and letter combinations that represent sounds. Students use the magnetized tiles to manipulate sounds and letters in fun activities that combine visual, auditory, tactile, and oral learning.

How to Use the Tile Kit

The Tile Kit is used for a variety of gentle, interactive procedures, such as "build words," "touch and say," and "word chains." Detailed instructions for these procedures are provided in the lessons. (You can also see the Tile Kit used in the K^{12} *PhonicsWorks* video.) The more you use the kit, the less you will need to consult the instructions, although the instructions are always available for you to use.

The Tile Kit helps students understand how speech is represented in print. For example, consider how we use the tiles to build the word *chin*. When students first build the word *chin*, they will be guided to select three tiles:

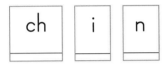

The single sound /ch/ is represented by two letters, *c* and *h*. Because those two letters are printed on a single tile, students get both visual and tactile reinforcement of the simple but important concept that two letters can represent one sound.

Basic Letter Tiles

In the PhonicsWorks Basic course, you receive the Tile Kit, which consists of a binder with pages for the Basic letter tiles. These tiles include the following:

- Color tiles
- All uppercase (capital) letters
- All lowercase letters (multiple tiles provided for each letter)
- Digraphs *sh, ch, th, wh, ph,* and *ck* and trigraph *tch* (multiple tiles provided for each)
- Common word endings *–s, –es, –ed, –ing, –er,* and *–est*
- Double letter endings *–ff, –ll, –ss, –zz,* and *–all*
- Basic punctuation marks: period, question mark, exclamation point, comma, and apostrophe
- Vowels printed in red (to provide a visual cue for identifying those letters)

Advanced Letter Tiles

In PhonicsWorks Advanced, you receive the PhonicsWorks Basic course Tile Kit and the Advanced letter tile pages, which include letter tiles with common spellings for sounds that can be spelled in more than one way. The pages are organized to group together the various letters or combinations of letters that represent one sound.

For example, in one section of the binder you will find the following tiles for the long *o* vowel sound:

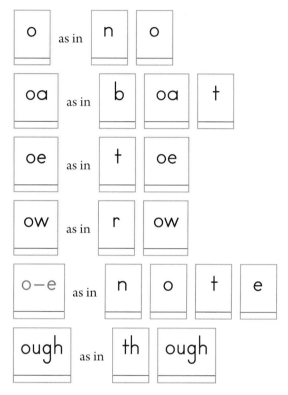

In another section you will find the following tiles to represent the consonant sound /j/:

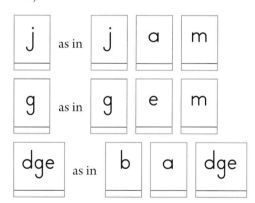

Here is the complete list of what you will receive (some tiles in multiples):

- All PhonicsWorks Basic tiles
- Word endings *ng, ang, ing, ong, ung*
- Word endings *nk, ank, ink, onk, unk*
- Long vowel sound /ā/: *a, e, ai, ay, eigh, a–e, ea*
- Long vowel sound /ē/: *e, e, ee, ea, ie, y, e–e*
- Long vowel sound /ī/: *i, e, ie, y, igh, i–e, y–e*
- Long vowel sound /ō/: *o, e, ow, oa, oe, o–e, ough*
- Long vowel sound /ū/: *u, e, u–e, ew, eu*
- Long double *o* sound (/o͞o/): *oo, e, u, ue, ew, u–e, ough*
- Short double *o* sound (/o͝o/): *oo, u, ou*
- Schwa sound: /ə/
- R-controlled vowels: *ar, or, er, ir, ur, ear, oar, ore*

My Accomplishments! Chart

Research shows that rewarding students for quality work can increase their motivation. To aid you in rewarding students, you will receive a My Accomplishments! chart and sticker sheet for use throughout the course. This chart gives students a tangible and concrete representation of their progress and accomplishments throughout the PhonicsWorks course (and other courses in which they may be enrolled), which they can proudly display and share with others. When students score 80% or above on a Unit Checkpoint, have them add a sticker for that unit to the My Accomplishments! chart. Encourage students to set goals and watch their stickers accumulate. Verbally reinforce their progress to help them understand the connection between their own growing skill set and the My Accomplishments! chart.

How to Correct Errors: "Accentuate the Positive"

All students will make mistakes as they learn to read. They may have to try repeatedly to grasp concepts that strike experienced readers as painfully obvious. When correcting mistakes, we need to remain patient and encouraging.

PhonicsWorks lessons suggest specific phrases for you to use when students make an error. These suggestions are meant to help make the experience of learning to read a positive one that focuses on success.

For example, imagine that you ask students to touch the letter *b* and they touch the letter *d*. You want to avoid a negative (and potentially discouraging) response such as, "No, that's not right. Try again." Instead, say, "You touched the letter *d*. This is the letter *b*. Touch this letter and say *b*." These words inform students that they did indeed touch a letter, and they serve as a reminder of the name of the letter touched. They also provide immediate and gentle guidance about how to give the right answer.

PhonicsWorks Keywords

accent – the emphasis, by stress or pitch, on a word or syllable. For example, in the word *garden*, the accent falls on the first syllable, *gar*.

base word – the part of a word that contains a prefix, suffix, or both. A base word can stand on its own.

blend – a combination of two or three consonants in which you hear the sound of each consonant; for example, the two letters *st* can each be heard in the word *stop*, and the three letters *str* can each be heard in the word *string*.

compound word – a word made from two smaller words (for example, baseball)

decode – the ability to translate written forms into their corresponding speech sounds. For example, students decode when they recognize that *d* represents /d/, *o* represents /ŏ/, *g* represents /g/, and therefore that combination of letters (*d-o-g*) is the word *dog*.

digraph – two letters together that make one sound. For example, the two letters *sh* in the word *fish* make one sound.

onset – the part of a word preceding the first vowel. For example, in the word *smart*, *sm* is the onset.

phonemes – the smallest units of sound. Phonemes are combined to make words.

phonological awareness – the ability to identify and manipulate sound parts in words. The ability to identify similar sounds in words, create rhyming words, and count syllables are all signs of phonological awareness.

rime – the part of a word that includes the first vowel and what follows it. For example, in the word *smart*, *art* is the rime.

schwa – an unstressed vowel indistinct in pronunciation, often similar to short *u*. In the word *garden*, the unstressed syllable *den* contains the schwa sound. In the word *alone*, the unstressed syllable *a* is the schwa sound. The schwa sound is represented by the symbol ə.

trigraph – three letters together that make one sound. For example, the three letters *tch* in the word *match* make one sound.

Sounds /m/ and /t/

Unit Overview

In this unit, students will
- ▸ Practice right hand awareness.
- ▸ Identify letters in the alphabet.
- ▸ Distinguish between beginning, ending, and middle locations.
- ▸ Identify and say the sounds /m/, /t/, /n/, /p/, /h/, /ē/, /d/, and /ŏ/.
- ▸ Identify beginning and ending sounds in words.

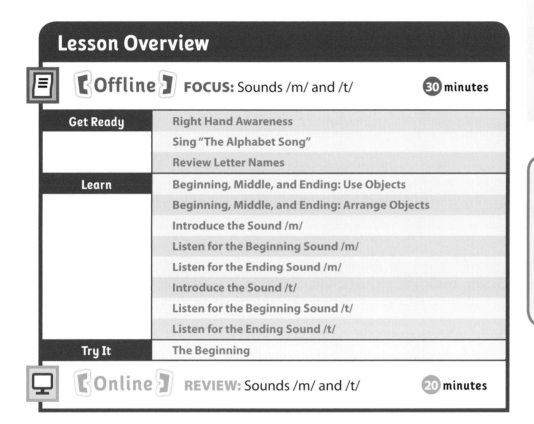

Lesson Overview

Offline FOCUS: Sounds /m/ and /t/   30 minutes

Get Ready	Right Hand Awareness
	Sing "The Alphabet Song"
	Review Letter Names
Learn	Beginning, Middle, and Ending: Use Objects
	Beginning, Middle, and Ending: Arrange Objects
	Introduce the Sound /m/
	Listen for the Beginning Sound /m/
	Listen for the Ending Sound /m/
	Introduce the Sound /t/
	Listen for the Beginning Sound /t/
	Listen for the Ending Sound /t/
Try It	The Beginning

Online REVIEW: Sounds /m/ and /t/   20 minutes

Materials

Supplied
- *K¹² PhonicsWorks Basic Activity Book*, p. PH 1
- whiteboard, Learning Coach
- Tile Kit

Also Needed
- household objects – glass, spoon, book (any 3 objects will do)

Keywords
phonemic awareness – ability to identify and manipulate individual sounds in words

phonological awareness – ability to identify and manipulate sound parts in words

Advance Preparation

Place uppercase letter tiles in alphabetical order on your whiteboard.

Big Ideas

- ▸ Phonological awareness is a critical pre-reading component of early literacy instruction.
- ▸ Phonological awareness activities deal with sounds only.
- ▸ Phonemic awareness is a subset of phonological awareness.

 **30 minutes**

FOCUS: Sounds /m/ and /t/

Work **together** with students to complete offline Get Ready, Learn, and
Try It activities.

Get Ready

Right Hand Awareness

Students read from left to right, so play a game to develop right hand awareness.
To avoid confusion, focus on the right hand only.

1. Say each sentence and do each action. Have students repeat your words
   and actions.

   ▸ I'm shaking your right hand.
   ▸ Now I'm touching my right ankle.
   ▸ Now I'm waving my right hand in the air.
   ▸ Now I'm touching my right toe.
   ▸ Now I'm touching my right cheek.

2. Repeat the actions and mix up the order. To end the activity, shake right
   hands again.

Objectives
- Develop right hand awareness.
- Identify letters of the alphabet.
- Identify capital and lowercase letters.

Sing "The Alphabet Song"

To help students become familiar and comfortable with the alphabet, sing
"The Alphabet Song" with them. Sing slowly, so that students may touch
each letter on your whiteboard as they sing the letter's name.

Review Letter Names

To help students learn the alphabet, have them practice identifying and naming the
letters *A, F, G, L, M, S, T,* and *Z.* Grab your whiteboard with letters.

1. Point to each letter and have students touch and name each one.

   A   G   M   T   F   L   S   Z

2. Say the name of each letter. After each one, have students repeat the name and
   touch the tile.

   A   G   M   T   F   L   S   Z

TIP If students don't know the names of the letters when you say them, start with
A, B, C, and *D.* Write each letter about two to three inches high on a sheet of paper.
Have students trace the shape of each letter while saying its name.

Learn •

Beginning, Middle, and Ending: Use Objects

Reinforce with students interchangeable words used to describe position.

1. Line up three objects, such as a book, glass, and spoon, about two inches apart on the table. For example,

    book   glass   spoon

2. Explain to students that when we read,

    ▸ We always start here (point to the book), at the **beginning**.
    ▸ We always stop here (point to the spoon), at the **end**.

3. Have students touch the first object on the table.

    ▸ Is the book first, second, or last? first
    ▸ Which place is it in—beginning, middle, or ending? beginning

4. Have students touch the last object on the table.

    ▸ Is the spoon first, second, or last? last
    ▸ Which place is it in—beginning, middle, or ending? ending

5. Explain that when three objects are lined up, the **middle** object is also called the **second** object.

    ▸ Is the glass first, second, or last? second
    ▸ Which place is it in—beginning, middle, or ending? middle

6. Have students

    ▸ Touch the middle object.
    ▸ Touch the ending object.
    ▸ Touch the beginning object.
    ▸ Touch the first object.
    ▸ Touch the last object.

Objectives
- Identify and use the sound /m/.
- Identify and use the sound /t/.
- Identify beginning sounds in words.
- Identify ending sounds in words.
- Identify beginning, middle, and ending positions.

Beginning, Middle, and Ending: Arrange Objects

Have students practice identifying beginning, middle, and ending positions.

1. Place three objects, such as a book, glass, and spoon, on a table. Move the spoon so that it is first.

    ▸ What is last now? glass
    ▸ What is in the middle? book
    ▸ What is at the beginning? spoon

2. Move the glass so that it is in the middle.

    ▸ What is first now? spoon
    ▸ What is at the end? book
    ▸ What is second? glass

Introduce the Sound /m/

Teach the sound /m/, as in *mop*, *mat*, and *most*.

1. **Say:** We're going to play a game to practice the **sound /m/**. Your job is to say the sound just like me and do what I do, too. Now we're going to learn.

2. Rub your belly like something tastes good and say the sound /m/. Have students do this, too.

3. **Say:** We make many sounds with our tongue, our teeth, and our lips. Say /m/ again and feel whether your tongue, teeth, or lips are making the sound.

   ▸ Did you feel your lips making a sound? Yes

4. **Say:** We make some sounds with a whisper and some sounds with our voice. Let's figure out whether the sound /m/ is whispered or voiced. Say /m/ and put your fingers on the lump in your throat called your voice box.

   ▸ Do you feel your voice box vibrate? Yes, /m/ is a noisy sound because we use our voice box when we make the sound.

5. **Say:** I'll say some words that start with the sound /m/ and you'll repeat them, saying /m/ just the way I do.

   mop   *mat*   *most*

6. **Say:** Now I'll say some words that end with the sound /m/ and you'll repeat them, saying /m/ just the way I do.

   same   *Tom*   *foam*

TIP When you teach the sound /m/, make sure to enunciate clearly. Students should say /m/, not *muh*.

Listen for the Beginning Sound /m/

Present pairs of words to help students recognize beginning sounds.

1. **Say:** I'm going to say two words. Listen for the **beginning sound /m/**. Then tell me the word that has that beginning sound. For example, if I say *Mars* and *tiger*, you'll say *Mars* because /m/ is the first sound in *Mars*.

2. Say each pair of words. Have students identify the word that begins with the sound /m/.

   ▸ *sun* or *moon* moon
   ▸ *mountain* or *hill* mountain
   ▸ *dog* or *mouse* mouse

Listen for the Ending Sound /m/

Present pairs of words to help students recognize ending sounds.

1. **Say:** I'm going to say two words. Listen for the **ending sound** /**m**/. Then tell me the word with that ending sound. For example, if I say *time* and *clock*, you'll say *time* because /m/ is the last sound in *time*.

2. Say each pair of words. Have students identify the word that ends with the sound /m/.

   ▸ *ram* or *deer* ram
   ▸ *stand* or *same* same
   ▸ *sing* or *hum* hum

Introduce the Sound /t/

Teach the sound /t/, as in *toes*, *teeth*, and *tap*.

1. **Say:** We're going to play a game to practice the **sound** /**t**/. Your job is to say the sound just like me and do what I do, too.

2. Touch your toes and say the sound /t/. Have students do this, too.

3. **Say:** We make many sounds with our tongue, our teeth, and our lips. Say /t/ again and feel whether your tongue, teeth, or lips are making the sound.

   ▸ Did you feel your tongue making a sound? Yes

4. **Say:** We make some sounds with a whisper and some sounds with our voice. Let's figure out whether the sound /t/ is whispered or voiced. Say /t/ and put your fingers on the lump in your throat called your voice box.

   ▸ Do you feel your voice box vibrate? No, /t/ is a whispered sound because we don't use our voice box when we make the sound.

5. **Say:** I'll say some words that start with the sound /t/ and you'll repeat them, saying /t/ just the way I do.

   tap   Tom   take

6. **Say:** Now I'll say some words that end with the sound /t/ and you'll repeat them, saying /t/ just the way I do.

   sit   mat   cut

TIP When you teach the sound /t/, make sure students say the sound correctly and do not add *uh* after pronouncing it. Students should say /t/, not *tuh*.

Listen for the Beginning Sound /t/

Present pairs of words to help students recognize beginning sounds.

1. **Say:** I'm going to say two words. Listen for the **beginning sound** /t/. Then tell me the word that has that beginning sound. For example, if I say *toad* and *frog*, you'll say *toad* because /t/ is the first sound in *toad*.

2. Say each pair of words. Have students identify the word that begins with the sound /t/.

   ▸ *yellow* or *tan* *tan*
   ▸ *top* or *bottom* *top*
   ▸ *wind* or *tornado* *tornado*

Listen for the Ending Sound /t/

Present pairs of words to help students recognize ending sounds.

1. **Say:** I'm going to say two words. Listen for the **ending sound** /t/. Then tell me the word with that ending sound. For example, if I say *eat* and *fork*, you'll say *eat* because /t/ is the last sound in *eat*.

2. Say each pair of words. Have students identify the word that ends with the sound /t/.

   ▸ *went* or *came* *went*
   ▸ *dog* or *cat* *cat*
   ▸ *cookie* or *kite* *kite*

Try It

The Beginning

Have students complete page PH 1 in *K¹² PhonicsWorks Basic Activity Book* for more practice with the sounds /m/ and /t/. First have students say the name of each picture. Then have them circle pictures whose name begins with the sound /m/ and draw an X over pictures whose name begins with the sound /t/.

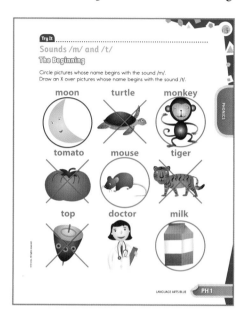

Objectives
- Identify and use the sound /m/.
- Identify and use the sound /t/.
- Identify beginning sounds in words.

Online — 20 minutes

REVIEW: Sounds /m/ and /t/

Students will work online independently to

▶ Practice the sounds /m/ and /t/.

Help students locate the online activities and provide support as needed.

Objectives
- Identify and use the sound /m/.
- Identify and use the sound /t/.
- Identify beginning sounds in words.
- Identify ending sounds in words.

Offline Alternative

No computer access? Have students point out and name things that begin or end with the sounds /m/ and /t/ (for example, *mop* and *cat*).

Sounds /n/ and /p/

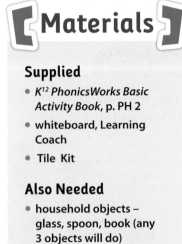

Lesson Overview

Offline FOCUS: Sounds /n/ and /p/ — **30** minutes

Get Ready	Right Hand Awareness
	Sing "The Alphabet Song"
	Review Letter Names
	Secret Sound
	Beginning, Middle, and Ending: Use Objects and Sounds
Learn	Introduce the Sound /n/
	Listen for the Beginning Sound /n/
	Listen for the Ending Sound /n/
	Introduce the Sound /p/
	Listen for the Beginning Sound /p/
	Listen for the Ending Sound /p/
Try It	The Beginning

Online REVIEW: Sounds /n/ and /p/ — **20** minutes

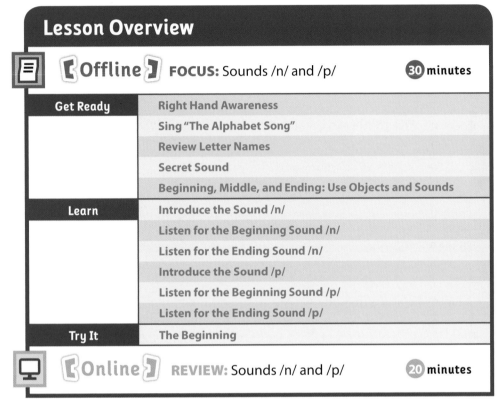

[Materials]

Supplied
- *K¹² PhonicsWorks Basic Activity Book*, p. PH 2
- whiteboard, Learning Coach
- Tile Kit

Also Needed
- household objects – glass, spoon, book (any 3 objects will do)

Advance Preparation

Place uppercase letter tiles in alphabetical order on your whiteboard.

Big Ideas

Phonemic awareness is the ability to hear and manipulate individual sounds in words.

Offline · 30 minutes

FOCUS: Sounds /n/ and /p/

Work **together** with students to complete offline Get Ready, Learn, and Try It activities.

Get Ready

Right Hand Awareness
Students read from left to right, so play a game to develop right hand awareness. To avoid confusion, focus on the right hand only.

1. Say each sentence and do each action. Have students repeat your words and actions.

   ▸ I'm shaking your right hand.
   ▸ Now I'm touching my right ankle.
   ▸ Now I'm waving my right hand in the air.
   ▸ Now I'm touching my right toe.
   ▸ Now I'm touching my right cheek.

2. Repeat the actions and mix up the order. To end the activity, shake right hands again.

Sing "The Alphabet Song"
To help students become familiar and comfortable with the alphabet, sing "The Alphabet Song" with them. Sing slowly, so that students may touch each letter on your whiteboard as they sing the letter's name.

Review Letter Names
To help students learn the alphabet, have them practice identifying and naming the letters *A, F, G, L, M, S, T,* and *Z.* Grab your whiteboard with letters.

1. Point to each letter and have students touch and name each one.

   Z   S   L   F   T   M   G   A

2. Say the name of each letter. After each one, have students repeat the name and touch the tile.

   Z   S   L   F   T   M   G   A

3. Redirect students if they name a letter incorrectly.

   ▸ Name the letter students missed.
   ▸ Have students touch the letter and say its name.
   ▸ Have students trace the shape of the letter with their finger on the brown side of their board, and have them say the letter's name as they trace the shape.
   ▸ If students name a letter incorrectly twice, point to the letter and tell them its name. Have students touch the letter and say its name.

> **Objectives**
> - Develop right hand awareness.
> - Identify letters of the alphabet.
> - Identify capital and lowercase letters.
> - Identify and use the sound /m/.
> - Identify and use the sound /t/.
> - Identify beginning, middle, and ending positions.

Secret Sound

Say groups of words that begin with the same letter to help students recognize **beginning** sounds.

1. **Say:** I am going to say some groups of words. Listen for a secret sound at the beginning of each word. Then tell me what sound you hear at the beginning of each group of words.

2. Say each of the following groups of words. Have students identify the secret sound in each group.

    ▸ *move, meal, monster, mix* /m/
    ▸ *time, tomato, taxi, towel* /t/
    ▸ *munch, middle, mouse, many* /m/

3. Repeat any groups of words for which students couldn't identify the secret sound. Have students repeat each word in that group. Then have them say what sound they hear at the beginning of each word.

Beginning, Middle, and Ending: Use Objects and Sounds

Help students recognize the order of sounds in words by having them identify the order of three objects, and then identify a sequence of sounds.

1. Line up three objects, such as a book, glass, and spoon, about two inches apart on a table. For example,

    book   glass   spoon

2. Have students

    ▸ Touch the middle object.
    ▸ Touch the last object.
    ▸ Touch the beginning object.
    ▸ Touch the first object.
    ▸ Touch the last object.
    ▸ Touch the middle object.

3. **Say:** Just as we have a **first**, **middle**, and **last** object, we can also have a **first**, **middle**, and **last** sound. I'm going to make three noises, and then I'm going to ask you what the first, middle, and last sounds were. Close your eyes and listen.

4. Slam the book shut, drop the spoon into the glass, and clap your hands.

5. Have students identify the sounds you made.

    ▸ What was the first sound? book slamming shut
    ▸ What was the middle sound? spoon dropping into glass
    ▸ What was the last sound? hands clapping

Learn ••

Introduce the Sound /n/

Teach the sound /n/, as in *nap*, *nest*, and *not*.

1. **Say:** We're going to play a game to practice the **sound /n/**. Your job is to say the sound just like me and do what I do.

2. Shake your head and say the sound /n/. Have students do this, too.

3. **Say:** We make many sounds with our tongue, our teeth, and our lips. Say /n/ again and feel whether your tongue, teeth, or lips are making the sound.

   ▶ Do you feel your tongue and teeth help make the sound /n/? Yes

4. **Say:** We make some sounds with a whisper and some sounds with our voice. Let's figure out whether the sound /n/ is whispered or voiced. Say /n/ and put your fingers on the lump in your throat called your voice box.

   ▶ Do you feel your voice box vibrate? Yes, /n/ is a noisy sound because we use our voice box when we make the sound.

5. **Say:** I'll say some words that start with the sound /n/ and you'll repeat them, saying /n/ just the way I do.

   nap   nest   not

6. **Say:** Now I'll say some words that end with the sound /n/ and you'll repeat them, saying /n/ just the way I do.

   line   fun   ran

(TIP) When you teach the sound /n/, make sure students say the sound correctly and do not add *uh* after pronouncing it. Students should say /n/, not *nuh*.

Listen for the Beginning Sound /n/

Present pairs of words to help students recognize beginning sounds.

1. **Say:** I'm going to say two words. Listen for the **beginning sound /n/**. Then tell me the word that has that beginning sound. For example, if I say *nine* and *six*, you'll say *nine* because /n/ is the first sound in *nine*.

2. Say each pair of words. Have students identify the word that begins with the sound /n/.

   ▶ *night* or *day* night
   ▶ *mat* or *not* not
   ▶ *dish* or *nut* nut

Objectives
- Identify and use the sound /n/.
- Identify and use the sound /p/.
- Identify beginning sounds in words.
- Identify ending sounds in words.

Listen for the Ending Sound /n/

Present pairs of words to help students recognize ending sounds.

1. **Say:** I'm going to say two words. Listen for the **ending sound /n/**. Then tell me the word with that ending sound. For example, if I say *pin* and *sharp*, you'll say *pin* because /n/ is the last sound in *pin*.

2. Say each pair of words. Have students identify the word that ends with the sound /n/.

   ▸ *pot* or *pan* *pan*
   ▸ *sad* or *tin* *tin*
   ▸ *fan* or *fly* *fan*

Introduce the Sound /p/

Teach the sound /p/, as in *pan*, *pass*, and *pie*.

1. **Say:** We're going to play a game to practice the **sound /p/**. Your job is to say the sound just like me and do what I do, too.

2. Move your hands as if you were pushing and say the sound /p/. Have students do this, too.

3. **Say:** We make many sounds with our tongue, our teeth, and our lips. Say /p/ again and feel whether your tongue, teeth, or lips are making the sound.

   ▸ Did you feel your lips making a sound? Yes

4. **Say:** We make some sounds with a whisper and some sounds with our voice. Let's figure out whether the sound /p/ is whispered or voiced. Say /p/ and put your fingers on the lump in your throat called your voice box.

   ▸ Do you feel your voice box vibrate? No, /p/ is a whispered sound because we don't use our voice box when we make the sound.

5. **Say:** I'll say some words that start with the sound /p/ and you'll repeat them, saying /p/ just the way I do.

   pan   pass   pie

6. **Say:** Now I'll say some words that end with the sound /p/ and you'll repeat them, saying /p/ just the way I do.

   tip   cup   lamp

(TIP) When you teach the sound /p/, make sure students say the sound correctly and do not add *uh* after pronouncing it. Students should say /p/, not *puh*.

Listen for the Beginning Sound /p/

Present pairs of words to help students recognize beginning sounds.

1. **Say:** I'm going to say two words. Listen for the **beginning sound** /p/. Then tell me the word that has that beginning sound. For example, if I say *pie* and *cake*, you'll say *pie* because /p/ is the first sound in *pie*.

2. Say each pair of words. Have students identify the word that begins with the sound /p/.

   ▸ *tea or pot* pot
   ▸ *pants or shirt* pants
   ▸ *pail or bucket* pail

Listen for the Ending Sound /p/

Present pairs of words to help students recognize ending sounds.

1. **Say:** I'm going to say two words. Listen for the **ending sound** /p/. Then tell me the word with that ending sound. For example, if I say *scrape* and *scratch*, you'll say *scrape* because /p/ is the last sound in *scrape*.

2. Say each pair of words. Have students identify the word that ends with the sound /p/.

   ▸ *sip or crunch* sip
   ▸ *flop or dog* flop
   ▸ *mouth or lip* lip

Try It •••

The Beginning

Have students complete page PH 2 in *K¹² PhonicsWorks Basic Activity Book* for more practice with the sounds /n/ and /p/. First have students say the name of each picture. Then have them circle pictures whose name begins with the sound /p/ and draw an X over pictures whose name begins with the sound /n/.

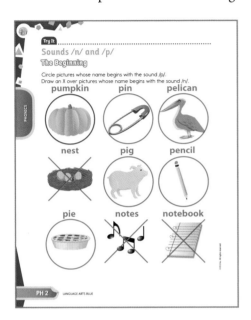

Online 20 minutes

REVIEW: Sounds /n/ and /p/

Students will work online independently to

▸ Practice the sounds /n/ and /p/.

Help students locate the online activities and provide support as needed.

Offline Alternative

No computer access? Have students point out and name things that begin or end with the sounds /n/ and /p/ (for example, *noodle* and *mop*).

Sounds /ē/ and /h/

Materials

Supplied
- *K¹² PhonicsWorks Basic Activity Book*, p. PH 3
- whiteboard, Learning Coach
- Tile Kit

Keywords
letter name knowledge – the ability to name a given letter, in or out of alphabetical order

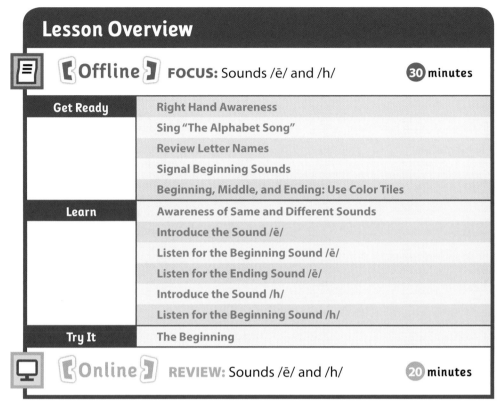

Lesson Overview

Offline FOCUS: Sounds /ē/ and /h/ — **30** minutes

Get Ready	Right Hand Awareness
	Sing "The Alphabet Song"
	Review Letter Names
	Signal Beginning Sounds
	Beginning, Middle, and Ending: Use Color Tiles
Learn	Awareness of Same and Different Sounds
	Introduce the Sound /ē/
	Listen for the Beginning Sound /ē/
	Listen for the Ending Sound /ē/
	Introduce the Sound /h/
	Listen for the Beginning Sound /h/
Try It	The Beginning

Online REVIEW: Sounds /ē/ and /h/ — **20** minutes

Advance Preparation

Place uppercase letter tiles in alphabetical order on your whiteboard.

Big Ideas

Letter name knowledge is a key indicator of future reading ability.

Offline   30 minutes

FOCUS: Sounds /ē/ and /h/

Work **together** with students to complete offline Get Ready, Learn, and Try It activities.

Get Ready

Right Hand Awareness

Students read from left to right, so play a game to develop right hand awareness. To avoid confusion, focus on the right hand only.

1. Say each sentence and do each action. Have students repeat your words and actions.

   ▸ I'm shaking your right hand.
   ▸ Now I'm touching my right ankle.
   ▸ Now I'm waving my right hand in the air.
   ▸ Now I'm touching my right toe.
   ▸ Now I'm touching my right cheek.

2. Repeat the actions and mix up the order. To end the activity, shake right hands again.

Objectives
- Develop right hand awareness.
- Identify letters of the alphabet.
- Identify capital and lowercase letters.
- Identify individual sounds in words.

Sing "The Alphabet Song"

To help students become familiar and comfortable with the alphabet, sing "The Alphabet Song" with them. Sing slowly, so that students may touch each letter on your whiteboard as they sing the letter's name.

Review Letter Names

To help students learn the alphabet, have them practice identifying and naming the letters *B, E, H, K, N, R, U,* and *Y.* Grab your whiteboard with letters.

1. Point to each letter and have students touch and name each one.

   B   H   N   U   E   K   R   Y

2. Say the name of each letter. After each one, have students repeat the name and touch the tile.

   B   H   N   U   E   K   R   Y

3. Redirect students if they name a letter incorrectly.

   ▸ Name the letter students missed.
   ▸ Have students touch the letter and say its name.
   ▸ Have students trace the shape of the letter with their finger on the brown side of their board, and have them say the letter's name as they trace the shape.
   ▸ If students name a letter incorrectly twice, point to the letter and tell them its name. Have students touch the letter and say its name.

Signal Beginning Sounds

Use a special signal to help students identify the **beginning sound** in words.

1. **Say:** I'm going to tell you a special sound, and then I'll say some words. Repeat each word I say and make a special signal to tell me where the special sound is. If the special sound is at the beginning of the word, tug your ear. If the special sound is **not** at the beginning of the word, just smile at me. For example,

   ▸ If I ask you to listen for the sound /m/ and I say the word *map*, you'll repeat the word *map* and tug your ear because *map* has the sound /m/ at the beginning.

   ▸ If I say the word *dog*, you'll repeat the word *dog* and smile at me because *dog* has the sound /d/, not /m/, at the beginning.

2. Say each sound and group of words. Have students make the special signal to identify the beginning sound.

   ▸ /m/: *map, mustard, ketchup, mayonnaise, pickles, meatballs* tug ear: *map, mustard, mayonnaise, meatballs*

   ▸ /t/: *chin, tooth, nose, toes, tongue, cheek* tug ear: *tooth, toes, tongue*

   ▸ /p/: *pie, cake, peanut, popcorn, snack, pizza* tug ear: *pie, peanut, popcorn, pizza*

   ▸ /n/: *day, night, noon, morning, nine, never* tug ear: *night, noon, nine, never*

TIP If students can't identify the beginning sound of each word, say the word again and emphasize the beginning sound by repeating it three times (for example, *taste* /t/ /t/ /t/). You can also draw out the beginning sound when you say the word (for example, *mmmustard*). If necessary, have students look at your mouth while you repeat the sounds.

Beginning, Middle, and Ending: Use Color Tiles

Use this activity to reinforce the concepts of beginning, middle, and ending (or first, second, and last). Grab three different color tiles from the Tile Kit.

1. Line up the tiles from left to right, about two inches apart, on a table.

2. Have students

   ▸ Touch the middle tile.
   ▸ Touch the last tile.
   ▸ Touch the beginning tile.
   ▸ Touch the first tile.
   ▸ Touch the last tile.
   ▸ Touch the middle tile.

Learn

Awareness of Same and Different Sounds

Play a game with color tiles to help students identify sounds that are the same and sounds that are different. Grab the color tiles from the Tile Kit.

1. Place the tiles on a table.

2. **Say:** I am going to make two sounds. If the sounds are the same, you'll pick out two tiles that are the same color and put them next to each other. If the sounds are different, you'll pick out two tiles that are different colors and put them next to each other. For example,

   ▸ If I make the sounds /mmm/, /mmm/, you'll pick out two tiles that are the same color and put them next to each other because both sounds are the same.

   ▸ If I make the sounds /mmm/, /ēēē/, you'll pick out two tiles that are different colors because both sounds are different.

3. Say each pair of sounds. Have students pick out and place tiles to indicate whether the sounds are the same or different.

   ▸ /sss/, /mmm/
   ▸ /mmm/, /mmm/
   ▸ /nnn/, /sss/
   ▸ /nnn/, /nnn/
   ▸ /nnn/, /mmm/

TIP If students have difficulty hearing the differences between two sounds, have them watch your mouth as you make each sound.

Introduce the Sound /ē/

Teach the sound /ē/, as in *eagle, eat,* and *even.* It's important that you explain this as closely as possible to what you see below.

1. **Say:** We're going to play a game to practice the **sound /ē/.** Your job is to say the sound just like me and do what I do, too.

2. Flap your wings like an eagle and say, "It's eeeasy to fly if you're an eeeagle!" Have students do this, too.

3. **Say:** We make some sounds with a whisper and some sounds with our voice. Let's figure out whether the sound /ē/ is whispered or voiced. Say /ē/ and put your fingers on the lump in your throat called your voice box.

   ▸ Do you feel your voice box vibrate? Yes, /ē/ is a noisy sound because we use our voice box when we make the sound.

Objectives

- Identify and use the sound /ē/.
- Identify and use the sound /h/.
- Identify beginning sounds in words.
- Identify ending sounds in words.
- Identify individual sounds in words.

4. **Say:** I'll say some words that start with the sound /ē/ and you'll repeat them, saying /ē/ just the way I do.

eagle   even   eat

5. **Say:** Now I'll say some words that end with the sound /ē/ and you'll repeat them, saying /ē/ just the way I do.

bee   me   knee

Listen for the Beginning Sound /ē/

Present pairs of words to help students recognize beginning sounds.

1. **Say:** I'm going to say two words. Listen for the **beginning sound** /ē/. Then tell me the word that has that beginning sound. For example, if I say *eat* and *drink*, you'll say *eat* because /ē/ is the first sound in *eat*.

2. Say each pair of words. Have students identify the word that begins with the sound /ē/.

   - *west* or *east east*
   - *even* or *odd even*
   - *tough* or *easy easy*

Listen for the Ending Sound /ē/

Present pairs of words to help students recognize ending sounds.

1. **Say:** I'm going to say two words. Listen for the **ending sound** /ē/. Then tell me the word with that ending sound. For example, if I say *tree* and *try*, you'll say *tree* because /ē/ is the last sound in *tree*.

2. Say each pair of words. Have students identify the word that ends with the sound /ē/.

   - *we* or *why we*
   - *by* or *be be*
   - *me* or *moo me*
   - *so* or *see see*
   - *wasp* or *flea flea*
   - *happy* or *mad happy*

Introduce the Sound /h/

Teach the sound /h/, as in *hot*, *hat*, and *head*.

1. **Say:** We're going to play a game to practice the **sound /h/**. Your job is to say the sound just like me and do what I do, too.

2. Pretend to tip your hat and say the sound /h/. Have students do this, too.

3. **Say:** We make some sounds with a whisper and some sounds with our voice. Let's figure out whether the sound /h/ is whispered or voiced. Say /h/ and put your fingers on the lump in your throat called your voice box.

   ▸ Do you feel your voice box vibrate? No, /h/ is a whispered sound because we don't use our voice box when we make the sound.

4. **Say:** I'll say some words that start with the sound /h/ and you'll repeat them, saying /h/ just the way I do.

   hot   *hat*   *head*

(**TIP**) When you teach the sound /h/, make sure students say the sound correctly and do not add *uh* after pronouncing it. Students should say /h/, not *huh*.

Listen for the Beginning Sound /h/

Present pairs of words to help students recognize beginning sounds.

1. **Say:** I'm going to say two words. Listen for the **beginning sound /h/**. Then tell me the word that has that beginning sound. For example, if I say *help* and *yelp*, you'll say *help* because /h/ is the first sound in *help*.

2. Say each pair of words. Have students identify the word that begins with the sound /h/.

   ▸ *sharp* or *hurt* hurt
   ▸ *heavy* or *light* heavy
   ▸ *cold* or *heat* heat

Try It

The Beginning

Have students complete page PH 3 in *K¹² PhonicsWorks Basic Activity Book* for more practice with the sounds /ē/ and /h/. First have students say the name of each picture. Then have them circle pictures whose name begins with the sound /h/ and draw an X over pictures whose name begins with the sound /ē/.

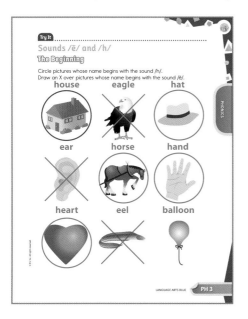

Online 20 minutes

REVIEW: Sounds /ē/ and /h/

Students will work online independently to

▶ Practice the sounds /ē/ and /h/.

Help students locate the online activities and provide support as needed.

Offline Alternative

No computer access? Have students point out and name things or words that start with the sounds /ē/ and /h/ (for example, *eat* or *house*).

Sounds /d/ and /ŏ/

Lesson Overview

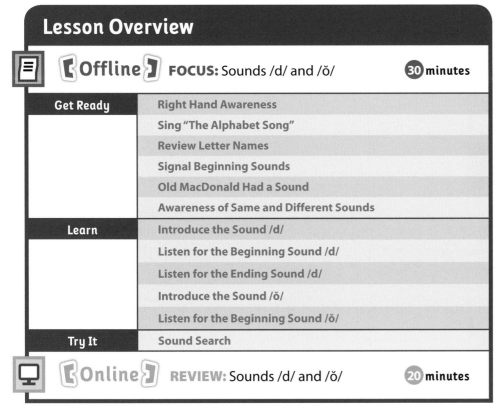

【Offline】 FOCUS: Sounds /d/ and /ŏ/ — **30** minutes

Get Ready	Right Hand Awareness
	Sing "The Alphabet Song"
	Review Letter Names
	Signal Beginning Sounds
	Old MacDonald Had a Sound
	Awareness of Same and Different Sounds
Learn	Introduce the Sound /d/
	Listen for the Beginning Sound /d/
	Listen for the Ending Sound /d/
	Introduce the Sound /ŏ/
	Listen for the Beginning Sound /ŏ/
Try It	Sound Search

【Online】 REVIEW: Sounds /d/ and /ŏ/ — **20** minutes

【Materials】

Supplied

- *K¹² PhonicsWorks Basic Activity Book*, p. PH 4
- whiteboard, Learning Coach
- Tile Kit

Advance Preparation

Place uppercase letter tiles in alphabetical order on your whiteboard.

Offline ⏱ 30 minutes

FOCUS: Sounds /d/ and /ŏ/

Work **together** with students to complete offline Get Ready, Learn, and Try It activities.

Get Ready

Right Hand Awareness

Students read from left to right, so play a game to develop right hand awareness. To avoid confusion, focus on the right hand only.

1. Say each sentence and do each action. Have students repeat your words and actions.

   ▸ I'm shaking your right hand.
   ▸ Now I'm touching my right ankle.
   ▸ Now I'm waving my right hand in the air.
   ▸ Now I'm touching my right toe.
   ▸ Now I'm touching my right cheek.

2. Repeat the actions and mix up the order. To end the activity, shake right hands again.

> **Objectives**
> - Develop right hand awareness.
> - Identify letters of the alphabet.
> - Identify capital and lowercase letters.
> - Identify beginning sounds in words.
> - Identify individual sounds in words.

Sing "The Alphabet Song"

To help students become familiar and comfortable with the alphabet, sing "The Alphabet Song" with them. Sing slowly, so that students may touch each letter on your whiteboard as they sing the letter's name.

Review Letter Names

To help students learn the alphabet, have them practice identifying and naming the letters *C, F, G, J, O, Q, V,* and *X.* Grab your whiteboard with letters.

1. Point to each letter and have students touch and name each one.

   C   G   O   V   F   J   Q   X

2. Say the name of each letter. After each one, have students repeat the name and touch the tile.

   C   G   O   V   F   J   Q   X

3. Redirect students if they name a letter incorrectly.

   ▸ Name the letter students missed.
   ▸ Have students touch the letter and say its name.
   ▸ Have students trace the shape of the letter with their finger on the brown side of their board, and have them say the letter's name as they trace the shape.
   ▸ If students name a letter incorrectly twice, point to the letter and tell them its name. Have students touch the letter and say its name.

Signal Beginning Sounds

Use a special signal to help students identify the **beginning sound** in words.

1. **Say:** I'm going to tell you a special sound, and then I'll say some words. Repeat each word I say and make a special signal to tell me where the special sound is. If the special sound is at the beginning of the word, tug your ear. If the special sound is **not** at the beginning of the word, just smile at me. For example,

   ▶ If I ask you to listen for the sound /ē/ and I say the word *eagle*, you'll repeat the word *eagle* and tug your ear because *eagle* has the sound /ē/ at the beginning.
   ▶ If I say the word *octopus*, you'll repeat the word *octopus* and smile at me, because *octopus* has the sound /ŏ/, not /ē/, at the beginning.

2. Say each sound and group of words. Have students make the special signal to identify the beginning sound.

   ▶ /ē/: *even, east, October, equal, inside* tug ear: *even, east, equal*
   ▶ /h/: *sad, happy, hide, show, help, hurt* tug ear: *happy, hide, help, hurt*
   ▶ /p/: *pen, book, paper, write, print, read* tug ear: *pen, paper, print*
   ▶ /n/: *yes, no, night, day, nice, mean* tug ear: *no, night, nice*
   ▶ /m/: *Mike, Ken, Mark, Jeff, Dave, Matt* tug ear: *Mike, Mark, Matt*

TIP If students can't identify the beginning sound of each word, say the word again and emphasize the beginning sound by repeating it three times (for example, *taste* /t/ /t/ /t/). You can also draw out the beginning sound when you say the word (for example, *mmmommy*). If necessary, ask students to watch your mouth as you repeat the sound.

Old MacDonald Had a Sound

To review sounds, sing "Old MacDonald's Farm" with students.

1. **Say:** Let's have some fun with "Old MacDonald's Farm." Instead of animals, we'll put vowel sounds on the farm. We'll sing "Old MacDonald had a farm, E-I-E-I-O. And on that farm he had a /m/, E-I-E-I-O. With a /m/, /m/ here and a /m/, /m/ there . . . ."

2. Continue singing the song with these sounds:

   ▶ /t/
   ▶ /n/
   ▶ /p/
   ▶ /ē/
   ▶ /h/

Awareness of Same and Different Sounds

Play a game with color tiles to help students identify sounds that are the same and sounds that are different. Grab the color tiles from the Tile Kit.

1. Place the tiles on a table.

2. **Say:** I am going to make three sounds. If the sounds are the same, you'll pick out three tiles that are the same color and put them next to each other. If the sounds are different, you'll pick out three tiles that are different colors and put them next to each other. For example,

   ▸ If I make the sounds /mmm/, /mmm/, /mmm/, you'll pick out three tiles that are all the same color and put them next to each other because all three sounds are the same.
   ▸ If I make the sounds /mmm/, /ēēē/, /t/ you'll pick out three tiles that are different colors because all three sounds are different.
   ▸ Finally if I make the sounds /t/, /t/, /ŏ/ you'll pick out two color tiles that are the same color and one color tile that is different because the first two sounds are the same and the last sound is different.

3. Say each group of sounds. Have students pick out and place tiles to indicate whether the sounds are the same or different.

   ▸ /d/, /d/, /m/
   ▸ /d/, /p/, /n/
   ▸ /p/, /p/, /ē/
   ▸ /ē/, /ē/, /s/
   ▸ /ŏ/, /ē/, /t/
   ▸ /m/, /p/, /d/

Learn

Introduce the Sound /d/

Teach the sound /d/, as in *dog*, *dime*, and *dip*.

1. **Say:** We're going to play a game to practice the **sound /d/**. Your job is to say the sound just like me and do what I do, too.

2. Dance and say, "It's delightful to dance with you!" Have students do this, too.

3. **Say:** We make many sounds with our tongue, our teeth, and our lips. Say /d/ again and feel whether your tongue, teeth, or lips are making the sound.

   ▸ Do you feel your tongue help make the sound /d/? Yes

4. **Say:** We make some sounds with a whisper and some sounds with our voice. Let's figure out whether the sound /d/ is whispered or voiced. Say /d/ and put your fingers on the lump in your throat called your voice box.

   ▸ Do you feel your voice box vibrate? Yes, /d/ is a noisy sound because we use our voice box when we make the sound.

Objectives

- Identify and use the sound /d/.
- Identify and use the sound /ŏ/.
- Identify beginning sounds in words.
- Identify ending sounds in words.

5. **Say:** I'll say some words that start with the sound /d/ and you'll repeat them, saying /d/ just the way I do.

dog   dime   dip

6. **Say:** Now I'll say some words that end with the sound /d/ and you'll repeat them, saying /d/ just the way I do.

bid   mud   sad

TIP When you teach the sound /d/, make sure students say the sound correctly and do not add *uh* after pronouncing it. Students should say /d/, not *duh*.

Listen for the Beginning Sound /d/

Present pairs of words to help students recognize beginning sounds.

1. **Say:** I'm going to say two words. Listen for the **beginning sound /d/**. Then tell me the word that has that beginning sound. For example, if I say *dish* and *cup*, you'll say *dish* because /d/ is the first sound in *dish*.

2. Say each pair of words. Have students identify the word that begins with the sound /d/.

   - *night* or *day* day
   - *wash* or *dirt* dirt
   - *dog* or *cat* dog

Listen for the Ending Sound /d/

Present pairs of words to help students recognize ending sounds.

1. **Say:** I'm going to say two words. Listen for the **ending sound /d/**. Then tell me the word with that ending sound. For example, if I say *good* and *fine*, you'll say *good* because /d/ is the last sound in *good*.

2. Say each pair of words. Have students identify the word that ends with the sound /d/.

   - *glad* or *smile* glad
   - *munch* or *food* food
   - *look* or *hide* hide

Introduce the Sound /ŏ/

Teach the sound /ŏ/, as in *odd*, *octopus*, and *opera*.

1. **Say:** We're going to play a game to practice the **sound /ŏ/**. Your job is to say the sound just like me and do what I do, too.

2. Wiggle your fingers as if they were octopus tentacles and say the sound /ŏ/. Have students do this, too.

3. **Say:** We make some sounds with a whisper and some sounds with our voice. Let's figure out whether the sound /ŏ/ is whispered or voiced. Say /ŏ/ and put your fingers on the lump in your throat called your voice box.

    ▸ Do you feel your voice box vibrate? Yes, /ŏ/ is a noisy sound because we use our voice box when we make the sound.

4. **Say:** I'll say some words that start with the sound /ŏ/ and you'll repeat them, saying /ŏ/ just the way I do.

    odd   *octopus*   *opera*

Listen for the Beginning Sound /ŏ/

Present pairs of words to help students recognize beginning sounds.

1. **Say:** I'm going to say two words. Listen for the **beginning sound /ŏ/**. Then tell me the word that has that beginning sound. For example, if I say *operate* and *cold*, you'll say *operate* because /ŏ/ is the first sound in *operate*.

2. Say each pair of words. Have students identify the word that begins with the sound /ŏ/.

    ▸ *otter* or *ant* otter
    ▸ *ink* or *Oliver* Oliver
    ▸ *eagle* or *ostrich* ostrich

Try It

Sound Search

Have students complete page PH 4 in *K¹² PhonicsWorks Basic Activity Book* for more practice with the sounds /d/ and /ŏ/. First have students say the name of each picture. Then have them circle pictures whose name ends with the sound /d/ and draw an X over pictures whose name has the sound /ŏ/.

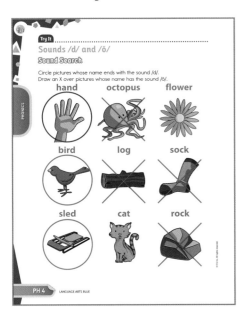

⌈ Online ⌉ 🔟 minutes

REVIEW: Sounds /d/ and /ŏ/

Students will work online independently to

▶ Practice the sounds /d/ and /ŏ/.

Help students locate the online activities and provide support as needed.

Offline Alternative

No computer access? Have students point out and name things that contain the sounds /d/ and /ŏ/ (for example, *door* or *log*).

Unit Checkpoint

Lesson Overview

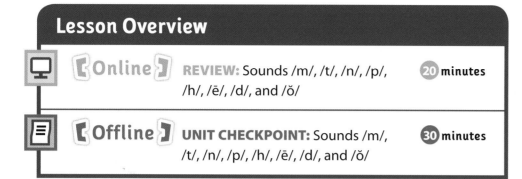

🖥	**[Online]** REVIEW: Sounds /m/, /t/, /n/, /p/, /h/, /ē/, /d/, and /ŏ/	**20** minutes
📄	**[Offline]** UNIT CHECKPOINT: Sounds /m/, /t/, /n/, /p/, /h/, /ē/, /d/, and /ŏ/	**30** minutes

[Materials]

Supplied
- *K¹² PhonicsWorks Basic Assessments*, pp. PH 1–4

Objectives

- Identify and use the sound /m/.
- Identify and use the sound /t/.
- Identify and use the sound /n/.
- Identify and use the sound /p/.
- Identify and use the sound /h/.
- Identify and use the sound /ē/.
- Identify and use the sound /d/.
- Identify and use the sound /ŏ/.
- Identify beginning sounds in words.
- Identify ending sounds in words.
- Identify individual sounds in words.
- Identify beginning, middle, and ending positions.

[Online] **20** minutes

REVIEW: **Sounds /m/, /t/, /n/, /p/, /h/, /ē/, /d/, and /ŏ/**

Students will review the sounds /m/, /t/, /n/, /p/, /h/, /ē/, /d/, and /ŏ/ to prepare for the Unit Checkpoint. Help students locate the online activities and provide support as needed.

 **30** minutes

UNIT CHECKPOINT: Sounds /m/, /t/, /n/, /p/, /h/, /ē/, /d/, and /ŏ/

Explain that students are going to show what they have learned about sounds.

1. Give students the Unit Checkpoint pages for the Sounds /m/, /t/, /n/, /p/, /h/, /ē/, /d/, and /ŏ/unit and print the Unit Checkpoint Answer Key, if you'd like.

2. Use the instructions below to help administer the Checkpoint to students. On the Answer Key or another sheet of paper, note student answers to oral response questions to help with scoring the Checkpoint later.

3. Use the Answer Key to score the Checkpoint, and then enter the results online.

Part 1. Beginning, Middle, or End? Have students color the beginning car black, the middle car yellow, and the ending car red.

Part 2. Match Beginning Sounds Have students say the name of each picture and draw a line to connect pictures that begin with the same sound.

Part 3. Beginning Sounds Say each group of words and have students say which words begin with the same sound. Repeat the words, as necessary. Note any incorrect responses.

8. *moon, bike, mask*

9. *test, tent, foot*

10. *boat, piano, paint*

11. *nickel, match, needle*

12. *otter, eagle, eating*

13. *book, duckling, deer*

14. *hippo, thermometer, horn*

15. *even, octopus, ox*

Part 4. Ending Sounds Say each group of words and have students say which words end with the same sound. Repeat the words, as necessary. Note any incorrect responses.

16. *ham, pot, jam*

17. *hot, pin, hat*

18. *lap, lip, gum*

19. *green, peach, line*

20. *bee, day, we*

21. *read, band, rib*

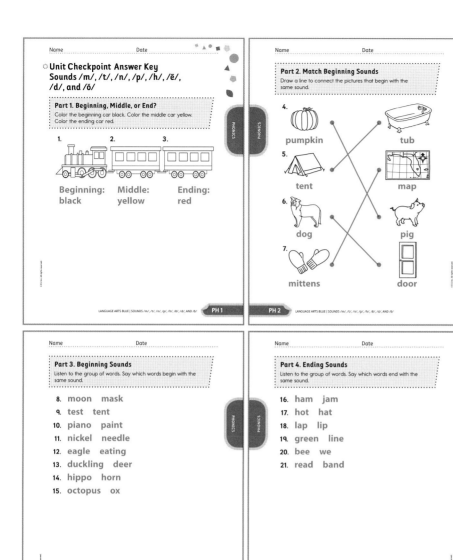

Name _____ **Date** _____

○ **Unit Checkpoint Answer Key**
Sounds /m/, /t/, /n/, /p/, /h/, /ē/,
/d/, and /ŏ/

Part 1. Beginning, Middle, or End?
Color the beginning car black. Color the middle car yellow.
Color the ending car red.

1.   2.   3.

Beginning: Middle: Ending:
black   yellow   red

Name _____ **Date** _____

Part 2. Match Beginning Sounds
Draw a line to connect the pictures that begin with the
same sound.

4. pumpkin — tub

5. tent — map

6. dog — pig

7. mittens — door

Name _____ **Date** _____

Part 3. Beginning Sounds
Listen to the group of words. Say which words begin with the
same sound.

8. moon   mask
9. test   tent
10. piano   paint
11. nickel   needle
12. eagle   eating
13. duckling   deer
14. hippo   horn
15. octopus   ox

Name _____ **Date** _____

Part 4. Ending Sounds
Listen to the group of words. Say which words end with the
same sound.

16. ham   jam
17. hot   hat
18. lap   lip
19. green   line
20. bee   we
21. read   band

Sounds /b/ and /f/

Unit Overview

In this unit, students will
- Identify letters in the alphabet.
- Identify and say the sounds /b/, /f/, /ā/, /g/, /ō/, and /j/.
- Distinguish between words that rhyme or sound different.
- Identify individual sounds within words.

Lesson Overview

[Offline] FOCUS: Sounds /b/ and /f/ — **30** minutes

Get Ready	Sing "The Alphabet Song"
	Learn Lowercase Letters *a* and *b*
	Review Letter Names
	Sound Chains
	Rhyming Practice
	Find Rhyming Words in Poems
Learn	Introduce the Sound /b/
	Listen for the Beginning Sound /b/
	Listen for the Ending Sound /b/
	Introduce the Sound /f/
	Listen for the Beginning Sound /f/
	Listen for the Ending Sound /f/
Try It	The Beginning

[Online] REVIEW: Sounds /b/ and /f/ — **20** minutes

Advance Preparation

Place uppercase letter tiles in alphabetical order on your whiteboard. Place lowercase letter tiles *a* and *b* on students' whiteboard.

Big Ideas

The ability to hear, identify, and create rhyming words is a demonstration of phonological awareness.

 **30 minutes**

FOCUS: Sounds /b/ and /f/

Work **together** with students to complete offline Get Ready, Learn, and Try It activities.

Get Ready ··

Sing "The Alphabet Song"
To help students become familiar and comfortable with the alphabet, sing "The Alphabet Song" with them. Sing slowly, so that students may touch each letter on your whiteboard as they sing the letter's name.

_____

Learn Lowercase Letters *a* and *b*
To help students learn lowercase letters of the alphabet, have them practice identifying and naming the letters *a* and *b*.

1. **Say:** There are two different kinds of letters in our alphabet. The ones you already know are called capital, or uppercase, letters. The other kind of letters are called lowercase, or small, letters. These letters are smaller than capital letters.

2. **Say:** We're going to learn two lowercase letters today. They are *a* and *b*.

3. Have students touch each lowercase letter on their whiteboard and say its name.

4. **Say:** I'm going to put these letters on my whiteboard in place of the capital letters for *a* and *b*.

5. Move the uppercase *A* and *B* tiles from your whiteboard to the Tile Kit, and replace them with the lowercase *a* and *b* tiles.

6. Have students sing "The Alphabet Song," touching the lowercase letters *a* and *b*, then moving back to the capital letters.

_____

Review Letter Names
To help students learn the alphabet, have them practice identifying and naming the letters *a, b, C, F, I, M, P,* and *Z*. Grab your whiteboard with letters.

1. Point to each letter and have students touch and name each one.

        C   F   I   a   P   M   b   Z

2. Say the name of each letter. After each one, have students repeat the name and touch the tile.

        C   F   I   a   P   M   b   Z

Objectives
- Match capital letters to lowercase letters.
- Identify letters of the alphabet.
- Identify capital and lowercase letters.
- Identify individual sounds in words.
- Identify words that rhyme.

3. Redirect students if they name a letter incorrectly.

   ▸ Name the letter students missed.
   ▸ Have students touch the letter and say its name.
   ▸ Have students trace the shape of the letter with their finger on the brown side of their board, and have them say the letter's name as they trace the shape.
   ▸ If students name a letter incorrectly twice, point to the letter and tell them its name. Have students touch the letter and say its name.

Sound Chains

Play a game with color tiles to help students identify sounds that are the same and sounds that are different. Grab the color tiles from the Tile Kit.

1. Place the tiles on a table.

2. **Say:** I am going to make two sounds. If the sounds are the same, you'll pick out two tiles that are the same color and put them next to each other. If the sounds are different, you'll pick out two tiles that are different colors and put them next to each other. For example,

   ▸ When I make the sounds /mmm/ and /ēēē/, you'll pick out two tiles that are different colors because the two sounds are different. Remember, the two sounds I made were /mmm/ and /ēēē/.
   ▸ Now listen carefully to the next two sounds: /mmm/, /t/. The first sound—/mmm/—stayed the same, but the second sound changed from /ēēē/ to /t/. To show that the second sound changed, you will change the second color tile to a tile of a different color.

3. Say each pair of sounds. Have students pick out and place tiles to indicate whether the sounds are the same or different. Note that students should **not** choose two new tiles for each pair of sounds; they should begin with two tiles and replace those tiles as necessary throughout the "chain."

   ▸ /d/, /t/
   ▸ /d/, /d/
   ▸ /n/, /d/
   ▸ /s/, /d/
   ▸ /f/, /d/
   ▸ /f/, /f/
   ▸ /ŏ/, /f/
   ▸ /ŏ/, /s/

TIP If you have not done so already, watch the *K¹² PhonicsWorks* video, which models using color tiles.

Rhyming Practice

Discuss rhyming words with students.

1. **Say:** Let's talk about words that rhyme. Rhyming words are words that sound almost alike. If the beginning sound of each word is different but the rest of the sounds are the same, the words rhyme. For example, these words rhyme:

   ▸ *fun* and *sun*
   ▸ *bag* and *rag*
   ▸ *fight* and *light*
   ▸ *cat* and *hat*

2. **Say:** When I say two words, say *Yes* if they rhyme and *No* if they don't.

   ▸ *bat* and *hat* Yes
   ▸ *hat* and *top* No
   ▸ *stop* and *top* Yes
   ▸ *cat* and *bat* Yes
   ▸ *cat* and *hat* Yes

Find Rhyming Words in Poems

Use common poems and nursery rhymes to practice identifying rhyming words.

1. **Say:** I'm going to say part of a poem. You'll tell me which words rhyme. For example, if I say, "Hickory, dickory, dock. The mouse ran up the clock," you will tell me that *dock* and *clock* rhyme.

2. Say the following couplets. Have students identify the words that rhyme.

   ▸ "Twinkle, twinkle, little star / How I wonder what you are." *star* and *are*
   ▸ "Up above the world so high / Like a diamond in the sky." *high* and *sky*

Learn

Introduce the Sound /b/

Teach the sound /b/, as in *bell*, *bat*, and *bean*.

1. **Say:** We're going to play a game to practice the **sound /b/**. Your job is to say the sound just like me and do what I do, too.

2. Pretend to bounce a ball and say the sound /b/. Have students do this, too.

3. **Say:** We make many sounds with our tongue, our teeth, and our lips. Say /b/ again and feel whether your tongue, teeth, or lips are making the sound.

   ▸ Did you feel your lips making a sound? Yes

4. **Say:** We make some sounds with a whisper and some sounds with our voice. Let's figure out whether the sound /b/ is whispered or voiced. Say /b/ and put your fingers on the lump in your throat called your voice box.

   ▸ Do you feel your voice box vibrate? Yes, /b/ is a noisy sound because we use our voice box when we make the sound.

Objectives

- Identify and use the sound /b/.
- Identify and use the sound /f/.
- Identify beginning sounds in words.
- Identify ending sounds in words.

5. **Say:** I'll say some words that start with the sound /b/ and you'll repeat them, saying /b/ just the way I do.

bell   bat   bean

6. **Say:** Now I'll say some words that end with the sound /b/ and you'll repeat them, saying /b/ just the way I do.

lab   sub   cab

(TIP) When you teach the sound /b/, make sure students say the sound correctly and do not add *uh* after pronouncing it. Students should say /b/, not *buh*.

Listen for the Beginning Sound /b/

Present pairs of words to help students recognize beginning sounds.

1. **Say:** I'm going to say two words. Listen for the **beginning sound /b/**. Then tell me the word that has that beginning sound. For example, if I say *bend* and *straight*, you'll say *bend* because /b/ is the first sound in *bend*.

2. Say each pair of words. Have students identify the word that begins with the sound /b/.

    ▸ *mitt* or *button* button
    ▸ *ball* or *cat* ball
    ▸ *bat* or *sing* bat

Listen for the Ending Sound /b/

Present pairs of words to help students recognize ending sounds.

1. **Say:** I'm going to say two words. Listen for the **ending sound /b/**. Then tell me the word with that ending sound. For example, if I say *rib* and *lid*, you'll say *rib* because /b/ is the last sound in *rib*.

2. Say each pair of words. Have students identify the word that ends with the sound /b/.

    ▸ *sun* or *knob* knob
    ▸ *grab* or *stick* grab
    ▸ *scrub* or *wash* scrub

Introduce the Sound /f/

Teach the sound /f/, as in *fan*, *first*, and *fuss*.

1. **Say:** We're going to play a game to practice the **sound /f/**. Your job is to say the sound just like me and do what I do, too.

2. Fan yourself with your hand and say, "My hand makes a f-f-fantastic f-f-fan." Have students do this, too.

3. **Say:** We make many sounds with our tongue, our teeth, and our lips. Say /f/ again and feel whether your tongue, teeth, or lips are making the sound.

    ▸ Did you feel your teeth and lips making a sound? Yes

4. **Say:** We make some sounds with a whisper and some sounds with our voice. Let's figure out whether the sound /f/ is whispered or voiced. Say /f/ and put your fingers on the lump in your throat called your voice box.

    ▸ Do you feel your voice box vibrate? No, /f/ is a whispered sound because we don't use our voice box when we make the sound.

5. **Say:** I'll say some words that start with the sound /f/ and you'll repeat them, saying /f/ just the way I do.

            fan   *first*   *fuss*

6. **Say:** Now I'll say some words that end with the sound /f/ and you'll repeat them, saying /f/ just the way I do.

            leaf   *if*   *stuff*

(TIP) When you teach the sound /f/, make sure students say the sound correctly and do not add *uh* after pronouncing it. Students should say /f/, not *fuh*.

Listen for the Beginning Sound /f/

Present pairs of words to help students recognize beginning sounds.

1. **Say:** I'm going to say two words. Listen for the **beginning sound /f/**. Then tell me the word that has that beginning sound. For example, if I say *fun* and *man*, you'll say *fun* because /f/ is the first sound in *fun*.

2. Say each pair of words. Have students identify the word that begins with the sound /f/.

    ▸ *moon* or *fix* fix
    ▸ *field* or *grass* field
    ▸ *sack* or *fountain* fountain

Listen for the Ending Sound /f/

Present pairs of words to help students recognize ending sounds.

1. **Say:** I'm going to say two words. Listen for the **ending sound /f/**. Then tell me the word with that ending sound. For example, if I say *golf* and *fly*, you'll say *golf* because /f/ is the last sound in *golf*.

2. Say each pair of words. Have students identify the word that ends with the sound /f/.

    ▸ *leaf* or *twig* leaf
    ▸ *on* or *off* off
    ▸ *smooth* or *rough* rough

Try It

The Beginning

Have students complete page PH 5 in *K¹² PhonicsWorks Basic Activity Book* for more practice with the sounds /b/ and /f/. First have students say the name of each picture. Then have them circle pictures whose name begins with the sound /b/ and draw an X over pictures whose name begins with the sound /f/.

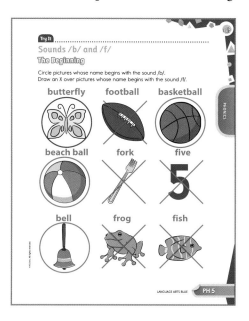

> **Objectives**
> - Identify and use the sound /b/.
> - Identify and use the sound /f/.
> - Identify beginning sounds in words.

Online 20 minutes

REVIEW: **Sounds /b/ and /f/**

Students will work online independently to

► Practice the sounds /b/ and /f/.

Help students locate the online activities and provide support as needed.

___

Offline Alternative

No computer access? Have students point out and name things that begin or end with the sounds /b/ and /f/ (for example, *knob* or *foot*).

> **Objectives**
> - Identify and use the sound /b/.
> - Identify and use the sound /f/.
> - Identify beginning sounds in words.
> - Identify ending sounds in words.

Sound /ā/

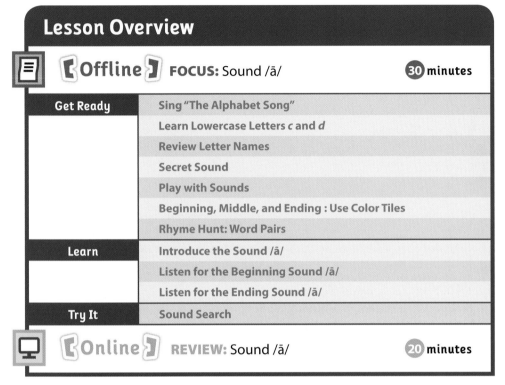

Lesson Overview

Offline FOCUS: Sound /ā/ — **30** minutes

Get Ready	Sing "The Alphabet Song"
	Learn Lowercase Letters *c* and *d*
	Review Letter Names
	Secret Sound
	Play with Sounds
	Beginning, Middle, and Ending : Use Color Tiles
	Rhyme Hunt: Word Pairs
Learn	Introduce the Sound /ā/
	Listen for the Beginning Sound /ā/
	Listen for the Ending Sound /ā/
Try It	Sound Search

Online REVIEW: Sound /ā/ — **20** minutes

Materials

Supplied

- *K¹² PhonicsWorks Basic Activity Book*, p. PH 6
- whiteboard, Learning Coach
- whiteboard, student
- Tile Kit

Advance Preparation

Place lowercase letter tiles *a* and *b* and uppercase letter tiles *C* through *Z* in alphabetical order on your whiteboard. Place lowercase letter tiles *c* and *d* on students' whiteboard.

 **30** minutes

FOCUS: Sound /ā/

Work **together** with students to complete offline Get Ready, Learn, and Try It activities.

Get Ready •••

Sing "The Alphabet Song"

To help students become familiar and comfortable with the alphabet, sing "The Alphabet Song" with them. Sing slowly, so that students may touch each letter on your whiteboard as they sing the letter's name.

Objectives
- Match capital letters to lowercase letters.
- Identify letters of the alphabet.
- Identify capital and lowercase letters.
- Identify individual sounds in words.
- Identify beginning, middle, and ending positions.
- Identify words that rhyme.

Learn Lowercase Letters *c* and *d*

To help students learn lowercase letters of the alphabet, have them practice identifying and naming the letters *c* and *d*.

1. **Say:** There are two different kinds of letters in our alphabet. The ones you already know are called capital, or uppercase, letters. The other kind of letters are called lowercase, or small, letters. These letters are smaller than capital letters.

2. **Say:** We're going to learn two lowercase letters today. They are *c* and *d*.

3. Have students touch each lowercase letter on their whiteboard and say its name.

4. **Say:** I'm going to put these letters on my whiteboard in place of the capital letters for *c* and *d*.

5. Move the uppercase *C* and *D* tiles from your whiteboard to the Tile Kit, and replace them with the lowercase *c* and *d* tiles.

6. Have students sing "The Alphabet Song," touching the lowercase letters *c* and *d*, then moving back to the capital letters.

Review Letter Names

To help students learn the alphabet, have them practice identifying and naming the letters *a, b, c, d, O, P, Q,* and *T*. Grab your whiteboard with letters.

1. Point to each letter and have students touch and name each one.

    c   O   T   a   P   b   Q   d

2. Say the name of each letter. After each one, have students repeat the name and touch the tile.

    c   O   T   a   P   b   Q   d

3. Redirect students if they name a letter incorrectly.

> ► Name the letter students missed.
> ► Have students touch the letter and say its name.
> ► Have students trace the shape of the letter with their finger on the brown side of their board, and have them say the letter's name as they trace the shape.
> ► If students name a letter incorrectly twice, point to the letter and tell them its name. Have students touch the letter and say its name.

Secret Sound

Say groups of words that begin with the same letter to help students recognize **beginning sounds** in words.

1. **Say**: I am going to say some groups of words. Listen for a secret sound at the beginning of each word. Then tell me what sound you hear at the beginning of each group of words.

2. Say each of the following groups of words. Have students identify the secret sound in each group.

> ► *bug, brunch, bike, bless* /b/
> ► *fun, flip, fine, fowl* /f/
> ► *eat, easy, eel, eagle* /ē/
> ► *head, heel, heart, hands* /h/

3. Repeat any groups of words for which students couldn't identify the secret sound. Have students repeat each word in that group. Then have them say what sound they hear at the beginning of each word.

Play with Sounds

Review the actions and sounds for the letter sounds students have learned so far.

1. **Say:** You have learned some sounds and movements that go with those sounds. Let's go over them. I am going to make a sound, and you make the movement that goes with that sound. For example, if I make the sound /m/, you rub your belly.

2. Make the following sounds. Have students make the signals that go with the sounds.

> ► /m/ rub belly "Mmm, that tastes good!"
> ► /p/ push hands out
> ► /ē/ flap wings like an eagle
> ► /d/ pretend to dance
> ► /b/ bounce a ball
> ► /t/ touch toes
> ► /n/ shake head "No"
> ► /h/ tip imaginary hat
> ► /ŏ/ wiggle fingers as if they were octopus tentacles
> ► /f/ make fanning motion with hand

TIP If students forget the signal that goes with a sound, show them the signal and have them repeat both the sound and the signal.

Beginning, Middle, and Ending: Use Color Tiles

Use this activity to reinforce the concepts of beginning, middle, and ending (or first, middle, and last). Grab three different color tiles from the Tile Kit.

1. Line up the tiles from left to right, about two inches apart, on a table.

2. **Say:** When we read, we always start here [point to the color tile on the far left], at the **beginning**, and stop here [point to the color tile on the far right], at the **end**.

3. Have students touch the first tile on the table and have them say, "The [color] tile is first on the table. It is at the **beginning**."

4. Have students touch the last tile on the table and have them say, "The [color] tile is last on the table. It is at the **ending**."

5. **Say:** When three objects are lined up, the middle object is also called the second object.

6. Have students touch the second tile on the table and have them say, "The [color] tile is second on the table. It is in the **middle**."

7. Have students

  ▸ Touch the middle tile.
  ▸ Touch the last tile.
  ▸ Touch the beginning tile.
  ▸ Touch the first tile.
  ▸ Touch the last tile.
  ▸ Touch the middle tile.

8. **Say:** Please move the middle tile so it is first.

  ▸ What is last now?
  ▸ What is in the middle?
  ▸ What is at the beginning?

9. **Say:** Please move the last tile so it is in the middle.

  ▸ What is first now?
  ▸ What is at the end?
  ▸ What is second?

10. Repeat this activity until students are comfortable with arranging the tiles from left to right and they understand what beginning, middle, and ending (or first, second, and last) mean.

Rhyme Hunt: Word Pairs

Play a game with students to reinforce awareness of words that rhyme.

1. **Say:** Words that rhyme sound almost alike. If the beginning sound of each word is different but the other sounds are the same, the words rhyme.

2. Review rhyming words with students before beginning the game.

   Say: Let's talk about words that rhyme. Can you give me some examples of rhyming words?

   ▸ Does *tin* rhyme with *spin*? Yes
   ▸ Does *rock* rhyme with *roll*? No

3. Have students play the Rhyme Hunt game. When you say a word, students try to think of a rhyming word or find an object in the room that rhymes. If they have trouble with one word, provide a rhyme for them and then go to the next word.

   label Possible rhyme: *table*
   dock Possible rhyme: *clock*
   men Possible rhyme: *pen*
   bear Possible rhyme: *chair*
   look Possible rhyme: *book*
   mug Possible rhyme: *rug*
   door Possible rhyme: *floor*
   taper Possible rhyme: *paper*

Learn

Introduce the Sound /ā/

Teach the sound /ā/, as in *aim, age,* and *ache.*

1. **Say:** We're going to play a game to practice the **sound** /ā/. Your job is to say the sound just like me and do what I do, too.

2. Cheer and say, "Yay! Yay! For the sound of A!" Have students do this, too.

3. **Say:** We make some sounds with a whisper and some sounds with our voice. Let's figure out whether the sound /ā/ is whispered or voiced. Say /ā/ and put your fingers on the lump in your throat called your voice box.

   ▸ Do you feel your voice box vibrate? Yes, /ā/ is a noisy sound because we use our voice box when we make the sound.

4. **Say:** I'll say some words that start with the sound /ā/ and you'll repeat them, saying /ā/ just the way I do.

   aim   age   ache

5. **Say:** Now I'll say some words that end with the sound /ā/ and you'll repeat them, saying /ā/ just the way I do.

   May   day   play

Objectives

- Identify and use the sound /ā/.
- Identify beginning sounds in words.
- Identify ending sounds in words.

Listen for the Beginning Sound /ā/

Present pairs of words to help students recognize beginning sounds.

1. **Say:** I'm going to say two words. Listen for the **beginning sound** /ā/. Then tell me the word that has that beginning sound. For example, if I say *April* and *August*, you'll say *April* because /ā/ is the first sound in *April*.

2. Say each pair of words. Have students identify the word that begins with the sound /ā/.

   ▸ *Asia* or *Africa Asia*
   ▸ *strong* or *able able*
   ▸ *one* or *eight eight*

Listen for the Ending Sound /ā/

Present pairs of words to help students recognize ending sounds.

1. **Say:** I'm going to say two words. Listen for the **ending sound** /ā/. Then tell me the word with that ending sound. For example, if I say *day* and *dough*, you'll say *day* because /ā/ is the last sound in *day*.

2. Say each pair of words. Have students identify the word that ends with the sound /ā/.

   ▸ *pie* or *pay pay*
   ▸ *gray* or *grow gray*
   ▸ *sigh* or *say say*

Try It ....

Sound Search

Have students complete page PH 6 in *K¹² PhonicsWorks Basic Activity Book* for more practice with the sound /ā/. First have students say the name of each picture. Then have them circle pictures whose name has the sound /ā/.

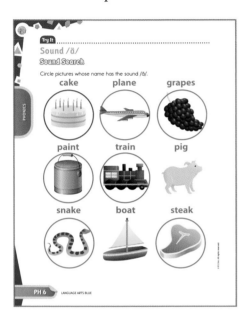

Objectives
- Identify and use the sound /ā/.
- Identify individual sounds in words.

   **minutes**

REVIEW: Sound /ā/

Students will work online independently to

▸ Practice the sound /ā/.

Help students locate the online activities and provide support as needed.

Objectives
- Identify and use the sound /ā/.
- Identify beginning sounds in words.
- Identify ending sounds in words.

Offline Alternative

No computer access? Have students point out and name things that begin or end with the sound /ā/ (for example, *acorn* or *tray*).

Sounds /g/ and /ō/

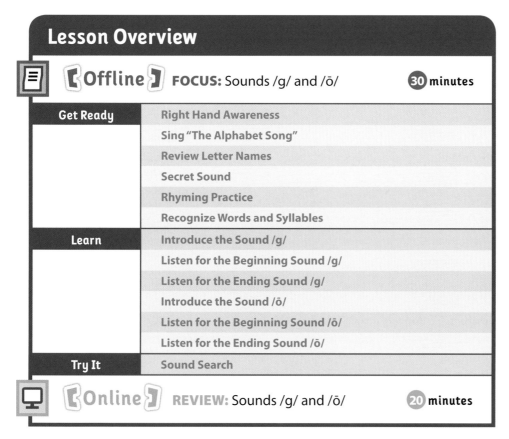

Lesson Overview

Offline FOCUS: Sounds /g/ and /ō/ — **30** minutes

Get Ready	
	Right Hand Awareness
	Sing "The Alphabet Song"
	Review Letter Names
	Secret Sound
	Rhyming Practice
	Recognize Words and Syllables
Learn	
	Introduce the Sound /g/
	Listen for the Beginning Sound /g/
	Listen for the Ending Sound /g/
	Introduce the Sound /ō/
	Listen for the Beginning Sound /ō/
	Listen for the Ending Sound /ō/
Try It	
	Sound Search

Online REVIEW: Sounds /g/ and /ō/ — **20** minutes

Materials

Supplied
- *K¹² PhonicsWorks Basic Activity Book*, p. PH 7
- whiteboard, Learning Coach
- whiteboard, student
- Tile Kit

Keywords

syllable – a unit of spoken language; a syllable contains only one vowel sound

Advance Preparation

Place lowercase letter tiles *a* through *d* and uppercase letter tiles *E* through *Z* in alphabetical order on your whiteboard.

Big Ideas

▶ The ability to identify syllables is a demonstration of phonological awareness.
▶ A syllable always contains a vowel sound, and it may or may not contain consonant sounds before or after the vowel sound.

[Offline] **30** minutes

FOCUS: Sounds /g/ and /ō/

Work **together** with students to complete offline Get Ready, Learn, and
Try It activities.

Get Ready

Right Hand Awareness
Students read from left to right, so play a game to develop right hand awareness.
To avoid confusion, focus on the right hand only.

1. Say each sentence and do each action. Have students repeat your words
   and actions.

   ▸ I'm shaking your right hand.
   ▸ Now I'm touching my right ankle.
   ▸ Now I'm waving my right hand in the air.
   ▸ Now I'm touching my right toe.
   ▸ Now I'm touching my right cheek.

2. Repeat the actions and mix up the order. To end the activity, shake right
   hands again.

> **Objectives**
> - Develop right hand awareness.
> - Identify letters of the alphabet.
> - Identify capital and lowercase letters.
> - Identify ending sounds in words.
> - Identify words that rhyme.
> - Identify individual sounds in words.

Sing "The Alphabet Song"
To help students become familiar and comfortable with the alphabet, sing
"The Alphabet Song" with them. Sing slowly, so that students may touch
each letter on your whiteboard as they sing the letter's name.

Review Letter Names
To help students learn the alphabet, have them practice identifying and naming the
letters *a, b, c, d, E, K, L,* and *M.* Grab your whiteboard with letters.

1. Point to each letter and have students touch and name each one.

   a b M K L c d E

2. Say the name of each letter. After each one, have students repeat the name and
   touch the tile.

   a b M K L c d E

3. Redirect students if they name a letter incorrectly.

   ▸ Name the letter students missed.
   ▸ Have students touch the letter and say its name.
   ▸ Have students trace the shape of the letter with their finger on the brown side
     of their board, and have them say the letter's name as they trace the shape.
   ▸ If students name a letter incorrectly twice, point to the letter and tell them
     its name. Have students touch the letter and say its name.

Secret Sound

Say groups of words that end with the same letter to help students recognize **ending sounds** in words.

1. **Say:** I am going to say some groups of words. Listen for a secret sound at the end of each word. Then tell me what sound you hear at the end of each group of words.

2. Say each of the following groups of words. Have students identify the secret sound in each group.

   ▸ *rub, rib, slab, grab* /b/
   ▸ *if, cliff, staff, laugh* /f/
   ▸ *me, be, tree, funny* /ē/
   ▸ *sun, tan, in, on* /n/

3. Repeat any groups of words for which students couldn't identify the secret sound. Have students repeat each word in that group. Then have them say what sound they hear at the beginning of each word.

Rhyming Practice

Use common poems and nursery rhymes to practice identifying rhyming words.

1. **Say:** I am going to start reading a poem. When you hear words that rhyme, raise your hand and tell me the words. I will continue reading the poem. As I read, keep raising your hand when you hear words that rhyme and tell me the words.

2. Read the poem. Have students raise their hand when they hear rhyming words and have them tell you which words rhyme. Continue reading the poem.

   Baa, baa, black sheep,
   Have you any wool?
   Yes, sir, yes, sir,
   Three bags full.

3. Continue this activity with other poems that have obvious rhyming words. Here are some choices:

   ▸ "One, Two, Buckle My Shoe"
   ▸ "A-Tisket, A-Tasket, a Green and Yellow Basket"

Learn

Recognize Words and Syllables

Introduce the concept of syllables to students.

1. **Say:** When we talk, we make words by pushing air out of our mouths. Each push of air in a word is called a **syllable**. Each word has one or more syllables. You can think of syllables as chunks of words.

2. **Say:** Let's break some words into syllables.

   ▸ I'll say a word. I'll repeat the word.
   ▸ You'll say the word after me, and you'll break it into syllables by saying the separate chunks of the word and tapping your fist on the table as you say each chunk.
   ▸ For example, I'll say *hammer,* and then I'll say it again.
   ▸ You'll say *ham / mer* and tap your fist on the table as you say each syllable.

3. Say each word and repeat it. Have students fist tap on the table as they say the syllables in each word.

   ▸ *river* ri / ver
   ▸ *sunset* sun / set
   ▸ *inside* in / side
   ▸ *outside* out / side
   ▸ *backpack* back / pack
   ▸ *pigpen* pig / pen
   ▸ *laptop* lap / top
   ▸ *smile* smile
   ▸ *fun* fun

   ▸ *baseball* base / ball
   ▸ *game* game
   ▸ *football* foot / ball
   ▸ *window* win / dow
   ▸ *forget* for / get
   ▸ *maybe* may / be
   ▸ *lightbulb* light / bulb
   ▸ *toenail* toe / nail

TIP You can practice syllables with students wherever you are. Have students name items in the room and fist tap the syllables with you. For example, have them name and fist tap words such as *ta / ble* and *win / dow.* Challenge students to name and fist tap something with several syllables (for example, *tel / e / vi / sion*).

Objectives

- Identify syllables in words.
- Identify and use the sound /g/.
- Identify and use the sound /ō/.
- Identify beginning sounds in words.
- Identify ending sounds in words.
- Identify individual sounds in words.

Introduce the Sound /g/

Teach the sound /g/, as in *gift, go,* and *game.*

1. **Say:** We're going to play a game to practice the **sound /g/**. Your job is to say the sound just like me and do what I do, too.

2. Put your hand to your mouth and pretend to giggle. Have students do this, too.

3. **Say:** We make many sounds with our tongue, our teeth, and our lips. Say /g/ again and feel whether your tongue, teeth, or lips are making the sound.

   ▸ Did you feel the back of your tongue make the sound /g/? Yes

4. **Say:** We make some sounds with a whisper and some sounds with our voice. Let's figure out whether the sound /g/ is whispered or voiced. Say /g/ and put your fingers on the lump in your throat called your voice box.

   ▸ Do you feel your voice box vibrate? Yes, /g/ is a noisy sound because we use our voice box when we make the sound.

5. **Say:** I'll say some words that start with the sound /g/ and you'll repeat them, saying /g/ just the way I do.

   gift   go   game

6. **Say:** Now I'll say some words that end with the sound /g/ and you'll repeat them, saying /g/ just the way I do.

   big   rag   jug

Listen for the Beginning Sound /g/

Present pairs of words to help students recognize beginning sounds.

1. **Say:** I'm going to say two words. Listen for the **beginning sound /g/**. Then tell me the word that has that beginning sound. For example, if I say *go* and *kid*, you'll say *go* because /g/ is the first sound in *go*.

2. Say each pair of words. Have students identify the word that begins with the sound /g/.

   ▸ *gust* or *cab* gust
   ▸ *show* or *grow* grow
   ▸ *girl* or *boy* girl

Listen for the Ending Sound /g/

Present pairs of words to help students recognize ending sounds.

1. **Say:** I'm going to say two words. Listen for the **ending sound /g/**. Then tell me the word with that ending sound. For example, if I say *mug* and *cup*, you'll say *mug* because /g/ is the last sound in *mug*.

2. Say each pair of words. Have students identify the word that ends with the sound /g/.

   ▸ *floor* or *rug* rug
   ▸ *slug* or *snail* slug
   ▸ *pull* or *jug* jug

Introduce the Sound /ō/

Teach sound /ō/, as in *open*, *over*, and *oak*.

1. **Say:** We're going to play a game to practice the **sound** /ō/. Your job is to say the sound just like me and do what I do, too.

2. Make the okay sign with your fingers and say, "O is Okay!" Have students do this, too.

3. **Say:** We make some sounds with a whisper and some sounds with our voice. Let's figure out whether the sound /ō/ is whispered or voiced. Say /ō/ and put your fingers on the lump in your throat called your voice box.

   ▸ Do you feel your voice box vibrate? Yes, /ō/is a noisy sound because we use our voice box when we make the sound.

4. **Say:** I'll say some words that start with the sound /ō/ and you'll repeat them, saying /ō/ just the way I do.

   open   over   oak

5. **Say:** Now I'll say some words that end with the sound /ō/ and you'll repeat them, saying /ō/ just the way I do.

   low   go   so

Listen for the Beginning Sound /ō/

Present pairs of words to help students recognize beginning sounds.

1. **Say:** I'm going to say two words. Listen for the **beginning sound** /ō/. Then tell me the word that has that beginning sound. For example, if I say *over* and *under*, you'll say *over* because /ō/ is the first sound in *over*.

2. Say each pair of words. Have students identify the word that begins with the sound /ō/.

   ▸ *apple* or *oats* oats
   ▸ *oboe* or *harp* oboe
   ▸ *each* or *own* own

Listen for the Ending Sound /ō/

Present pairs of words to help students recognize ending sounds.

1. **Say:** I'm going to say two words. Listen for the **ending sound** /ō/. Then tell me the word with that ending sound. For example, if I say *toe* and *tree*, you'll say *toe* because /ō/ is the last sound in *toe*.

2. Say each pair of words. Have students identify the word that ends with the sound /ō/.

   ▸ *mow* or *me* mow
   ▸ *agree* or *below* below
   ▸ *know* or *by* know

Try It •••

Sound Search

Have students complete page PH 7 in *K¹² PhonicsWorks Basic Activity Book* for more practice with the sounds /g/ and /ō/. First have students say the name of each picture. Then have them circle pictures whose name ends with the sound /g/ and draw an X over pictures whose name has the sound /ō/.

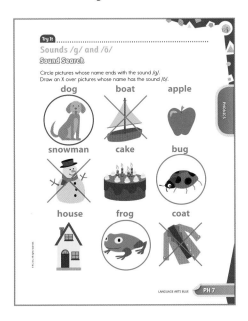

 **20 minutes**

REVIEW: **Sounds /g/ and /ō/**

Students will work online independently to

► Practice the sounds /g/ and /ō/.

Help students locate the online activities and provide support as needed.

Offline Alternative

No computer access? Have students point out and name things that begin or end with the sounds /g/ and /ō/ (for example, *rag* or *dough*).

Sound /j/

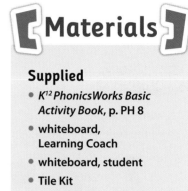

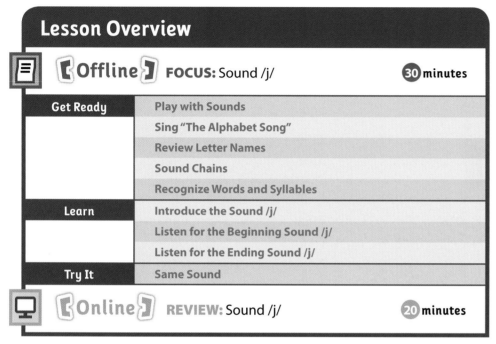

Lesson Overview

Offline FOCUS: Sound /j/ — **30** minutes

Get Ready	Play with Sounds
	Sing "The Alphabet Song"
	Review Letter Names
	Sound Chains
	Recognize Words and Syllables
Learn	Introduce the Sound /j/
	Listen for the Beginning Sound /j/
	Listen for the Ending Sound /j/
Try It	Same Sound

Online REVIEW: Sound /j/ — **20** minutes

[Materials]

Supplied

- *K¹² PhonicsWorks Basic Activity Book*, p. PH 8
- whiteboard, Learning Coach
- whiteboard, student
- Tile Kit

Advance Preparation

Place lowercase letter tiles *a* through *d* and uppercase letter tiles *E* through *Z* in alphabetical order on your whiteboard.

 **30 minutes**

FOCUS: Sound /j/

Work **together** with students to complete offline Get Ready, Learn, and Try It activities.

Get Ready

Play with Sounds

Review the actions and sounds for the letter sounds students have learned so far.

1. **Say:** You have learned some sounds and movements that go with those sounds. Let's go over them. I am going to make a sound, and you make the movement that goes with that sound. For example, if I make the sound /m/, you rub your belly.

2. Make the following sounds. Have students make the signals that go with the sounds.

   ▶ /m/ rub belly "Mmm, that tastes good!"
   ▶ /p/ push hands out
   ▶ /ē/ flap wings like an eagle
   ▶ /d/ pretend to dance
   ▶ /b/ bounce a ball
   ▶ /t/ touch toes
   ▶ /n/ shake head "No"
   ▶ /h/ tip imaginary hat
   ▶ /ŏ/ wiggle fingers as if they were octopus tentacles
   ▶ /f/ make fanning motion with hand
   ▶ /ā/ cheer motion, while saying "Yea, yea for the sound of A!"
   ▶ /ō/ make okay sign with your fingers
   ▶ /g/ put your hand to your mouth and pretend to giggle

    If students forget the signal that goes with a sound, show them the signal and have them repeat both the sound and the signal.

Objectives

- Identify capital and lowercase letters.
- Identify letters of the alphabet.
- Identify beginning sounds in words.
- Identify ending sounds in words.
- Identify individual sounds in words.
- Identify syllables in words.

Sing "The Alphabet Song"

To help students become familiar and comfortable with the alphabet, sing "The Alphabet Song" with them. Sing slowly, so that students may touch each letter on your whiteboard as they sing the letter's name.

Review Letter Names

To help students learn the alphabet, have them practice identifying and naming the letters *a, b, c, d, V, W, Y,* and *Z.* Grab your whiteboard with letters.

1. Point to each letter and have students touch and name each one.

   a   b   c   d   Z   Y   W   V

2. Say the name of each letter. After each one, have students repeat the name and touch the tile.

a   b   c   d   Z   Y   W   V

3. Redirect students if they name a letter incorrectly.

- ▶ Name the letter students missed.
- ▶ Have students touch the letter and say its name.
- ▶ Have students trace the shape of the letter with their finger on the brown side of their whiteboard, and have them say the letter's name as they trace the shape.
- ▶ If students name a letter incorrectly twice, point to the letter and tell them its name. Have students touch the letter and say its name.

Sound Chains

Play a game with color tiles to help students identify sounds that are the same and sounds that are different. Grab the color tiles from the Tile Kit.

1. Place the tiles on a table.

2. **Say:** I am going to make two sounds. If the sounds are the same, you'll pick out two tiles that are the same color and put them next to each other. If the sounds are different, you'll pick out two tiles that are different colors and put them next to each other. For example,

- ▶ With the sounds /n/ and /ēēē/, you'll pick out two tiles that are different colors because the two sounds are different. Remember, the two sounds I made were /n/, /ēēē/.
- ▶ Now listen carefully to the next two sounds: /n/, /n/. The first sound— /n/—stayed the same, but the second sound changed from /ēēē/ to /n/.
- ▶ Since both sounds are now the same (/n/, /n/), you will change the color of the second tile to one that matches the color of the first tile.

3. Say each pair of sounds. Have students pick out and place tiles to indicate whether the sounds are the same or different. Note that students should **not** choose two new tiles for each pair of sounds; they should begin with two tiles and replace those tiles as necessary throughout the "chain."

- ▶ /n/, /ā/
- ▶ /s/, /ā/
- ▶ /ā/, /ā/
- ▶ /g/, /ā/
- ▶ /g/, /g/
- ▶ /b/, /g/
- ▶ /b/, /d/
- ▶ /b/, /b/

TIP If students name a letter incorrectly, name the letter students missed. Have them touch the letter and say its name. Have students trace the shape of the letter with their finger on the brown side of their whiteboard and have them say the letter's name as they trace the shape.

Recognize Words and Syllables
Introduce the concept of syllables to students.

1. **Say:** When we talk, we make words by pushing air out of our mouths. Each push of air in a word is called a **syllable**. Each word has one or more syllables. You can think of syllables as chunks of words.

2. **Say:** Let's break some words into syllables.

   ▸ I'll say a word. I'll repeat the word.
   ▸ You'll say the word after me, and you'll break it into syllables by saying the separate chunks of the word and tapping your fist on the table as you say each chunk.
   ▸ For example, I'll say *table,* and then I'll say it again.
   ▸ You'll say *ta / ble* and tap your fist on the table as you say each syllable.

3. Say each word and repeat it. Have students fist tap on the table as they say the syllables in each word.

   ▸ *picture* pic / ture
   ▸ *inside* in / side
   ▸ *outside* out / side
   ▸ *untie* un / tie
   ▸ *under* un / der
   ▸ *understand* un / der / stand
   ▸ *important* im / por / tant
   ▸ *sunshine* sun / shine
   ▸ *elephant* el / e / phant
   ▸ *cartoon* car / toon
   ▸ *nature* na / ture
   ▸ *animal* an / i / mal
   ▸ *napkin* nap / kin

Learn

Introduce the Sound /j/
Teach the sound /j/, as in *jump, joke,* and *joy.*

1. **Say:** We're going to play a game to practice the **sound /j/**. Your job is to say the sound just like me and do what I do, too.

2. Jump and make the sound /j/. Have students do this, too.

3. **Say:** We make some sounds with a whisper and some sounds with our voice. Let's figure out whether the sound /j/ is whispered or voiced. Say /j/ and put your fingers on the lump in your throat called your voice box.

   ▸ Do you feel your voice box vibrate? Yes, /j/ is a noisy sound because we use our voice box when we make the sound.

Objectives
• Identify and use the sound /j/.
• Identify beginning sounds in words.
• Identify ending sounds in words.

4. **Say:** I'll say some words that start with the sound /j/ and you'll repeat them, saying /j/ just the way I do.

jump   *joke*   *joy*

5. **Say:** Now I'll say some words that end with the sound /j/ and you'll repeat them, saying /j/ just the way I do.

age   *fudge*   *stage*

Listen for the Beginning Sound /j/

Present pairs of words to help students recognize beginning sounds.

1. **Say:** I'm going to say two words. Listen for the **beginning sound /j/**. Then tell me the word that has that beginning sound. For example, if I say *job* and *work*, you'll say *job* because /j/ is the first sound in *job*.

2. Say each pair of words. Have students identify the word that begins with the sound /j/.

   ▸ *ship* or *jam* *jam*
   ▸ *jog* or *run* *jog*
   ▸ *jelly* or *bread* *jelly*

Listen for the Ending Sound /j/

Present pairs of words to help students recognize ending sounds.

1. **Say:** I'm going to say two words. Listen for the **ending sound /j/**. Then tell me the word with that ending sound. For example, if I say *cage* and *pen*, you'll say *cage* because /j/ is the last sound in *cage*.

2. Say each pair of words. Have students identify the word that ends with the sound /j/.

   ▸ *age* or *church* *age*
   ▸ *big* or *huge* *huge*
   ▸ *strange* or *odd* *strange*

Try It

Same Sound

Have students complete page PH 8 in *K¹² PhonicsWorks Basic Activity Book* for more practice with the sound /j/. Have students say the name of the pictures in each row. Then have students circle pictures whose name begins with the same sound in each row.

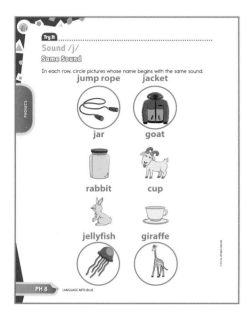

Try It
....
Sound /j/
Same Sound

In each row, circle pictures whose name begins with the same sound.

jump rope   jacket

jar   goat

rabbit   cup

jellyfish   giraffe

PH 8   LANGUAGE ARTS BLUE

[Online] 20 minutes

REVIEW: Sound /j/

Students will work online independently to

► Practice the sound /j/.

Help students locate the online activities and provide support as needed.

Offline Alternative

No computer access? Have students point out and name things that begin or end with the sound /j/ (for example, *jacket* or *badge*).

Unit Checkpoint

Lesson Overview

🖥	【Online】 **REVIEW:** Sounds /b/, /f/, /ā/, /g/, /ō/, and /j/	**20** minutes
📄	【Offline】 **UNIT CHECKPOINT:** Sounds /b/, /f/, /ā/, /g/, /ō/, and /j/	**30** minutes

【Materials】

Supplied
- *K¹² PhonicsWorks Basic Assessments,* pp. PH 5–8

⭐ Objectives

- Identify and use the sound /b/.
- Identify and use the sound /f/.
- Identify and use the sound /ā/.
- Identify and use the sound /g/.
- Identify and use the sound /ō/.
- Identify and use the sound /j/.
- Identify letters of the alphabet.
- Identify beginning sounds in words.
- Identify ending sounds in words.
- Identify words that rhyme.

【Online】 **20** minutes

REVIEW: Sounds /b/, /f/, /ā/, /g/, /ō/, and /j/

Students will review the sounds /b/, /f/, /ā/, /g/, /ō/, and /j/ to prepare for the Unit Checkpoint. Help students locate the online activities and provide support as needed.

Offline 30 minutes

UNIT CHECKPOINT: Sounds /b/, /f/, /ā/, /g/, /ō/, and /j/

Explain that students are going to show what they have learned about letters and sounds.

1. Give students the Unit Checkpoint pages for the Sounds /b/, /f/, /ā/, /g/, /ō/, and /j/ unit and print the Unit Checkpoint Answer Key, if you'd like.
2. Use the instructions below to help administer the Checkpoint to students. On the Answer Key or another sheet of paper, note student answers to oral response questions to help with scoring the Checkpoint later.
3. Use the Answer Key to score the Checkpoint, and then enter the results online.

Part 1. Letter Matching Moving from left to right, have students read the letters aloud and circle the letters that match the first letter in the row.

Part 2. Match Ending Sounds Have students say the name of each picture and draw a line to connect pictures that end with the same sound.

Part 3. Rhymes Say each pair of words and have students say if the word pairs rhyme. Note any incorrect responses.

9. *log, dog*
10. *pig, wig*
11. *cake, bike*
12. *bone, cone*
13. *page, cage*
14. *soap, sap*

Part 4. Beginning Sounds Say each group of three words, and have students say which words begin with the same sound. Repeat the words, as necessary. Note any incorrect responses.

15. *bike, moon, bag*
16. *shrimp, fan, fit*
17. *octopus, apple, ax*
18. *gorilla, piano, game*
19. *open, okay, apron*
20. *jam, jelly, gum*

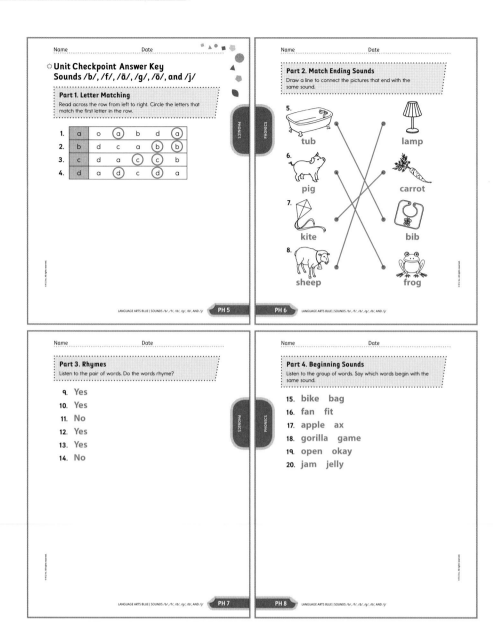

Name _____ Date _____

Unit Checkpoint Answer Key
Sounds /b/, /f/, /ā/, /g/, /ō/, and /j/

Part 1. Letter Matching
Read across the row from left to right. Circle the letters that match the first letter in the row.

1.	a	o	(a)	b	d	(a)
2.	b	d	c	a	(b)	(b)
3.	c	d	a	(c)	(c)	b
4.	d	a	(d)	c	(d)	a

Part 2. Match Ending Sounds
Draw a line to connect the pictures that end with the same sound.

5. tub — lamp
6. pig — carrot
7. kite — bib
8. sheep — frog

Part 3. Rhymes
Listen to the pair of words. Do the words rhyme?

9. Yes
10. Yes
11. No
12. Yes
13. Yes
14. No

Part 4. Beginning Sounds
Listen to the group of words. Say which words begin with the same sound.

15. bike   bag
16. fan   fit
17. apple   ax
18. gorilla   game
19. open   okay
20. jam   jelly

Sound /s/

Unit Overview

In this unit, students will
► Identify letters in the alphabet.
► Identify and say the sounds /s/, /ă/, /w/, /z/, /ī/, and /l/.
► Distinguish between words that rhyme or do not rhyme.
► Identify individual sounds within words.
► Learn and practice blends.

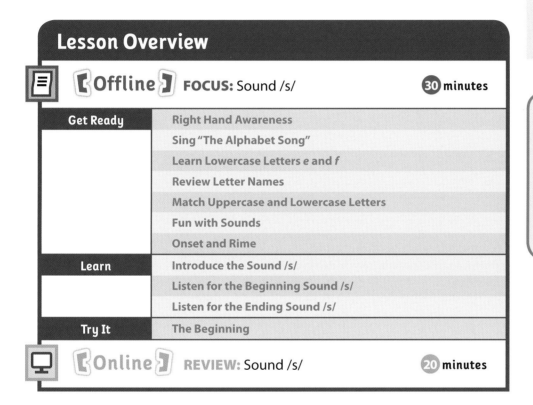

Lesson Overview

Offline FOCUS: Sound /s/ **30** minutes

Get Ready	Right Hand Awareness
	Sing "The Alphabet Song"
	Learn Lowercase Letters *e* and *f*
	Review Letter Names
	Match Uppercase and Lowercase Letters
	Fun with Sounds
	Onset and Rime
Learn	Introduce the Sound /s/
	Listen for the Beginning Sound /s/
	Listen for the Ending Sound /s/
Try It	The Beginning

Online REVIEW: Sound /s/ **20** minutes

{ Materials }

Supplied
● *K¹² PhonicsWorks Basic Activity Book,* p. PH 9
● whiteboard, Learning Coach
● whiteboard, student
● Tile Kit

Keywords

onset – the part of a word preceding the first vowel; in the word *smart, sm*– is the onset

rime – the part of a word that includes the first vowel and what follows it; in the word *smart, –art* is the rime

Advance Preparation

Place lowercase letter tiles *a* through *d* and uppercase letter tiles *E* through *Z* in alphabetical order on both your and students' whiteboards. Place lowercase letter tiles *e* and *f* on the bottom of students' whiteboard.

Big Ideas

The ability to blend onset and rime into a word demonstrates phonological awareness.

 **30 minutes**

FOCUS: Sound /s/

Work **together** with students to complete offline Get Ready, Learn, and Try It activities.

Get Ready

Right Hand Awareness

Students read from left to right, so play a game to develop right hand awareness. To avoid confusion, focus on the right hand only.

1. Say each sentence and do each action. Have students repeat your words and actions.

   ▸ I'm shaking your right hand.
   ▸ Now I'm touching my right ankle.
   ▸ Now I'm waving my right hand in the air.
   ▸ Now I'm touching my right toe.
   ▸ Now I'm touching my right cheek.

2. Repeat the actions and mix up the order. To end the activity, shake right hands again.

Sing "The Alphabet Song"

To help students become familiar and comfortable with the alphabet, sing "The Alphabet Song" with them. Sing slowly, so that students may touch each letter on your whiteboard as they sing the letter's name.

Learn Lowercase Letters *e* and *f*

To help students learn lowercase letters of the alphabet, have them practice identifying and naming the letters *e* and *f*. Grab your whiteboard with letters.

1. **Say:** There are two different kinds of letters in our alphabet. The ones you already know are called capital, or uppercase, letters. The other kind of letters is called small, or lowercase, letters. These letters are smaller than capital letters.

2. **Say:** We're going to learn two lowercase letters today. They are *e* and *f*.

3. Have students touch each lowercase letter on their whiteboard and say its name.

4. **Say:** I'm going to put these letters on my whiteboard in place of the capital letters for *e* and *f*.

5. Move the uppercase *E* and *F* tiles from your whiteboard to the Tile Kit, and replace them with the lowercase *e* and *f* tiles.

6. Have students sing "The Alphabet Song," touching the lowercase letters *a* through *f*, then moving back to the capital letters.

> **Objectives**
> - Develop right hand awareness.
> - Identify letters of the alphabet.
> - Identify capital and lowercase letters.
> - Match capital letters to lowercase letters.
> - Identify individual sounds in words.
> - Blend sounds to create words.
> - Identify a word when given the onset and rime.

Review Letter Names

To help students learn the alphabet, have them practice identifying and naming the letters *a, b, c, e, f, G,* and *H.* Grab your whiteboard with letters.

1. Point to each letter and have students touch and name each one.

   a   f   e   G   H   b   c

2. Say the name of each letter. After each one, have students repeat the name and touch the tile.

   a   f   e   G   H   b   c

3. Redirect students if they name a letter incorrectly.

   ▸ Name the letter students missed.
   ▸ Have students touch the letter and say its name.
   ▸ Have students trace the shape of the letter with their finger on the brown side of their board, and have them say the letter's name as they trace the shape.
   ▸ If students name a letter incorrectly twice, point to the letter and tell them its name. Have students touch the letter and say its name.

Match Uppercase and Lowercase Letters

To help students learn to recognize the difference between lowercase and uppercase letters of the alphabet, have them practice identifying and naming letters. Grab your whiteboard with letters.

1. Place the following uppercase letters on students' whiteboard in a horizontal row: *A, B, C, D, E,* and *F.*

2. Point to a letter and have students name it.

3. Have students select the matching lowercase letter from your whiteboard.

4. Have students place the lowercase letter next to the uppercase letter to make a pair.

TIP If students have difficulty with this activity, have them practice naming the letters in the alphabet. When they can name all the letters in the correct order, have them touch and name the lowercase and uppercase letters for each letter.

Fun with Sounds

Play a game with color tiles to help students identify sounds that are the same and sounds that are different. Grab the color tiles from the Tile Kit.

1. Place the tiles on a table.

2. **Say:** I am going to make three sounds. If the sounds are the same, you'll pick out three tiles that are the same color and put them next to each other. If the sounds are different, you'll pick out three tiles that are different colors and put them next to each other. For example,

   ▶ When I make the sounds /m/, /m/, /m/, you'll pick out three tiles of the same color and put them next to each other because all three sounds are the same.
   ▶ Now listen carefully to the next three sounds: /m/, /m/, /ă/. The first and second sounds —/m/— stayed the same, but the third sound changed from /m/ to /ă/. To show that the third sound changed, you will change the third tile to a tile of a different color.
   ▶ Each time I say a group of sounds, you will change one color tile to show that one of the sounds changed.

3. Say each group of sounds. Have students pick out and place tiles to identify the sounds that change. Note that students should **not** choose three new tiles for each group of sounds; they should begin with three tiles and replace those tiles as necessary throughout the "chain."

   ▶ /j/, /j/, /t/
   ▶ /j/, /k/, /t/
   ▶ /ē/, /k/, /t/
   ▶ /ē/, /k/, /d/
   ▶ /ŏ/, /k/, /d/
   ▶ /ā/, /k/, /d/
   ▶ /ā/, /k/, /m/
   ▶ /ā/, /f/, /m/

TIP If you have not done so already, watch the *K¹² PhonicsWorks* video, which models using color tiles.

Onset and Rime

In a word, the part of the syllable before the first vowel sound is the **onset**. The part of the syllable after the first vowel sound is the **rime**. For example, in *dog*, /d/ is the onset and *og* is the rime. Help students put together words that are broken down into parts by onset and rime.

1. **Say:** I'm going to break a word into two parts. Your job is to put the parts together and say the word. If the first part of a word is /r/ and the last part of the word is *oad*, then the whole word is *road*: /r/ . . . *oad* . . . *road*.

2. Say the following pairs of word parts. Have students tell you the word that each pair forms.

   ▶ /j/ . . . *et jet*
   ▶ /h/ . . . *ot hot*
   ▶ /p/ . . . *est pest*
   ▶ /g/ . . . *ame game*

Learn

Introduce the Sound /s/

Teach the sound /s/, as in *sip, sing,* and *such.*

1. **Say:** We're going to play a game to practice the **sound /s/.** Your job is to say the sound just like me and do what I do, too.

2. Pretend to gently slap your hand on the table and say the sound /s/. Have students do this, too.

3. **Say:** We make some sounds with a whisper and some sounds with our voice. Let's figure out whether the sound /s/ is whispered or voiced. Say /s/ and put your fingers on the lump in your throat called your voice box.

   ▶ Do you feel your voice box vibrate? No, /s/ is a whispered sound because we don't use our voice box when we make the sound.

4. **Say:** I'll say some words that start with the sound /s/ and you'll repeat them, saying /s/ just the way I do.

   sip   sing   such

5. **Say:** Now I'll say some words that end with the sound /s/ and you'll repeat them, saying /s/ just the way I do.

   pass   fuss   chase

TIP When you teach the sound /s/, make sure students say the sound correctly and do not add *uh* after pronouncing it. Students should say /s/, not *suh.*

Listen for the Beginning Sound /s/

Present pairs of words to help students recognize beginning sounds.

1. **Say:** I'm going to say two words. Listen for the **beginning sound /s/.** Then tell me the word that has that beginning sound. For example, if I say *sun* and *moon,* you'll say *sun* because /s/ is the first sound in *sun.*

2. Say each pair of words. Have students identify the word that begins with the sound /s/.

   ▶ *bag* or *sack* sack
   ▶ *fun* or *silly* silly
   ▶ *sing* or *clap* sing

Objectives
- Identify and use the sound /s/.
- Identify beginning sounds in words.
- Identify ending sounds in words.

Listen for the Ending Sound /s/
Present pairs of words to help students recognize ending sounds.

1. **Say:** I'm going to say two words. Listen for the **ending sound /s/**. Then tell me the word with that ending sound. For example, if I say *miss* and *mitt*, you'll say *miss* because /s/ is the last sound in *miss*.

2. Say each pair of words. Have students identify the word that ends with the sound /s/.

    ▶ *duck* or *goose* goose
    ▶ *pass* or *path* pass
    ▶ *run* or *race* race

Try It

The Beginning
Have students complete page PH 9 in *K¹² PhonicsWorks Basic Activity Book* for more practice with the sound /s/. First have students say the name of each picture. Then have them circle pictures whose name begins with the sound /s/.

Objectives
- Identify and use the sound /s/.
- Identify beginning sounds in words.

 **20 minutes**

REVIEW: **Sound /s/**

Students will work online independently to

► Practice the sound /s/.

Help students locate the online activities and provide support as needed.

Objectives
- Identify and use the sound /s/.
- Identify beginning sounds in words.
- Identify ending sounds in words.

Offline Alternative

No computer access? Have students point out and name things that begin or end with the sound /s/ (for example, *sink* or *face*).

Sounds /ă/ and /w/

Lesson Overview

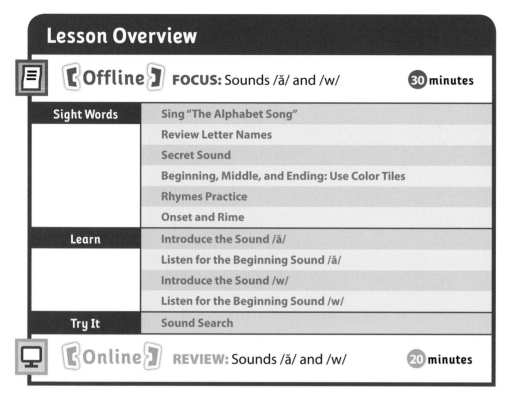

Offline FOCUS: Sounds /ă/ and /w/ — 30 minutes

Sight Words	Sing "The Alphabet Song"
	Review Letter Names
	Secret Sound
	Beginning, Middle, and Ending: Use Color Tiles
	Rhymes Practice
	Onset and Rime
Learn	Introduce the Sound /ă/
	Listen for the Beginning Sound /ă/
	Introduce the Sound /w/
	Listen for the Beginning Sound /w/
Try It	Sound Search

Online REVIEW: Sounds /ă/ and /w/ — 20 minutes

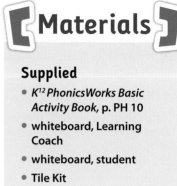

Materials

Supplied

- *K¹² PhonicsWorks Basic Activity Book,* p. PH 10
- whiteboard, Learning Coach
- whiteboard, student
- Tile Kit

Advance Preparation

Place lowercase letter tiles *a* through *f* and uppercase letter tiles *G* through *Z* in alphabetical order on both your and students' whiteboards.

Big Ideas

Phonological awareness activities are most effective when done separately from letter-naming activities.

 **30 minutes**

FOCUS: Sounds /ă/ and /w/

Work **together** with students to complete offline Get Ready, Learn, and Try It activities.

Get Ready

Sing "The Alphabet Song"
To help students become familiar and comfortable with the alphabet, sing "The Alphabet Song" with them. Sing slowly, so that students may touch each letter on your whiteboard as they sing the letter's name.

Review Letter Names
To help students learn the alphabet, have them practice identifying and naming the letters *a, b, c, d, e, f, J, K,* and *L*. Grab your whiteboard with letters.

1. Point to each letter and have students touch and name each one.

   e f a b J K L c d

2. Say the name of each letter. After each one, have students repeat the name and touch the tile.

   e f a b J K L c d

3. Redirect students if they name a letter incorrectly.

   ► Name the letter students missed.
   ► Have students touch the letter and say its name.
   ► Have students trace the shape of the letter with their finger on the brown side of their board, and have them say the letter's name as they trace the shape.
   ► If students name a letter incorrectly twice, point to the letter and tell them its name. Have students touch the letter and say its name.

Secret Sound
Say groups of words that begin with the same letter to help students recognize **beginning sounds** in words.

1. **Say:** I am going to say some groups of words. Listen for a secret sound at the beginning of each word. Then tell me what sound you hear at the beginning of each group of words.

> ★ **Objectives**
> - Identify letters of the alphabet.
> - Identify capital and lowercase letters.
> - Identify individual sounds in words.
> - Identify beginning sounds in words.
> - Identify words that rhyme.
> - Blend sounds to create words.
> - Identify a word when given the onset and rime.

2. Say each of the following groups of words. Have students identify the secret sound in each group.

> ▶ *tune, time, take, total* /t/
> ▶ *sip, sister, sun, sardine* /s/
> ▶ *each, equal, eat, ear* /ē/
> ▶ *help, heart, heal, hope* /h/

3. Repeat any groups of words for which students couldn't identify the secret sound. Have students repeat each word in that group. Then have them say what sound they hear at the beginning of each word.

Beginning, Middle, and Ending: Use Color Tiles

Reinforce the concepts of beginning, middle, and ending (or first, second, and last). Grab three different color tiles from the Tile Kit.

1. Line up the tiles from left to right, about two inches apart, on a table.

2. Have students

> ▶ Touch the middle tile.
> ▶ Touch the last tile.
> ▶ Touch the beginning tile.
> ▶ Touch the first tile.
> ▶ Touch the last tile.
> ▶ Touch the middle tile.

Rhymes Practice

Use common songs and nursery rhymes to practice identifying rhyming words.

1. **Say:** I am going to start reading a poem. When you hear words that rhyme, raise your hand and tell me the words. I will continue reading the poem. As I read, keep raising your hand when you hear words that rhyme and tell me the words.

2. Read the poem. Have students raise their hand when they hear rhyming words and have them tell you which words rhyme. Continue reading the poem.

> *I've got a mule, her name is Sal,*
> *Fifteen miles on the Erie Canal.*
> *She's a good ole' worker and a good ole' pal,*
> *Fifteen miles on the Erie Canal.*

3. Continue this activity with other poems that have obvious rhyming words. Here are some choices:

- "Jack and Jill"
- "The Owl and the Pussycat"
- "Lullaby and Goodnight"
- "Rock-a-Bye, Baby"
- "Winkin, Blinkin, and Nod"
- "The Pied Piper of Hamlin"
- "Twinkle, Twinkle, Little Star"
- "Hush, Little Baby"
- "Bye, Baby Bunting"
- "Little Miss Muffet"
- "Higglety, Pigglety, Pop"
- "Sing a Song of Sixpence"
- "Three Little Kittens"

Onset and Rime

In a word, the part of the syllable before the first vowel sound is the **onset**. The part of the syllable after the first vowel sound is the **rime**. For example, in *dog*, /d/ is the onset and *og* is the rime. Help students put together words that are broken down into parts by onset and rime.

1. **Say:** I'm going to break a word into two parts. Your job is to put the parts together and say the word. If the first part of a word is /s/ and the last part of the word is *oap*, then the whole word is *soap*: /s/ . . . *oap* . . .*soap*.

2. Say the following pairs of word parts. Have students tell you the word that each pair forms.

- /h/ . . . *ope* hope
- /f/ . . . *ace* face
- /d/ . . . *ust* dust
- /b/ . . . *ust* bust
- /f/ . . . *ast* fast
- /m/ . . . *ask* mask
- /t/ . . . *ask* task

Learn ....

Introduce the Sound /ă/

Teach the sound /ă/, as in *apple, act,* and *after.*

1. **Say:** We're going to play a game to practice the **sound /ă/**. Your job is to say the sound just like me and do what I do, too.

2. Pretend to bite an apple and say the sound /ă/. Have students do this, too.

3. **Say:** We make some sounds with a whisper and some sounds with our voice. Let's figure out whether the sound /ă/ is whispered or voiced. Say /ă/ and put your fingers on the lump in your throat called your voice box.

   ▸ Do you feel your voice box vibrate? Yes, /ă/ is a noisy sound because we do use our voice box when we make the sound.

4. **Say:** I'll say some words that start with the sound /ă/ and you'll repeat them, saying /ă/ just the way I do.

   apple   act   after

Listen for the Beginning Sound /ă/

Present pairs of words to help students recognize beginning sounds.

1. **Say:** I'm going to say two words. Listen for the **beginning sound /ă/**. Then tell me the word that has that beginning sound. For example, if I say *after* and *over,* you'll say *after* because /ă/ is the first sound in *after.*

2. Say each pair of words. Have students identify the word that begins with the sound /ă/.

   ▸ *each* or *at* at
   ▸ *Asia* or *Africa* Africa
   ▸ *Allen* or *Mike* Allen

Introduce the Sound /w/

Teach the sound /w/, as in *wave, wind,* and *wild.*

1. **Say:** We're going to play a game to practice the **sound /w/**. Your job is to say the sound just like me and do what I do, too.

2. Wave your hand and say the sound /w/. Have students do this, too.

3. **Say:** We make many sounds with our tongue, our teeth, and our lips. Say /w/ again and feel whether your tongue, teeth, or lips are making the sound.

   ▸ Did you feel your lips make the sound /w/? Yes

Objectives

- Identify and use the sound /ă/.
- Identify and use the sound /w/.
- Identify beginning sounds in words.

4. **Say:** We make some sounds with a whisper and some sounds with our voice. Let's figure out whether the sound /w/ is whispered or voiced. Say /w/ and put your fingers on the lump in your throat called your voice box.

   ► Do you feel your voice box vibrate? Yes, /w/ is a noisy sound because we do use our voice box when we make the sound.

5. **Say:** I'll say some words that start with the sound /w/ and you'll repeat them, saying /w/ just the way I do.

   wave   wind   wild

Listen for the Beginning Sound /w/

Present pairs of words to help students recognize beginning sounds.

1. **Say:** I'm going to say two words. Listen for the **beginning sound /w/**. Then tell me the word that has that beginning sound. For example, if I say *went* and *past*, you'll say *went* because /w/ is the first sound in *went*.

2. Say each pair of words. Have students identify the word that begins with the sound /w/.

   ► *big* or *wig* wig
   ► *win* or *van* win
   ► *wish* or *hope* wish
   ► *want* or *get* want
   ► *pancake* or *waffle* waffle

Try It

Sound Search

Have students complete page PH 10 in *K[12] PhonicsWorks Basic Activity Book* for more practice with the sounds /ă/ and /w/. First have students say the name of each picture. Then have them circle pictures whose name has the sound /ă/ and draw an X over pictures whose name has the sound /w/.

Objectives
- Identify and use the sound /ă/.
- Identify and use the sound /w/.
- Identify individual sounds in words.

Online 20 minutes

REVIEW: Sounds /ă/ and /w/

Students will work online independently to

▶ Practice the sounds /ă/ and /w/.

Help students locate the online activities and provide support as needed.

Objectives
- Identify and use the sound /ă/.
- Identify and use the sound /w/.
- Identify individual sounds in words.

Offline Alternative

No computer access? Have students point out and name things that contain the sounds /ă/ and /w/ (for example, *pat* or *water*).

Sounds /z/ and /ī/

Lesson Overview

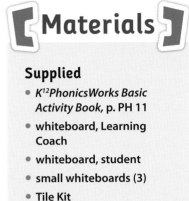

Materials

Supplied
- *K¹²PhonicsWorks Basic Activity Book*, p. PH 11
- whiteboard, Learning Coach
- whiteboard, student
- small whiteboards (3)
- Tile Kit

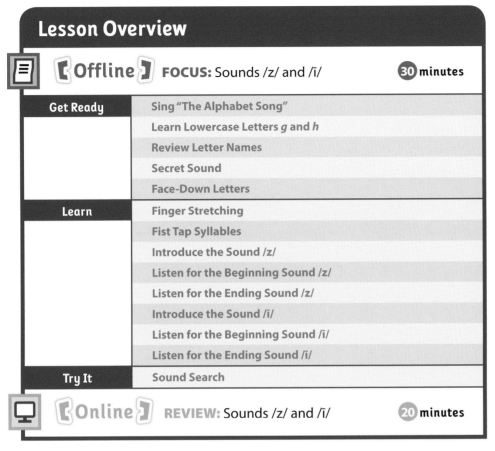

Offline FOCUS: Sounds /z/ and /ī/   **30** minutes

Get Ready	Sing "The Alphabet Song"
	Learn Lowercase Letters *g* and *h*
	Review Letter Names
	Secret Sound
	Face-Down Letters
Learn	Finger Stretching
	Fist Tap Syllables
	Introduce the Sound /z/
	Listen for the Beginning Sound /z/
	Listen for the Ending Sound /z/
	Introduce the Sound /ī/
	Listen for the Beginning Sound /ī/
	Listen for the Ending Sound /ī/
Try It	Sound Search

Online REVIEW: Sounds /z/ and /ī/   **20** minutes

Advance Preparation

Place lowercase letter tiles *a* through *f* and uppercase letter tiles *G* through *Z* in alphabetical order on both your and students' whiteboards. Place lowercase letter tiles *g* and *h* on the bottom of students' whiteboard.

 **30** minutes

FOCUS: Sounds /z/ and /ī/

Work **together** with students to complete offline Get Ready, Learn, and Try It activities.

Get Ready

Sing "The Alphabet Song"

To help students become familiar and comfortable with the alphabet, sing "The Alphabet Song" with them. Sing slowly, so that students may touch each letter on your whiteboard as they sing the letter's name.

Learn Lowercase Letters *g* and *h*

To help students learn lowercase letters of the alphabet, have them practice identifying and naming the letters *g* and *h*.

1. **Say:** We're going to learn two lowercase letters today. They are *g* and *h*.

2. Have students touch each lowercase letter on their whiteboard and say its name.

3. **Say:** I'm going to put these letters on my whiteboard in place of the capital letters for *g* and *h*.

4. Move the uppercase *G* and *H* tiles from your whiteboard to the Tile Kit, and replace them with the lowercase *g* and *h* tiles.

5. Have students sing "The Alphabet Song," touching the lowercase letters *a* through *h*, then moving back to the capital letters.

Review Letter Names

To help students learn the alphabet, have them practice identifying and naming the letters *a, d, e, f, g, h, J,* and *l*. Grab your whiteboard with letters.

1. Point to each letter and have students touch and name each one.

    a   d   e   f   g   h   l   J

2. Say the name of each letter. After each one, have students repeat the name and touch the tile.

    a   d   e   f   g   h   l   J

3. Redirect students if they name a letter incorrectly.

   ▸ Name the letter students missed.
   ▸ Have students touch the letter and say its name.
   ▸ Have students trace the shape of the letter with their finger on the brown side of their board, and have them say the letter's name as they trace the shape.
   ▸ If students name a letter incorrectly twice, point to the letter and tell them its name. Have students touch the letter and say its name.

Secret Sound

Say groups of words that end with the same sound to help students recognize **ending sounds** in words.

1. **Say:** I am going to say some groups of words. Listen for a secret sound at the end of each word. Then tell me what sound you hear at the end of each group of words.

2. Say each of the following groups of words. Have students identify the secret sound in each group.

   ▸ *mess, pass, chase* /s/
   ▸ *edge, page, huge, cringe* /j/
   ▸ *toe, glow, mow, potato* /ō/
   ▸ *play, May, today, weigh* /ā/

3. Repeat any groups of words for which students couldn't identify the secret sound. Have students repeat each word in that group. Then have them say what sound they hear at the beginning of each word.

Face-Down Letters

To help students learn to recognize the letters of the alphabet, have them practice identifying and naming letters. Grab your whiteboard with letters placed in alphabetical order.

1. Lay your whiteboard down on a flat surface and flip over the following letter tiles so they are face down on the whiteboard: *b, f, K,* and *N.*

2. **Say:** These letters are face down. We are looking at the back of them. Name each letter and then turn it over to see if you were right.

TIP If students miss any of the letters, have them turn over the missed ones and try again.

Learn

Finger Stretching

Use finger stretching to help students identify individual sounds in words.

1. **Say:** Let's review finger stretching. In the word *pat*, the first sound is /p/, the next sound is /ă/, and the last sound is /t/. I will finger stretch each sound as I say it. Then I'll say the word, while pulling my fist toward my body.

2. Finger stretch the word *pat* for students.

3. **Say:** I'm going to say words with several sounds in them. You'll say each word and then finger stretch it while you say each sound in the word.

4. Say the following words and have students finger stretch them. After they finger stretch each word, ask them the question for that word.

   ▸ *mop* /m/ /ŏ/ /p/   What is the first sound? /m/
   ▸ *mad* /m/ /ă/ /d/   What is the middle sound? /ă/
   ▸ *cat* /k/ /ă/ /t/   What is the first sound? /k/
   ▸ *dog* /d/ /ŏ/ /g/   What is the last sound? /g/

 Refer to the *K¹² PhonicsWorks* video for a demonstration of finger stretching.

Fist Tap Syllables

Help students practice listening for syllables. Grab the small whiteboards.

1. **Say:** Let's practice breaking words into syllables. I'll say a word and you'll repeat it. Then you'll pull down one whiteboard for each syllable and fist tap the board for each syllable.

2. Say the word *happy*. After students repeat the word, have them pull down another small whiteboard for each syllable and then fist tap the syllables.

   ▸ How many syllable boards did you use? two
   ▸ How many syllables are there? two
   ▸ What are the syllables? *hap / py*

3. Continue the activity with the following words:

   ▸ *puppy* pup / py
   ▸ *kitten* kit / ten
   ▸ *giraffe* gi / raffe
   ▸ *snake* snake
   ▸ *monkey* mon / key
   ▸ *elephant* e / le / phant
   ▸ *tiger* ti / ger

Objectives

- Identify individual sounds in words.
- Identify and use the sound /ī/.
- Identify and use the sound /z/.
- Identify syllables in words.
- Identify beginning sounds in words.
- Identify ending sounds in words.

Introduce the Sound /z/

Teach the sound /z/, as in *zip*, *zoo*, and *zebra*.

1. **Say:** We're going to play a game to practice the **sound /z/**. Your job is to say the sound just like me and do what I do, too.

2. Pretend to zip your coat and say the sound /z/. Have students do this, too.

3. **Say:** We make many sounds with our tongue, our teeth, and our lips. Say /z/ again and feel whether your tongue, teeth, or lips are making the sound.

   ▸ Did you feel the back of your tongue and teeth make the sound /z/? Yes

4. **Say:** We make some sounds with a whisper and some sounds with our voice. Let's figure out whether the sound /z/ is whispered or voiced. Say /z/ and put your fingers on the lump in your throat called your voice box.

   ▸ Do you feel your voice box vibrate? Yes, /z/ is a noisy sound because we use our voice box when we make the sound.

5. **Say:** I'll say some words that start with the sound /z/ and you'll repeat them, saying /z/ just the way I do.

   zip   *zoo*   *zebra*

6. **Say:** Now I'll say some words that end with the sound /z/ and you'll repeat them, saying /z/ just the way I do.

   buzz   *prize*   *nose*

TIP When you teach the sound /z/, make sure students say the sound correctly and do not add *uh* after pronouncing it. Students should say /z/, not *zuh*.

Listen for the Beginning Sound /z/

Present pairs of words to help students recognize beginning sounds.

1. **Say:** I'm going to say two words. Listen for the **beginning sound /z/**. Then tell me the word that has that beginning sound. For example, if I say *zoo* and *school*, you'll say *zoo* because /z/ is the first sound in *zoo*.

2. Say each pair of words. Have students identify the word that begins with the sound /z/.

   ▸ *three* or *zero* zero
   ▸ *zap* or *drop* zap
   ▸ *bone* or *zone* zone

Listen for the Ending Sound /z/

Present pairs of words to help students recognize ending sounds.

1. **Say:** I'm going to say two words. Listen for the **ending sound /z/**. Then tell me the word with that ending sound. For example, if I say *fuzz* and *fluff,* you'll say *fuzz* because /z/ is the last sound in *fuzz.*

2. Say each pair of words. Have students identify the word that ends with the sound /z/.

   ▸ *chips* or *cheese* cheese
   ▸ *prize* or *big* prize
   ▸ *pick* or *choose* choose

Introduce the Sound /ī/

Teach the sound /ī/, as in *ice, ivy,* and *idea.*

1. **Say:** We're going to play a game to practice the **sound /ī/**. Your job is to say the sound just like me and do what I do, too.

2. Pretend to shiver as if you were icy cold and say the sound /ī/. Have students do this, too.

3. **Say:** We make many sounds with our tongue, our teeth, and our lips. Say /ī/ again and feel whether your tongue, teeth, or lips are making the sound.

   ▸ Do you feel your tongue help you make the sound /ī/? Yes

4. **Say:** We make some sounds with a whisper and some sounds with our voice. Let's figure out whether the sound /ī/ is whispered or voiced. Say /ī/ and put your fingers on the lump in your throat called your voice box.

   ▸ Do you feel your voice box vibrate? Yes, /ī/ is a noisy sound because we use our voice box when we make the sound.

5. **Say:** I'll say some words that start with the sound /ī/ and you'll repeat them, saying /ī/ just the way I do.

   ice   ivy   idea

6. **Say:** Now I'll say some words that end with the sound /ī/ and you'll repeat them, saying /ī/ just the way I do.

   try   by   my

Listen for the Beginning Sound /ī/

Present pairs of words to help students recognize beginning sounds.

1. **Say:** I'm going to say two words. Listen for the **beginning sound** /ī/. Then tell me the word that has that beginning sound. For example, if I say *ocean* and *island*, you'll say *island* because /ī/ is the first sound in *island*.

2. Say each pair of words. Have students identify the word that begins with the sound /ī/.

   ▸ *violet* or *iris* *iris*
   ▸ *idea* or *erase* *idea*
   ▸ *ivy* or *flower* *ivy*

Listen for the Ending Sound /ī/

Present pairs of words to help students recognize ending sounds.

1. **Say:** I'm going to say two words. Listen for the **ending sound** /ī/. Then tell me the word with that ending sound. For example, if I say *try* and *tree*, you'll say *try* because /ī/ is the last sound in *try*.

2. Say each pair of words. Have students identify the word that ends with the sound /ī/.

   ▸ *by* or *be* *by*
   ▸ *zoo* or *pie* *pie*
   ▸ *high* or *low* *high*

Try It

Sound Search

Have students complete page PH 11 in *K¹² PhonicsWorks Basic Activity Book* for more practice with the sounds /z/ and /ī/. First have students say the name of each picture. Then have them circle pictures whose has the sound /z/ and draw an X over pictures whose name has the sound /ī/.

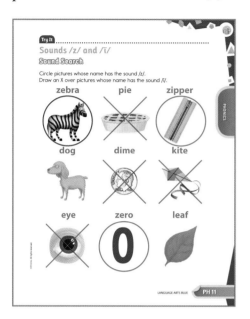

Objectives
- Identify and use the sound /ī/.
- Identify and use the sound /z/.
- Identify individual sounds in words.

[Online] 20 minutes

REVIEW: Sounds /z/ and /ī/

Students will work online independently to

▸ Practice the sounds /z/ and /ī/.

Help students locate the online activities and provide support as needed.

Objectives
- Identify and use the sound /ī/.
- Identify and use the sound /z/.
- Identify individual sounds in words.

___

Offline Alternative

No computer access? Have students point out and name things that contain the sounds /z/ and /ī/ (for example, *zoo* and *slide*).

Sound /l/

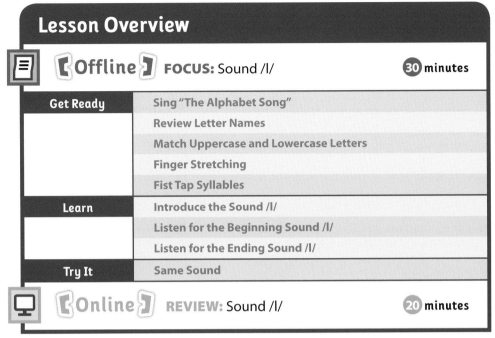

Lesson Overview

Offline FOCUS: Sound /l/ — **30** minutes

Get Ready	Sing "The Alphabet Song"
	Review Letter Names
	Match Uppercase and Lowercase Letters
	Finger Stretching
	Fist Tap Syllables
Learn	Introduce the Sound /l/
	Listen for the Beginning Sound /l/
	Listen for the Ending Sound /l/
Try It	Same Sound

Online REVIEW: Sound /l/ — **20** minutes

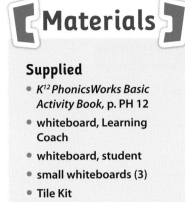

Materials

Supplied

- *K¹² PhonicsWorks Basic Activity Book,* p. PH 12
- whiteboard, Learning Coach
- whiteboard, student
- small whiteboards (3)
- Tile Kit

Advance Preparation

Place lowercase letter tiles *a* through *h* and uppercase letter tiles *I* through *Z* in alphabetical order on both your and students' whiteboards.

 **30 minutes**

FOCUS: Sound /l/

Work **together** with students to complete offline Get Ready, Learn, and Try It activities.

Get Ready

Sing "The Alphabet Song"

To help students become familiar and comfortable with the alphabet, sing "The Alphabet Song" with them. Sing slowly, so that students may touch each letter on your whiteboard as they sing the letter's name.

Review Letter Names

To help students learn the alphabet, have them practice identifying and naming the letters c, d, e, f, g, h, V, W, X, Y, and Z. Grab your whiteboard with letters.

1. Point to each letter and have students touch and name each one.

   c   d   e   f   g   h   Z   Y   X   W   V

2. Say the name of each letter. After each one, have students repeat the name and touch the tile.

   c   d   e   f   g   h   Z   Y   X   W   V

3. Redirect students if they name a letter incorrectly.

   ▸ Name the letter students missed.
   ▸ Have students touch the letter and say its name.
   ▸ Have students trace the shape of the letter with their finger on the brown side of their board, and have them say the letter's name as they trace the shape.
   ▸ If students name a letter incorrectly twice, point to the letter and tell them its name. Have students touch the letter and say its name.

Match Uppercase and Lowercase Letters

To help students learn to recognize the difference between lowercase and uppercase letters of the alphabet, have them practice identifying and naming letters. Grab your whiteboard with letters.

1. Place the following uppercase letters on students' whiteboard in a horizontal row: A, B, C, G, and H.

2. Point to a letter and have students name it.

3. Have students select the matching lowercase letter from your whiteboard.

4. Have students place the lowercase letter under the uppercase letter to make a pair.

TIP If students have difficulty with this activity, have them practice naming the letters in the alphabet. When they can name all the letters in the correct order, have them touch and name the lowercase and uppercase letters for each letter.

> **Objectives**
> - Identify letters of the alphabet.
> - Identify capital and lowercase letters.
> - Match capital letters to lowercase letters.
> - Identify individual sounds in words.
> - Identify syllables in words.
> - Identify the number of syllables in a word.

Finger Stretching

Use finger stretching to help students identify individual sounds in words.

1. **Say:** Let's review finger stretching. In the word *and*, the first sound is /ă/, the middle sound is /n/, and the last sound is /d/. I will finger stretch each sound as I say it. Then I'll say the word, while pulling my fist toward my body.

2. Finger stretch the word *and* for students.

3. **Say:** I'm going to say words with several sounds in them. You'll say the word and then finger stretch it while you say each sound in the word.

4. Say the following words and have students finger stretch them. After they finger stretch each word, ask them the question for that word.

    ▸ *zig* /z/ /ĭ/ /g/   What is the first sound? /z/
    ▸ *base* /b/ /ā/ /s/   What is the middle sound? /ā/
    ▸ *wide* /w/ /ī/ /d/   What is the first sound? /w/
    ▸ *sad* /s/ /ă/ /d/   What is the last sound? /d/
    ▸ *neat* /n/ /ē/ /t/   What is the middle sound? /ē/
    ▸ *page* /p/ /ā/ /j/   What is the first sound? /p/
    ▸ *sail* /s/ /ā/ /l/   What is the middle sound? /ā/

 Refer to the *K¹² PhonicsWorks* video for a demonstration of finger stretching.

Fist Tap Syllables

Help students practice listening for syllables. Grab the small whiteboards.

1. **Say:** Let's practice breaking words into syllables. I'll say a word and you'll repeat it. Then you'll pull down one whiteboard for each syllable and fist tap the board for each syllable.

2. Say the word *sunset*. After students repeat the word, have them pull down a whiteboard for each syllable and then fist tap the syllables.

    ▸ How many whiteboards did you use? two
    ▸ How many syllables are there? two
    ▸ What are the syllables? *sun / set*

3. Continue the activity with the following words:

    ▸ *running* run / ning
    ▸ *stopping* stop / ping
    ▸ *enjoying* en / joy / ing
    ▸ *toasted* toast / ed
    ▸ *stopped* stopped
    ▸ *landed* land / ed
    ▸ *camped* camped
    ▸ *pretended* pre / tend / ed
    ▸ *ended* end / ed

Learn

Introduce the Sound /l/

Teach the sound /l/, as in *lamp*, *light*, and *laugh*.

1. **Say:** We're going to play a game to practice the **sound /l/**. Your job is to say the sound just like me and do what I do, too.

2. Pretend to turn on a lamp and say the sound /l/. Have students do this, too.

3. **Say:** We make some sounds with a whisper and some sounds with our voice. Let's figure out whether the sound /l/ is whispered or voiced. Say /l/ and put your fingers on the lump in your throat called your voice box.

   ▶ Do you feel your voice box vibrate? Yes, /l/ is a noisy sound because we use our voice box when we make the sound.

4. **Say:** I'll say some words that start with the sound /l/ and you'll repeat them, saying /l/ just the way I do.

   lamp   light   laugh

5. **Say:** Now I'll say some words that end with the sound /l/ and you'll repeat them, saying /l/ just the way I do.

   will   pull   smile

TIP When you teach the sound /l/, make sure students say the sound correctly and do not add *uh* after pronouncing it. Students should say /l/, not *luh*.

Objectives
- Identify and use the sound /l/.
- Identify beginning sounds in words.
- Identify ending sounds in words.

Listen for the Beginning Sound /l/

Present pairs of words to help students recognize beginning sounds.

1. **Say:** I'm going to say two words. Listen for the **beginning sound /l/**. Then tell me the word that has that beginning sound. For example, if I say *like* and *take*, you'll say *like* because /l/ is the first sound in *like*.

2. Say each pair of words. Have students identify the word that begins with the sound /l/.

   ▶ *tick* or *lick* *lick*
   ▶ *laugh* or *vote* *laugh*
   ▶ *wish* or *live* *live*
   ▶ *lucky* or *rabbit* *lucky*
   ▶ *sheep* or *lamb* *lamb*

Listen for the Ending Sound /l/

Present pairs of words to help students recognize ending sounds.

1. **Say:** I'm going to say two words. Listen for the **ending sound** /l/. Then tell me the word with that ending sound. For example, if I say *Don* and *doll*, you'll say *doll* because /l/ is the last sound in *doll*.

2. Say each pair of words. Have students identify the word that ends with the sound /l/.

   ▸ *will* or *wind* *will*
   ▸ *trip* or *fall* *fall*
   ▸ *home* or *school* *school*
   ▸ *win* or *fail* *fail*
   ▸ *all* or *some* *all*

Try It

Same Sound

Have students complete page PH 12 in *K¹² PhonicsWorks Basic Activity Book* for more practice with beginning sounds. First have students say the name of each picture. Then, in each row, have them circle pictures whose names begin with the same sound.

Objectives
• Identify beginning sounds in words.

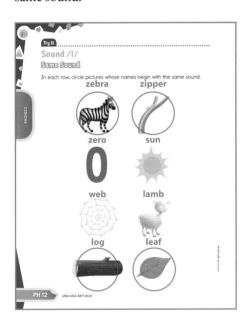

 **minutes**

REVIEW: **Sound /l/**

Students will work online independently to

► Practice the sound /l/.

Help students locate the online activities and provide support as needed.

Offline Alternative

No computer access? Have students point out and name things that begin or end with the sound /l/ (for example, *lid* or *ball*).

Objectives

- Identify and use the sound /l/.
- Identify beginning sounds in words.
- Identify ending sounds in words.

Unit Checkpoint

Lesson Overview

 Online REVIEW: Sounds /s/, /ă/, /w/, /z/, /ī/, and /l/ **20** minutes

Offline UNIT CHECKPOINT: Sounds /s/, /ă/, /w/, /z/, /ī/, and /l/ **30** minutes

Materials

Supplied
- *K¹² PhonicsWorks Basic Assessments,* pp. PH 9–12

Objectives
- Identify and use the sound /s/.
- Identify and use the sound /ă/.
- Identify and use the sound /w/.
- Identify and use the sound /z/.
- Identify and use the sound /ī/.
- Identify and use the sound /l/.
- Identify individual sounds in words.
- Identify beginning sounds in words.
- Identify ending sounds in words.
- Identify words that rhyme.
- Identify letters of the alphabet.

Online **20** minutes

REVIEW: Sounds /s/, /ă/, /w/, /z/, /ī/, and /l/

Students will review the sounds /s/, /ă/, /w/, /z/, /ī/, and /l/ to prepare for the Unit Checkpoint. Help students locate the online activities and provide support as needed.

 **30 minutes**

UNIT CHECKPOINT: Sounds /s/, /ă/, /w/, /z/, /ī/, and /l/

Explain that students are going to show what they have learned about letters and sounds.

1. Give students the Unit Checkpoint pages for the Sounds /s/, /ă/, /w/, /z/, /ī/, and /l/ unit and print the Unit Checkpoint Answer Key, if you'd like.

2. Use the instructions below to help administer the Checkpoint to students. On the Answer Key or another sheet of paper, note student answers to oral response questions to help with scoring the Checkpoint later.

3. Use the Answer Key to score the Checkpoint, and then enter the results online.

Part 1. Letter Matching Moving from left to right, have students read the letters aloud and circle the letters that match the first letter in the row.

Part 2. Match Ending Sounds Have students say the name of each picture and draw a line to connect pictures that end with the same sound.

Part 3. Rhymes Say each pair of words and have students say if the word pairs rhyme. Note any incorrect responses.

9. *light, bright*

10. *like, lake*

11. *match, catch*

12. *path, bath*

13. *fine, lime*

14. *cry, say*

Part 4. Beginning Sounds Say each group of three words, and have students say which words begin with the same sound. Repeat the words, as necessary. Note any incorrect responses.

15. *star, sun, planet*

16. *apple, ox, alligator*

17. *movie, work, window*

18. *lion, bear, lamb*

19. *ship, zipper, zig-zag*

20. *island, iron, ape*

Name _____ Date _____

☼ Unit Checkpoint Answer Key
Sounds /s/, /ă/, /w/, /z/, /ī/, and /l/

Part 1. Letter Matching
Read across the row from left to right. Circle the letters that match the first letter in the row.

1.	e	a	(e)	c	g	(e)
2.	g	f	h	(g)	e	(g)
3.	f	d	(f)	a	(f)	b
4.	h	e	g	(h)	f	(h)

Name _____ Date _____

Part 2. Match Ending Sounds
Draw a line to connect the pictures that end with the same sound.

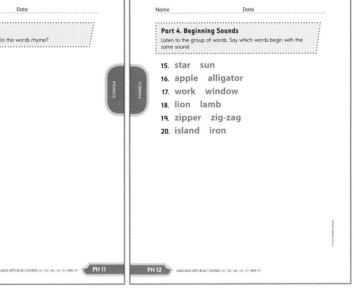

5. bus — nose
6. tie — shell
7. bell — dress
8. rose — pie

Name _____ Date _____

Part 3. Rhymes
Listen to the pair of words. Do the words rhyme?

9. Yes
10. No
11. Yes
12. Yes
13. No
14. No

Name _____ Date _____

Part 4. Beginning Sounds
Listen to the group of words. Say which words begin with the same sound.

15. star   sun
16. apple   alligator
17. work   window
18. lion   lamb
19. zipper   zig-zag
20. island   iron

Sounds /th/ and /<u>th</u>/

Unit Overview

In this unit, students will
- ► Identify letters in the alphabet.
- ► Identify and say the sounds /th/, /<u>th</u>/, /ĕ/, /k/, /v/, and /r/.
- ► Distinguish between words that rhyme or sound different.
- ► Identify individual sounds within words.
- ► Learn and practice blends.

【Materials】

Supplied
- ● *K¹² PhonicsWorks Basic Activity Book*, p. PH 13
- ● whiteboard, Learning Coach
- ● whiteboard, student
- ● Tile Kit

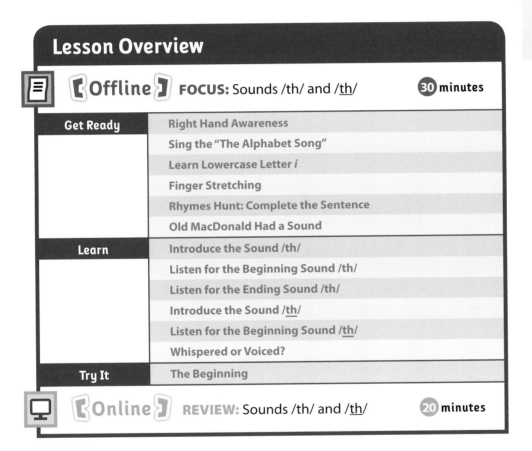

Lesson Overview

【Offline】 FOCUS: Sounds /th/ and /<u>th</u>/   30 minutes

Get Ready	Right Hand Awareness
	Sing the "The Alphabet Song"
	Learn Lowercase Letter *i*
	Finger Stretching
	Rhymes Hunt: Complete the Sentence
	Old MacDonald Had a Sound
Learn	Introduce the Sound /th/
	Listen for the Beginning Sound /th/
	Listen for the Ending Sound /th/
	Introduce the Sound /<u>th</u>/
	Listen for the Beginning Sound /<u>th</u>/
	Whispered or Voiced?
Try It	The Beginning

【Online】 REVIEW: Sounds /th/ and /<u>th</u>/   20 minutes

Advance Preparation

Place lowercase letter tiles *a* through *h* and uppercase letter tiles *I* through *Z* in alphabetical order on your whiteboard. Place the lowercase letter tile *i* on students' whiteboard.

 **30 minutes**

FOCUS: Sounds /th/ and /th/

Work **together** with students to complete offline Get Ready, Learn, and Try It activities.

Get Ready

Right Hand Awareness

Students read from left to right, so play a game to develop right hand awareness. To avoid confusion, focus on the right hand only.

1. Say each sentence and do each action. Have students repeat your words and actions.

   ▸ I'm shaking your right hand.
   ▸ Now I'm touching my right ankle.
   ▸ Now I'm waving my right hand in the air.
   ▸ Now I'm touching my right toe.
   ▸ Now I'm touching my right cheek

2. Repeat the actions and mix up the order. To end the activity, shake right hands again.

Sing the "The Alphabet Song"

To help students become familiar and comfortable with the alphabet, sing "The Alphabet Song" with them. Sing slowly, so that students may touch each letter on your whiteboard as they sing the letter's name.

Learn Lowercase Letter *i*

To help students learn lowercase letters of the alphabet, have them practice identifying and naming the letter *i*.

1. **Say:** We're going to learn one lowercase letter today. The letter is *i*.

2. Have students touch the letter on their whiteboard and say its name.

3. **Say:** I'm going to put this letter on my whiteboard in place of the capital letter for *i*.

4. Move the uppercase *I* tile from your whiteboard to the Tile Kit, and replace it with the lowercase *i* tile.

5. Have students sing "The Alphabet Song," touching the lowercase letters *a* through *i*, then moving back to the capital letters.

> **Objectives**
> - Develop right hand awareness.
> - Identify letters of the alphabet.
> - Identify capital and lowercase letters.
> - Match capital letters to lowercase letters.
> - Identify individual sounds in words.
> - Blend sounds to create words.
> - Identify words that rhyme.

Finger Stretching

Use finger stretching to help students identify individual sounds in words.

1. **Say:** Let's review finger stretching. In the word *doll*, the first sound is /d/, the next sound is /ŏ/, and the last sound is /l/. I will finger stretch each sound as I say it. Then I'll say the word, while pulling my fist toward my body.

2. Finger stretch the word *doll* for students.

3. **Say:** I'm going to say words with several sounds in them. You'll say each word and then finger stretch it while you say each sound in the word.

4. Say the following words and have students finger stretch them. After they finger stretch each word, ask them the question for that word.

   ▸ *hot* /h/ /ŏ/ /t/   What is the first sound? /h/
   ▸ *got* /g/ /ŏ/ /t/   What is the middle sound? /ŏ/
   ▸ *goat* /g/ /ō/ /t/   What is the first sound? /g/
   ▸ *vote* /v/ /ō/ /t/   What is the last sound? /t/
   ▸ *boat* /b/ /ō/ /t/   What is the middle sound? /ō/
   ▸ *bone* /b/ /ō/ /n/   What is the first sound? /b/

 Refer to the *K¹² PhonicsWorks* video for a demonstration of finger stretching.

Rhymes Hunt: Complete the Sentence

Play a game with students to reinforce awareness of words that rhyme.

1. **Say:** Let's have some fun with rhymes. Listen to this sentence: "Smell this rose with your nose." What word rhymes with *rose*? *nose*

2. **Say:** Now I'm going to give you a sentence with the rhyming word missing. Your job is to think of a word to complete the sentence. Remember, the word needs to rhyme.

   ▸ Listen: "For something to do, you can tie your _____ ."
   ▸ What rhymes with *do*?
   ▸ The word *shoe* rhymes with *do*. Now it's your turn.

3. Continue the procedure with the following sentences:

   Look at the cat *wearing a* _____ . *hat*
   It isn't very hard *to pick up an index* _____ . *card*
   I saw a pig *that was wearing a* _____ . *wig*
   If it's cold on the boat, *please wear a* _____ . *coat*
   I want a cake. *I think I'll* _____ . *bake*
   Do you care *if I sit in this* _____? *chair*

 If students have difficulty thinking of a rhyming word to complete the sentence, tell them the completed sentence and then have them identify the two rhyming words.

Old MacDonald Had a Sound

To review sounds, sing the song "Old MacDonald's Farm" with students.

1. **Say:** Let's have some fun with "Old MacDonald's Farm." Instead of animals, we'll put sounds on the farm. We'll sing, "Old MacDonald had a farm, E-I-E-I-O, and on that farm he had a /m/, E-I-E-I-O. With a /m/, /m/ here, and a /m/, /m/ there . . . ."

2. Continue singing the song. Alternate singing and having students sing until you have finished all of the following sounds: /ă/, /l/, /s/, /w/, and /z/.

Learn

Introduce the Sound /th/

Teach the sound /th/, as in *think*, *thin*, and *thank*.

1. **Say:** We're going to play a game to practice the **sound /th/**. Your job is to say the sound just like me and do what I do, too.

2. Pretend to touch your forehead and say, "I will think a thought." Have students do this, too.

3. **Say:** We make many sounds with our tongue, our teeth, and our lips. Say /th/ again and feel whether your tongue, teeth, or lips are making the sound.

   ▶ Did you feel your tongue and teeth make the sound /th/? Yes

4. **Say:** We make some sounds with a whisper and some sounds with our voice. Let's figure out whether the sound /th/ is whispered or voiced. Say /th/ and put your fingers on the lump in your throat called your voice box.

   ▶ Do you feel your voice box vibrate? No, /th/ is a whispered sound because we don't use our voice box when we make the sound.

5. **Say:** I'll say some words that start with the sound /th/ and you'll repeat them, saying /th/ just the way I do.

think   thin   thank

6. **Say:** Now, I'll say some words that end with the sound /th/ and you'll repeat them, saying /th/ just the way I do.

both   teeth   math

 TIP When you teach the sound /th/, make sure students say the sound correctly and do not add *uh* after pronouncing it. Students should say /th/, not *thuh*.

Objectives
- Identify and use the sound /th/.
- Identify and use the sound /th/.
- Identify beginning sounds in words.
- Identify ending sounds in words.

Listen for the Beginning Sound /th/

Present pairs of words to help students recognize beginning sounds.

1. **Say:** I'm going to say two words. Listen for the **beginning sound /th/**. Then tell me the word that has that beginning sound. For example, if I say *thrill* and *frill*, you'll say *thrill* because /th/ is the first sound in *thrill*.

2. Say each pair of words. Have students identify the word that begins with the sound /th/.

   ▸ *three* or *four* three
   ▸ *movie* or *theater* theater
   ▸ *drink* or *thirsty* thirsty

Listen for the Ending Sound /th/

Present pairs of words to help students recognize ending sounds.

1. **Say:** I'm going to say two words. Listen for the **ending sound /th/**. Then tell me the word with that ending sound. For example, if I say *math* and *man*, you'll say *math* because /th/ is the last sound in *math*.

2. Say each pair of words. Have students identify the word that ends with the sound /th/.

   ▸ *pass* or *path* path
   ▸ *did* or *cloth* cloth
   ▸ *moth* or *bug* moth

Introduce the Sound /th/

Teach the sound /th /, as in *this*, *that*, and *there*.

1. **Say:** We're going to play a game to practice the **sound /th/**. Your job is to say the sound just like me and do what I do, too.

2. Point to the table and say, "This is fun." Have students do this, too.

3. Make the sound /th/ and say, "This is fun" again.

4. **Say:** We make many sounds with our tongue, our teeth, and our lips. Say /th/ again and feel whether your tongue, teeth, or lips are making the sound. It feels like our tongue and teeth are in the same place when we say /th/.

5. **Say:** We make some sounds with a whisper and some sounds with our voice. Let's figure out whether the sound /th/ is whispered or voiced. Say /th/ and put your fingers on the lump in your throat called your voice box.

   ▸ Do you feel your voice box vibrate? Yes, /th/ is a voiced sound because we do use our voice box when we make the sound. That's why it's different from /th/. The sound /th/ uses our voice box.

6. **Say:** I'll say some words that start with the sound /<u>th</u>/ and you'll repeat them, saying /<u>th</u>/ just the way I do.

this   *that*   *there*

7. **Say:** Now I'll say some words that end with the sound /<u>th</u>/ and you'll repeat them, saying /<u>th</u>/ just the way I do.

bathe   *breathe*

(TIP) When you teach the sound /<u>th</u>/, make sure students say the sound correctly, such as *bathe* and *breathe*, not *bath* or *breath*.

(TIP) Some students may have difficulty hearing the difference between the sounds /<u>th</u>/ and /th/. Take time during the day to point out and name things for students that illustrate this difference.

Listen for the Beginning Sound /<u>th</u>/

Present pairs of words to help students recognize beginning sounds.

1. **Say:** I'm going to say two words. Listen for the **beginning sound /<u>th</u>/**. Then tell me the word that has that beginning sound. For example, if I say *those* and *size*, you'll say *those* because /<u>th</u>/ is the first sound in *those*.

2. Say each pair of words. Have students identify the word that begins with the sound /<u>th</u>/.

   - *them* or *meet* them
   - *that* or *fat* that
   - *here* or *there* there

Listen for the Ending Sound /<u>th</u>/

Present pairs of words to help students recognize ending sounds.

1. **Say:** I'm going to say two words. Listen for the **ending sound /<u>th</u>/**. Then tell me the word with that ending sound. For example, if I say *bathe* and *bat*, you'll say *bathe* because /<u>th</u>/ is the last sound in *bathe*.

2. Say each pair of words. Have students identify the word that ends with the sound /<u>th</u>/.

   - *smooth* or *hard* smooth
   - *dog* or *teethe* teethe
   - *breathe* or *steam* breathe

Whispered or Voiced?

Help students recognize the difference between the whispered sound /th/ and the voiced sound /th/. Grab students the green and red color tiles from the Tile Kit.

1. Explain that you will be playing a game with students, and their job is to listen carefully to the words you say. If the sound /th/ in the word is voiced, students should hold up the green color tile. If the sound /th/ is whispered, they should hold up the red tile. If needed, allow time for students to repeat the words and feel their throats.

2. Use the following words:

   - ▸ *bath* whispered (red tile)
   - ▸ *cloth* whispered (red tile)
   - ▸ *breathe* voiced (green tile)
   - ▸ *these* voiced (green tile)
   - ▸ *them* voiced (green tile)
   - ▸ *three* whispered (red tile)

Try It

The Beginning

Have students complete page PH 13 in *K¹² PhonicsWorks Basic Activity Book* for more practice with the sound /th/. First have students say the name of each picture. Then have them circle pictures whose name begins with the sound /th/.

Objectives
- Identify and use the sound /th/.
- Identify beginning sounds in words.

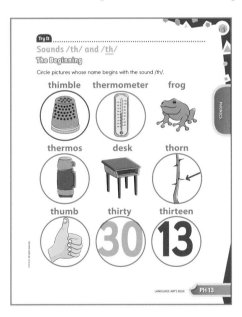

 20 minutes

REVIEW: Sounds /th/ and /<u>th</u>/

Students will work online independently to

▸ Practice the sounds /th/ and /<u>th</u>/.

Help students locate the online activities and provide support as needed.

Offline Alternative

No computer access? Have students think of words that begin or end with the sounds /th/ and /<u>th</u>/ (for example, *thirst* and *thud*, or *there* and *this*).

Objectives

- Identify and use the sound /th/.
- Identify and use the sound /<u>th</u>/.
- Identify beginning sounds in words.
- Identify ending sounds in words.

Sounds /ĕ/ and /k/

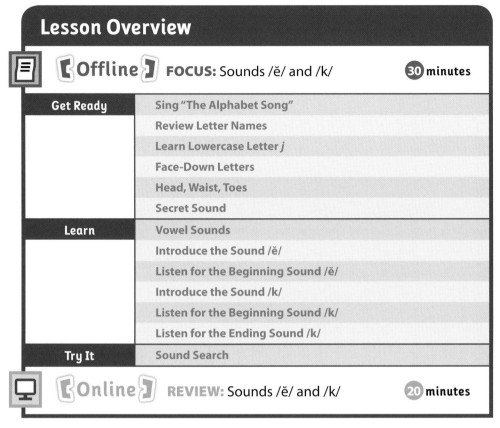

Lesson Overview

Offline FOCUS: Sounds /ĕ/ and /k/ — **30** minutes

Get Ready	Sing "The Alphabet Song"
	Review Letter Names
	Learn Lowercase Letter *j*
	Face-Down Letters
	Head, Waist, Toes
	Secret Sound
Learn	Vowel Sounds
	Introduce the Sound /ĕ/
	Listen for the Beginning Sound /ĕ/
	Introduce the Sound /k/
	Listen for the Beginning Sound /k/
	Listen for the Ending Sound /k/
Try It	Sound Search

Online REVIEW: Sounds /ĕ/ and /k/ — **20** minutes

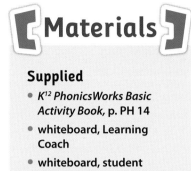

Materials

Supplied

- *K¹² PhonicsWorks Basic Activity Book*, p. PH 14
- whiteboard, Learning Coach
- whiteboard, student
- Tile Kit

Advance Preparation

Place lowercase letter tiles *a* through *i* and uppercase letter tiles *J* through *Z* in alphabetical order on your whiteboard. Place the lowercase letter tile *j* on students' whiteboard.

Big Ideas

Phonological awareness is a critical pre-reading component of early literacy instruction.

 **30** minutes

FOCUS: Sounds /ĕ/ and /k/

Work **together** with students to complete offline Get Ready, Learn, and Try It activities.

Get Ready

Sing "The Alphabet Song"

To help students become familiar and comfortable with the alphabet, sing "The Alphabet Song" with them. Sing slowly, so that students may touch each letter on your whiteboard as they sing the letter's name.

Review Letter Names

To help students learn the alphabet, have them practice identifying and naming the letters *a*, *b*, *e*, *f*, *i*, *j*, *M*, and *W*. Grab your whiteboard with letters.

1. Point to each letter and have students touch and name each one.

   i   j   e   f   a   b   W   M

2. Say the name of each letter. After each one, have students repeat the name and touch the tile.

   i   j   e   f   a   b   W   M

3. Redirect students if they name a letter incorrectly.

   ▸ Name the letter students missed.
   ▸ Have students touch the letter and say its name.
   ▸ Have students trace the shape of the letter with their finger on the brown side of their board, and have them say the letter's name as they trace the shape.
   ▸ If students name a letter incorrectly twice, point to the letter and tell them its name. Have students touch the letter and say its name.

Learn Lowercase Letter *j*

To help students learn lowercase letters of the alphabet, have them practice identifying and naming the letter *j*.

1. **Say:** We're going to learn a lowercase letter today. It is the letter *j*.

2. Have students touch the letter and say its name.

3. **Say:** I'm going to put the letter on my whiteboard in place of the capital letter for *j*.

4. Move the uppercase *J* tile from your whiteboard to the Tile Kit, and replace it with the lowercase *j* tile.

5. Have students sing "The Alphabet Song," touching the lowercase letters *a* through *j*, then moving back to the capital letters.

Objectives

- Identify letters of the alphabet.
- Identify capital and lowercase letters.
- Match capital letters to lowercase letters.
- Identify individual sounds in words.

Face-Down Letters

To help students learn to recognize the letters of the alphabet, have them practice identifying and naming letters. Grab your whiteboard with letters placed in alphabetical order.

1. Lay your whiteboard down on a flat surface and flip over the following letter tiles so they are face down on the whiteboard: *c, f, i, O,* and *S.*

2. **Say:** These letters are face down. We are looking at the back of them. Name each letter and then turn it over to see if you were right.

TIP If students miss any of the letters, have them turn over the missed ones and try again.

Head, Waist, Toes

Help students practice identifying the sounds in words.

1. **Say:** Let's identify sounds in words by touching parts of our body as we say each sound. For example, I'll say *van,* which has three sounds, and you'll repeat the word. Do these steps with me:

   ▸ The first sound in *van* is /v/, so I touch my head as I say /v/.
   ▸ The middle sound is /ă/, so I touch my waist as I say /ă/.
   ▸ The last sound is /n/, so I touch my toes as I say /n/.

2. Say the words below. Have students repeat each word and then touch their head, waist, and toes as they say each sound in the word. After they say the sounds in each word, ask them the question for that word.

   ▸ map /m/ /ă/ /p/   What is the middle sound? /ă/
   ▸ thin /th/ /ĭ/ /n/   What is the middle sound? /ĭ/
   ▸ hide /h/ /ī/ /d/   What is the last sound? /d/
   ▸ late /l/ /ā/ /t/   What is the last sound? /t/
   ▸ fat /f/ /ă/ /t/   What is the first sound? /f/
   ▸ Sam /s/ /ă/ /m/   What is the last sound? /m/

TIP If students have difficulty with this activity, be sure they can identify beginning, middle, and ending. If students still have difficulty with this activity, try finger stretching the words instead.

Secret Sound

Say groups of words that have the same letter to help students recognize **middle sounds** in words.

1. **Say:** I am going to say some groups of words. Listen for a secret sound in the middle of each word. Then tell me what sound you hear at the middle of each group of words.

2. Say each of the following groups of words. Have students identify the secret sound in each group.

   ▸ *take, safe, cane, place* /ā/
   ▸ *home, goat, rope, pole* /ō/
   ▸ *cat, sad, rag, tap* /ă/
   ▸ *side, night, sign, time* /ī/

(TIP) Repeat any groups of words for which students couldn't identify the secret sound. Have them repeat each word in that group. Then have them say what sound they hear in the middle of each word.

Learn

Vowel Sounds

Review the vowel sounds /ē/, /ŏ/, /ā/, /ī/, /ă/, and /ō/ with students.

1. **Say:** We make vowel sounds with our mouths open and without our tongue, teeth, or lips blocking the sound. Our mouths are open wide when we make some vowel sounds, like /ā/. Our mouths are open only a little for other vowel sounds, like /ī/.

2. **Say:** Let's review the vowel sounds you have learned. Say each sound and feel how your mouth is open when you say the sound.

   ▸ /ē/ as in *me*
   ▸ /ŏ/ as in *octopus*
   ▸ /ā/ as in *ace*
   ▸ /ī/ as in *ice*
   ▸ /ă/ as in *apple*
   ▸ /ō/ as in *oak*

3. **Say:** We can sing all vowel sounds because we can stretch them out. When we say /t/, our tongue blocks the sound. When we say /p/, our lips block the sound. That means /t/ and /p/ aren't vowel sounds. We can't sing them without adding vowel sounds.

4. **Say:** I'm going to say two sounds. Your job is to tell me which one is the vowel sound.

5. Say each pair of sounds and have students identify the vowel sound. After they have identified it, ask them the question about the other sound.

   ▸ /ē/ and /m/   What part of the mouth blocks the sound /m/? lips
   ▸ /d/ and /ŏ/   What part of the mouth blocks the sound /d/? tongue
   ▸ /ā/ and /s/   What parts of the mouth block the sound /s/? tongue and teeth
   ▸ /f/ and /ō/   What part of the mouth blocks the sound /f/? teeth against the lips

Objectives
- Identify and use the sound /k/.
- Identify and use the sound /ĕ/.
- Identify beginning sounds in words.
- Identify ending sounds in words.
- Identify individual sounds within words.
- Identify and distinguish between consonants and vowels.

Introduce the Sound /ĕ/

Teach the sound /ĕ/, as in *Ed*, *exit*, and *enter*.

1. **Say:** We're going to play a game to practice the **sound /ĕ/**. Your job is to say the sound just like me and do what I do, too.

2. Move your finger along the edge of the table and say the sound /ĕ/. Have students do this, too.

3. **Say:** We make some sounds with a whisper and some sounds with our voice. Let's figure out whether the sound /ĕ/ is whispered or voiced. Say /ĕ/ and put your fingers on the lump in your throat called your voice box.

   ▸ Do you feel your voice box vibrate? Yes, /ĕ/ is a voiced sound because we do use our voice box when we make the sound.

4. **Say:** The sound /ĕ/ is a vowel sound. Can you sing the sound /ĕ/? Yes

5. **Say:** I'll say some words that start with the sound /ĕ/ and you'll repeat them, saying /ĕ/ just the way I do.

   Ed   exit   enter   edge

Listen for the Beginning Sound /ĕ/

Present pairs of words to help students recognize beginning sounds.

1. **Say:** I'm going to say two words. Listen for the **beginning sound /ĕ/**. Then tell me the word that has that beginning sound. For example, if I say *extra* and *open*, you'll say *extra* because /ĕ/ is the first sound in *extra*.

2. Say each pair of words. Have students identify the word that begins with the sound /ĕ/.

   ▸ *ice* or *echo* echo
   ▸ *ask* or *effort* effort
   ▸ *Edward* or *Allen* Edward

Introduce the Sound /k/

Teach the sound /k/, as in *key*, *kick*, and *can*.

1. **Say:** We're going to play a game to practice the **sound /k/**. Your job is to say the sound just like me and do what I do, too.

2. Carefully kick the air and say the sound /k/. Have students do this, too.

3. **Say:** We make some sounds with a whisper and some sounds with our voice. Let's figure out whether the sound /k/ is whispered or voiced. Say /k/ and put your fingers on the lump in your throat called your voice box.

4. **Say:** The sound /k/ is a whispered sound because we do not use our voice box when we make the sound.

   ▸ Is /k/ a vowel sound? No, because we block the sound with the back of our tongue.

5. **Say:** I'll say some words that start with the sound /k/ and you'll repeat them, saying /k/ just the way I do.

key   kick   can

6. **Say:** Now I'll say some words that end with the sound /k/ and you'll repeat them, saying /k/ just the way I do.

pack   pink   sock

TIP When you teach the sound /k/, make sure students say the sound correctly and do not add *uh* after pronouncing it. Students should say /k/, not *kuh*.

Listen for the Beginning Sound /k/

Present pairs of words to help students recognize beginning sounds.

1. **Say:** I'm going to say two words. Listen for the **beginning sound /k/**. Then tell me the word that has that beginning sound. For example, if I say *can* and *tan*, you'll say *can* because /k/ is the first sound in *can*.

2. Say each pair of words. Have students identify the word that begins with the sound /k/.
   - ► *car* or *far* *car*
   - ► *clip* or *slip* *clip*
   - ► *toast* or *coast* *coast*

Listen for the Ending Sound /k/

Present pairs of words to help students recognize ending sounds.

1. **Say:** I'm going to say two words. Listen for the **ending sound /k/**. Then tell me the word with that ending sound. For example, if I say *buck* and *ram*, you'll say *buck* because /k/ is the last sound in *buck*.

2. Say each pair of words. Have students identify the word that ends with the sound /k/.
   - ► *trick* or *trip* *trick*
   - ► *lake* or *late* *lake*
   - ► *lime* or *like* *like*

Try It

....

Sound Search

Have students complete page PH 14 in *K¹² PhonicsWorks Basic Activity Book* for more practice with the sounds /ĕ/ and /k/. First have students say the name of each picture. Then have them circle pictures whose name has the sound the /k/ and draw an X over pictures whose name has the sound /ĕ/.

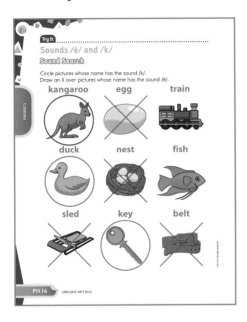

Objectives

- Identify and use the sound /ĕ/.
- Identify and use the sound /k/.
- Identify individual sounds in words.

⟦Online⟧ ⑳ minutes

REVIEW: Sounds /ĕ/ and /k/

Students will work online independently to

▸ Practice the sounds /ĕ/ and /k/.

Help students locate the online activities and provide support as needed.

_____

Offline Alternative

No computer access? Have students point out and name things that begin or end with the sounds /ĕ/ and /k/ (for example, *edge* or *kiss*).

Objectives

- Identify and use the sound /ĕ/.
- Identify and use the sound /k/.
- Identify beginning sounds in words.
- Identify ending sounds in words.

Sound /v/

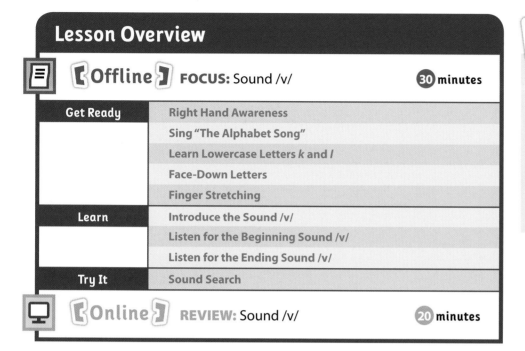

Lesson Overview

Offline FOCUS: Sound /v/ — **30** minutes

Get Ready	Right Hand Awareness
	Sing "The Alphabet Song"
	Learn Lowercase Letters *k* and *l*
	Face-Down Letters
	Finger Stretching
Learn	Introduce the Sound /v/
	Listen for the Beginning Sound /v/
	Listen for the Ending Sound /v/
Try It	Sound Search

Online REVIEW: Sound /v/ — **20** minutes

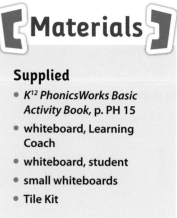

Materials

Supplied

- *K¹² PhonicsWorks Basic Activity Book,* p. PH 15
- whiteboard, Learning Coach
- whiteboard, student
- small whiteboards
- Tile Kit

Advance Preparation

Place lowercase letter tiles *a* through *j* and uppercase letter tiles *K* through *Z* in alphabetical order on both your and students' whiteboards. Place lowercase letter tiles *k* and *l* at the bottom of students' whiteboard.

 30 minutes

FOCUS: Sound /v/

Work **together** with students to complete offline Get Ready, Learn, and Try It activities.

Get Ready

Right Hand Awareness

Students read from left to right, so play a game to develop right hand awareness. To avoid confusion, focus on the right hand only.

1. Say each sentence and do each action. Have students repeat your words and actions.

   ► I'm shaking your right hand.
   ► Now I'm touching my right ankle.
   ► Now I'm waving my right hand in the air.
   ► Now I'm touching my right toe.
   ► Now I'm touching my right cheek

2. Repeat the actions and mix up the order. To end the activity, shake right hands again.

Objectives
- Develop right hand awareness.
- Identify capital and lowercase letters.
- Match capital letters to lowercase letters.
- Identify individual sounds in words.
- Blend sounds to create words.

Sing "The Alphabet Song"

To help students become familiar and comfortable with the alphabet, sing "The Alphabet Song" with them. Sing slowly, so that students may touch each letter on the whiteboard as they sing the letter's name.

Learn Lowercase Letters *k* and *l*

To help students learn lowercase letters of the alphabet, have them practice identifying and naming the letters *k* and *l*.

1. **Say:** We're going to learn two lowercase letters today. They are *k* and *l*.

2. Have students touch each lowercase letter on their whiteboard and say its name.

3. **Say:** I'm going to put these letters on my whiteboard in place of the capital letters for *k* and *l*.

4. Move the uppercase *K* and *L* tiles from your whiteboard to the Tile Kit, and replace them with the lowercase *k* and *l* tiles.

5. Have students sing "The Alphabet Song," touching the lowercase letters *a* through *l*, then moving back to the capital letters.

Face-Down Letters

To help students learn to recognize the letters of the alphabet, have them practice identifying and naming letters. Grab your whiteboard with letters placed in alphabetical order.

1. Lay your whiteboard down on a flat surface and flip over the following letter tiles so they are face down on the whiteboard: *c*, *i*, *k*, *P*, and *Z*.

2. **Say:** These letters are face down. We are looking at the back of them. Name each letter and then turn it over to see if you were right.

TIP If students miss any of the letters, have them turn over the missed ones and try again.

Finger Stretching

Use finger stretching to help students identify individual sounds in words.

1. **Say:** Let's review finger stretching. In the word *fed*, the first sound is /f/, the next sound is /ĕ/, and the last sound is /d/. I will finger stretch each sound as I say it. Then I'll say the word and while pulling my fist toward my body.

2. Finger stretch the word *fed* for students.

3. **Say:** I'm going to say words with several sounds in them. You'll say each word and then finger stretch it while you say each sound in the word.

4. Say the following words and have students finger stretch them. After they finger stretch each word, ask them the question for that word.

   ▸ *fed* /f/ /ĕ/ /d/   What is the first sound in the word? /f/
   ▸ *hope* /h/ /ō/ /p/   What is the middle sound? /ō/
   ▸ *mile* /m/ /ī/ /l/   What is the last sound? /l/
   ▸ *bad* /b/ /ă/ /d/   What is the last sound? /d/
   ▸ *cap* /c/ /ă/ /p/   What is the middle sound? /ă/
   ▸ *meal* /m/ /ē/ /l/   What is the middle sound? /ē/
   ▸ *ham* /h/ /ă/ /m/   What is the last sound? /m/

TIP Refer to the *K¹² PhonicsWorks* video for a demonstration of finger stretching.

Learn ••

Introduce the Sound /v/

Teach the sound /v/, as in *Vicky*, *vote*, and *Val*.

1. **Say:** We're going to play a game to practice the **sound /v/**. Your job is to say the sound just like me and do what I do, too.

2. Make a "V for victory" sign with your fingers and say the sound /v/. Have students do this, too.

3. **Say:** We make many sounds with our tongue, our teeth, and our lips. Say /v/ again and feel whether your tongue, teeth, or lips are making the sound.

   ▸ Do you feel your teeth and lower lip when you make the sound /v/? Yes

> **Objectives**
> • Identify and use the sound /v/.
> • Identify beginning sounds in words.
> • Identify ending sounds in words.
> • Identify individual sounds in words.

4. **Say:** We make some sounds with a whisper and some sounds with our voice. Let's figure out whether the sound /v/ is whispered or voiced. Say /v/ and put your fingers on the lump in your throat called your voice box.

   ▸ Do you feel your voice box vibrate? Yes, /v/ is a noisy sound because we use our voice box when we make the sound.

5. **Say:** I'll say some words that start with the sound /v/ and you'll repeat them, saying /v/ just the way I do.

   Vicky   vote   Val

6. **Say:** Now I'll say some words that end with the sound /v/ and you'll repeat them, saying /v/ just the way I do.

   have   love   live

TIP When you teach the sound /v/, make sure students say the sound correctly and do not add *uh* after pronouncing it. Students should say /v/, not *vuh*.

Listen for the Beginning Sound /v/
Present pairs of words to help students recognize beginning sounds.

1. **Say:** I'm going to say two words. Listen for the **beginning sound /v/**. Then tell me the word that has that beginning sound. For example, if I say *vowel* and *letter*, you'll say *vowel* because /v/ is the first sound in *vowel*.

2. Say each pair of words. Have students identify the word that begins with the sound /v/.

   ▸ *verse* or *purse verse*
   ▸ *rent* or *vent vent*
   ▸ *sound* or *voice voice*

Listen for the Ending Sound /v/
Present pairs of words to help students recognize ending sounds.

1. **Say:** I'm going to say two words. Listen for the **ending sound /v/**. Then tell me the word with that ending sound. For example, if I say *shave* and *shape*, you'll say *shave* because /v/ is the last sound in *shave*.

2. Say each pair of words. Have students identify the word that ends with the sound /v/.

   ▸ *five* or *ten five*
   ▸ *cook* or *stove stove*
   ▸ *lead* or *love love*

Try It ●

Sound Search

Have students complete page PH 15 in *K¹² PhonicsWorks Basic Activity Book* for more practice with the sound /v/. First have students say the name of each picture. Then have them circle pictures whose name has the sound /v/.

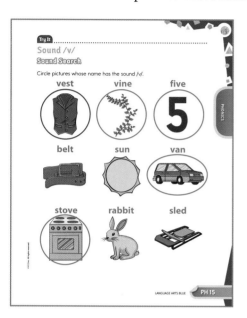

> **Objectives**
> • Identify and use the sound /v/.
> • Identify individual sounds in words.

 **20 minutes**

REVIEW: Sound /v/

Students will work online independently to

▶ Practice the sound /v/.

Help students locate the online activities and provide support as needed.

Offline Alternative

No computer access? Have students point out and name things that begin or end with the sound /v/ (for example, *vest* or *glove*).

> **Objectives**
> • Identify and use the sound /v/.
> • Identify beginning sounds in words.
> • Identify ending sounds in words.

Sound /r/

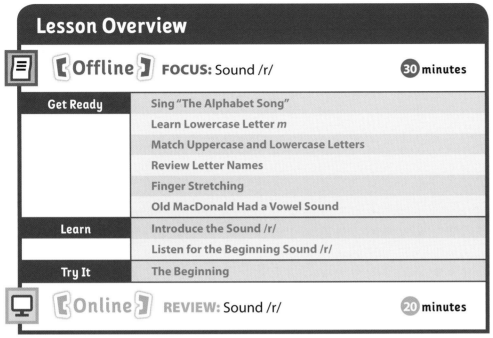

Lesson Overview

Offline FOCUS: Sound /r/ — **30** minutes

Get Ready	Sing "The Alphabet Song"
	Learn Lowercase Letter *m*
	Match Uppercase and Lowercase Letters
	Review Letter Names
	Finger Stretching
	Old MacDonald Had a Vowel Sound
Learn	Introduce the Sound /r/
	Listen for the Beginning Sound /r/
Try It	The Beginning

Online REVIEW: Sound /r/ — **20** minutes

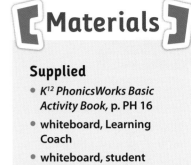

Materials

Supplied
- *K¹² PhonicsWorks Basic Activity Book,* p. PH 16
- whiteboard, Learning Coach
- whiteboard, student
- Tile Kit

Advance Preparation

Place lowercase letter tiles *a* through *k* and uppercase letter tiles *L* through *Z* in alphabetical order on your whiteboard. Place lowercase letter tile *m* on students' whiteboard.

 **30 minutes**

FOCUS: Sound /r/

Work **together** with students to complete offline Get Ready, Learn, and Try It activities.

Get Ready

Sing "The Alphabet Song"

To help students become familiar and comfortable with the alphabet, sing "The Alphabet Song" with them. Sing slowly, so that students may touch each letter on your whiteboard as they sing the letter's name.

Learn Lowercase Letter *m*

To help students learn lowercase letters of the alphabet, have them practice identifying and naming the letter *m*.

1. **Say:** We're going to learn a lowercase letter today. The letter is *m*.

2. Have students touch the letter and say its name.

3. **Say:** I'm going to put this letter on my whiteboard in place of the capital letter for *m*.

4. Move the uppercase letter *M* tile from your whiteboard to the Tile Kit, and replace it with the lowercase *m* tile.

5. Have students sing "The Alphabet Song," touching the lowercase letters *a* through *m*, then moving back to the capital letters.

Match Uppercase and Lowercase Letters

To help students learn to recognize the difference between lowercase and uppercase letters of the alphabet, have them practice identifying and naming letters. Grab your whiteboard with letters.

1. Place the following uppercase letters on students' whiteboard in a horizontal row: *A*, *B*, *I*, *J*, *K*, *L*, and *M*.

2. Point to a letter and have students name it.

3. Have students select the matching lowercase letter from your whiteboard.

4. Have students place the lowercase letter under the uppercase letter to make a pair.

 TIP If students have difficulty with this activity, have them practice naming the letters in the alphabet. When they can name all the letters in the correct order, have them touch and name the lowercase and uppercase letters for each letter.

Objectives

- Identify capital and lowercase letters.
- Match capital letters to lowercase letters.
- Identify letters of the alphabet.
- Identify individual sounds in words.
- Identify long vowel sounds.
- Blend sounds to create words.

Review Letter Names

To help students learn the alphabet, have them practice identifying and naming the letters *i, k, l, m, N, O, P,* and *Q.* Grab your whiteboard with letters.

1. Point to each letter and have students touch and name each one.

   i   k   l   m   N   O   P   Q

2. Say the name of each letter. After each one, have students repeat the name and touch the tile.

   i   k   l   m   N   O   P   Q

3. Redirect students if they name a letter incorrectly.

   ▸ Name the letter students missed.
   ▸ Have students touch the letter and say its name.
   ▸ Have students trace the shape of the letter with their finger on the brown side of their board, and have them say the letter's name as they trace the shape.
   ▸ If students name a letter incorrectly twice, point to the letter and tell them its name. Have students touch the letter and say its name.

Finger Stretching

Use finger stretching to help students identify individual sounds in words.

1. **Say:** Let's review finger stretching. In the word *tack*, the first sound is /t/, the middle sound is /ă/, and the last sound is /k/. I will finger stretch each sound as I say it. Then I'll say the word, while pulling my fist toward my body.

2. Finger stretch the word *tack* for students.

3. **Say:** I'm going to say words with several sounds in them. You'll say each word and then finger stretch it while you say each sound in the word.

4. Say the following words and have students finger stretch them. After they finger stretch each word, ask them the question for that word.

   ▸ *that* /th/ /ă /t/   What is the first sound in the word? /th/
   ▸ *mop* /m/ /ŏ/ /p/   What is the first sound? /m/
   ▸ *both* /b/ /ō/ /th/   What is the last sound? /th/
   ▸ *Beth* /b/ /ĕ/ /th/   What is the middle sound? /ĕ/
   ▸ *bath* /b/ /ă/ /th/   What is the middle sound? /ă/
   ▸ *dive* /d/ /ī/ /v/   What is the middle sound? /ī/

TIP Refer to the *K¹² PhonicsWorks* video for a demonstration of finger stretching.

Old MacDonald Had a Vowel Sound
To review sounds, sing "Old MacDonald's Farm" with students.

1. **Say:** Let's have some fun with "Old MacDonald's Farm." Instead of animals, we'll put sounds on the farm. We'll sing, "Old MacDonald had a farm, E-I-E-I-O, and on that farm he had an /ē/, E-I-E-I-O. With an /ē/, /ē/ here and an /ē/, /ē/ there . . . ."

2. Continue singing the song. Alternate singing and having students sing until you have finished all of the long vowel sounds: /ā/, /ē/, /ī/, /ō/, and /ū/.

Learn

Introduce the Sound /r/
Teach the sound /r/, as in *run, rip,* and *ride.*

1. **Say:** We're going to play a game to practice the **sound /r/.** Your job is to say the sound just like me and do what I do, too.

2. March and say, "Rrrrrobots are marrrrrching, rrrright, left, rrrright!" Have students do this, too.

3. **Say:** We make sounds with our tongues, our teeth, or our lips. Say the sound /r/ again and feel whether your tongue, teeth, or lips are making the sound.

   ► Do you feel your tongue and teeth when you make the sound /r/? Yes

4. **Say:** I'll say some words that start with the sound /r/ and you'll repeat them, saying /r/ just the way I do.

   run   rip   ride

(TIP) When you teach the sound /r/, make sure students say the sound correctly and do not say *are.* It might help students if they say /rrrrr/, making a sound like a bear growling. Note that this sound is /rrrrr/, not /grrrr/.

Listen for the Beginning Sound /r/
Present pairs of words to help students recognize beginning sounds.

1. **Say:** I'm going to say two words. Listen for the **beginning sound /r/.** Then tell me the word that has that beginning sound. For example, if I say *rice* and *nice,* you'll say *rice* because /r/ is the first sound in *rice.*

2. Say each pair of words. Have students identify the word that begins with the sound /r/.

   ► *rocks* or *box* rocks
   ► *sing* or *ring* ring
   ► *toad* or *road* road

Objectives
- Identify and use the sound /r/.
- Identify beginning sounds in words.
- Identify ending sounds in words.

Try It

The Beginning

Have students complete page PH 16 in *K¹² PhonicsWorks Basic Activity Book* for more practice with the sound /r/. First have students say the name of each picture. Then have students circle pictures whose name begins with the sound /r/.

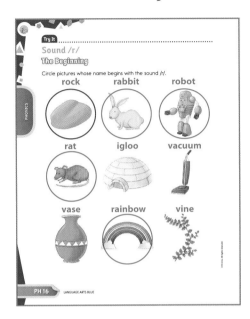

Online 20 minutes

REVIEW: Sound /r/

Students will work online independently to

▶ Practice the sound /r/.

Help students locate the online activities and provide support as needed.

Objectives

- Identify and use the sound /r/.
- Identify beginning sounds in words.

Offline Alternative

No computer access? Have students point out and name things that begin with the sound /r/ (for example, *ribbon* or *rug*).

Unit Checkpoint

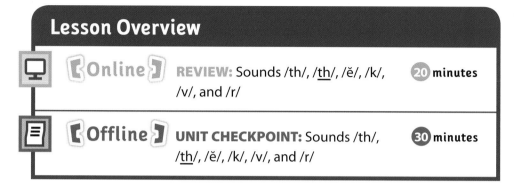

Lesson Overview

[Online] **REVIEW:** Sounds /th/, /<u>th</u>/, /ĕ/, /k/, /v/, and /r/ — **20** minutes

[Offline] **UNIT CHECKPOINT:** Sounds /th/, /<u>th</u>/, /ĕ/, /k/, /v/, and /r/ — **30** minutes

Materials

Supplied
- *K¹² PhonicsWorks Basic Assessments,* pp. PH 13–17

Objectives
- Identify and use the sound /th/.
- Identify and use the sound /<u>th</u>/.
- Identify and use the sound /ĕ/.
- Identify and use the sound /k/.
- Identify and use the sound /v/.
- Identify and use the sound /r/.
- Identify beginning sounds in words.
- Identify ending sounds in words.
- Identify individual sounds in words.
- Identify letters of the alphabet.
- Identify a word when given the onset and rime.

[Online] **20** minutes

REVIEW: **Sounds /th/, /<u>th</u>/, /ĕ/, /k/, /v/, and /r/**

Students will review the sounds /th/, /<u>th</u>/, /ĕ/, /k/, /v/, and /r/ to prepare for the Unit Checkpoint. Help students locate the online activities and provide support as needed.

[Offline] 🔞 minutes

UNIT CHECKPOINT: /th/, /<u>th</u>/, /ĕ/, /k/, /v/, and /r/

Explain that students are going to show what they have learned about letters, sounds, and words.

1. Give students the Unit Checkpoint pages for the Sounds /th/, /<u>th</u>/, /ĕ/, /k/, /v/, and /r/ unit and print the Unit Checkpoint Answer Key, if you'd like.

2. Use the instructions below to help administer the Checkpoint to students. On the Answer Key or another sheet of paper, note student answers to oral response questions to help with scoring the Checkpoint later.

3. Use the Answer Key to score the Checkpoint, and then enter the results online.

Part 1. Letter Matching Moving from left to right, have students read the letters aloud and circle the letters that match the first letter in the row.

Part 2. Match Ending Sounds Have students say the name of each picture and draw a line to connect the pictures that end with the same sound.

Part 3. Rhymes Say each pair of words and have students say if the word pairs rhyme. Note any incorrect responses.

9. *head, bread*
10. *feather, leather*
11. *nest, naps*
12. *rubber, blubber*
13. *math, calf*
14. *van, vine*

Part 4. Middle Sounds Say each pair of words and have students say if the words have the same middle sound. Repeat the words, as necessary. Note any incorrect responses.

15. *math, fan*
16. *bed, let*
17. *light, lock*
18. *sash, hat*
19. *bone, pot*
20. *sheep, beach*

Part 5. Onset and Rime Say the first sound of each word. Pause briefly and then say the rest of the word. Have students say the whole word. Note any incorrect responses.

21. /f/ . . . eet
22. /v/ . . . an
23. /m/ . . . ap
24. /s/ . . . and
25. /th/ . . . ink
26. /s/ . . . eat

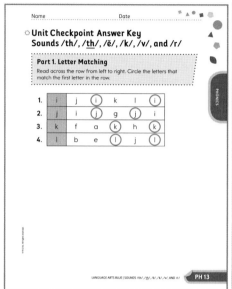
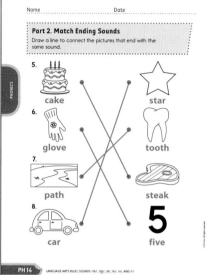
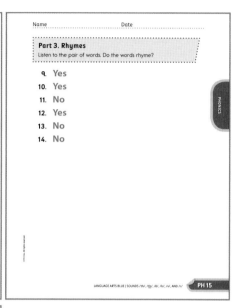
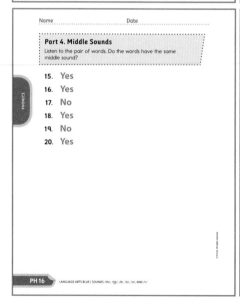
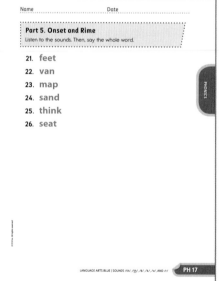

Sound /ĭ/

Unit Overview

In this unit, students will

- ▸ Identify letters in the alphabet.
- ▸ Identify and say the sounds /ĭ/, /ŭ/, /ch/, and /y/.
- ▸ Distinguish between words that rhyme or sound different.
- ▸ Identify individual sounds in words.
- ▸ Learn and practice blends.
- ▸ Learn to put phrases together to make sentences.

[Materials]

Supplied

- *K¹² PhonicsWorks Basic Activity Book,* p. PH 17
- whiteboard, Learning Coach
- whiteboard, student
- Tile Kit

Also Needed

- crayons

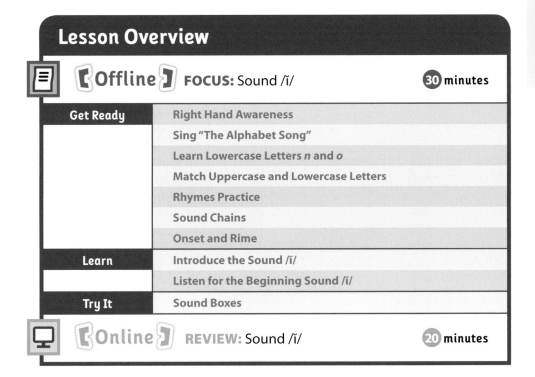

Lesson Overview

☰ [Offline] FOCUS: Sound /ĭ/	**30** minutes

Get Ready	Right Hand Awareness
	Sing "The Alphabet Song"
	Learn Lowercase Letters *n* and *o*
	Match Uppercase and Lowercase Letters
	Rhymes Practice
	Sound Chains
	Onset and Rime
Learn	Introduce the Sound /ĭ/
	Listen for the Beginning Sound /ĭ/
Try It	Sound Boxes

🖥 [Online] REVIEW: Sound /ĭ/	**20** minutes

Advance Preparation

Place lowercase letter tiles *a* through *m* and uppercase letter tiles *N* through *Z* in alphabetical order on your whiteboard. Place lowercase letter tiles *n* and *o* on students' whiteboard.

⟦ Offline ⟧ ③ minutes

FOCUS: Sound /ĭ/

Work **together** with students to complete offline Get Ready, Learn, and Try It activities.

Get Ready

Right Hand Awareness

Students read from left to right, so play a game to develop right hand awareness. To avoid confusion, focus on the right hand only.

1. Say each sentence and do each action. Have students repeat your words and actions.

   ▶ I'm shaking your right hand.
   ▶ Now I'm touching my right ankle.
   ▶ Now I'm waving my right hand in the air.
   ▶ Now I'm touching my right toe.
   ▶ Now I'm touching my right cheek

2. Repeat the actions and mix up the order. To end the activity, shake right hands again.

Sing "The Alphabet Song"

To help students become familiar and comfortable with the alphabet, sing "The Alphabet Song" with them. Sing slowly, so that students may touch each letter on your whiteboard as they sing the letter's name.

Learn Lowercase Letters *n* and *o*

To help students learn lowercase letters of the alphabet, have them practice identifying and naming the letters *n* and *o*. Grab your whiteboard with letters in alphabetical order.

1. **Say:** There are two different kinds of letters in our alphabet. Can you name them? lowercase or small, uppercase or capital

2. **Say:** We're going to learn two lowercase letters today. The letters are *n* and *o*.

3. Have students touch each lowercase letter on their whiteboard and say its name.

4. **Say:** I'm going to put these letters on my whiteboard in place of the capital letters for *n* and *o*.

5. Move the uppercase *N* and *O* tiles from your whiteboard to the Tile Kit, and replace them with the lowercase *n* and *o* tiles.

6. Have students sing "The Alphabet Song," touching the lowercase letters *a* through *o*, then moving back to the capital letters.

> **Objectives**
> - Develop right hand awareness.
> - Identify letters of the alphabet.
> - Identify capital and lowercase letters.
> - Match capital letters to lowercase letters.
> - Identify words that rhyme.
> - Identify individual sounds in words.
> - Identify a word when given the onset and rime.
> - Blend sounds to create words.

Match Uppercase and Lowercase Letters

To help students learn to recognize the difference between lowercase and uppercase letters of the alphabet, have them practice identifying and naming letters. Grab your whiteboard with letters in alphabetical order..

1. Place the following uppercase letters on students' whiteboard in a horizontal row: *A, B, C, I, J, K, L, M,* and *N.*

2. Point to a letter and have students name it.

3. Have students select the matching lowercase letter from your whiteboard.

4. Have students place the lowercase letter under the uppercase letter to make a pair.

TIP If students have difficulty with this activity, have them practice naming the letters in the alphabet. When they can name all the letters in the correct order, have them touch and name the lowercase and uppercase letters for each letter.

Rhymes Practice

Use common poems and nursery rhymes to practice identifying rhyming words.

1. **Say:** I am going to start reading a poem. When you hear words that rhyme, raise your hand and tell me the words. I will continue reading the poem. As I read, keep raising your hand when you hear words that rhyme and tell me the words.

2. Read the poem. Have students raise their hand when they hear rhyming words and have them tell you which words rhyme. Continue reading the poem.

   A swarm of bees in May
   Is worth a load of hay.
   A swarm of bees in June
   Is worth a silver spoon.
   A swarm of bees in July
   Is not worth a fly.

3. Continue this activity with other poems that have obvious rhyming words. Here are some choices:

   ▶ "Jack and Jill"
   ▶ "Twinkle, Twinkle, Little Star"
   ▶ "Little Miss Muffet"
   ▶ "Baa, Baa, Black Sheep"

Sound Chains

Play a game with color tiles to help students identify sounds that are the same and sounds that are different. Grab the color tiles from the Tile Kit.

1. Place the tiles on a table.

2. **Say:** I am going to make three sounds. If the sounds are the same, you'll pick out three tiles that are the same color and put them next to each other. If the sounds are different, you'll pick out three tiles that are different colors and put them next to each other. For example,

   ▸ When I make the sounds /m/, /m/, /m/, you'll pick out three tiles all the same color and put them next to each other because all three sounds are the same.
   ▸ Now listen carefully to the next three sounds: /m/, /m/, /ă/. The first and second sounds —/m/— stayed the same but the third sound changed from /m/ to /ă/, so you will change the third tile to a tile of a different color.
   ▸ Each time I say a group of sounds, you will change one color tile to show that one of the sounds changed.

3. Say each group of sounds. Have students pick out and place tiles to identify the sounds that change. Note that students should **not** choose three new tiles for each group of sounds; they should begin with three tiles and replace those tiles as necessary throughout the "chain."

   ▸ /k/, /k/, /ă/
   ▸ /k/, /k/, /v/
   ▸ /m/, /k/, /v/
   ▸ /m/, /f/, /v/
   ▸ /m/, /f/, /ŏ/
   ▸ /th/, /f/, /ŏ/
   ▸ /f/, /f/, /ŏ/
   ▸ /f/, /f/, /ă/

Onset and Rime

In a word, the part of the syllable before the first vowel sound is the **onset**. The part of the syllable after the first vowel sound is the **rime**. For example, in *dog*, /d/ is the onset and *og* is the rime. Help students put together words that are broken down into parts by onset and rime

1. **Say:** I'm going to break a word into two parts. Your job is to put the parts together and say the word. If the first part of a word is /r/ and the last part of the word is *oad*, then the whole word is *road*: /r/ . . . *oad* . . . *road*.

2. Say the following pairs of word parts. Have students tell you the word that each pair forms.

   ▸ /p/ . . . *ack pack*
   ▸ /h/ . . . *ope hope*
   ▸ /k/ . . . *ite kite*

Learn

Introduce the Sound /ĭ/

Teach the sound /ĭ/, as in *itch*, *in*, and *it*.

1. **Say:** We're going to play a game to practice the **sound** /ĭ/. Your job is to say the sound just like me and do what I do, too.

2. Make a scratching motion and say, "This is an i-i-icky i-i-itch!" Have students do this, too.

3. **Say:** We make some sounds with a whisper and some sounds with our voice. Let's figure out whether the sound /ĭ/ is whispered or voiced. Say /ĭ/ and put your fingers on the lump in your throat called your voice box.

   ▶ Do you feel your voice box vibrate? Yes, /ĭ/ is a noisy sound because we do use our voice box when we make the sound.

4. **Say:** The sound /ĭ/ is a vowel sound. You can sing the sound /ĭ/ without your lips, tongue, or teeth blocking the sound. Let's try it.

5. Sing the vowel sound /ĭ/ with students.

6. **Say:** I'll say some words that start with the sound /ĭ/ and you'll repeat them, saying /ĭ/ just the way I do.

itch   *in*   *it*

TIP When you teach the sound /ĭ/, have students say the sound and not the letter name. Remind them to feel how their mouth is open when the sound is said.

Listen for the Beginning Sound /ĭ/

Present pairs of words to help students recognize beginning sounds.

1. **Say:** I'm going to say two words. Listen for the **beginning sound** /ĭ/. Then tell me the word that has that beginning sound. For example, if I say *inside* and *open*, you'll say *inside* because /ĭ/ is the first sound in *inside*.

2. Say each pair of words. Have students identify the word that begins with the sound /ĭ/.

   ▶ *ask* or *itch* *itch*
   ▶ *if* or *off* *if*
   ▶ *inch* or *pie* *inch*

Objectives
- Identify and use the sound /ĭ/.
- Identify beginning sounds in words.

Try It

Sound Boxes

Have students complete page PH 17 in *K¹² PhonicsWorks Basic Activity Book* for more practice with the sound /ĭ/. First have students say the name of each picture. Then have them color in the box that corresponds to the position (beginning, middle, or ending) of the sound /ĭ/ in the word.

Objectives
- Identify and use the sound /ĭ/.
- Identify individual sounds in words.

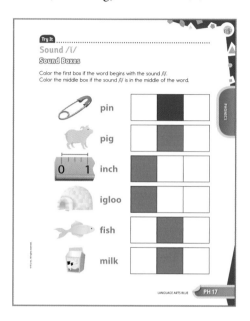

Online 20 minutes

REVIEW: Sound /ĭ/

Students will work online independently to

▸ Practice the sound /ĭ/.

Help students locate the online activities and provide support as needed.

Objectives
- Identify and use the sound /ĭ/.
- Identify individual sounds in words.
- Identify beginning sounds in words.
- Identify middle sounds in words.

Offline Alternative

No computer access? Have students point out and name things that begin with the sound /ĭ/. They should listen for the sound /ĭ/ in the middle of words, too. (Examples: *inches* or *mitt*).

Sound /ŭ/

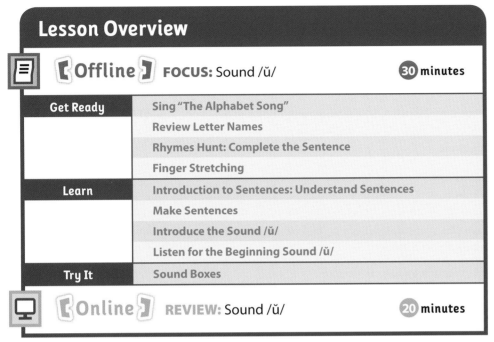

Lesson Overview

[Offline] FOCUS: Sound /ŭ/ — **30** minutes

Get Ready	Sing "The Alphabet Song"
	Review Letter Names
	Rhymes Hunt: Complete the Sentence
	Finger Stretching
Learn	Introduction to Sentences: Understand Sentences
	Make Sentences
	Introduce the Sound /ŭ/
	Listen for the Beginning Sound /ŭ/
Try It	Sound Boxes

[Online] REVIEW: Sound /ŭ/ — **20** minutes

Materials

Supplied
- K¹² PhonicsWorks Basic Activity Book, p. PH 18
- whiteboard, Learning Coach
- Tile Kit

Also Needed
- crayons

Advance Preparation

Place lowercase letter tiles *a* through *o* and uppercase letter tiles *P* through *Z* in alphabetical order on your whiteboard.

Big Ideas

Letters are put together to make words. Words are put together to make sentences. Understanding this fundamental concept is necessary to understanding written language.

 **30 minutes**

FOCUS: Sound /ŭ/

Work **together** with students to complete offline Get Ready, Learn, and Try It activities.

Get Ready ....

Sing "The Alphabet Song"

To help students become familiar and comfortable with the alphabet, sing "The Alphabet Song" with them. Sing slowly, so that students may touch each letter on your whiteboard as they sing the letter's name.

Objectives
- Identify letters of the alphabet.
- Identify words that rhyme.
- Identify individual sounds in words.
- Identify the number of sounds within words.

Review Letter Names

To help students learn the alphabet, have them practice identifying and naming the letters *e*, *f*, *m*, *n*, and *o*. Grab your whiteboard with letters.

1. Point to each letter and have students touch and name each one.

    e   f   m   n   o

2. Say the name of each letter. After each one, have students repeat the name and touch the tile.

    e   f   m   n   o

3. Redirect students if they name a letter incorrectly.

    ▸ Name the letter students missed.
    ▸ Have students touch the letter and say its name.
    ▸ Have students trace the shape of the letter with their finger on the brown side of their board, and have them say the letter's name as they trace the shape.
    ▸ If students name a letter incorrectly twice, point to the letter and tell them its name. Have students touch the letter and say its name.

Rhymes Hunt: Complete the Sentence

Play a game with students to reinforce awareness of words that rhyme.

1. **Say:** Let's have some fun with rhymes. Listen to this sentence: "I think I will take my boat to the lake." What word rhymes with *take*? *lake*

2. **Say:** Now I'm going to give you a sentence with the rhyming word missing. Your job is to think of a word to complete the sentence. Remember, the word needs to rhyme.

    ▸ Listen: "If you drop a cup, it goes down, not _____ ."
    ▸ What rhymes with *cup* and completes the sentence?
    ▸ The word *up* rhymes with *cup* and completes the sentence. Now it's your turn.

3. Continue the procedure with the following sentences:

  ▶ *If you look in the* sky, *you will see things that* _____ . *fly*
  ▶ *When day turns to* night, *we turn on the* _____ . *light*
  ▶ *My cat likes to* nap *when he sits on my* _____ . *lap*

TIP If students have difficulty thinking of a rhyming word to complete the sentence, tell them the completed sentence and then ask them to identify the two rhyming words.

Finger Stretching

Use finger stretching to help students identify individual sounds in words.

1. **Say:** Let's review finger stretching. In the word *sick*, the first sound is /s/, the middle sound is /ĭ/, and the last sound is /k/. I will finger stretch each sound as I say it. Then I'll say the word, while pulling my fist toward my body.

2. Finger stretch the word *sick* for students.

3. **Say:** I'm going to say words. You'll say each word and then finger stretch it while you say each sound in the word.

4. Say the following words and have students finger stretch them. After they finger stretch each word, ask them the question for that word.

  ▶ *bath* /b/ /ă/ /th/   How many sounds are in the word? three
  ▶ *mile* /m/ /ī/ /l/   How many sounds are in the word? three
  ▶ *most* /m/ /ō/ /s/ /t/   How many sounds are in the word? four
  ▶ *fan* /f/ /ă/ /n/   How many sounds are in the word? three
  ▶ *milk* /m/ /ĭ/ /l/ /k/   How many sounds are in the word? four

TIP Refer to the *K¹² PhonicsWorks* video for a demonstration of finger stretching.

Learn ....

Introduction to Sentences: Understand Sentences

Introduce students to sentences and have them choose if a set of words make a sentence.

1. **Say:** When we talk, we use words. When we put words together to say a complete thought, we make a sentence.

2. **Say:** This is a sentence: "The child plays with Roger." The sentence tells you what is happening (playing), and it tells you who is playing (the child). I will say a sentence and you repeat it. Then I will ask you a question about the sentence.

   ▸ *Robin has red hair.*   In the sentence, who has red hair? Robin
   ▸ *Tom likes to play with his cat.*   What does Tom like to do? play with his cat

3. **Say:** Those two examples are sentences because they tell what is happening, and who or what is doing it.

4. **Say:** I will say some words and you repeat them. Tell me whether the words make a sentence or not.

   ▸ *the ball* No
   ▸ *in the house* No
   ▸ *I have fun playing.* Yes
   ▸ *Mark ran around the house.* Yes

Make Sentences

Help students practice using phrases to make sentences.

1. **Say:** A sentence is made up of words. A phrase is a part of a sentence. Let's make some sentences from phrases. I'll say some words and you'll repeat them. Then you'll find different ways to make those words into a sentence. For example,

   ▸ If I say, "catches the ball," you might say, "Sally catches the ball" or "Rex the dog catches the ball."
   ▸ If I say "the dog," you might say, "The dog howled all night" or "I like to walk the dog."

2. Say the following phrases. Have students use each phrase to make two different sentences.

   ▸ *stood up quickly*
   ▸ *until it got dark*
   ▸ *the red ball*
   ▸ *hid under the chair*

Objectives
- Identify complete sentences.
- Orally create sentences from phrases.
- Identify and use the sound /ŭ/.
- Identify beginning sounds in words.

Introduce the Sound /ŭ/

Teach the sound /ŭ/, as in *up*, *us*, and *until*.

1. **Say:** We're going to play a game to practice the **sound /ŭ/.** Your job is to say the sound just like me and do what I do, too.

2. Point your finger up and say, "up." Have students do this, too.

3. **Say:** We make some sounds with a whisper and some sounds with our voice. Let's figure out whether the sound /ŭ/ is whispered or voiced. Say /ŭ/ and put your fingers on the lump in your throat called your voice box.

   ► Do you feel your voice box vibrate? Yes, /ŭ/ is a noisy sound because we do use our voice box when we make the sound.

4. **Say:** The sound /ŭ/ is a vowel sound. We can sing the sound /ŭ/ without our lips, our tongue, or our teeth stopping the sound.

5. Sing the vowel sound /ŭ/ with students.

6. **Say:** I'll say some words that start with the sound /ŭ/ and you'll repeat them, saying /ŭ/ just the way I do.

   up   us   until

Listen for the Beginning Sound /ŭ/

Present pairs of words to help students recognize beginning sounds.

1. **Say:** I'm going to say two words. Listen for the **beginning sound /ŭ/.** Then tell me the word that has that beginning sound. For example, if I say *cousin* and *uncle*, you'll say *uncle* because /ŭ/ is the first sound in *uncle*.

2. Say each pair of words. Have students identify the word that begins with the sound /ŭ/.

   ► *us* or *off us*
   ► *in* or *untie untie*
   ► *ugly* or *after ugly*

Try It ....

Sound Boxes

Have students complete page PH 18 in *K¹² PhonicsWorks Basic Activity Book* for more practice with the sound /ŭ/. First have students say the name of each picture. Then have them color in the box that corresponds to the position (beginning, middle, or ending) of the sound /ŭ/ in the word.

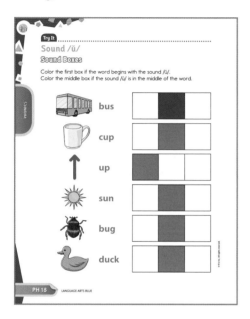

Objectives
- Identify and use the sound /ŭ/.
- Identify individual sounds in words.

Online · 20 minutes

REVIEW: Sound /ŭ/

Students will work online independently to

▸ Practice the sound /ŭ/.

Help students locate the online activities and provide support as needed.

Objectives
- Identify and use the sound /ŭ/.
- Identify individual sounds in words.

Offline Alternative

No computer access? Have students point out and name things that contain the sound /ŭ/. Many of the things may not be spelled with the letter *u* but will sound as if they contain the sound /ŭ/ (for example, *wagon* or *around*).

Sound /ch/

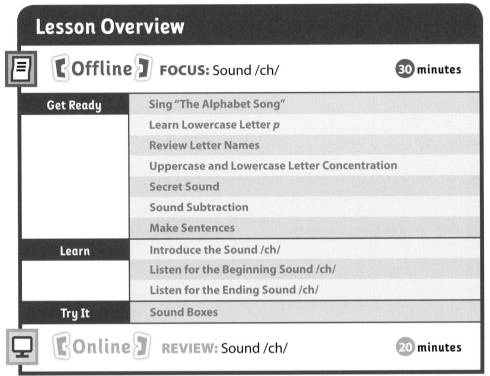

Lesson Overview

Offline FOCUS: Sound /ch/ — **30** minutes

Get Ready	Sing "The Alphabet Song"
	Learn Lowercase Letter *p*
	Review Letter Names
	Uppercase and Lowercase Letter Concentration
	Secret Sound
	Sound Subtraction
	Make Sentences
Learn	Introduce the Sound /ch/
	Listen for the Beginning Sound /ch/
	Listen for the Ending Sound /ch/
Try It	Sound Boxes

Online REVIEW: Sound /ch/ — **20** minutes

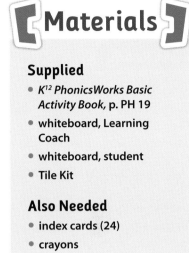

Materials

Supplied
- *K¹² PhonicsWorks Basic Activity Book,* p. PH 19
- whiteboard, Learning Coach
- whiteboard, student
- Tile Kit

Also Needed
- index cards (24)
- crayons

Advance Preparation

Place lowercase letter tiles *a* through *o* and uppercase letter tiles *P* through *Z* in alphabetical order on your whiteboard. Place lowercase letter tile *p* on students' whiteboard.

For Uppercase and Lowercase Letter Concentration, print the uppercase letters *A* through *L* and the lowercase letters *a* through *l* on index cards, using one card per letter.

[Offline] 30 minutes

FOCUS: Sound /ch/

Work **together** with students to complete offline Get Ready, Learn, and Try It activities.

Get Ready ....

Sing "The Alphabet Song"
To help students become familiar and comfortable with the alphabet, sing "The Alphabet Song" with them. Sing slowly, so that students may touch each letter on your whiteboard as they sing the letter's name.

Learn Lowercase Letter *p*
To help students learn lowercase letters of the alphabet, have them practice identifying and naming the letter *p*. Grab your whiteboard with letters.

1. **Say:** There are two different kinds of letters in our alphabet. The ones you already know are called capital, or uppercase, letters. The other kind of letters is called small, or lowercase, letters. These letters are smaller than capital letters.

2. **Say:** We're going to learn one lowercase letter today. It is the letter *p*.

3. Have students touch the lowercase letter on their whiteboard and say its name.

4. **Say:** I'm going to put this letter on my whiteboard in place of the capital letter for *p*.

5. Move the uppercase *P* tile from your whiteboard to the Tile Kit, and replace it with the lowercase *p* tile.

6. Have students sing "The Alphabet Song," touching the lowercase letters *a* through *p*, then moving back to the capital letters.

Review Letter Names
To help students learn the alphabet, have them practice identifying and naming the letters *a*, *b*, *c*, *f*, *g*, *n*, *p*, and *R*. Grab your whiteboard with letters.

1. Point to each letter and have students touch and name each one.

   a   b   c   n   p   f   g   R

2. Say the name of each letter. After each one, have students repeat the name and touch the tile.

   a   b   c   n   p   f   g   R

> **Objectives**
> - Identify letters of the alphabet.
> - Identify capital and lowercase letters.
> - Match capital letters to lowercase letters.
> - Identify individual sounds in words.
> - Orally create sentences from phrases.
> - Identify complete sentences.
> - Identify the new word when one sound is removed from a word.

3. Redirect students if they name a letter incorrectly.

   ▸ Name the letter students missed.
   ▸ Have students touch the letter and say its name.
   ▸ Have students trace the shape of the letter with their finger on the brown side of their board, and have them say the letter's name as they trace the shape.
   ▸ If students name a letter incorrectly twice, point to the letter and tell them its name. Have students touch the letter and say its name.

Uppercase and Lowercase Letter Concentration

Help students practice pairing uppercase and lowercase letters.

1. Gather the index cards you prepared.

2. Select five or six pairs of index cards with uppercase and lowercase letters.

3. Mix up the index cards and place them face down on the table or floor.

4. **Say:** Let's practice matching uppercase and lowercase letters. We can also call these letters big letters and small letters.

5. **Say:** You'll turn over the cards two at a time. If you turn over a card that has a lowercase letter and a card that has the uppercase form of the same letter, the cards match and you can keep them. If the cards don't match, turn them back over.

6. Continue the activity until all of the cards are paired.

7. Repeat the procedure with the remaining cards.

Secret Sound

Say groups of words that have the same letter to help students recognize **beginning sounds** in words.

1. **Say:** I am going to say some groups of words. Listen for a secret sound at the beginning of each word. Then tell me what sound you hear at the beginning of each group of words.

2. Say each of the following groups of words. Have students identify the secret sound in each group.

   ▸ *up, umpire, under* /ŭ/
   ▸ *voice, video, vote* /v/
   ▸ *think, thick, throw* /th/
   ▸ *kiss, kit, kite* /k/

TIP If students can't identify the secret sound, have them listen while you say each word again and then have them repeat each word. Have students say what sound they hear at the beginning of each word.

Sound Subtraction

Present pairs of words to improve students' ability to distinguish between sounds.

1. **Say:** Let's play a game with the sounds in words. I'll say a word and you'll repeat it. Then I'll subtract the first sound from the word and say a new word. Your job is to say the new word and tell me what sound I took away. For example,

   ▸ If I say *fear*, you'll repeat the word.
   ▸ Then I'll take away the first sound from *fear* and say the new word, which is *ear*.
   ▸ When I ask you what sound I subtracted from *fear*, you'll say /f/.

2. Say each pair of words. Have students tell you what sound you subtracted from the first word.

   ▸ *think* and *ink* /th/
   ▸ *mice* and *ice* /m/
   ▸ *phone* and *own* /f/
   ▸ *hair* and *air* /h/

Make Sentences

Help students practice using phrases to make sentences.

1. **Say:** A sentence is made up of words. A phrase is a part of a sentence. Let's make some sentences from phrases. I'll say some words and you'll repeat them. Then you'll find different ways to make those words into a sentence. For example,

   ▸ If I say, "the stove," you might say, "The stove is in the kitchen."
   ▸ If I say "rolled over," you might say, "My dog Rover rolled over."

2. Say the following phrases. Have students use each phrase to make two different sentences.

   ▸ *my right hand*
   ▸ *went bouncing down the hall*
   ▸ *smiled at me*

Learn

Introduce the Sound /ch/

Teach the sound /ch/, as in *chin*, *cheek*, and *child*.

1. **Say:** We're going to play a game to practice the **sound /ch/**. Your job is to say the sound just like me and do what I do, too.

2. Touch your chin and say the sound /ch/. Have students do this, too.

3. **Say:** We make many sounds with our tongue, our teeth, and our lips. Say /ch/ again and feel whether your tongue, teeth, or lips are making the sound.

   ▸ Do you feel your teeth making the sound /ch/? Yes

Objectives

- Identify and use the sound /ch/.
- Identify beginning sounds in words.
- Identify ending sounds in words.
- Identify individual sounds in words.

4. **Say:** We make some sounds with a whisper and some sounds with our voice. Let's figure out whether the sound /ch/ is whispered or voiced. Say /ch/ and put your fingers on the lump in your throat called your voice box.

   ▶ **Do you feel your voice box vibrate?** No, /ch/ is a whispered sound because we don't use our voice box when we make the sound.

5. **Say:** I'll say some words that start with the sound /ch/ and you'll repeat them, saying /ch/ just the way I do.

   chin   cheek   child

6. **Say:** Now I'll say some words that end with the sound /ch/ and you'll repeat them, saying /ch/ just the way I do.

   which   coach   teach

TIP When you teach the sound /ch/, make sure students say the sound correctly and do not add *uh* after pronouncing it. Students should say /ch/, not *chuh*.

Listen for the Beginning Sound /ch/

Present pairs of words to help students recognize beginning sounds.

1. **Say:** I'm going to say two words. Listen for the **beginning sound /ch/**. Then tell me the word that has that beginning sound. For example, if I say *chin* and *thin*, you'll say *chin* because /ch/ is the first sound in *chin*.

2. Say each pair of words. Have students identify the word that begins with the sound /ch/.

   ▶ *chop* or *shop* *chop*
   ▶ *wild* or *child* *child*
   ▶ *thick* or *chick* *chick*

Listen for the Ending Sound /ch/

Present pairs of words to help students recognize ending sounds.

1. **Say:** I'm going to say two words. Listen for the **ending sound /ch/**. Then tell me the word with that ending sound. For example, if I say *March* and *miles*, you'll say *March* because /ch/ is the last sound in *March*.

2. Say each pair of words. Have students identify the word that ends with the sound /ch/.

   ▶ *peek* or *peach* *peach*
   ▶ *such* or *sun* *such*
   ▶ *lunch* or *lend* *lunch*

Try It

Sound Boxes

Have students complete page PH 19 in *K¹² PhonicsWorks Basic Activity Book* for more practice with the sound /ch/. First have students say the name of each picture. Then have them color in the box that corresponds to the position (beginning, middle, or ending) of the sound /ch/ in the word.

Objectives
- Identify and use the sound /ch/.
- Identify individual sounds in words.

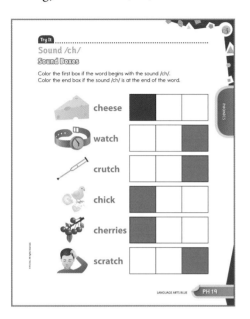

Online 20 minutes

REVIEW: Sound /ch/

Students will work online independently to

▶ Practice the sound /ch/.

Help students locate the online activities and provide support as needed.

Objectives
- Identify and use the sound /ch/.
- Identify beginning sounds in words.
- Identify ending sounds in words.

Offline Alternative

No computer access? Have students point out and name things that begin or end with the sound /ch/ (for example, *chair* or *watch*).

Sound /y/

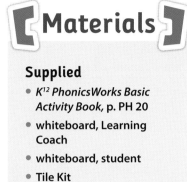

Lesson Overview

Offline FOCUS: Sound /y/ — **30** minutes

Get Ready	Right Hand Awareness
	Sing "The Alphabet Song"
	Learn Lowercase Letters *qu*
	Review Letter Names
	Sound Subtraction
	Finger Stretching
	Recognize Words and Syllables
Learn	Introduce the Sound /y/
	Listen for the Beginning Sound /y/
Try It	The Beginning

Online REVIEW: Sound /y/ — **20** minutes

Materials

Supplied
- *K¹² PhonicsWorks Basic Activity Book,* p. PH 20
- whiteboard, Learning Coach
- whiteboard, student
- Tile Kit

Advance Prep

Place lowercase letter tiles *a* through *p* and uppercase letter tiles Q through Z in alphabetical order on your whiteboard. Place lowercase letter tile *qu* on students' whiteboard.

 **Offline** ⏱ **30 minutes**

FOCUS: Sound /y/

Work **together** with students to complete offline Get Ready, Learn, and Try It activities.

Get Ready ....

Right Hand Awareness

Students read from left to right, so play a game to develop right hand awareness. To avoid confusion, focus on the right hand only.

1. Say each sentence and do each action. Have students repeat your words and actions.

   ‣ I'm shaking your right hand.
   ‣ Now I'm touching my right ankle.
   ‣ Now I'm waving my right hand in the air.
   ‣ Now I'm touching my right toe.
   ‣ Now I'm touching my right cheek

2. Repeat the actions and mix up the order. To end the activity, shake right hands again.

Sing "The Alphabet Song"

To help students become familiar and comfortable with the alphabet, sing "The Alphabet Song" with them. Sing slowly, so that students may touch each letter on your whiteboard as they sing the letter's name.

Learn Lowercase Letters *qu*

To help students learn lowercase letters of the alphabet, have them practice identifying and naming the letters *qu*. Grab your whiteboard with letters.

1. **Say:** There are two different kinds of letters in our alphabet. They are called capital, or uppercase, letters and lowercase, or small, letters.

2. **Say:** We're going to learn a lowercase letter pair today. This tile has two letters because *q* doesn't like to be by itself. In our language, it is always followed by the letter *u*. We call *q* and *u* "glue letters," because they are always seen together. We will say the letter *q* every time we touch the letter tile *qu*.

3. Have students touch the letter tile on their whiteboard and say its name.

4. **Say:** I'm going to put this letter tile on my whiteboard in place of the capital letter Q.

5. Move the uppercase letter Q tile from your whiteboard to the Tile Kit, and replace it with the lowercase *qu* tile.

6. Have students sing "The Alphabet Song," touching the lowercase letters *a* through *qu*, then moving back to the capital letters.

Objectives

- Develop right hand awareness.
- Identify letters of the alphabet.
- Identify capital and lowercase letters.
- Match capital letters to lowercase letters.
- Identify the new word when one sound is removed from a word.
- Identify individual sounds in words.
- Identify syllables in words.
- Identify the number of syllables in a word.

Review Letter Names

To help students learn the alphabet, have them practice identifying and naming the letters *e*, *f*, *g*, *h*, *j*, *l*, and *qu*. Grab your whiteboard with letters.

1. Point to each letter and have students touch and name each one.

j   l   h   g   f   e   qu

2. Say the name of each letter. After each one, have students repeat the name and touch the tile.

j   l   h   g   f   e   qu

3. Redirect students if they name a letter incorrectly.

   ▸ Name the letter students missed.
   ▸ Have students touch the letter and say its name.
   ▸ Have students trace the shape of the letter with their finger on the brown side of their board, and have them say the letter's name as they trace the shape.
   ▸ If students name a letter incorrectly twice, point to the letter and tell them its name. Have students touch the letter and say its name.

Sound Subtraction

Present pairs of words to improve students' ability to distinguish between sounds.

1. **Say:** Let's play a game with the sounds in words. I'll say a word and you'll repeat it. Then I'll subtract the first sound from the word and say a new word. Your job is to say the new word and tell me what sound I took away. For example,

   ▸ If I say *fact*, you'll repeat the word.
   ▸ Then I'll take away the first sound from *fact* and say the new word, which is *act*.
   ▸ When I ask you what sound I subtracted from *fact*, you'll say /f/.

2. Say each pair of words. Have students tell you what sound you subtracted from the first word.

   ▸ *size* and *eyes* /s/
   ▸ *soak* and *oak* /s/
   ▸ *neat* and *eat* /n/
   ▸ *fake* and *ache* /f/

Finger Stretching

Use finger stretching to help students identify individual sounds in words.

1. **Say:** Let's review finger stretching. In the word *send*, the first sound is /s/, the next sound is /ĕ/, the next sound is /n/, and the last sound is /d/. I will finger stretch each sound as I say it. Then I'll say the word, while pulling my fist toward my body.

2. Finger stretch the word *send* for students.

3. **Say:** I'm going to say words with several sounds in them. You'll say each word and then finger stretch it while you say each sound in the word.

4. Say the following words and have students finger stretch them. After they finger stretch each word, ask them the question for that word.

   ▸ *hop* /h/ /ŏ/ /p/   What is the first sound in the word? /h/
   ▸ *sack* /s/ /ă/ /k/   What is the middle sound? /ă/
   ▸ *ask* /ă/ /s/ /k/   What is the first sound? /ă/
   ▸ *gift* /g/ /ĭ/ /f/ /t/   What is the last sound? /t/
   ▸ *me* /m/ /ē/   What is the first sound? /m/

TIP Refer to the *K¹² PhonicsWorks* video for a demonstration of finger stretching.

Recognize Words and Syllables

Introduce the concept of syllables to students.

1. **Say:** When we talk, we make words by pushing air out of our mouths. Each push of air in a word is called a **syllable**. Each word has one or more syllables. You can think of syllables as chunks of words.

2. **Say:** Let's break some words into syllables.

   ▸ I'll say a word. I'll repeat the word.
   ▸ You'll say the word after me, and you'll break it into syllables by saying the separate chunks of the word and tapping your fist on the table as you say each chunk.
   ▸ For example, I'll say *hammer,* and then I'll say it again.
   ▸ You will say *ham / mer* and tap your fist on the table as you say each syllable.

3. Say each word and repeat it. Have students fist tap on the table as they say the syllables in each word.

   ▸ *river* ri / ver
   ▸ *roasted* roast / ed
   ▸ *flew* flew
   ▸ *erase* e / rase
   ▸ *even* e / ven
   ▸ *over* o / ver
   ▸ *out* out
   ▸ *radio* ra / di / o

TIP Have students name items in the room and fist tap the syllables with you. For example, have them name and fist tap words such as *ta / ble* and *win / dow*. Challenge students to name and fist tap something with several syllables, such as *com / pu / ter*.

Learn

Introduce the Sound /y/

Teach the sound /y/, as in *yes*, *you*, and *yet*.

1. **Say:** We're going to play a game to practice the **sound /y/**. Your job is to say the sound just like me and do what I do, too.

2. Pretend to yawn and say, "Y-y-yes, I can y-y-yawn." Have students do this, too.

3. **Say:** We make some sounds with a whisper and some sounds with our voice. Let's figure out whether the sound /y/ is whispered or voiced. Say /y/ and put your fingers on the lump in your throat called your voice box.

   ▸ Do you feel your voice box vibrate? Yes, /y/ is a noisy sound because we do use our voice box when we make the sound.

4. **Say:** I'll say some words that start with the sound /y/ and you'll repeat them, saying /y/ just the way I do.

yes   *you*   *yet*

TIP When you teach the sound /y/, make sure students say the sound correctly and do not add *uh* after pronouncing it. Students should say /y/, not *yuh*.

Listen for the Beginning Sound /y/

Present pairs of words to help students recognize beginning sounds.

1. **Say:** I'm going to say two words. Listen for the **beginning sound /y/**. Then tell me the word that has that beginning sound. For example, if I say *yes* and *less*, you'll say *yes* because /y/ is the first sound in *yes*.

2. Say each pair of words. Have students identify the word that begins with the sound /y/.

   ▸ *yelp* or *bark* yelp
   ▸ *front* or *yard* yard
   ▸ *plum* or *yum* yum

> **Objectives**
> - Identify and use the sound /y/.
> - Identify beginning sounds in words.

Try It

The Beginning

Have students complete page PH 20 in *K¹² PhonicsWorks Basic Activity Book* for more practice with the sound /y/. First have students say the name of each picture. Then have students circle pictures whose name begins with the sound /y/.

Objectives
- Identify and use the sound /y/.
- Identify beginning sounds in words.

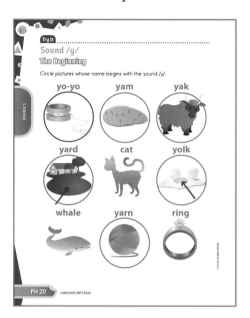

Online · 20 minutes

REVIEW: Sound /y/

Students will work online independently to

▶ Practice the sound /y/.

Help students locate the online activities and provide support as needed.

Objectives
- Identify and use the sound /y/.
- Identify beginning sounds in words.

Offline Alternative

No computer access? Have students point out and name things that begin with the sound /y/ (for example, *yo-yo*).

Unit Checkpoint

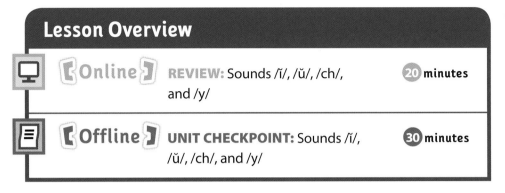

Lesson Overview

《Online》 REVIEW: Sounds /ĭ/, /ŭ/, /ch/, and /y/ — **20** minutes

《Offline》 UNIT CHECKPOINT: Sounds /ĭ/, /ŭ/, /ch/, and /y/ — **30** minutes

Objectives
- Identify and use the sound /ĭ/.
- Identify and use the sound /ŭ/.
- Identify and use the sound /ch/.
- Identify and use the sound /y/.
- Identify words that rhyme.
- Identify the number of syllables in a word.
- Identify a word when given the onset and rime.
- Identify middle sounds in words.

Materials

Supplied
- *K¹² PhonicsWorks Basic Assessments*, pp. PH 19–23

《Online》 **20** minutes

REVIEW: Sounds /ĭ/, /ŭ/, /ch/, and /y/

Students will review the sounds /ĭ/, /ŭ/, /ch/, and /y/ to prepare for the Unit Checkpoint. Help students locate the online activities and provide support as needed.

 **30 minutes**

UNIT CHECKPOINT: Sounds /ĭ/, /ŭ/, /ch/, and /y/

Explain that students are going to show what they have learned about letters, sounds, and words.

1. Give students the Unit Checkpoint pages for the Sounds /ĭ/, /ŭ/, /ch/, and /y/ unit and print the Unit Checkpoint Answer Key, if you'd like.

2. Use the instructions below to help administer the Checkpoint to students. On the Answer Key or another sheet of paper, note student answers to oral response questions to help with scoring the Checkpoint later.

3. Use the Answer Key to score the Checkpoint, and then enter the results online.

Part 1. Letter Matching Moving left to right, have students read the letters aloud and circle the letter or letters that match the first letter in the row.

Part 2. Match Middle Sounds Have students say the name of each picture and draw a line to connect pictures that have the same middle sound.

Part 3. Rhymes Say each pair of words and have students say if the word pairs rhyme. Note any incorrect responses.

10. *crust, rust*   13. *hut, hot*

11. *bump, lamp*   14. *rock, block*

12. *rich, which*   15. *brick, stick*

Part 4. Beginning Sounds Say each pair of words and have students say if the words have the same beginning sound. Repeat the words, as necessary. Note any incorrect responses.

16. *chin, chest*   19. *children, suitcase*

17. *year, yarn*   20. *yellow, wheel*

18. *sheep, cheap*   21. *yesterday, yardstick*

Part 5. Onset and Rime Say the first sound of each word. Pause briefly and then say the rest of the word. Have students say the whole word. Note any incorrect responses.

22. /y/ . . . *ear*

23. /ch/ . . . *ick*

24. /y/ . . . *es*

25. /y/ . . . *ell*

26. /ch/ . . . *eese*

27. /ch/ . . . *ampion*

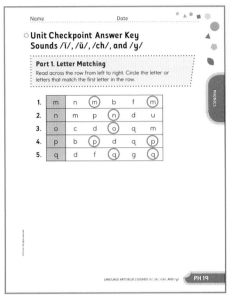

Name _____ Date _____

○ **Unit Checkpoint Answer Key**
Sounds /ĭ/, /ŭ/, /ch/, and /y/

Part 1. Letter Matching
Read across the row from left to right. Circle the letter or letters that match the first letter in the row.

1.	m	n	(m)	b	f	(m)
2.	n	m	p	(n)	d	u
3.	o	c	d	(o)	q	m
4.	p	b	(p)	d	q	(p)
5.	q	d	f	(q)	g	(q)

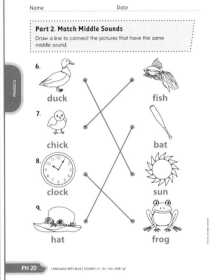

Name _____ Date _____

Part 2. Match Middle Sounds
Draw a line to connect the pictures that have the same middle sound.

6. duck — fish

7. chick — bat

8. clock — sun

9. hat — frog

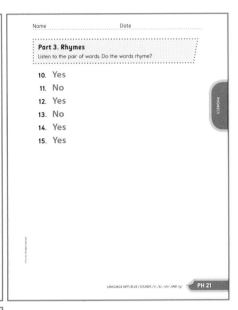

Name _____ Date _____

Part 3. Rhymes
Listen to the pair of words. Do the words rhyme?

10. Yes
11. No
12. Yes
13. No
14. Yes
15. Yes

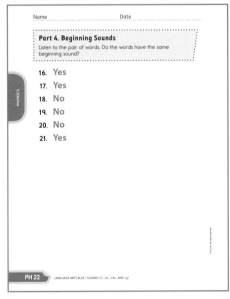

Name _____ Date _____

Part 4. Beginning Sounds
Listen to the pair of words. Do the words have the same beginning sound?

16. Yes
17. Yes
18. No
19. No
20. No
21. Yes

Name _____ Date _____

Part 5. Onset and Rime
Listen to the sounds. Then, say the whole word.

22. year
23. chick
24. yes
25. yell
26. cheese
27. champion

Sound /sh/

Unit Overview

In this unit, students will
- ▶ Identify letters of the alphabet.
- ▶ Identify and say the sounds /sh/, /aw/, and /kw/.
- ▶ Distinguish between words that rhyme and sound different.
- ▶ Identify individual sounds and syllables in words.
- ▶ Learn and practice blends.
- ▶ Learn to put phrases together to make sentences.

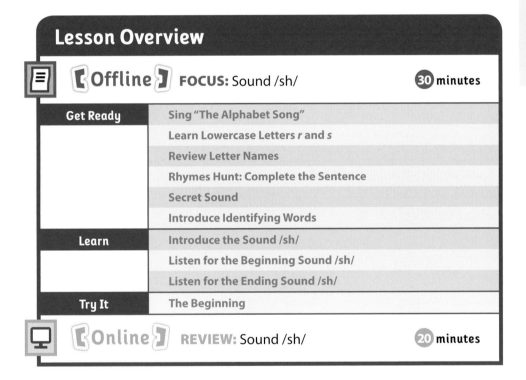

Lesson Overview

【 Offline 】 FOCUS: Sound /sh/ — 30 minutes

Get Ready	Sing "The Alphabet Song"
	Learn Lowercase Letters *r* and *s*
	Review Letter Names
	Rhymes Hunt: Complete the Sentence
	Secret Sound
	Introduce Identifying Words
Learn	Introduce the Sound /sh/
	Listen for the Beginning Sound /sh/
	Listen for the Ending Sound /sh/
Try It	The Beginning

【 Online 】 REVIEW: Sound /sh/ — 20 minutes

Advance Preparation

Place lowercase letter tiles *a* through *qu* and uppercase letter tiles *R* through *Z* in alphabetical order on your whiteboard. Place lowercase letter tiles *r* and *s* on students' whiteboard.

 ⏱ **30 minutes**

FOCUS: Sound /sh/

Work **together** with students to complete offline Get Ready, Learn, and Try It activities.

Get Ready ....

Sing "The Alphabet Song"

To help students become familiar and comfortable with the alphabet, sing "The Alphabet Song" with them. Sing slowly, so that students may touch each letter on your whiteboard as they sing the letter's name.

Learn Lowercase Letters *r* and *s*

To help students learn lowercase letters of the alphabet, have them practice identifying and naming the letters *r* and *s*.

1. **Say:** There are two different kinds of letters in our alphabet. Can you name them? lowercase or small, uppercase or capital

2. **Say:** We're going to learn two lowercase letters today. The letters are *r* and *s*.

3. Have students touch each lowercase letter on their whiteboard and say its name.

4. **Say:** I'm going to put these letters on my whiteboard in place of the capital letters for *r* and *s*.

5. Move the uppercase *R* and *S* tiles from your whiteboard to the Tile Kit, and replace them with the lowercase *r* and *s* tiles.

6. Have students sing "The Alphabet Song," touching the lowercase letters *a* through *s*, then moving back to the capital letters.

> **Objectives**
> - Identify letters of the alphabet.
> - Identify capital and lowercase letters.
> - Match capital letters to lowercase letters.
> - Identify individual sounds in words.
> - Identify words that rhyme.
> - Identify middle sounds in words.
> - Demonstrate one-to-one correspondence.

Review Letter Names

To help students learn the alphabet, have them practice identifying and naming the letters *p*, *qu*, *r*, *s*, *T*, *U*, *V*, *W*, *X*, *Y*, and *Z*. Grab your whiteboard with letters.

1. Point to each letter and have students touch and name each one.

   Z   Y   X   W   V   U   T   s   r   qu   p

2. Say the name of each letter. After each one, have students repeat the name and touch the tile.

   Z   Y   X   W   V   U   T   s   r   qu   p

3. Redirect students if they name a letter incorrectly.

    ▸ Name the letter students missed.
    ▸ Have students touch the letter and say its name.
    ▸ Have students trace the shape of the letter with their finger on the brown side of their board, and have them say the letter's name as they trace the shape.
    ▸ If students name a letter incorrectly twice, point to the letter and tell them its name. Have students touch the letter and say its name.

Rhymes Hunt: Complete the Sentence

Play a game with students to reinforce awareness of words that rhyme.

1. **Say:** Let's have some fun with rhymes. Listen to this sentence: "Count to ten, I will tell you when." What word rhymes with *ten*? *when*

2. **Say:** Now I am going to say the first part of a sentence. Your job is to finish the sentence with a rhyme of your own.

    ▸ The first one is: "That goat spends all *day* eating lots of _____ ."
    ▸ Can you think of a rhyming word to finish the sentence? The word *hay* rhymes with *day*. Let's try some more.

3. Continue the procedure with the following sentences:

    ▸ *Come take a* look *at this fifty-page* _____ . *book*
    ▸ *My friend* Dan *cools himself with a* _____ . *fan*
    ▸ *If it's a sunny* day, *I like to go out and* _____ . *play*

TIP If students have difficulty thinking of a rhyming word to complete the sentence, tell them the completed sentence and then ask them to identify the two rhyming words.

Secret Sound

Say groups of words that have the same letter to help students recognize **middle sounds** in words.

1. **Say:** I am going to say some groups of words. Listen for a secret sound in the middle of each word. Then tell me what sound you hear at the middle of each group of words.

2. Say each of the following groups of words. Have students identify the secret sound in each group.

    ▸ *sit, lip, fin, hid* /ĭ/
    ▸ *take, late, mane* /ā/
    ▸ *sack, lap, mash, had* /ă/
    ▸ *shop, moth, rock* /ŏ/

TIP If students can't identify the secret sound, have them listen while you say each word again and then have them repeat each word. Have students say what sound they hear in the middle of each word.

Introduce Identifying Words
Help students identify the number of words in a phrase.

1. Gather five index cards.

2. **Say:** A sentence is made up of words. A phrase is a part of a sentence. We read words in a sentence or phrase from left to right.

3. **Say:** Let's use index cards to stand for words in phrases.

   ▸ The phrase *the red box* has three words, so I'll place three index cards on the table and put them next to each other.
   ▸ I'll say *the* as I touch the first card, *red* as I touch the second card, and *box* as I touch the third card.
   ▸ Now you touch the cards and say the words *the red box*.

4. Remove the cards from the table. Give students the stack of cards.

5. Say the following phrases. Have students put one card on the table for each word you say. Have them repeat the word as they put down the card. Have students pick up the cards between each example.

   ▸ *a big horse farm*
   ▸ *purring gray cat*
   ▸ *one spotted pony*
   ▸ *pencil and eraser*
   ▸ *the white sandy beach*
   ▸ *on a long car trip*
   ▸ *at the soccer game*

TIP If students can't identify the number of words in a phrase, say the phrase again and lay down an index card for each word you say. Have students count the cards and say how many words are in the phrase.

Learn •

Introduce the Sound /sh/
Teach the sound /sh/, as in *she*, *ship*, and *shut*.

1. **Say:** We're going to play a game to practice the **sound /sh/**. Your job is to say the sound just like me and do what I do, too.

2. Put your index finger to your lips and say, "Shhh!" Have students do this, too.

3. **Say:** We make many sounds with our tongue, our teeth, and our lips. Say /sh/ again and feel whether your tongue, teeth, or lips are making the sound.

   ▸ Did you feel your teeth make the sound /sh/? Yes

4. **Say:** We make some sounds with a whisper and some sounds with our voice. Let's figure out whether the sound /sh/ is whispered or voiced. Say /sh/ and put your fingers on the lump in your throat called your voice box.

   ▸ Do you feel your voice box vibrate? No

Objectives
- Identify and use the sound /sh/.
- Identify beginning sounds in words.
- Identify ending sounds in words.

5. **Say:** I'll say some words that start with the sound /sh/ and you'll repeat them, saying /sh/ just the way I do.

she   *ship*   *shut*

6. **Say:** Now I'll say some words that end with the sound /sh/ and you'll repeat them, saying /sh/ just the way I do.

fish   *ash*   *wash*

Listen for the Beginning Sound /sh/

Present pairs of words to help students recognize beginning sounds.

1. **Say:** I'm going to say two words. Listen for the **beginning sound /sh/**. Then tell me the word that has that beginning sound. For example, if I say *show* and *see*, you'll say *show* because /sh/ is the first sound in *show*.

2. Say each pair of words. Have students identify the word that begins with the sound /sh/.

   ▸ *light* or *shine* *shine*
   ▸ *shirt* or *off* *shirt*
   ▸ *third* or *sharp* *sharp*

Listen for the Ending Sound /sh/

Present pairs of words to help students recognize ending sounds.

1. **Say:** I'm going to say two words. Listen for the **ending sound /sh/**. Then tell me the word with that ending sound. For example, if I say *marsh* and *muck*, you'll say *marsh* because /sh/ is the last sound in *marsh*.

2. Say each pair of words. Have students identify the word that ends with the sound /sh/.

   ▸ *fin* or *fish* *fish*
   ▸ *push* or *put* *push*
   ▸ *with* or *wish* *wish*

Try It

The Beginning

Have students complete page PH 21 in *K¹² PhonicsWorks Basic Activity Book* for more practice with the sound /sh/. First have students say the name of each picture. Then have them circle pictures whose name begins with the sound /sh/.

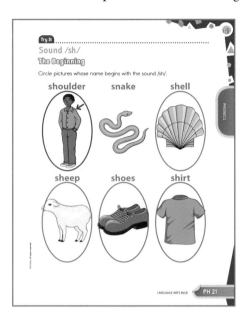

Try It
Sound /sh/
The Beginning
Circle pictures whose name begins with the sound /sh/.

shoulder   snake   shell

sheep   shoes   shirt

LANGUAGE ARTS BLUE   PH 21

Online   20 minutes

REVIEW: Sound /sh/

Students will work online independently to

▶ Practice the sound /sh/.

Help students locate the online activities and provide support as needed.

Offline Alternative

No computer access? Have students point out and name things or words that begin and end with the sound /sh/ (for example, *ship* or *wish*).

Sound /aw/

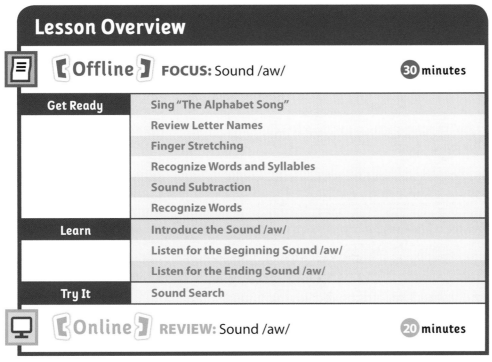

Lesson Overview

Offline FOCUS: Sound /aw/ — 30 minutes

Get Ready	Sing "The Alphabet Song"
	Review Letter Names
	Finger Stretching
	Recognize Words and Syllables
	Sound Subtraction
	Recognize Words
Learn	Introduce the Sound /aw/
	Listen for the Beginning Sound /aw/
	Listen for the Ending Sound /aw/
Try It	Sound Search

Online REVIEW: Sound /aw/ — 20 minutes

Materials

Supplied
- *K¹² PhonicsWorks Basic Activity Book*, p. PH 22
- whiteboard, Learning Coach
- whiteboard, student
- Tile Kit

Also Needed
- index cards (12)

Advance Preparation

Place lowercase letter tiles *a* through *s* and uppercase letter tiles *T* through *Z* in alphabetical order on your whiteboard.

For Recognize Words, print a single word of your choice on six index cards, using one card per word. On another six cards, print a short sentence of your choice that includes one of the single words you wrote on the first six cards. Students will not be asked to read the index cards. Single word suggestions include *house, food, chair, books, flower,* and *toys.* Sentence suggestions include the following:

- ► *My house is on the left.*
- ► *The food is on the table.*
- ► *Please sit in the chair.*
- ► *Where are the books?*
- ► *Don't pick the flower!*
- ► *Jack shares his toys.*

 **Offline** **30** minutes

FOCUS: Sound /aw/
Work **together** with students to complete offline Get Ready, Learn, and Try It activities.

Get Ready

Sing "The Alphabet Song"
To help students become familiar and comfortable with the alphabet, sing "The Alphabet Song" with them. Sing slowly, so that students may touch each letter on your whiteboard as they sing the letter's name.

 Objectives
- Identify letters of the alphabet.
- Identify capital and lowercase letters.
- Identify individual sounds in words.
- Identify the new word when one sound is changed in a word.
- Identify the number of syllables in a word.
- Identify syllables in words.

Review Letter Names
To help students learn the alphabet, have them practice identifying and naming the letters *d*, *e*, *p*, *qu*, *r*, *s*, *Y*, and *Z*. Grab your whiteboard with letters.

1. Point to each letter and have students touch and name each one.

    d   e   Z   p   qu   r   s   Y

2. Say the name of each letter. After each one, have students repeat the name and touch the tile.

    d   e   Z   p   qu   r   s   Y

3. Redirect students if they name a letter incorrectly.

   ▸ Name the letter students missed.
   ▸ Have students touch the letter and say its name.
   ▸ Have students trace the shape of the letter with their finger on the brown side of their board, and have them say the letter's name as they trace the shape.
   ▸ If students name a letter incorrectly twice, point to the letter and tell them its name. Have students touch the letter and say its name.

Finger Stretching
Use finger stretching to help students identify individual sounds in words.

1. **Say:** Let's review finger stretching. In the word *shape*, the first sound is /sh/, the middle sound is /ā/, and the last sound is /p/. I will finger stretch each sound as I say it. Then I'll say the word and while pulling my fist toward my body.

2. Finger stretch the word *shape* for students.

3. **Say:** I'm going to say words with several sounds in them. You'll say each word, and then finger stretch it while you say each sound in the word.

4. Say the following words and have students finger stretch them. After they finger stretch each word, ask them the question for that word.

> ► *shone* /sh/ /ō/ /n/   What is the middle sound? /ō/
> ► *mile* /m/ /ī/ /l/   What is the first sound? /m/
> ► *page* /p/ /ā/ /j/   What is the last sound? /j/
> ► *mat* /m/ /ă/ /t/   What is the first sound? /m/

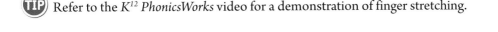 **TIP** Refer to the *K¹² PhonicsWorks* video for a demonstration of finger stretching.

Recognize Words and Syllables

Practice syllables with students

1. **Say:** When we talk, we make words by pushing air out of our mouths. Each push of air in a word is called a **syllable**. Each word has one or more syllables. You can think of syllables as chunks of words.

2. **Say:** Let's break some words into syllables.

> ► I'll say a word. I'll repeat the word.
> ► You'll say the word after me and you'll break it into syllables by saying the separate chunks of the word and tapping your fist on the table as you say each chunk.
> ► For example, I'll say *pumpkin,* and then I'll say it again.
> ► You will say *pump / kin* and you will tap your fist on the table as you say each syllable.

3. Say each word and repeat it. Have students fist tap on the table as they say the syllables in each word.

> ► *apple* ap / ple
> ► *tomato* to / ma / to
> ► *squash* squash
> ► *lemon* le / mon
> ► *coconut* co / co / nut

TIP Have students name items in the room and fist tap the syllables with you. For example, have them name and fist tap words such as *ta / ble* and *win / dow.* Challenge students to name and fist tap something with several syllables, such as *com / pu / ter.*

Sound Subtraction

Present pairs of words to improve students' ability to distinguish between sounds.

1. **Say:** Let's play a game with the sounds in words. I'll say a word and you'll repeat it. Then I'll subtract the first sound from the word and say a new word. Your job is to say the new word and tell me what sound I took away. For example,

   ▶ If I say *fear*, you'll repeat the word.
   ▶ Then I'll take away the first sound from *fear* and say the new word, which is *ear*.
   ▶ When I ask you what sound I subtracted from *fear*, you'll say /f/.

2. Say each pair of words. Have students tell you what sound you subtracted from the first word.

   ▶ *wait* and *ate* /w/
   ▶ *meat* and *eat* /m/
   ▶ *sold* and *old* /s/
   ▶ *sink* and *ink* /s/

Recognize Words

Help students differentiate between words and sentences.

1. Gather the index cards you prepared.

2. **Say:** Let's play a sorting game.

   ▶ You'll pick an index card, and I'll read what's on it.
   ▶ You'll repeat what I said, and if it's a single word, you'll put it in one pile.
   ▶ If it's a complete sentence, you'll put it in the other pile.

3. Be sure to point to each word on the index cards as you read them so you can model one-to-one correspondence for the students.

4. When you have completed the activity, shuffle all of the cards and ask students to sort them again. Point out that students don't need to read the cards in order to sort them. They should look for indicators (capital letter, more than one word, punctuation at the end) to help them sort the cards.

Learn

Introduce the Sound /aw/

Teach the sound /aw/, as in *all*, *awful*, and *author*.

1. **Say:** We're going to play a game to practice the **sound /aw/**. Your job is to say the sound just like me and do what I do, too.

2. Say /aw/ and say the sentence, "Awwww, you poor thing!" Have students do this, too.

Objectives

- Identify and use the sound /aw/.
- Identify beginning sounds in words.
- Identify ending sounds in words.

3. **Say:** We make some sounds with a whisper and some sounds with our voice. Let's figure out whether the sound /aw/ is whispered or voiced. Say /aw/ and put your fingers on the lump in your throat called your voice box.

   ▶ Do you feel your voice box vibrate? Yes, /aw/ is a noisy sound because we use our voice box when we make the sound.

4. **Say:** I'll say some words that start with the sound /aw/ and you'll repeat them, saying /aw/ just the way I do.

   all   awful   author

5. **Say:** Now I'll say some words that end with the sound /aw/ and you'll repeat them, saying /aw/ just the way I do.

   saw   law   draw

Listen for the Beginning Sound /aw/
Present pairs of words to help students recognize beginning sounds.

1. **Say:** I'm going to say two words. Listen for the **beginning sound /aw/**. Then tell me the word that has that beginning sound. For example, if I say *author* and *idea*, you'll say *author* because /aw/ is the first sound in *author*.

2. Say each pair of words. Have students identify the word that begins with the sound /aw/.

   ▶ *icky* or *awful* awful
   ▶ *auction* or *sale* auction
   ▶ *eagle* or *autograph* autograph

Listen for the Ending Sound /aw/
Present pairs of words to help students recognize ending sounds.

1. **Say:** I'm going to say two words. Listen for the **ending sound /aw/**. Then tell me the word with that ending sound. For example, if I say *straw* and *tree*, you'll say *straw* because /aw/ is the last sound in *straw*.

2. Say each pair of words. Have students identify the word that ends with the sound /aw/.

   ▶ *true* or *law* law
   ▶ *saw* or *see* saw
   ▶ *foot* or *paw* paw

Try It

Sound Search

Have students complete page PH 22 in *K¹² PhonicsWorks Basic Activity Book* for more practice with the sound /aw/. First have students say the name of each picture. Then have them circle words that contain the sound /aw/.

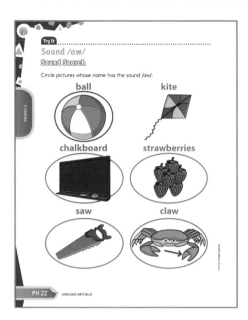

Objectives
- Identify and use the sound /aw/.
- Identify individual sounds in words.

Online 20 minutes

REVIEW: Sound /aw/

Students will work online independently to

► Practice the sound /aw/.

Help students locate the online activities and provide support as needed.

Objectives
- Identify and use the sound /aw/.
- Identify individual sounds in words.

Offline Alternative

No computer access? Have students point out and name things or words that contain the sound /aw/ (for example, *awning* or *draw*).

Sound /kw/

Lesson Overview

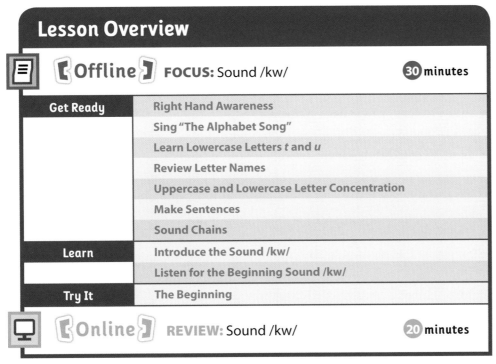

Offline FOCUS: Sound /kw/ — **30** minutes

Get Ready	Right Hand Awareness
	Sing "The Alphabet Song"
	Learn Lowercase Letters *t* and *u*
	Review Letter Names
	Uppercase and Lowercase Letter Concentration
	Make Sentences
	Sound Chains
Learn	Introduce the Sound /kw/
	Listen for the Beginning Sound /kw/
Try It	The Beginning

Online REVIEW: Sound /kw/ — **20** minutes

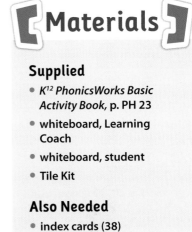

[Materials]

Supplied
- *K¹² PhonicsWorks Basic Activity Book,* p. PH 23
- whiteboard, Learning Coach
- whiteboard, student
- Tile Kit

Also Needed
- index cards (38)

Advance Preparation

Place lowercase letter tiles *a* through *s* and uppercase letter tiles *T* through *Z* in alphabetical order on your whiteboard. Place lowercase letter tiles *t* and *u* on students' whiteboard.

For Uppercase and Lowercase Letter Concentration, print the uppercase letters *A* through *S* and the lowercase letters *a* through *s* on index cards, using one card per letter.

 **30 minutes**

FOCUS: Sound /kw/

Work **together** with students to complete offline Get Ready, Learn, and Try It activities.

Get Ready

Right Hand Awareness

Students read from left to right, so play a game to develop right hand awareness. To avoid confusion, focus on the right hand only.

1. Say each sentence and do each action. Have students repeat your words and actions.

   ▸ I'm shaking your right hand.
   ▸ Now I'm touching my right ankle.
   ▸ Now I'm waving my right hand in the air.
   ▸ Now I'm touching my right toe.
   ▸ Now I'm touching my right cheek

2. Repeat the actions and mix up the order. To end the activity, shake right hands again.

Sing "The Alphabet Song"

To help students become familiar and comfortable with the alphabet, sing "The Alphabet Song" with them. Sing slowly, so that students may touch each letter on your whiteboard as they sing the letter's name.

Learn Lowercase Letters *t* and *u*

To help students learn lowercase letters of the alphabet, have them practice identifying and naming the letters *t* and *u*. Grab your whiteboard with letters.

1. **Say:** We're going to learn two lowercase letters today. They are the letters *t* and *u*.

2. Have students touch each lowercase letter on their whiteboard and say its name.

3. **Say:** I'm going to put these letters on my whiteboard in place of the capital letters for *t* and *u*.

4. Move the uppercase *T* and *U* tiles from your whiteboard to the Tile Kit, and replace them with the lowercase *t* and *u* tiles.

5. Have students sing "The Alphabet Song," touching the lowercase letters *a* through *u*, then moving back to the capital letters.

> **Objectives**
> - Develop right hand awareness.
> - Identify capital and lowercase letters.
> - Match capital letters to lowercase letters.
> - Identify individual sounds in words.
> - Orally create sentences from phrases.

Review Letter Names

To help students learn the alphabet, have them practice identifying and naming the letters g, h, i, j, k, l, qu, r, s, t, u, and V. Grab your whiteboard with letters.

1. Point to each letter and have students touch and name each one.

    g   h   i   j   k   l   qu   r   s   t   u   V

2. Say the name of each letter. After each one, have students repeat the name and touch the tile.

    g   h   i   j   k   l   qu   r   s   t   u   V

3. Redirect students if they name a letter incorrectly.

    ▸ Name the letter students missed.
    ▸ Have students touch the letter and say its name.
    ▸ Have students trace the shape of the letter with their finger on the brown side of their board, and have them say the letter's name as they trace the shape.
    ▸ If students name a letter incorrectly twice, point to the letter and tell them its name. Have students touch the letter and say its name.

Uppercase and Lowercase Letter Concentration

Help students practice pairing uppercase and lowercase letters.

1. Gather the index cards you prepared.

2. Select five or six pairs of index cards with uppercase and lowercase letters.

3. Mix up the index cards and place them face down on the table or floor.

4. **Say:** Let's practice matching uppercase and lowercase letters.

5. **Say:** You'll turn over the cards two at a time. If you turn over a card that has a lowercase letter and a card that has the uppercase form of the same letter, the cards match and you can keep them. If the cards don't match, turn them back over.

6. Continue the activity until all of the cards are paired.

7. Repeat the procedure with the remaining cards.

Make Sentences

Help students practice using phrases to make sentences.

1. **Say:** A sentence is made up of words. A phrase is a part of a sentence.

2. **Say:** Let's make some sentences from phrases. I'll say some words and you'll repeat them. Then you'll find different ways to make those words into a sentence. For example,

   ▸ If I say, "catches the ball," you might say, "Sally catches the ball" or "Rex the dog catches the ball."
   ▸ If I say "the dog," you might say, "The dog howled all night" or "The dog was scratching at the door."

3. Say the following phrases. Have students use each phrase to make two different sentences.

   ▸ *until it got dark*
   ▸ *the red ball*
   ▸ *hid under the chair*

Sound Chains

Help students use color tiles to represent the sounds in words. Grab the color tiles from the Tile Kit.

1. Place the tiles on a table.

2. **Say:** Let's use tiles to stand for sounds in words.

   ▸ I'll say a word and the sounds in that word. The word *see* has two sounds: /s/ and /ē/.
   ▸ I'll put a tile down for each sound in the word. The sounds are different, so I'll use two different colors. Then I'll touch each tile and say the sound it represents.
   ▸ Next I'll blend the sounds into a word and say the word while running my finger under the two color tiles: /s/.../ē/...*see*.

3. **Say:** I'll say another word, *me*. *Me* has two sounds: /m/ and /ē/. Listen for the sound that changed in the word: *see, me*.

   ▸ Let's change the color of the tile for the first sound only, because the sound /s/ in *see* changed to /m/ in *me*, while the second sound, /ē/, stayed the same.
   ▸ Touch each tile and say the sound it represents. Then you'll blend the two sounds into a word and say the word while running your finger under the two color tiles: /m/.../ē/...*me*.

4. Now make the word *tea*. Have students answer the following questions to reinforce the process.

   ▸ What are the sounds in the word *tea*? /t/, /ē/
   ▸ Which sound stays the same when we change *me* to *tea*? /ē/
   ▸ Which sound changes when we change *me* to *tea*? /m/ changes to /t/

5. Say each of the following words. Have students change the color tile for the sound that changes.

- ▸ *tie* the second tile changes
- ▸ *lie* the first tile changes
- ▸ *lay* the second tile changes
- ▸ *day* the first tile changes
- ▸ *bay* the first tile changes
- ▸ *by* the second tile changes

Learn

Introduce the Sound /kw/

Teach the sound /kw/, as in *queen, quick,* and *quit.*

1. **Say:** We're going to play a game to practice the **sound /kw/**. All words are made up of sounds. Your job is to say the sound just like me and do what I do, too.

2. Make a duck mouth with your hands and say, "Quack, quack!" Have students do this, too.

3. **Say:** I'll say some words that start with the sound /kw/ and you'll repeat them, saying /kw/ just the way I do.

queen   quick   quit

quack   quiet

Objectives

- Identify and use the sound /kw/.
- Identify beginning sounds in words.

Listen for the Beginning Sound /kw/

Present pairs of words to help students recognize beginning sounds.

1. **Say:** I'm going to say two words. Listen for the **beginning sound /kw/**. Then tell me the word that has that beginning sound. For example, if I say *queen* and *prince,* you'll say *queen* because /kw/ is the first sound in *queen.*

2. Say each pair of words. Have students identify the word that begins with the sound /kw/.

- ▸ *trick* or *quick quick*
- ▸ *quack* or *bite quack*
- ▸ *loud* or *quiet quiet*
- ▸ *blanket* or *quilt quilt*

Try It

The Beginning

Have students complete page PH 23 in *K¹² PhonicsWorks Basic Activity Book* for more practice with the sound /kw/. First have students say the name of each picture. Then have them circle pictures whose name begins with the sound /kw/.

Objectives
- Identify and use the sound /kw/.
- Identify beginning sounds in words.

⟦Online⟧ ⑳ minutes

REVIEW: Sound /kw/

Students will work online independently to

▶ Practice the sound /kw/.

Help students locate the online activities and provide support as needed.

Objectives
- Identify and use the sound /kw/.
- Identify individual sounds in words.

Offline Alternative

No computer access? Have students point out and name things or words that contain the sound /kw/ (for example, *quiet* or *quilt*).

Syllables and Sounds

Lesson Overview

Offline FOCUS: Syllables and Sounds — **30** minutes

Get Ready	Sing "The Alphabet Song"
	Review Letter Names
	Face-Down Letters
Learn	Head, Waist, Toes
	Identify Words
	Rhymes Practice
	Sound Chains
	Recognize Words and Syllables
Try It	Careful Counting

Online REVIEW: Syllables and Sounds — **20** minutes

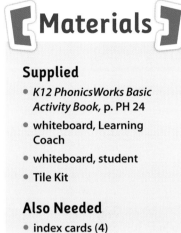

Materials

Supplied
- *K12 PhonicsWorks Basic Activity Book,* p. PH 24
- whiteboard, Learning Coach
- whiteboard, student
- Tile Kit

Also Needed
- index cards (4)

Keywords

phonological awareness – ability to identify and manipulate sound parts in words

Advance Preparation

Place lowercase letter tiles *a* through *u* and uppercase letter tiles *V* through *Z* in alphabetical order on your whiteboard.

Big Ideas

The ability to segment words into individual phonemes is an indicator of phonological awareness.

 **Offline** ⏱ **30 minutes**

FOCUS: Syllables and Sounds
Work **together** with students to complete offline Get Ready, Learn, and Try It activities.

Get Ready

Sing "The Alphabet Song"
To help students become familiar and comfortable with the alphabet, sing "The Alphabet Song" with them. Sing slowly, so that students may touch each letter on your whiteboard as they sing the letter's name.

_____

Review Letter Names
To help students learn the alphabet, have them practice identifying and naming the letters *a, s, t, u, V, W, X, Y,* and *Z*. Grab your whiteboard with letters.

1. Point to each letter and have students touch and name each one.

    Z   Y   X   W   V   u   t   s   a

2. Say the name of each letter. After each one, have students repeat the name and touch the tile.

    Z   Y   X   W   V   u   t   s   a

3. Redirect students if they name a letter incorrectly.

    ► Name the letter students missed.
    ► Have students touch the letter and say its name.
    ► Have students trace the shape of the letter with their finger on the brown side of their board, and have them say the letter's name as they trace the shape.
    ► If students name a letter incorrectly twice, point to the letter and tell them its name. Have students touch the letter and say its name.

_____

Face-Down Letters
To help students learn to recognize the letters of the alphabet, have them practice identifying and naming letters. Grab your whiteboard with letters placed in alphabetical order.

1. Lay your whiteboard down on a flat surface and flip over the letter tiles *a, k, l, r, V,* and *Y*.

2. **Say:** These letters are face down. We are looking at the back of them. Name each letter and then turn it over to see if you were right.

TIP If students miss any of the letters, have them turn over the missed ones and try again.

Objectives
- Identify letters of the alphabet.
- Identify capital and lowercase letters.
- Match capital letters to lowercase letters.
- Identify individual sounds in words.

Learn

Head, Waist, Toes
Help students practice identifying the sounds in words.

1. **Say:** Let's identify sounds in words by touching parts of our body as we say each sound. For example, I'll say *yes*, which has three sounds, and you'll repeat the word. Do these steps with me:

    ▸ The first sound in *yes* is /y/, so I touch my head as I say /y/.
    ▸ The middle sound is /ĕ/, so I touch my waist as I say /ĕ/.
    ▸ The last sound is /s/, so I touch my toes as I say /s/.

2. Say the words below. Have students repeat each word and then touch their head, waist, and toes as they say each sound in the word. After they say the sounds in each word, ask them the question for that word.

    ▸ *fit* /f/ /ĭ/ /t/   What is the middle sound? /ĭ/
    ▸ *fat* /f/ /ă/ /t/   What is the middle sound? /ă/
    ▸ *hat* /h/ /ă/ /t/   What is the last sound? /t/
    ▸ *had* /h/ /ă/ /d/   What is the last sound? /d/
    ▸ *mad* /m/ /ă/ /d/   What is the first sound? /m/
    ▸ *mash* /m/ /ă/ /sh/   What is the last sound? /sh/

Objectives
- Identify individual sounds in words.
- Orally create sentences from phrases.
- Identify words that rhyme.
- Identify the new word when one sound is changed in a word.
- Identify the number of syllables in a word.
- Identify syllables in words.

Identify Words
Help students identify the number of words in a phrase or sentence.

1. Gather four index cards.

2. **Say:** A sentence is made up of words. A phrase is a part of a sentence. We read words in a sentence or phrase from left to right.

3. **Say:** Let's use index cards to stand for words in phrases.

    ▸ The phrase *walk away quickly* has three words, so I'll place three index cards on the table and put them next to each other.
    ▸ I'll say *walk* as I touch the first card, *away* as I touch the second card, and *quickly* as I touch the third card.
    ▸ Now you touch the cards and say the words *walk away quickly*.

4. Remove the cards from the table. Give students the stack of cards.

5. Say the following words and phrases. Have students put one card on the table for each word you say. Have them repeat each word as they put down each card. Have students pick up the cards between each example.

    ▸ *shop*   ▸ *bus*
    ▸ *dress shop*   ▸ *school bus*
    ▸ *busy dress shop*   ▸ *yellow school bus*

TIP If students can't identify the number of words in a phrase, say the phrase again and lay down an index card for each word you say. Have students count the cards and say how many words are in the phrase.

Rhymes Practice

Use common phrases to practice identifying rhyming words.

1. **Say:** Let's play a game. I am going to name something that is loaded into a big pretend truck. Your job is to think of something else that rhymes with what I put into the truck.

   ▸ For example, if I say, "I've got a truck and it's loaded with *coats,*" you might say, "I've got a truck and it's loaded with *goats!*"
   ▸ We will take turns thinking of rhyming words. I'll go first.
   ▸ "I've got a truck and it's loaded with *hats.*" What can you put in the truck that rhymes with *hats*?

2. Continue this activity with these words: *logs, cars, rocks.*

TIP If students have difficulty thinking of a word, say the beginning sound of a possible word.

Sound Chains

Help students use color tiles to represent the sounds in words. Grab the color tiles from the Tile Kit.

1. Place the tiles on the table.

2. **Say:** Let's use tiles to stand for sounds in words.

   ▸ I'll say a word and the sounds in that word. The word *two* has two sounds: /t/ and /o͞o/.
   ▸ I'll put a tile down for each sound in the word. The sounds are different, so I'll use two different colors. Then I'll touch each tile and say the sound it represents.
   ▸ Next I'll blend the sounds into a word and say the word while running my finger under the two color tiles: /t/ . . . /o͞o/ . . . *too.*

3. **Say:** I'll say another word, *do. Do* has two sounds: /d/ and /o͞o/. Listen for the sound that changed in the word: *two, do.*

   ▸ Let's change the color of the tile for the first sound only, because the sound /t/ in *two* changed to /d/ in *do,* but the second sound, /o͞o/, stayed the same.
   ▸ Touch each tile and say the sound it represents. Then you'll blend the two sounds into a word and say the word while running your finger under the two color tiles: /d/ . . . /o͞o/ . . . *do.*

4. Make the word *day*. Have students answer the following questions to reinforce the process.

   ▸ What are the sounds in the word *day*? /d/, /ā/
   ▸ Which sound stays the same when we change *do* to *day*? /d/
   ▸ Which sound changes when we change *do* into *day*? /o͞o/ changes to /ā/

5. Say each of the following words. Have students change the color of the tile for the sound that changes.

   ▸ *say* the first tile changes
   ▸ *may* the first tile changes
   ▸ *my* the second tile changes
   ▸ *pie* the first tile changes
   ▸ *sigh* the first tile changes
   ▸ *see* the second tile changes

Recognize Words and Syllables

Review the concept of syllables with students.

1. **Say:** When we talk, we make words by pushing air out of our mouths. Each push of air in a word is called a **syllable**. Each word has one or more syllables. You can think of syllables as chunks of words.

2. **Say:** Let's break some words into syllables.

   ▸ I'll say a word. I'll repeat the word.
   ▸ You'll say the word after me, and you'll break it into syllables by saying the separate chunks of the word and tapping your fist on the table as you say each chunk.
   ▸ For example, I'll say *kitten,* and then I'll say it again.
   ▸ You will say *kit / ten* and tap your fist on the table as you say each syllable.

3. Say each word and repeat it. Have students fist tap on the table as they say the syllables in each word.

   ▸ *puppy pup / py*
   ▸ *robin ro / bin*
   ▸ *kangaroo kan / ga / roo*
   ▸ *lion li / on*
   ▸ *opossum o / pos / sum*
   ▸ *squid squid*
   ▸ *tuna tu / na*

TIP Have students name items in the room and fist tap the syllables with you. For example, have them name and fist tap words such as *ta / ble* and *win / dow*. Challenge students to name and fist tap something with several syllables, such as *com / pu / ter*.

Try It •••

Careful Counting

Have students complete page PH 24 in *K¹² PhonicsWorks Basic Activity Book* for more practice with syllables. First have students say the name of each picture. Then have students count the number of syllables in each word and write the number.

Objectives
- Identify individual sounds in words.
- Identify the number of syllables in a word.

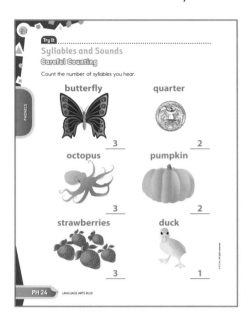

Online 20 minutes

REVIEW: Syllables and Sounds

Students will work online independently to

- ▶ Practice the sounds /sh/, /aw/, and /kw/.
- ▶ Identify rhyming words.
- ▶ Identify the number of syllables in words.

Help students locate the online activities and provide support as needed.

Objectives
- Identify individual sounds in words.
- Identify syllables in words.
- Identify the number of syllables in a word.

Offline Alternative

No computer access? Have students point out and name things or words that contain the sounds /sh/, /aw/, and /kw/; name words that rhyme; and count the number of syllables in words.

Unit Checkpoint

Lesson Overview

[Online] **REVIEW:** Sounds /sh/, /aw/, & /kw/ and Syllables — **20** minutes

[Offline] **UNIT CHECKPOINT:** Sounds /sh/, /aw/, & /kw/ and Syllables — **30** minutes

Materials

Supplied

- *K¹² PhonicsWorks Basic Assessments*, pp. PH 25–30

Objectives

- Identify and use the sound /sh/.
- Identify and use the sound /aw/.
- Identify and use the sound /kw/.
- Identify letters of the alphabet.
- Identify capital and lowercase letters.
- Match capital letters to lowercase letters.
- Identify words that rhyme.
- Identify beginning sounds in words.
- Identify a word when given the onset and rime.
- Blend sounds to create words.
- Identify the number of syllables in a word
- Identify syllables in words.

[Online] **20** minutes

REVIEW: **Sounds /sh/, /aw/, & /kw/ and Syllables**

Students will review the sounds /sh/, /aw/, and /kw/; rhyming words; and syllables to prepare for the Unit Checkpoint. Help students locate the online activities and provide support as needed.

 **30 minutes**

UNIT CHECKPOINT: Sounds /sh/, /aw/, & /kw/ and Syllables

Explain that students are going to show what they have learned about letters, sounds, syllables, and words.

1. Give students the Unit Checkpoint pages for the Sounds /sh/, /aw/, & /kw/ and Syllables unit and print the Unit Checkpoint Answer Key, if you'd like.

2. Use the instructions below to help administer the Checkpoint to students. On the Answer Key or another sheet of paper, note student answers to oral response questions to help with scoring the Checkpoint later.

3. Use the Answer Key to score the Checkpoint, and then enter the results online.

Part 1. Letter Matching Moving from left to right, have students read the letters aloud and circle the letter or letters that match the first letter in the row.

Part 2. Match Beginning Sounds Have students say the name of each picture and draw a line to connect pictures that have the same beginning sound.

Part 3. Rhymes Say each pair of words and have students say if the word pairs rhyme. Note any incorrect responses.

9. *paw, claw*   12. *box, lip*

10. *ball, fall*   13. *ship, chip*

11. *saw, say*   14. *much, such*

Part 4. Beginning Sounds Say each group of three words and have students say which words begin with the same sound. Repeat the words, as necessary. Note any incorrect responses.

15. *moon, bike, monkey*   19. *quicksand, yellow, yarn*

16. *ship, shave, sink*   20. *chain, shine, chair*

17. *queen, kick, quit*   21. *awful, eagle, awesome*

18. *quilt, quiet, keen*   22. *monkey, raccoon, rat*

Part 5. Onset and Rime Say the first sound of each word. Pause briefly and then say the rest of the word. Have students say the whole word aloud. Note any incorrect responses.

23. /s/ . . . *at*   **26.** /k/ . . . *law*

24. /sh/ . . . *ip*   **27.** /b/ . . . *all*

25. /kw/ . . . *ilt*   **28.** /kw/ . . . *een*

Part 6. Blend Sounds Say each sound in the word. Pause briefly between sounds. Have students repeat the sounds and then blend them together to say a word. Note any incorrect responses.

29. /sh/ /ĭ/ /p/   **32.** /p/ /aw/

30. /kw/ /ē/ /n/   **33.** /kw/ /ĭ/ /t/

31. /t/ /aw/ /l/   **34.** /f/ /ĭ/ /sh/

Part 7. Syllables Say each word. Have students repeat the word and then fist tap the word to identify the number of syllables. Note any incorrect responses.

35. *autumn*   **38.** *strawberry*

36. *quilt*   **39.** *quiet*

37. *machine*   **40.** *watermelon*

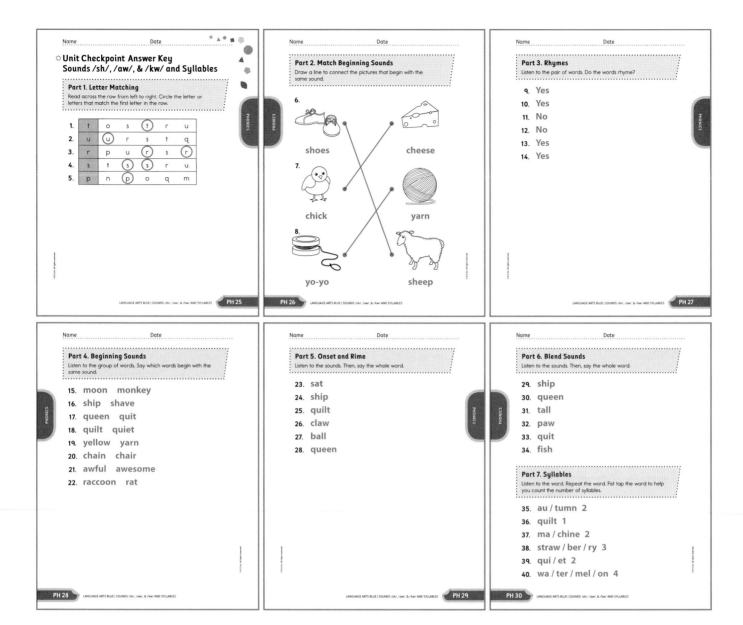

Unit Checkpoint Answer Key
Sounds /sh/, /aw/, & /kw/ and Syllables

Part 1. Letter Matching
Read across the row from left to right. Circle the letter or letters that match the first letter in the row.

1. t o s (t) r u
2. u (u) r s t q
3. r p u (r) s (r)
4. s t (s) (s) r u
5. p n (p) o q m

Part 2. Match Beginning Sounds
Draw a line to connect the pictures that begin with the same sound.

6. shoes — cheese
7. chick — yarn
8. yo-yo — sheep

Part 3. Rhymes
Listen to the pair of words. Do the words rhyme?

9. Yes
10. Yes
11. No
12. No
13. Yes
14. Yes

Part 4. Beginning Sounds
Listen to the group of words. Say which words begin with the same sound.

15. moon   monkey
16. ship   shave
17. queen   quit
18. quilt   quiet
19. yellow   yarn
20. chain   chair
21. awful   awesome
22. raccoon   rat

Part 5. Onset and Rime
Listen to the sounds. Then, say the whole word.

23. sat
24. ship
25. quilt
26. claw
27. ball
28. queen

Part 6. Blend Sounds
Listen to the sounds. Then, say the whole word.

29. ship
30. queen
31. tall
32. paw
33. quit
34. fish

Part 7. Syllables
Listen to the word. Repeat the word. Fist tap the word to help you count the number of syllables.

35. au / tumn 2
36. quilt 1
37. ma / chine 2
38. straw / ber / ry 3
39. qui / et 2
40. wa / ter / mel / on 4

Sound /oi/

Unit Overview

In this unit, students will
- Identify the letters of the alphabet.
- Identify and say the sounds /oi/, /ū/, and /ks/.
- Distinguish between words that rhyme or sound different.
- Identify individual sounds and syllables in words.
- Learn and practice blends.
- Learn to put phrases together to make sentences.

Materials

Supplied
- *K¹² PhonicsWorks Basic Activity Book,* p. PH 25
- whiteboard, Learning Coach
- whiteboard, student
- Tile Kit

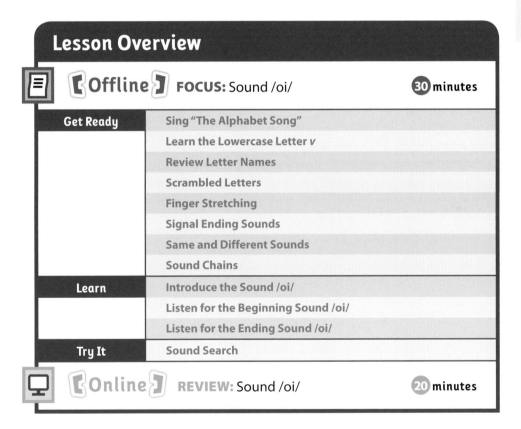

Lesson Overview

【Offline】 FOCUS: Sound /oi/   **30** minutes

Get Ready	Sing "The Alphabet Song"
	Learn the Lowercase Letter *v*
	Review Letter Names
	Scrambled Letters
	Finger Stretching
	Signal Ending Sounds
	Same and Different Sounds
	Sound Chains
Learn	Introduce the Sound /oi/
	Listen for the Beginning Sound /oi/
	Listen for the Ending Sound /oi/
Try It	Sound Search

【Online】 REVIEW: Sound /oi/   **20** minutes

Advance Preparation

Place lowercase letter tiles *a* through *u* and uppercase letter tiles *V* through *Z* in alphabetical order on your whiteboard. Place lowercase letter tile *v* on students' whiteboard.

 **30** minutes

FOCUS: Sound /oi/

Work **together** with students to complete offline Get Ready, Learn, and Try It activities.

Get Ready

Sing "The Alphabet Song"
To help students become familiar and comfortable with the alphabet, sing "The Alphabet Song" with them. Sing slowly, so that students may touch each letter on your whiteboard as they sing the letter's name.

Learn the Lowercase Letter *v*
To help students learn lowercase letters of the alphabet, have them practice identifying and naming the letter *v*.

1. **Say:** There are two different kinds of letters in our alphabet. The ones you already know are called capital, or uppercase, letters. The other kind of letters are called lowercase, or small, letters. These letters are smaller than capital letters.

2. **Say:** We're going to learn one lowercase letter today. The letter is *v*.

3. Have students touch the lowercase letter on their whiteboard and say its name.

4. **Say:** I'm going to put this letter on my whiteboard in place of the capital letter for *v*.

5. Move the uppercase *V* tile from your whiteboard to the Tile Kit, and replace it with the lowercase *v* tile.

6. Have students sing "The Alphabet Song," touching the lowercase letters *a* through *v*, then moving back to the capital letters.

Review Letter Names
To help students learn the alphabet, have them practice identifying and naming the letters *a, b, C, F, I, P, Y,* and *Z*. Grab your whiteboard with letters.

1. Point to each letter and have students touch and name each one.

    a   b   C   F   I   P   Y   Z

2. Say the name of each letter. After each one, have students repeat the name and touch the tile.

    a   b   C   F   I   P   Y   Z

Objectives
- Identify letters of the alphabet.
- Identify capital and lowercase letters.
- Match capital letters to lowercase letters.
- Identify ending sounds in words.
- Identify individual sounds in words.
- Blend sounds to create words.
- Identify the new word when one sound is changed in a word.

3. Redirect students if they name a letter incorrectly.

- ▸ Name the letter students missed.
- ▸ Have students touch the letter and say its name.
- ▸ Have students trace the shape of the letter with their finger on the brown side of their board, and have them say the letter's name as they trace the shape.
- ▸ If students name a letter incorrectly twice, point to the letter and tell them its name. Have students touch the letter and say its name.

Scrambled Letters

To help students learn the alphabet, have them practice identifying and naming letters.

1. Place the following letter tiles in random order on students' whiteboard: *c, d, e, f,* and *g.*

2. Have students arrange the letters in alphabetical order.

TIP Students may find this activity easier if they slowly sing "The Alphabet Song" to themselves as they work.

Finger Stretching

Use finger stretching to help students identify individual sounds in words.

1. **Say:** Let's review finger stretching. In the word *mash,* the first sound is /m/, the next sound is /ă/, and the last sound is /sh/. I will finger stretch each sound as I say it. Then I'll say the word, while pulling my fist toward my body.

2. Finger stretch the word *mash* for students.

3. **Say:** I'm going say words with several sounds in them. You'll say each word and then finger stretch it while you say each sound in the word.

4. Say the following words and have students finger stretch them. After they finger stretch each word, ask them the question for that word.

- ▸ *smash* /s/ /m/ /ă/ /sh/   What is the first sound? /s/
- ▸ *fat* /f/ /ă/ /t/   What is the middle sound? /ă/
- ▸ *list* /l/ /ĭ/ /s/ /t/   What is the last sound? /t/
- ▸ *fist* /f/ /ĭ/ /s/ /t/   What is the last sound? /t/
- ▸ *rag* /r/ /ă/ /g/   What is the first sound? /r/
- ▸ *rust* /r/ /ŭ/ /s/ /t/   What is the last sound? /t/

TIP Refer to the *K¹² PhonicsWorks* video for a demonstration of finger stretching.

Signal Ending Sounds

Use a special signal to help students identify **ending sounds** in words.

1. **Say:** I'm going to tell you a special sound, and then I'll say some words. Repeat each word I say and make a special signal to tell me where the special sound is. If the special sound is at the end of the word, pat your cheek. If the special sound is **not** at the end of the word, just smile at me. For example,

   ▸ If I ask you to listen for /th/ and I say the word *with*, you will repeat the word *with* and pat your cheek because *with* has the sound /th/ at the end.
   ▸ If I say the word *wig*, you will repeat the word and just smile at me because *wig* has the sound /g/, not /th/, at the end.

2. Say each sound and group of words. Have students make the special signals to identify the ending sounds.

   ▸ /d/: *wide, mail, like, ride, bride* pat cheek: *wide, ride, bride*
   ▸ /t/: *bun, bit, fall, fault, meant* pat cheek: *bit, fault, meant*
   ▸ /p/: *yelp, yell, gull, gulp, snip* pat cheek: *yelp, gulp, snip*
   ▸ /m/: *same, Mike, Mom, time, end* pat cheek: *same, Mom, time*

TIP If students can't identify the ending sound of each word, say the word again and emphasize the ending sound by repeating it three times (for example, *sit* /t/ /t/ /t/). You can also draw out the ending sound when you say the word (for example, *kissssssss*). If necessary, have students look at your mouth while you repeat the sounds.

Same and Different Sounds

Play a game with color tiles to help students identify sounds that are the same and sounds that are different. Grab the color tiles from the Tile Kit.

1. Place the tiles on a table.

2. **Say:** I am going to make two sounds. If the sounds are the same, you'll pick out two tiles that are the same color and put them next to each other. If the sounds are different, you'll pick out two tiles that are different colors and put them next to each other. For example,

   ▸ For the sounds /ē/, /t/ in the word *eat,* you'll pick out two tiles that are different colors because the two sounds are different. Remember, the last two sounds I made were /ē/, /t/.
   ▸ Let's add the sound /m/ to *eat* and make a three-sound word, *meat*. I will add a new color tile to make the three sounds, /m/, /ē/, /t/, for the word *meat*.

3. Say each pair of words. Have students pick out and place tiles to indicate whether the sounds are the same or different. Have students add a third letter tile to change the two-sound word to a three-sound word. Note that students should **not** choose new tiles for each group of sounds; they should begin with two tiles, replace, and add to those tiles as necessary throughout the "chain."

   ▸ *age* and *page*
   ▸ *oak* and *soak*

TIP If students have difficulty with words with three sounds, continue the activity with the following two-sound words: *eat, age, me, see, he, mow, low*.

Sound Chains

Help students use color tiles to represent the sounds in words. Grab the color tiles from the Tile Kit.

1. Place the tiles on a table.

2. **Say:** Let's use tiles to stand for sounds in words.

   ▸ I'll say a word and the sounds in that word. The word *meat* has three sounds: /m/ /ē/ /t/.
   ▸ I'll put a tile down for each sound in the word. The sounds are different, so I'll use three different colors of tiles. Then I'll touch each tile and say the sound it represents.
   ▸ Next I'll blend the sounds into a word and say the word while running my finger under the three color tiles: /m/ . . . /ē/ . . . /t/ . . . *meat*.

3. **Say:** I'll say another word, *seat*, which has three sounds: /s/ /ē/ /t/. Listen for the sound that changed in the word: *meat, seat*.

   ▸ You'll change the color of the tile for the first sound only, because the sound /m/ in *meat* changed to /s/ in *seat*, but the second and third sounds stayed the same.
   ▸ You'll touch each tile and say the sound it represents. Then you'll blend the three sounds into a word and say the word while running your finger under the color tiles: /s/ . . . /ē/ . . . /t/ . . . *seat*.

4. Say the word *seat*. Ask students the questions for the word to reinforce the process.

   ▸ What are the sounds in the word? /s/ /ĕ/ /t/
   ▸ Which sounds stay the same? /ĕ/ and /t/
   ▸ Which sound changes? /m/ changes to /s/

5. Say each of the following words. Have students change the color of the tile for the sound that changes.

   ▸ *beam*
   ▸ *beat* last sound
   ▸ *feet* first sound
   ▸ *feed* last sound
   ▸ *read* first sound
   ▸ *lead* first sound

Learn

Introduce the Sound /oi/

Teach the sound /oi/, as in *oil*, *oink*, and *oyster*.

1. **Say:** We're going to play a game to practice the **sound /oi/**. Your job is to say the sound just like me and do what I do, too.

2. Push your nose up like a pig's nose and say, "Oink!" Have students do this, too.

3. **Say:** I'll say some words that start with the sound /oi/ and you'll repeat them, saying /oi/ just the way I do.

oil   oink   oyster

4. **Say:** Now I'll say some words that end with the sound /oi/ and you'll repeat them, saying /oi/ just the way I do.

boy   toy   enjoy

Listen for the Beginning Sound /oi/

Present pairs of words to help students recognize beginning sounds.

1. **Say:** I'm going to say two words. Listen for the **beginning sound /oi/**. Then tell me the word that has that beginning sound. For example, if I say *oil* and *oats*, you'll say *oil* because /oi/ is the first sound in *oil*.

2. Say each pair of words. Have students identify the word that begins with the sound /oi/.

   ▸ *eek* or *oink* oink
   ▸ *ointment* or *easy* ointment

Listen for the Ending Sound /oi/

Present pairs of words to help students recognize ending sounds.

1. **Say:** I'm going to say two words. Listen for the **ending sound /oi/**. Then tell me the word with that ending sound. For example, if I say *toy* and *tea*, you'll say *toy* because /oi/ is the last sound in *toy*.

2. Say each pair of words. Have students identify the word that ends with the sound /oi/.

   ▸ *decide* or *destroy* destroy
   ▸ *enjoy* or *embrace* enjoy
   ▸ *bee* or *boy* boy

Objectives
- Identify and use the sound /oi/.
- Identify beginning sounds in words.
- Identify ending sounds in words.

Try It

Sound Search

Have students complete page PH 25 in *K¹² PhonicsWorks Basic Activity Book* for more practice with the sound /oi/. First have students say the name of each picture. Then have them circle pictures whose name contains the sound /oi/.

Objectives
- Identify and use the sound /oi/.
- Identify individual sounds in words.

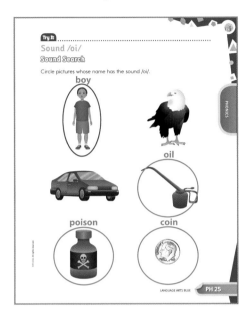

Online 20 minutes

REVIEW: Sound /oi/

Students will work online independently to

▸ Practice the sound /oi/.

Help students locate the online activities and provide support as needed.

Objectives
- Identify and use the sound /oi/.
- Identify individual sounds in words.

Offline Alternative

No computer access? Have students point out and name things or words that contain the sound /oi/ (for example, *soil* or *toy*).

Sound /ū/

Lesson Overview

Offline FOCUS: Sound /ū/ — **30** minutes

Get Ready	Sing "The Alphabet Song"
	Learn the Lowercase Letter *w*
	Review Letter Names
	Old MacDonald Had a Sound
	Rhymes Practice
	Sounds in Words
Learn	Introduce the Sound /ū/
	Listen for the Beginning Sound /ū/
Try It	The Beginning

Online REVIEW: Sound /ū/ — **20** minutes

Materials

Supplied

- *K¹² PhonicsWorks Basic Activity Book*, p. PH 26
- whiteboard, Learning Coach
- whiteboard, student
- Tile Kit

Advance Preparation

Place lowercase letter tiles *a* through *v* and uppercase letter tiles *W* through *Z* in alphabetical order on your whiteboard. Place lowercase letter tile *w* on students' whiteboard.

 **30 minutes**

FOCUS: Sound /ū/

Work **together** with students to complete offline Get Ready, Learn, and Try It activities.

Get Ready

Sing "The Alphabet Song"

To help students become familiar and comfortable with the alphabet, sing "The Alphabet Song" with them. Sing slowly, so that students may touch each letter on your whiteboard as they sing the letter's name.

Learn the Lowercase Letter w

To help students learn lowercase letters of the alphabet, have them practice identifying and naming the letter w.

1. **Say:** There are two different kinds of letters in our alphabet. The ones you already know are called capital, or uppercase, letters. The other kind of letters are called lowercase, or small, letters. These letters are smaller than capital letters.

2. **Say:** We're going to learn one lowercase letter today. The letter is w.

3. Have students touch the lowercase letter on their whiteboard and say its name.

4. **Say:** I'm going to put this letter on my whiteboard in place of the capital letter for w.

5. Move the uppercase W tile from your whiteboard to the Tile Kit, and replace it with the lowercase w tile.

6. Have students sing "The Alphabet Song," touching the lowercase letters a through w, then moving back to the capital letters.

Review Letter Names

To help students learn the alphabet, have them practice identifying and naming the letters s, t, u, v, w, X, Y, and Z. Grab your whiteboard with letters.

1. Point to each letter and have students touch and name each one.

   s   t   u   v   w   X   Y   Z

2. Say the name of each letter. After each one, have students repeat the name and touch the tile.

   s   t   u   v   w   X   Y   Z

Objectives
- Identify letters of the alphabet.
- Identify capital and lowercase letters.
- Match capital letters to lowercase letters.
- Identify words that rhyme.
- Identify individual sounds in words.
- Blend sounds to create words.

3. Redirect students if they name a letter incorrectly.

 ▸ Name the letter students missed.
 ▸ Have students touch the letter and say its name.
 ▸ Have students trace the shape of the letter with their finger on the brown side of their board, and have them say the letter's name as they trace the shape.
 ▸ If students name a letter incorrectly twice, point to the letter and tell them its name. Have students touch the letter and say its name.

Old MacDonald Had a Sound
To review sounds, sing "Old MacDonald's Farm" with students.

1. **Say:** Let's have some fun with "Old MacDonald's Farm." Instead of animals, we'll put sounds on the farm. We'll sing, "Old MacDonald had a farm, E-I-E-I-O, and on that farm he had a /ch/, E-I-E-I-O. With a /ch/, /ch/ here, and a /ch/, /ch/ there . . . ."

2. Continue singing the song. Alternate singing and having students sing until you have finished all of the following sounds: /oi/, /z/, /ē/, /ĭ/, /v/, and /d/.

Rhymes Practice
Use common phrases to practice identifying rhyming words.

1. **Say:** I am going to name something that is loaded into a big truck. Your job is to think of something else that rhymes with what I put into the truck.

 ▸ For example, if I say, "I've got a truck and it's loaded with *coats*," you might say, "I've got a truck and it's loaded with *goats*!"
 ▸ We will take turns thinking of rhyming words. I'll go first.
 ▸ "I've got a truck and it's loaded with *trees*." What can you put in the truck that rhymes with *trees*?

2. Continue this activity with these words: *books, chairs, flags.*

TIP If students have difficulty thinking of a word, say the beginning sound of a possible word.

Sounds in Words

Help students use color tiles to represent the sounds in words. Grab the color tiles from the Tile Kit.

1. Place the tiles on a table.

2. **Say:** Let's use tiles to stand for sounds in words.

   ▸ I'll say a word and the sounds in that word. I'll build the word *pop*: /p/ /ŏ/ /p/.

   ▸ I'll put a tile down for each sound in the word. The sounds are different, so I'll use three different colors of tiles. Then I'll touch each tile and say the sound it represents: *pop.* /p/ [put down first color tile], /ŏ/ [put down second color tile], /p/ [put down third color tile].

3. **Say:** Notice that I put down the same colors for the first and last sounds, because the sounds are the same. Next I'll blend the sounds into a word and say the word while running my finger under the three color tiles.

4. Since the first and last sounds in the word *pop* are the same, be sure to place the same color tile at the end of the chain that is at the beginning. Do not stress that the color represents the sound /p/, but rather that it shows that the word begins and ends with the same sound.

5. Say each of the following words. Have students place a color tile for each different sound in the word.

   ▸ *mom* /m/ /ŏ/ /m/
   ▸ *boat* /b/ /ō/ /t/
   ▸ *nun* /n/ /ŭ/ /n/
   ▸ *fan* /f/ /ă/ /n/
   ▸ *bib* /b/ /ĭ/ /b/
   ▸ *bob* /b/ /ŏ/ /b/
   ▸ *gag* /g/ /ă/ /g/
   ▸ *rug* /r/ /ŭ/ /g/

Learn

Introduce the Sound /ū/

Teach the sound /ū/, as in *United States, useful,* and *use.*

1. **Say:** We're going to play a game to practice the **sound /ū/**. Your job is to say the sound just like me and do what I do, too.

2. Use your index finger to make a horn on your head and say, "I am a unicorn." Have students do this, too.

3. **Say:** I'll say some words that start with the sound /ū/ and you'll repeat them, saying /ū/ just the way I do.

United States   useful   use

4. **Say:** Now I'll say some words that end with the sound /ū/ and you'll repeat them, saying /ū/ just the way I do.

menu   rescue   review

Objectives

- Identify and use the sound /ū/.
- Identify beginning sounds in words.
- Identify ending sounds in words

Listen for the Beginning Sound /ū/

Present pairs of words to help students recognize beginning sounds.

1. **Say:** I'm going to say two words. Listen for the **beginning sound** /ū/. Then tell me the word that has that beginning sound. For example, if I say *use* and *old*, you'll say *use* because /ū/ is the first sound in *use*.

2. Say each pair of words. Have students identify the word that begins with the sound /ū/.

   ► *bicycle* or *unicycle* *unicycle*
   ► *oboe* or *ukulele* *ukulele*
   ► *universe* or *Easter* *universe*

 If students have difficulty identifying the correct word, say the word again and draw out the beginning sound (for example, *uuuuuuse*). If students continue to have difficulty, give multiple words using the same beginning sound.

Try It

The Beginning

Have students complete page PH 26 in *K¹² PhonicsWorks Basic Activity Book* for more practice with the sound /ū/. First have students say the name of each picture. Then have them circle words that begin with the sound /ū/.

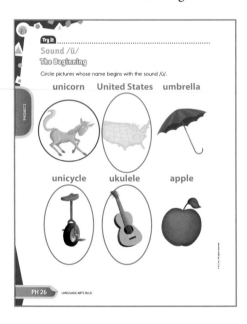

Objectives
- Identify and use the sound /ū/.
- Identify beginning sounds in words.

 20 minutes

REVIEW: **Sound /ū/**

Students will work online independently to

▸ Practice the sound /ū/.

Help students locate the online activities and provide support as needed.

Objectives
- Identify and use the sound /ū/.
- Identify individual sounds in words.

Offline Alternative

No computer access? Have the student point out and name things or words that contain the sound /ū/ (for example, *cube* or *use*).

Sound /ks/

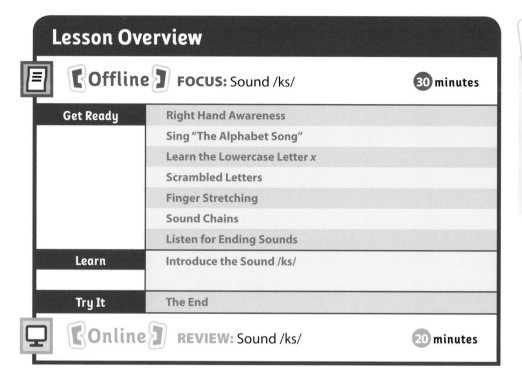

Lesson Overview

Offline FOCUS: Sound /ks/ — **30** minutes

Get Ready	Right Hand Awareness
	Sing "The Alphabet Song"
	Learn the Lowercase Letter x
	Scrambled Letters
	Finger Stretching
	Sound Chains
	Listen for Ending Sounds
Learn	Introduce the Sound /ks/
Try It	The End

Online REVIEW: Sound /ks/ — **20** minutes

Materials

Supplied

- *K¹²PhonicsWorks Basic Activity Book*, p. PH 27
- whiteboard, Learning Coach
- whiteboard, student
- Tile Kit

Advance Preparation

Place lowercase letter tiles *a* through *w* and uppercase letter tiles *X* through *Z* in alphabetical order on your whiteboard. Place lowercase letter tile *x* on students' whiteboard.

 **Offline** 🕥 **minutes**

FOCUS: Sound /ks/

Work **together** with students to complete offline Get Ready, Learn, and Try It activities.

Get Ready

Right Hand Awareness

Students read from left to right, so play a game to develop right hand awareness. To avoid confusion, focus on the right hand only.

1. Say each sentence and do each action. Have students repeat your words and actions.

   ‣ I'm shaking your right hand.
   ‣ Now I'm touching my right ankle.
   ‣ Now I'm waving my right hand in the air.
   ‣ Now I'm touching my right toe.
   ‣ Now I'm touching my right cheek.

2. Repeat the actions and mix up the order. To end the activity, shake right hands again.

Objectives

- Develop right hand awareness.
- Identify letters of the alphabet.
- Identify capital and lowercase letters.
- Match capital letters to lowercase letters.
- Identify individual sounds in words.
- Identify the number of sounds within words.
- Identify ending sounds in words.

Sing "The Alphabet Song"

To help students become familiar and comfortable with the alphabet, sing "The Alphabet Song" with them. Sing slowly, so that students may touch each letter on your whiteboard as they sing the letter's name.

Learn the Lowercase Letter *x*

To help students learn lowercase letters of the alphabet, have them practice identifying and naming the letter *x*.

1. **Say:** There are two different kinds of letters in our alphabet. The ones you already know are called capital, or uppercase, letters. The other kind of letters are called lowercase, or small, letters. These letters are smaller than capital letters.

2. **Say:** We're going to learn one lowercase letter today. The letter is *x*.

3. Have students touch the lowercase letter on their whiteboard and say its name.

4. **Say:** I'm going to put this letter on my whiteboard in place of the capital letter for *x*.

5. Move the uppercase *X* tile from your whiteboard to the Tile Kit, and replace it with the lowercase *x* tile.

6. Have students sing "The Alphabet Song," touching the lowercase letters *a* through *x*, then moving back to the capital letters.

Scrambled Letters

To help students learn the alphabet, have them practice identifying and naming letters.

1. Place the following letter tiles in random order on students' whiteboard: *c, d, e, f,* and *g.*

2. Have students arrange the letters in alphabetical order.

TIP Students may find this activity easier if they slowly sing "The Alphabet Song" to themselves as they work.

Finger Stretching

Use finger stretching to help students identify individual sounds in words.

1. **Say:** Let's review finger stretching. In the word *sell,* the first sound is /s/, the next sound is /ĕ/, and the last sound is /l/. I will finger stretch each sound as I say it. Then I'll say the word, while pulling my fist toward my body.

2. Finger stretch the word *sell* for students.

3. **Say:** I'm going to say words with several sounds in them. You'll say each word and then finger stretch it while you say each sound in the word.

4. Say the following words and have students finger stretch them. After they finger stretch each word, ask them the question for that word.

   ▸ *end* /ĕ/ /n/ /d/   How many sounds does the word have? three
   ▸ *both* /b/ /ō/ /th/   How many sounds does the word have? three
   ▸ *gift* /g/ /ĭ/ /f/ /t/   How many sounds does the word have? four
   ▸ *shift* /sh/ /ĭ/ /f/ /t/   How many sounds does the word have? four
   ▸ *task* /t/ /ă/ /s/ /k/   How many sounds does the word have? four
   ▸ *me* /m/ /ē/   How many sounds does the word have? two
   ▸ *lift* /l/ /ĭ/ /f/ /t/   How many sounds does the word have? four

TIP Refer to the *K¹² PhonicsWorks* video for a demonstration of finger stretching.

Sound Chains

Help students use color tiles to represent the sounds in words. Grab the color tiles from the Tile Kit.

1. Place the tiles on a table.

2. **Say:** Let's use tiles to stand for sounds in words.

   ▸ I'll say a word and the sounds in that word. The word *me* has two sounds: /m/ /ē/.
   ▸ I'll put a tile down for each sound in the word. The sounds are different, so I'll use two different colors of tiles. Then I'll touch each tile and say the sound it represents.
   ▸ Next I'll blend the sounds into a word and say the word while running my finger under the two color tiles: /m/ . . . /ē/ . . . *me.*

3. **Say:** I'll say another word, *we*, which has two sounds: /w/ /ē/. Listen for the sound that changed in the word.

   ▸ You'll change the color of the tile for the first sound only, because the sound /m/ in *me* changed to /w/ in *we*, but the second sound, /ē/, stayed the same.
   ▸ You'll touch each tile and say the sound it represents. Then you'll blend the two sounds into a word and say the word while running your finger under the two color tiles: /w/ . . . /ē/ . . . *we*.

4. Say the word *way*. Ask students the questions for the word to reinforce the process.

   ▸ What are the sounds in this word? /w/ /ā/
   ▸ Which sound stays the same? /w/
   ▸ Which sound changes? /ē/ changes to /ā/

5. Say each of the following words. Have students change the color of the tile for the sound that changes.

   ▸ *bay*
   ▸ *be* second sound
   ▸ *by* second sound
   ▸ *my* first sound
   ▸ *may* second sound
   ▸ *say* first sound
   ▸ *see* second sound
   ▸ *fee* first sound

Listen for Ending Sounds

Help students identify **ending sounds** in words.

1. **Say:** I am going to say a word. Your job is to listen for the ending sound you hear in the word. Then you can tell me that sound.

   ▸ For example, if I say *clap*, you will say /p/ because the last sound you hear in *clap* is /p/.
   ▸ Now it's your turn. Listen to the word I say. You repeat the word, and then tell me the last sound you hear in the word.

2. Repeat the process, using the following words to help students recognize ending sounds:

   ▸ *fish* /sh/
   ▸ *ask* /k/
   ▸ *match* /ch/
   ▸ *will* /l/
   ▸ *me* /ē/
   ▸ *try* /ī/
   ▸ *rub* /b/
   ▸ *laugh* /f/

Learn

Introduce the Sound /ks/

Teach the sound /ks/, as in *box*, *fix*, and *wax*.

1. **Say:** We're going to play a game to practice the **sound /ks/**. Your job is to say the sound just like me and do what I do, too.

2. Outline a box shape with your hands and say the word *box*. Have students do this, too.

3. **Say:** Now I'll say some words that end with the sound /ks/ and you'll repeat them, saying /ks/ just the way I do.

box   fix   wax

TIP The sound /x/ as in *fox* is represented by the sound /ks/. This representation is not a pure **phoneme**, but rather a special sound used in teaching reading.

Objectives
- Identify and use the sound /ks/.
- Identify ending sounds in words.

Try It

The End

Have students complete page PH 27 in *K¹² PhonicsWorks Basic Activity Book* for more practice with the sound /ks/. First have students say the name of each picture. Then have students circle pictures whose name ends with the sound /ks/.

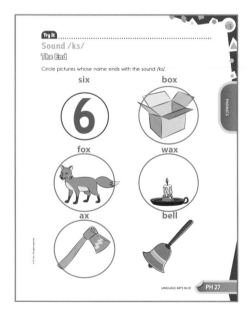

Objectives
- Identify and use the sound /ks/.
- Identify ending sounds in words.

 **minutes**

REVIEW: **Sound /ks/**

Students will work online independently to

▶ Practice the sound /ks/.

Help students locate the online activities and provide support as needed.

★ **Objectives**

- Identify and use the sound /ks/.
- Identify ending sounds in words.

Offline Alternative

No computer access? Have students point out and name things or words that end with the sound /ks/ (for example, *tax* and *sax*).

Sound Practice

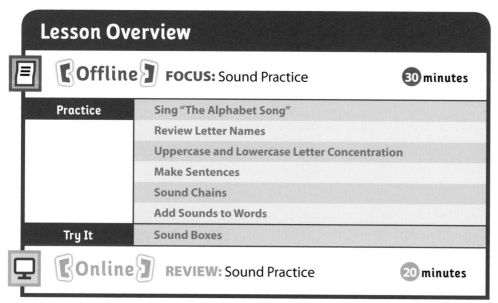

Lesson Overview

Offline FOCUS: Sound Practice — **30** minutes

Practice	Sing "The Alphabet Song"
	Review Letter Names
	Uppercase and Lowercase Letter Concentration
	Make Sentences
	Sound Chains
	Add Sounds to Words
Try It	Sound Boxes

Online REVIEW: Sound Practice — **20** minutes

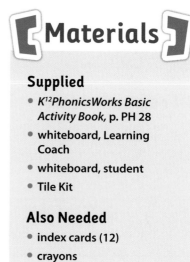

Materials

Supplied
- *K¹²PhonicsWorks Basic Activity Book,* p. PH 28
- whiteboard, Learning Coach
- whiteboard, student
- Tile Kit

Also Needed
- index cards (12)
- crayons

Advance Preparation

Place lowercase letter tiles *a* through *x* and uppercase letter tiles *Y* through *Z* in alphabetical order on your whiteboard.

For Uppercase and Lowercase Letter Concentration, print uppercase and lowercase letters on index cards, using one card per letter. Select six pairs of letters, such as *B, b; E, e; H, h; O, o; S, s;* and *T, t.*

 **30 minutes**

FOCUS: Sound Practice

Work **together** with students to complete offline Practice and Try It activities.

Practice

Sing "The Alphabet Song"

To help students become familiar and comfortable with the alphabet, sing "The Alphabet Song" with them. Sing slowly, so that students may touch each letter on your whiteboard as they sing the letter's name.

Review Letter Names

To help students learn the alphabet, have them practice identifying and naming the letters *b, c, d, e, f, g, h, i, t, u, v,* and *w.* Grab your whiteboard with letters.

1. Point to each letter and have students touch and name each one.

   b   c   d   e   f   g   h   i   t   u   v   w

2. Say the name of each letter. After each one, have students repeat the name and touch the tile.

   b   c   d   e   f   g   h   i   t   u   v   w

3. Redirect students if they name a letter incorrectly.

   ▶ Name the letter students missed.

   ▶ Have students touch the letter and say its name.

   ▶ Have students trace the shape of the letter with their finger on the brown side of their board, and have them say the letter's name as they trace the shape.

   ▶ If students name a letter incorrectly twice, point to the letter and tell them its name. Have students touch the letter and say its name.

Uppercase and Lowercase Letter Concentration

Help students practice pairing uppercase and lowercase letters.

1. Gather the uppercase and lowercase letter pairs of index cards you prepared.

2. Mix up the index cards and place them face down on the table or floor.

3. **Say:** Let's practice matching uppercase and lowercase letters. We can also call these letters big letters and small letters.

Objectives

- Identify letters of the alphabet.
- Identify capital and lowercase letters.
- Match capital letters to lowercase letters.
- Orally create sentences from phrases.
- Identify complete sentences.
- Identify individual sounds in words.
- Identify the new word when one sound is changed in a word.
- Identify beginning sounds in words.
- Identify and use vowels and vowel sounds.

4. **Say:** You'll turn over the cards two at a time. If you turn over a card that has a lowercase letter and a card that has the uppercase form of the same letter, the cards match and you can keep them. If the cards don't match, turn them back over.

5. Have students play until all of the cards are paired.

Make Sentences

Help students practice using phrases to make sentences.

1. **Say:** A sentence is made up of words. A phrase is a part of a sentence.

2. **Say:** Let's make some sentences from phrases. I'll say some words and you'll repeat them. Then you'll find different ways to make those words into a sentence. For example,

   ▸ If I say, "catches the ball," you might say, "Sally catches the ball" or "Rex the dog catches the ball."
   ▸ If I say "the dog," you might say, "The dog howled all night" or "The dog was scratching at the door."

3. Say the following phrases. Have students use each phrase to make two different sentences.

   ▸ *the old shirt*
   ▸ *for dinner last night*
   ▸ *shone brightly*

Sound Chains

Help students use color tiles to represent the sounds in words.

1. Gather the color tiles from the Tile Kit. Place the tiles on the table.

2. **Say:** Let's use tiles to stand for sounds in words.

   ▸ I'll say a word and the sounds in that word. The word *ad* has two sounds: /ă/ /d/.
   ▸ I'll put a tile down for each sound in the word. The sounds are different, so I'll use two different colors of tiles. Then I'll touch each tile and say the sound it represents.
   ▸ Next I'll blend the sounds into a word and say the word while running my finger under the two color tiles: /ă/ . . . /d/ . . . *ad*.

3. **Say:** I'll say another word, *mad*, which has three sounds: /m/ /ă/ /d/. Listen for the new sound in the word: *ad, mad*.

   ▸ You'll add a new color tile for the first sound, /m/. The other two sounds in *mad*, /ă/ and /d/, stay the same.
   ▸ You'll touch each tile and say the sound it represents. Then you'll blend the three sounds into a word and say the word while running your finger under the three color tiles: /m/ . . . /ă/ . . . /d/ . . . *mad*.

4. Say the word *sad*. Ask students the questions for the word to reinforce the process.

   ► What are the sounds in this word? /s/ /ă/ /d/
   ► Which sounds stay the same? /ă/, /d/
   ► Which sound changes? /m/ changes to /s/

5. Say each of the following words. Have students change the color of the tile for the sound that changes.

   ► *sax* last sound
   ► *fax* first sound
   ► *fix* second sound

6. Remove all the color tiles, and repeat the activity using the following words:

   ► *use*
   ► *muse* first sound
   ► *mute* last sound
   ► *moat* middle sound
   ► *meet* middle sound
   ► *me* last sound
   ► *bee* first sound
   ► *boy* last sound

Add Sounds to Words

Help students make new words by adding **beginning sounds** to words.

1. **Say:** Let's make new words by adding sounds. I'll say a word and you'll repeat it. Then I'll add a sound to the beginning of the word and you'll say the new word. For example, I'll say *ox* and you'll repeat it. Then I'll add the sound /f/ to *ox* and you'll say *fox*.

2. Say the following words and beginning sounds. Have students say the new word.

   ► *at* . . . /m/ *mat*
   ► *eat* . . . /s/ *seat*
   ► *eat* . . . /m/ *meat*
   ► *oat* . . . /g/ *goat*
   ► *oat* . . . /v/ *vote*
   ► *ice* . . . /n/ *nice*
   ► *ice* . . . /r/ *rice*

Try It

Sound Boxes

Have students complete page PH 28 in *K¹² PhonicsWorks Basic Activity Book* for more practice with sounds. First have students say the name of each picture. Be sure they say each separate sound slowly and clearly. As students say a sound, have them color a box. Have them use a different color to show each different sound.

Objectives

- Identify individual sounds in words.
- Identify and use vowels and vowel sounds.

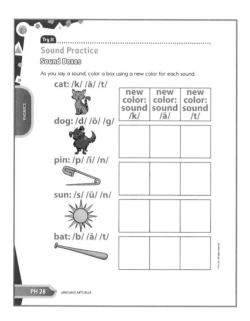

 Online ⑳ **minutes**

REVIEW: Sound Practice

Students will work online independently to

▶ Identify letters.
▶ Identify sounds in words.
▶ Add sounds to make new words.

Help students locate the online activities and provide support as needed.

Objectives

- Identify individual sounds in words.
- Identify and use the sound /oi/.
- Identify and use the sound /ū/.
- Identify and use the sound /ks/.

Offline Alternative

No computer access? Have students point out and name things or words that contain the sounds /oi/, /ū/, and /ks/ (for example, *joy, blue,* and *fox*). You might also ask students to name letters that they see, count the number of sounds in words, and practice making new words by adding sounds.

Unit Checkpoint

Lesson Overview

🖥	**【Online】**	**REVIEW:** Sounds /oi/, /ū/, & /ks/ and Sound Practice	**20** minutes
📄	**【Offline】**	**UNIT CHECKPOINT:** Sounds /oi/, /ū/, & /ks/ and Sound Practice	**30** minutes

Materials

Supplied
- *K¹² PhonicsWorks Basic Assessments*, pp. PH 31–36

⭐ Objectives

- Identify and use the sound /oi/.
- Identify and use the sound /ū/.
- Identify and use the sound /ks/.
- Identify words that rhyme.
- Identify capital and lowercase letters.
- Match capital letters to lowercase letters.
- Identify letters of the alphabet.
- Identify beginning sounds in words.
- Identify individual sounds in words.
- Identify a word when given the onset and rime.
- Blend sounds to create words.

【Online】 **20** minutes

REVIEW: **Sounds /oi/, /ū/, & /ks/ and Sound Practice**

Students will review the sounds /oi/, /ū/, and /ks/, and practice identifying letters and sounds, to prepare for the Unit Checkpoint. Help students locate the online activities and provide support as needed.

 **30 minutes**

UNIT CHECKPOINT: Sounds /oi/, /ū/, & /ks/ and Sound Practice

Explain that students are going to show what they have learned about letters, sounds, and words.

1. Give students the Unit Checkpoint pages for the Sounds /oi/, /ū/, & /ks/ and Sound Practice unit and print the Unit Checkpoint Answer Key, if you'd like.

2. Use the instructions below to help administer the Checkpoint to students. On the Answer Key or another sheet of paper, note student answers to oral response questions to help with scoring the Checkpoint later.

3. Use the Answer Key to score the Checkpoint, and then enter the results online.

Part 1. Letter Matching Moving from left to right, have students read the letters aloud and circle the letters that match the first letter in the row.

Part 2. Match Ending Sounds Have students say the name of each picture and draw a line to connect pictures that have the same ending sound.

Part 3. Rhymes Say each pair of words and have students say if the word pairs rhyme. Note any incorrect responses.

9. *boy, joy*
10. *tall, wall*
11. *cute, mute*
12. *fox, fix*
13. *toy, tea*
14. *shed, pet*

Part 4. Beginning Sounds Say each group of three words, and have students say which words begin with the same sound. Repeat the words, as necessary. Note any incorrect responses.

15. *unicorn, united, island*
16. *oyster, violin, velvet*
17. *chain, sweet, chip*
18. *wagon, weed, yellow*
19. *in, up, us*
20. *apple, alligator, ugly*
21. *pumpkin, quick, queen*
22. *onion, unicycle, universe*

Part 5. Onset and Rime Say the first sound of each word. Pause briefly and then say the rest of the word. Have students say the whole word aloud. Note any incorrect responses.

23. /b/ . . . *ox*

24. /f/ . . . *ix*

25. /oi/ . . . *ster*

26. /j/ . . . *oy*

27. /k/ . . . *ute*

28. /k/ . . . *ube*

Part 6. Blend Sounds Say each sound in the word. Pause briefly between sounds. Have students repeat the sounds and then blend them together to say a word. Note any incorrect responses.

29. /t/ /oi/

30. /f/ /ŏ/ /ks/

31. /s/ /ĭ/ /ks/

32. /kw/ /ĭ/ /k/

33. /ch/ /ŭ /m/

34. /y/ /ĕ/ /s/

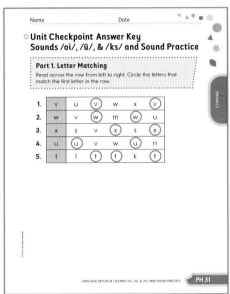

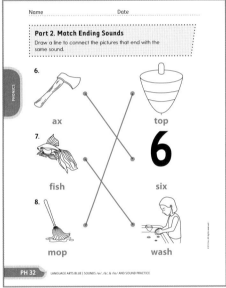

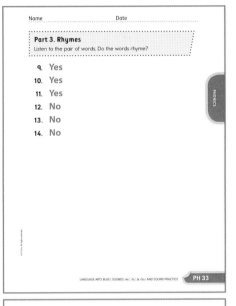

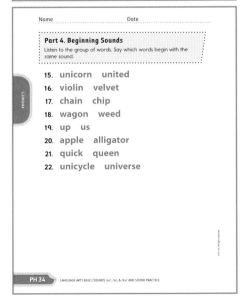

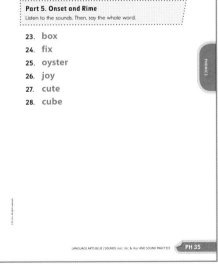

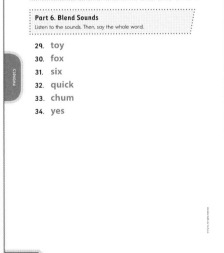

Long Double *o* Sound

Unit Overview

In this unit, students will
- ▸ Identify letters in the alphabet.
- ▸ Learn the sound /o͞o/.
- ▸ Learn the sound /ow/.
- ▸ Distinguish between words that rhyme or sound different.
- ▸ Identify individual sounds and syllables in words.
- ▸ Learn and practice blends.
- ▸ Learn to put phrases together to make sentences.

Materials

Supplied
- *K¹² PhonicsWorks Basic Activity Book*, p. PH 29
- whiteboard, Learning Coach
- whiteboard, student
- Tile Kit

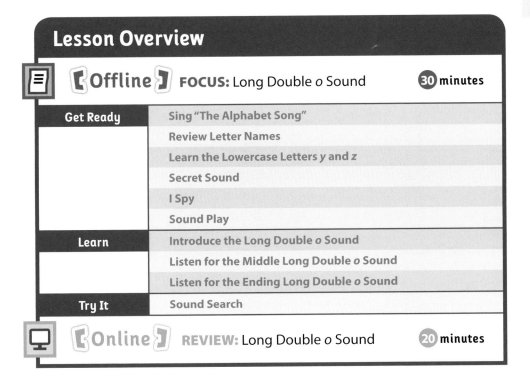

Lesson Overview

≡ [Offline] FOCUS: Long Double *o* Sound — **30 minutes**

Get Ready	Sing "The Alphabet Song"
	Review Letter Names
	Learn the Lowercase Letters *y* and *z*
	Secret Sound
	I Spy
	Sound Play
Learn	Introduce the Long Double *o* Sound
	Listen for the Middle Long Double *o* Sound
	Listen for the Ending Long Double *o* Sound
Try It	Sound Search

🖥 [Online] REVIEW: Long Double *o* Sound — **20 minutes**

Advance Preparation

Place lowercase letter tiles *a* through *x* and uppercase letter tiles *Y* through *Z* in alphabetical order on your whiteboard. Place lowercase letter tiles *y* and *z* at the bottom of students' whiteboard.

 **30 minutes**

FOCUS: Long Double *o* Sound

Work **together** with students to complete offline Get Ready, Learn, and Try It activities.

Get Ready

Sing the "Alphabet Song"

To help students become familiar and comfortable with the alphabet, sing "The Alphabet Song" with them. Sing slowly, so that students may touch each letter on your whiteboard as they sing the letter's name.

Objectives
- Identify letters of the alphabet.
- Identify capital and lowercase letters.
- Match capital letters to lowercase letters.
- Identify individual sounds in words.
- Identify ending sounds in words.

Review Letter Names

To help students learn the alphabet, have them practice identifying and naming the letters *g, h, l, j, x, y,* and *z*. Grab your whiteboard with letters.

1. Point to each letter and have students touch and name each one.

    g   h   l   j   x   y   z

2. Say the name of each letter. After each one, have students repeat the name and touch the tile.

    g   h   l   j   x   y   z

3. Redirect students if they name a letter incorrectly.

    ▸ Name the letter students missed.
    ▸ Have students touch the letter and say its name.
    ▸ Have students trace the shape of the letter with their finger on the brown side of their board, and have them say the letter's name as they trace the shape.
    ▸ If students name a letter incorrectly twice, point to the letter and tell them its name. Have students touch the letter and say its name.

Learn the Lowercase Letters *y* and *z*

To help students learn lowercase letters of the alphabet, have them practice identifying and naming the letters *y* and *z*.

1. **Say:** There are two different kinds of letters in our alphabet. The ones you already know are called capital, or uppercase, letters. The other kind of letters are called lowercase, or small, letters. These letters are smaller than capital letters.

2. **Say:** We're going to learn two lowercase letters today. The letters are *y* and *z*.

3. Have students touch each lowercase letter on their whiteboard and say its name.

4. **Say:** I'm going to put these letters on my whiteboard in place of the capital letters for *y* and *z*.

5. Move the uppercase *Y* and *Z* tiles from your whiteboard to the Tile Kit, and replace them with the lowercase *y* and *z* tiles.

6. Have students sing "The Alphabet Song," touching the lowercase letters *a* through *z*.

Secret Sound

Say groups of words to help students recognize **middle sounds** in words.

1. **Say:** I am going to say some groups of words. Listen for a secret sound in the middle of each word. Then tell me what sound you hear in the middle of each group of words.

2. Say each of the following groups of words. Have students identify the secret sound in each group.

   ▶ *box, shop, knob, stop* /ŏ/
   ▶ *make, shape, brave, cane* /ā/
   ▶ *point, join, foil, hoist* /oi/
   ▶ *mile, like, find, bride* /ī/

TIP If students can't identify the secret sound, have them listen while you say each word again and then have them repeat each word. Have students say what sound they hear in the middle of each word.

I Spy

Have students name and use common objects to help them recognize individual sounds in words.

1. Explain to students that you will be playing I Spy, and show them how to use the thumb and index finger to make a circle, simulating a spyglass.

2. **Say:** I say, "I spy, with my little eye, something that starts with the sound /l/." Your job is to guess what I spy. What I had in mind was the *light. Light* begins with the sound /l/.

3. Repeat Step 2 with a different object in the room.

4. **Say:** Are you ready to begin? I spy, with my little eye, something that starts with the sound [target sound]. Can you guess what it is?

5. After students have guessed the object, repeat Step 4 until you have spied six objects, or until students tire of the game. Possible words to use are *shirt, book, plant, floor, dust, leg,* and *wall.*

6. Redirect students if they name an object with an incorrect sound.

   Say: The sound that begins the word [word] is [sound]. We're looking for something that begins with the sound [target sound]. What is a word that begins with that sound? Now look around the room. What do you see that begins with that sound?

7. Narrow down the search to a certain part of the room if students become frustrated. If students continue to have trouble, narrow down the search to two objects.

   Say: What is the beginning sound of [target word]? What is the beginning sound of [another word]? Which one starts with the sound [target sound]?

Sound Play

Help students use color tiles to represent the sounds in words. Grab the color tiles from the Tile Kit.

1. Place the tiles on a table.

2. **Say:** Let's use tiles to stand for sounds in words.

   ▸ I'll say a word and the sounds in that word. I'll build the word *fish*: /f/ /ĭ/ /sh/.
   ▸ I'll put a tile down for each sound in the word. The sounds are different, so I'll use three different colors of tiles. Then I'll touch each tile and say the sound it represents.
   ▸ Next I'll blend the sounds into a word and say the word while running my finger under the three color tiles: /f/ . . . /ĭ/ . . . /sh/ . . . *fish*.

3. **Say:** I'll say another word, *same*. Listen for the different sounds you hear in the word.

   ▸ You'll place a different color tile for each sound in the word. There are three different sounds, so you'll use three different colors.
   ▸ If the word uses the same sound more than once, use the same color of the tile for sounds that are the same. For example in the word *none*, the sound /n/ is used at the beginning and end of the word, so you'll use the same color tile at the beginning and end.
   ▸ You'll touch each tile and say the sound it represents. Next you'll blend the sounds into a word and say the word while running your finger under the color tiles.

4. Say each of the following words. Have students place a different color tile for each different sound in the word.

   ▸ *same* /s/ /ā/ /m/
   ▸ *ridge* /r/ /ĭ/ /j/
   ▸ *match* /m/ /ă/ /ch/
   ▸ *at* /ă/ /t/
   ▸ *mat* /m/ /ă/ /t/
   ▸ *tub* /t/ /ŭ/ /b/
   ▸ *nine* /n/ /ī/ /n/

Learn

Introduce the Long Double *o* Sound
Teach the sound /o͞o/, as in *too*, *who*, and *moo*.

1. **Say:** We're going to play a game to practice the **sound /o͞o/**, which is the sound heard at the end of the word *too*. Listen: *tooooo*. Your job is to say the sound just like me and do what I do, too.

2. Put your hand over your mouth and say "Oooops." Have students do this, too.

3. **Say:** We make some sounds with a whisper and some sounds with our voice. Let's figure out whether the sound /o͞o/ is whispered or voiced. Say /o͞o/ and put your fingers on the lump in your throat called your voice box.

   ▸ Do you feel your voice box vibrate? Yes, /o͞o/ is a noisy sound because we do use our voice box when we make the sound.

4. **Say:** Now I'll say some words that end with the sound /o͞o/ and you'll repeat them, saying /o͞o/ just the way I do.

   too   *who*   *moo*

Objectives
- Identify and use the long double *o* sound.
- Identify ending sounds in words.
- Identify middle sounds in words.

Listen for the Middle Long Double *o* Sound
Present pairs of words to help students recognize middle sounds.

1. **Say:** I'm going to say two words. Listen for the **middle sound /o͞o/**. Then tell me the word that has that middle sound. For example, if I say *school* and *smile*, you'll say *school* because /o͞o/ is the middle sound in *school*.

2. Say each pair of words. Have students identify the word that has the middle sound /o͞o/.

   ▸ *moose* or *mouse* moose
   ▸ *pool* or *hound* pool
   ▸ *geese* or *goose* goose

Listen for the Ending Long Double *o* Sound
Present pairs of words to help students recognize ending sounds.

1. **Say:** I'm going to say two words. Listen for the **ending sound /o͞o/**. Then tell me the word that has that ending sound. For example, if I say *too* and *tea*, you'll say *too* because /o͞o/ is the ending sound in *too*.

2. Say each pair of words. Have students identify the word that has the ending sound /o͞o/.

   ▸ *shoe* or *slow* shoe
   ▸ *meow* or *moo* moo
   ▸ *bye* or *boo* boo

Try It

Sound Search

Have students complete page PH 29 in *K¹² PhonicsWorks Basic Activity Book* for more practice with the sound /o͞o/. First have students say the name of each picture. Then have them circle pictures whose name contains the sound /o͞o/.

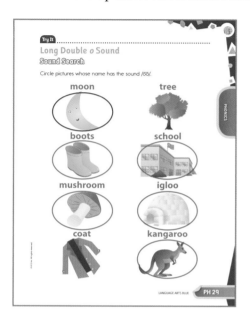

Objectives

- Identify and use the long double *o* sound.
- Identify middle sounds in words.

Online · 20 minutes

REVIEW: Long Double *o* Sound

Students will work online independently to

▶ Practice the sound /o͞o/.

Help students locate the online activities and provide support as needed.

Objectives

- Identify and use the long double *o* sound.
- Identify middle sounds in words.

Offline Alternative

No computer access? Have students point out and name things or words that contain the sound /o͞o/ (for example, *food* or *broom*).

Sound /ow/

Lesson Overview

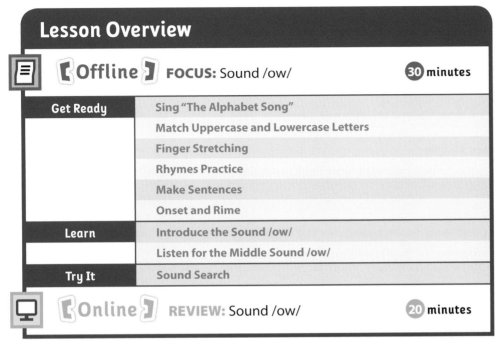

Offline FOCUS: Sound /ow/ — 30 minutes

Get Ready	Sing "The Alphabet Song"
	Match Uppercase and Lowercase Letters
	Finger Stretching
	Rhymes Practice
	Make Sentences
	Onset and Rime
Learn	Introduce the Sound /ow/
	Listen for the Middle Sound /ow/
Try It	Sound Search

Online REVIEW: Sound /ow/ — 20 minutes

Materials

Supplied
- *K¹² PhonicsWorks Basic Activity Book,* p. PH 30
- whiteboard, Learning Coach
- whiteboard, student
- Tile Kit

Advance Preparation

Place lowercase letter tiles in alphabetical order on your whiteboard.

 **Offline** 30 minutes

FOCUS: Sound /ow/

Work **together** with students to complete offline Get Ready, Learn, and Try It activities.

Get Ready •••

Sing "The Alphabet Song"

To help students become familiar and comfortable with the alphabet, sing "The Alphabet Song" with them. Sing slowly, so that students may touch each letter on your whiteboard as they sing the letter's name.

Objectives

- Identify letters of the alphabet.
- Identify capital and lowercase letters.
- Match capital letters to lowercase letters.
- Identify individual sounds in words.
- Identify the number of sounds within words.
- Identify words that rhyme.
- Orally create sentences from phrases.
- Identify a word when given the onset and rime.
- Blend sounds to create words.

Match Uppercase and Lowercase Letters

To help students learn to recognize the difference between lowercase and uppercase letters of the alphabet, have them practice identifying and naming letters. Grab your whiteboard with letters.

1. Place the following uppercase letters in random order on students' whiteboard in a horizontal row: *A, G, H, L, M, Q, R, Y,* and *Z.*

2. Point to a letter and have students name it.

3. Have students select the matching lowercase letter from your whiteboard.

4. Have students place the lowercase letter under the uppercase letter to make a pair.

TIP If students have difficulty with this activity, have them practice naming the letters in the alphabet. When they can name all the letters in the correct order, have them touch and name the lowercase and uppercase letters for each letter.

Finger Stretching

Use finger stretching to help students identify individual sounds in words.

1. **Say:** Let's review finger stretching. In the word *set,* the first sound is /s/, the middle sound is /ĕ/, and the last sound is /t/. I will finger stretch each sound as I say it. Then I'll say the word and while pulling my fist toward my body.

2. Finger stretch the word *set* for students.

3. **Say:** I'm going to say words with several sounds in them. You'll say each word and then finger stretch it while you say each sound in the word.

4. Say the following words and have students finger stretch them. After they finger stretch each word, ask them the questions for that word.

> ▸ *tell* /t/ /ĕ/ /l/   What is the first sound? /t/
>   How many sounds are there? three
> ▸ *shoe* /sh/ /o͞o/   What is the last sound? /o͞o/
>   How many sounds are there? two
> ▸ *desk* /d/ /ĕ/ /s/ /k/   What is the first sound? /d/
>   How many sounds are there? four
> ▸ *tool* /t/ /o͞o/ /l/   What is the middle sound? /o͞o/
>   How many sounds are there? three
> ▸ *itch* /ĭ/ /ch/   What is the first sound? /ĭ/
>   How many sounds are there? two
> ▸ *rich* /r/ /ĭ/ /ch/   What is the middle sound? /ĭ/
>   How many sounds are there? three

 TIP Refer to the *K¹² PhonicsWorks* video for a demonstration of finger stretching.

Rhymes Practice

Use common phrases to practice identifying rhyming words.

1. **Say:** I am going to name something that is loaded into a big truck. Your job is to think of something else that rhymes with what I put into the truck.

   > ▸ For example, if I say, "I've got a truck and it's loaded with *coats*," you might say, "I've got a truck and it's loaded with *goats*!"
   > ▸ We will take turns thinking of rhyming words. I'll go first.
   > ▸ "I've got a truck and it's loaded with *cars*." What can you put in the truck that rhymes with *cars*?

2. Continue this activity with these words: *dogs, hats, phones.*

TIP If students have difficulty thinking of a word, say the beginning sound of a possible word.

Make Sentences

Help students practice using phrases to make sentences.

1. **Say:** A sentence is made up of words. A phrase is a part of a sentence.

2. **Say:** Let's make some sentences from phrases. I'll say some words and you'll repeat them. Then you'll find different ways to make those words into a sentence. For example, if I say, "the dog," you might say, "The dog howled all night" or "The dog was scratching at the door."

3. Say the following phrases. Have students use each phrase to make two different sentences.

  ▸ *my friend Rick*
  ▸ *the path in the woods*
  ▸ *six little rabbits*
  ▸ *got up early in the morning*

Onset and Rime

In a word, the part of the syllable before the first vowel sound is the **onset**. The part of the syllable after the first vowel sound is the **rime**. For example, in *dog*, /d/ is the onset and *og* is the rime. Help students put together words that are broken down into parts by onset and rime.

1. **Say:** I'm going to break a word into two parts. Your job is to put the parts together and say the word. If the first part of a word is /h/ and the last part of the word is *ouse*, then the whole word is *house*: /h/ . . . *ouse* . . . *house*.

2. Say the following pairs of word parts. Have students tell you the word that each pair forms.

  ▸ /ch/ . . . *oice choice*
  ▸ /m/ . . . *ath math*
  ▸ /k/ . . . *ite kite*
  ▸ /kw/ . . . *ite quite*
  ▸ /kw/ . . . *ick quick*

Learn

Introduce the Sound /ow/

Teach the sound /ow/, as in *ouch*, *out*, and *ounce*.

1. **Say:** We're going to play a game to practice the **sound /ow/**. Your job is to say the sound just like me and do what I do, too.

2. Gently pinch yourself and say, "Ouch." Have students do this, too.

3. **Say:** We make some sounds with a whisper and some sounds with our voice. Let's figure out whether the sound /ow/ is whispered or voiced. Say /ow/ and put your fingers on the lump in your throat called your voice box.

  ▸ Do you feel your voice box vibrate? Yes, /ow/ is a noisy sound because we use our voice box when we make the sound.

4. **Say:** I'll say some words that start with the sound /ow/ and you'll repeat them, saying /ow/ just the way I do.

  ouch   out   ounce

5. **Say:** Now I'll say some words that end with the sound /ow/ and you'll repeat them, saying /ow/ just the way I do.

  now   cow   how

Objectives

- Identify and use the sound /ow/.
- Identify beginning sounds in words.
- Identify ending sounds in words.
- Identify middle sounds in words.

Listen for the Middle Sound /ow/

Present pairs of words to help students recognize middle sounds.

1. **Say:** I'm going to say two words. Listen for the **middle sound /ow/**. Then tell me the word that has that middle sound. For example, if I say *sound* and *end*, you'll say *sound* because /ow/ is the middle sound in *sound*.

2. Say each pair of words. Have students identify the word that has the middle sound /ow/.

   ► *blue* or *brown* brown
   ► *south* or *north* south
   ► *pound* or *scale* pound

TIP If students have difficulty identifying the correct word, say the words again and emphasize the middle sound.

Try It

Sound Search

Have students complete page PH 30 in *K¹² PhonicsWorks Basic Activity Book* for more practice with the sound /ow/. First have students say the name of each picture. Then have them circle pictures whose name contains the sound /ow/.

Objectives
- Identify and use the sound /ow/.
- Identify individual sounds in words.

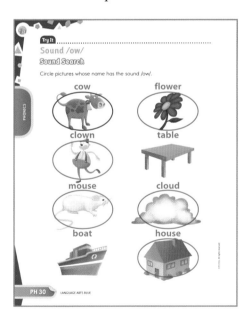

 **20 minutes**

REVIEW: **Sound /ow/**

Students will work online independently to

▶ Practice the sound /ow/.

Help students locate the online activities and provide support as needed.

Objectives
- Identify and use the sound /ow/.
- Identify individual sounds in words.

Offline Alternative

No computer access? Have students point out and name things or words that contain the sound /ow/ (for example, *frown* or *loud*).

Sound Practice (A)

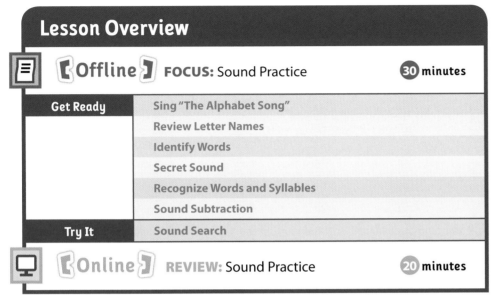

Lesson Overview

Offline FOCUS: Sound Practice — **30** minutes

Get Ready	Sing "The Alphabet Song"
	Review Letter Names
	Identify Words
	Secret Sound
	Recognize Words and Syllables
	Sound Subtraction
Try It	Sound Search

Online REVIEW: Sound Practice — **20** minutes

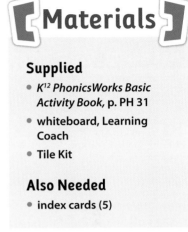

Materials

Supplied
- *K¹² PhonicsWorks Basic Activity Book*, p. PH 31
- whiteboard, Learning Coach
- Tile Kit

Also Needed
- index cards (5)

Advance Preparation

Place lowercase letter tiles in alphabetical order on your whiteboard.

 **30 minutes**

FOCUS: Sound Practice
Work **together** with students to complete offline Get Ready, Learn, and Try It activities.

Get Ready

Sing "The Alphabet Song"
To help students become familiar and comfortable with the alphabet, sing "The Alphabet Song" with them. Sing slowly, so that students may touch each letter on your whiteboard as they sing the letter's name.

Review Letter Names
To help students learn the alphabet, have them practice identifying and naming the letters *b, c, d, e, f, g, h, i, t, u, v,* and *w*. Grab your whiteboard with letters.

1. Point to each letter and have students touch and name each one.

    b   c   d   e   f   g   h   i   t   u   v   w

2. Say the name of each letter. After each one, have students repeat the name and touch the tile.

    b   c   d   e   f   g   h   i   t   u   v   w

3. Redirect students if they name a letter incorrectly.

    ► Name the letter students missed.
    ► Have students touch the letter and say its name.
    ► Have students trace the shape of the letter with their finger on the brown side of their board, and have them say the letter's name as they trace the shape.
    ► If students name a letter incorrectly twice, point to the letter and tell them its name. Have students touch the letter and say its name.

Identify Words
Help students identify the number of words in a phrase or sentence.

1. Gather five index cards.

2. **Say:** A sentence is made up of words. A phrase is a part of a sentence. We read words in a sentence or phrase from left to right

3. **Say:** Let's use index cards to stand for words in phrases.

    ► The phrase *the red box* has three words, so I'll place three index cards on the table and put them next to each other.
    ► I'll say *the* as I touch the first card, *red* as I touch the second card, and *box* as I touch the third card.
    ► Now you touch the cards and say the words *the red box*.

Objectives
- Identify letters of the alphabet.
- Demonstrate one-to-one correspondence.
- Identify middle sounds in words.
- Identify syllables in words.
- Identify the number of syllables in a word.
- Identify beginning sounds in words.

4. Remove the cards from the table. Give students the stack of cards.

5. Say the following words and phrases. Have students put one card on the table for each word you say. Have them repeat the word as they put down the card. Have students pick up the cards between each example.

> ► *red bicycle*
> ► *new red bicycle*
> ► *rusty red bicycle*
> ► *jar*
> ► *honey jar*
> ► *the honey jar*
> ► *moon*
> ► *The moon is full.*
> ► *shirt*
> ► *My shirt has short sleeves.*

TIP If students can't identify the number of words in a phrase, say the phrase again and lay down an index card for each word you say. Have students count the cards and say how many words are in the phrase.

Secret Sound

Say groups of words that have the same middle sound to help students recognize **middle sounds** in words.

1. **Say:** I am going to say some groups of words. Listen for a secret sound in the middle of each word. Then tell me what sound you hear at the middle of each group of words.

2. Say each of the following groups of words. Have students identify the secret sound in each group.

> ► *soon, scoop, choose, lose* /o͞o/
> ► *cast, pack, tag, laugh* /ă/
> ► *mint, hid, thick, his* /ĭ/
> ► *men, kept, shed, friend* /ĕ/

TIP If students can't identify the secret sound, have them listen while you say each word again and then have them repeat each word. Have them say what sound they hear in the middle of each word.

Recognize Words and Syllables

Practice syllables with students.

1. **Say:** When we talk, we make words by pushing air out of our mouths. Each push of air in a word is called a **syllable**. Each word has one or more syllables. You can think of syllables as chunks of words.

2. **Say:** Let's break some words into syllables.

   - I'll say a word. I'll repeat the word.
   - You'll say the word after me, and you'll break it into syllables by saying the separate chunks of the word and tapping your fist on the table as you say each chunk.
   - For example, I'll say *kitten,* and then I'll say it again.
   - You will say *kit / ten* and tap your fist on the table as you say each syllable.

3. Say each word and repeat it. Have students fist tap on the table as they say the syllables in each word.

   - *jacket* ja / cket
   - *coat* coat
   - *umbrella* um / brel / la
   - *sweater* swea / ter
   - *boots* boots
   - *parka* par / ka

   TIP Have students name items in the room and fist tap the syllables with you. For example, have them name and fist tap words such as foods, furniture, or animals.

Sound Subtraction

Present pairs of words to improve students' ability to distinguish between sounds.

1. **Say:** Let's play a game with the sounds in words. I'll say a word and you'll repeat it. Then I'll subtract the first sound from the word and say a new word. Your job is to say the new word and tell me what sound I took away. For example,

   - If I say *fear,* you'll repeat the word.
   - Then I'll take away the first sound from *fear* and say the new word, which is *ear.*
   - When I ask you what sound I subtracted from *fear,* you'll say /f/.

2. Say each pair of words. Have students tell you what sound or sounds you subtracted from the first word.

   - *sink* and *ink* /s/
   - *shore* and *or* /sh/
   - *pitch* and *itch* /p/
   - *cape* and *ape* /k/
   - *thunder* and *under* /th/
   - *stick* and *ick* /st/
   - *brick* and *rick* /b/
   - *blink* and *link* /b/

Try It

Sound Search

Have students complete page PH 31 in *K¹² PhonicsWorks Basic Activity Book* for more practice with the sound /o͞o/. First have students say the name of each picture. Then, have students circle pictures whose name contains the sound /o͞o/.

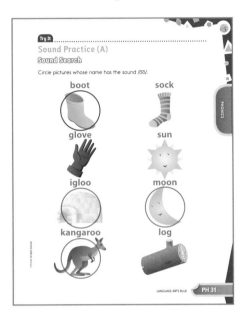

 **Online** **20** minutes

REVIEW: Sound Practice

Students will work online independently to

▶ Identify letters.
▶ Count sounds in words.
▶ Make new words by subtracting sounds.
▶ Count syllables in words.

Help students locate the online activities and provide support as needed.

Offline Alternative

No computer access? Have students point out and name things or words that contain the sounds /o͞o/ and /ow/ (for example, *food* and *brown*). You might also have students name letters that they see, count sounds in words, make new words by subtracting sounds, and count syllables in words.

Sound Practice (B)

Lesson Overview

Offline FOCUS: Sound Practice — **30** minutes

Practice	Right Hand Awareness
	Sing "The Alphabet Song"
	Review Letter Names
	Scrambled Letters
	Finger Stretching
	Add Sounds to Words
	Listen for Middle Sounds
	Sound Chains
Try It	Guide Words

Online REVIEW: Sound Practice — **20** minutes

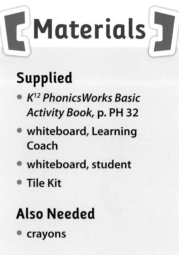

Materials

Supplied
- *K¹² PhonicsWorks Basic Activity Book*, p. PH 32
- whiteboard, Learning Coach
- whiteboard, student
- Tile Kit

Also Needed
- crayons

Advance Preparation

Place lowercase letter tiles in alphabetical order on both your and students' whiteboards.

 **30 minutes**

FOCUS: Sound Practice

Work **together** with students to complete offline Practice and Try It activities.

Practice

Right Hand Awareness

Students read from left to right, so play a game to develop right hand awareness. To avoid confusion, focus on the right hand only.

1. Say each sentence and do each action. Have students repeat your words and actions.

   ▸ I'm shaking your right hand.
   ▸ Now I'm touching my right ankle.
   ▸ Now I'm waving my right hand in the air.
   ▸ Now I'm touching my right toe.
   ▸ Now I'm touching my right cheek.

2. Repeat the actions and mix up the order. To end the activity, shake right hands again.

Sing "The Alphabet Song"

To help students become familiar and comfortable with the alphabet, sing "The Alphabet Song" with them. Sing slowly, so that students may touch each letter on your whiteboard as they sing the letter's name.

Review Letter Names

To help students learn the alphabet, have them practice identifying and naming the letters *c, f, i, l, r,* and *z.* Grab your whiteboard with letters.

1. Point to each letter and have students touch and name each one.

   c   f   i   l   r   z

2. Say the name of each letter. After each one, have students repeat the name and touch the tile.

   c   f   i   l   r   z

3. Redirect students if they name a letter incorrectly.

   ▸ Name the letter students missed.
   ▸ Have students touch the letter and say its name.
   ▸ Have students trace the shape of the letter with their finger on the brown side of their board, and have them say the letter's name as they trace the shape.
   ▸ If students name a letter correctly twice, point to the letter and tell them its name. Have students touch the letter and say its name.

Objectives

- Develop right hand awareness.
- Identify letters of the alphabet.
- Identify individual sounds in words.
- Identify the number of sounds within words.
- Identify and use the long double *o* sound.
- Identify and use the sound /ow/.
- Identify the new word when one sound is added to word.
- Identify middle sounds in words.
- Identify and use vowels and vowel sounds.
- Identify the new word when one sound is changed in a word.

Scrambled Letters

To help students learn the alphabet, have them practice identifying and naming letters.

1. Place the following letter tiles in random order on students' whiteboard: *b, c, d, j, k, l, x, y,* and *z.*

2. Have students arrange the letters in alphabetical order.

TIP Students may find this activity easier if they slowly sing "The Alphabet Song" to themselves as they work.

Finger Stretching

Use finger stretching to help students identify individual sounds in words.

1. **Say:** Let's review finger stretching. In the word *couch,* the first sound is /k/, the middle sound is /ow/, and the last sound is /ch/. I will finger stretch each sound as I say it. Then I'll say the word, while pulling my fist toward my body.

2. Finger stretch the word *couch* for students.

3. **Say:** I'm going to say words with several sounds in them. You'll say each word and then finger stretch it while you say each sound in the word.

4. Say the following words and have students finger stretch them. After they finger stretch each word, ask them the question for that word.

   ▸ *boot* /b/ /o͞o/ /t/   How many sounds are in the word? three
   ▸ *food* /f/ /o͞o/ /d/   How many sounds are in the word? three
   ▸ *town* /t/ /ow/ /n/   How many sounds are in the word? three
   ▸ *cow* /k/ /ow/   How many sounds are in the word? two
   ▸ *chow* /ch/ /ow/   How many sounds are in the word? two

TIP Refer to the *K¹² PhonicsWorks* video for a demonstration of finger stretching.

Add Sounds to Words

Help students make new words by adding **beginning sounds** to words.

1. **Say:** Let's make new words by adding sounds. I'll say a word and you'll repeat it. Then I'll add a sound to the beginning of the word and you'll say the new word. For example, I'll say *each* and you'll repeat it. Then I'll add the sound /r/ to *each* and you'll say *reach.*

2. Say the following words and beginning sounds. Have students say the new word.

   ▸ *ouch*…/k/ *couch*
   ▸ *itch*…/p/ *pitch*
   ▸ *ick*…/kw/ *quick*

Listen for Middle Sounds

Help students recognize **middle vowel sounds** in words.

1. **Say:** I'm going to say a word. Your job is to listen for the middle sound. For example, if I say *lap,* you'll say /ă/ because /ă/ is the middle sound in *lap.*

2. Say each word. Have students identify the middle sound.

  ► *fish* /ĭ/
  ► *match* /ă/
  ► *phone* /ō/
  ► *meet* /ē/
  ► *tribe* /ī/
  ► *rude* /o͞o/
  ► *read* /ē/
  ► *gown* /ow/

TIP If students incorrectly name the sound, say the word again and draw out or repeat the middle vowel sound (for example, *reeeead*).

Sound Chains
Help students use color tiles to represent the sounds in words. Grab the color tiles from a Tile Kit.

1. Place the tiles on the table.

2. **Say:** Let's use tiles to stand for sounds in words.

  ► I'll say a word and the sounds in that word. The word *run* has three sounds: /r/ /ŭ/ /n/.
  ► I'll put a tile down for each sound in the word. The sounds are different, so I'll use three different colors of tiles. Then I'll touch each tile and say the sound it represents.
  ► Next I'll blend the sounds into a word and say the word while running my finger under the three color tiles: /r/ . . . /ŭ/ . . . /n/ . . . *run.*

3. **Say:** I'll say another word, *sun*, which has three sounds: /s/ /ŭ/ /n/. Listen for the sound that changed in the word.

  ► You'll change the color of the tile for the first sound only, because the sound /r/ in *run* changed to /s/ in *sun*, but the second and third sounds, /ŭ/ and /n/, stayed the same.
  ► You'll touch each tile and say the sound it represents. Next you'll blend the three sounds into a word and say the word while running your finger under the three color tiles.

4. Say the word *bun*. Ask students the questions for the word to reinforce the process.

  ► What are the sounds in this word? /b/ /ŭ/ /n/
  ► Which sounds stay the same? /ŭ/ and /n/
  ► Which sound changes? /s/ changes to /b/

5. Say each of the following words. Have students change the color of the tile for the sound that changes.

  ► *bin* second sound
  ► *tin* first sound
  ► *tan* second sound
  ► *man* first sound
  ► *ran* first sound

TIP If students struggle, try using the following words with only two sounds: *see, bee, me, my, tie, toe,* and *so.*

Try It

Guide Words

Have students complete page PH 32 in *K¹² PhonicsWorks Basic Activity Book* for more practice with sounds. First have students say the name of each picture. Then have them say the vowel sound in the name of the picture while they color the picture. Finally have students say a word that has the same beginning vowel sound.

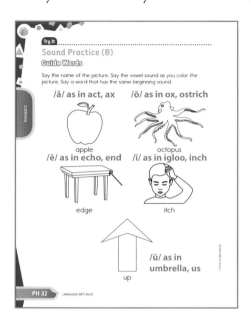

Objectives
- Identify beginning sounds in words.
- Identify short vowel sounds.
- Identify and use the long double *o* sound.
- Identify and use the sound /ow/.
- Identify individual sounds in words.

Online 20 minutes

REVIEW: Sound Practice

Students will work online independently to

- ▸ Identify letters.
- ▸ Count sounds in words.
- ▸ Make new words by adding sounds.
- ▸ Identify middle sounds in words.

Help students locate the online activities and provide support as needed.

Objectives
- Identify and use the long double *o* sound.
- Identify and use the sound /ow/.
- Identify individual sounds in words.

Offline Alternative

No computer access? Have students point out and name things or words that contain the sounds /o͞o/ and /ow/ (for example, *pool* and *town*). You might also have students name letters that they see, count sounds in words, make new words by adding sounds, and identify middle sounds in words.

Unit Checkpoint

Lesson Overview

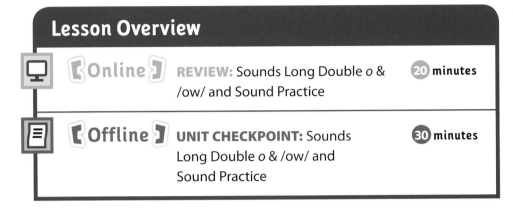

🖥	**〖Online〗**	**REVIEW:** Sounds Long Double *o* & /ow/ and Sound Practice	**20** minutes
📄	**〖Offline〗**	**UNIT CHECKPOINT:** Sounds Long Double *o* & /ow/ and Sound Practice	**30** minutes

Materials

Supplied
- *K¹² PhonicsWorks Basic Assessments,* pp. PH 37–42

Objectives
- Identify and use the long double *o* sound.
- Identify and use the sound /ow/.
- Identify letters of the alphabet.
- Identify capital and lowercase letters.
- Match capital letters to lowercase letters.
- Identify words that rhyme.
- Identify beginning sounds in words.
- Identify ending sounds in words.
- Identify individual sounds in words.
- Identify a word when given the onset and rime.
- Blend sounds to create words.

 **〖Online〗** **20** minutes

REVIEW: Sounds Long Double *o* & /ow/ and Sound Practice

Students will review the sounds /o͞o/ and /ow/, and practice identifying letters, sounds, and rhymes to prepare for the Unit Checkpoint. Help students locate the online activities and provide support as needed.

 **30 minutes**

UNIT CHECKPOINT: Sounds Long Double *o* & /ow/ and Sound Practice

Explain that students are going to show what they have learned about letters, sounds, syllables, and words.

1. Give students the Unit Checkpoint pages for the Sounds Long Double *o* & /ow/ and Sound Practice unit and print the Unit Checkpoint Answer Key, if you'd like.

2. Use the instructions below to help administer the Checkpoint to students. On the Answer Key or another sheet of paper, note student answers to oral response questions to help with scoring the Checkpoint later.

3. Use the Answer Key to score the Checkpoint, and then enter the results online.

Part 1. Letter Matching Moving from left to right, have students read the letters aloud and circle the letter or letters that match the first letter in the row.

Part 2. Match Middle Sounds Have students say the name of each picture and draw a line to connect pictures that have the same middle sound.

Part 3. Rhymes Say each pair of words and have students say if the word pairs rhyme. Note any incorrect responses.

9. *moon, soon*
10. *cow, so*
11. *mouse, blouse*

12. *book, shook*
13. *grow, show*
14. *loud, load*

Part 4. Ending Sounds Say each group of three words, and have students say which words end with the same sound. Repeat the words, as necessary. Note any incorrect responses.

15. *fox, lock, box*
16. *boy, boo, joy*
17. *ray, paw, claw*
18. *pinch, fish, wish*

19. *boat, nap, hat*
20. *show, go, me*
21. *hip, hill, tell*
22. *flag, bee, chug*

Part 5. Onset and Rime Say the first sound of each word. Pause briefly and then say the rest of the word. Have students say the whole word aloud. Note any incorrect responses.

23. /m/ . . . *oon*

24. /k/ . . . *ow*

25. /sh/ . . . *ow*

26. /w/ . . . *ood*

27. /h/ . . . *ole*

28. /w/ . . . *ax*

Part 6. Blend Sounds Say each sound in the word. Pause briefly between sounds. Have students repeat the sounds and then blend them together to say a word. Note any incorrect responses.

29. /m/ /$\overline{oo}$/ /n/

30. /s/ /$\overline{oo}$/ /n/

31. /b/ /$\breve{oo}$/ /k/

32. /t/ /ow/ /n/

33. /d/ /ow/ /n/

34. /k/ /$\breve{oo}$/ /k/

Name _____ Date _____

☼ **Unit Checkpoint Answer Key**
Sounds Long Double *o* & /ow/
and Sound Practice

Part 1. Letter Matching
Read across the row from left to right. Circle the letter that matches the first letter in the row.

1.	v	u	(v)	w	x	y
2.	w	n	(w)	m	b	a
3.	x	k	t	(x)	w	u
4.	y	h	v	q	u	(y)
5.	z	f	j	i	(z)	r

Name _____ Date _____

Part 2. Match Middle Sounds
Draw a line to connect the pictures that have the same middle sound.

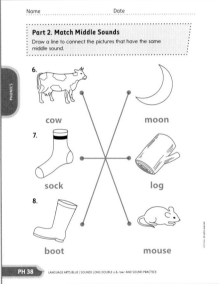

6. cow — moon
7. sock — log
8. boot — mouse

Name _____ Date _____

Part 3. Rhymes
Listen to the pair of words. Do the words rhyme?

9. Yes
10. No
11. Yes
12. Yes
13. Yes
14. No

Name _____ Date _____

Part 4. Ending Sounds
Listen to the group of words. Say which words end with the same sound.

15. fox   box
16. boy   joy
17. paw   claw
18. fish   wish
19. boat   hat
20. show   go
21. hill   tell
22. flag   chug

Name _____ Date _____

Part 5. Onset and Rime
Listen to the sounds. Then, say the whole word.

23. moon
24. cow
25. show
26. wood
27. hole
28. wax

Name _____ Date _____

Part 6. Blend Sounds
Listen to the sounds. Then, say the whole word.

29. moon
30. soon
31. book
32. town
33. down
34. cook

Sounds for Letters *a*, *m*, *s*, and *t*,

Unit Overview

In this unit, students will
- ▶ Identify the letters and sounds of the alphabet.
- ▶ Identify sounds for the letters *a, m, s, t, b, f, c, h,* and *j.*
- ▶ Identify beginning and ending sounds in words.
- ▶ Build words.
- ▶ Learn the sight words *the, and,* and *is.*

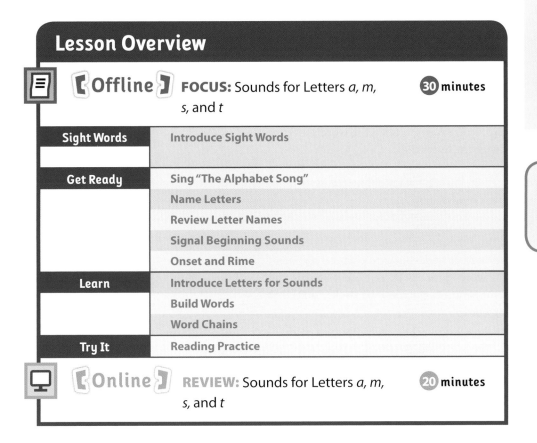

Lesson Overview

Offline FOCUS: Sounds for Letters *a, m, s,* and *t* — 30 minutes

Sight Words	Introduce Sight Words
Get Ready	Sing "The Alphabet Song"
	Name Letters
	Review Letter Names
	Signal Beginning Sounds
	Onset and Rime
Learn	Introduce Letters for Sounds
	Build Words
	Word Chains
Try It	Reading Practice

Online REVIEW: Sounds for Letters *a, m, s,* and *t* — 20 minutes

Advance Preparation

Place lowercase letter tiles in alphabetical order on your whiteboard.

If you have not already done so, create **two sets** of the sight words on 3½ x 5-index cards (the list of words can be found in the Sight Words section of the Lesson Guide introduction). Use a bold black marker and print each word in neat, large, lowercase letters. Keep the two sets of cards somewhere convenient. As you work through the Phonics lessons, you will gradually add these cards to the file box (sight words box).

Offline 30 minutes

FOCUS: Sounds for Letters *a, m, s,* and *t*

Work **together** with students to complete offline Sight Words, Get Ready, Learn, and Try It activities.

Sight Words

Introduce Sight Words

Help students learn the sight words *the, and,* and *is.*

1. Gather the sight word cards *the, and,* and *is.*

2. Show students the *the* card.

3. **Say:** This is the word *the.* We see this word so often that we want to be able to read and spell it quickly without thinking about it. Look closely at the word *the.* Spell the word *the* aloud. Take a picture of the word *the* in your mind. When you think you can spell *the* yourself, turn the card over and use your letter tiles to spell the word *the.* Check the card to see if you spelled the word *the* correctly. Read aloud the word you spelled with the letter tiles.

4. Repeat the activity with the remaining sight words.

5. Chart students' progress on the back of each card.

   ▸ Divide the back of the card into two columns.
   ▸ Label the first column "Read" and the second column "Spell."
   ▸ Record the dates that students read or spell the word correctly. When students can read and spell the word correctly three times in a row, they have mastered the word. You may want to put a star or sticker on the card when they have mastered that word.

6. Add the cards to students' sight words box.

TIP Sight words can be very difficult for some students. Let students work at their own pace and really master these words, as they occur frequently in reading and writing.

Objectives
- Read sight words.
- Spell sight words.

Get Ready

Sing "The Alphabet Song"

To help students become familiar and comfortable with the alphabet, sing "The Alphabet Song" with them. Sing slowly, so that students may touch each letter on your whiteboard as they sing the letter's name.

Name Letters

To help students learn the alphabet, have them practice identifying and naming letters. Grab your whiteboard with letters placed in alphabetical order.

1. **Say:** Let's practice naming letters.

2. Have students touch the first letter in each row on your whiteboard and say the letter's name.

3. Have students touch the last letter in each row and say the letter's name. Repeat the actions and mix up the order.

   ▸ If students name a letter incorrectly, name the letter they missed. Have students touch the letter and say its name. Have them trace the shape of the letter with their finger on the brown side of their board, and have them say the letter's name as they trace the shape.

   ▸ If students name a letter incorrectly twice, point to the letter and tell them its name. Have students touch the letter and say its name.

   ▸ If students continue to struggle with a letter, review that letter with them daily until understanding is achieved.

TIP To help students remember what a row is, run your finger from left to right along a row of letters. Have students do the same. Have them show you another row.

Review Letter Names

To help students learn the alphabet, have them practice identifying and naming the letters *b, j, o, r,* and *y*. Grab your whiteboard with letters.

1. Point to each letter and have students touch and name each one.

   b   j   o   r   y

2. Say the name of each letter. After each one, have students repeat the name and touch the tile.

   b   j   o   r   y

3. Redirect students if they name a letter incorrectly.

   ▸ Name the letter students missed.
   ▸ Have students touch the letter and say its name.
   ▸ Have students trace the shape of the letter with their finger on the brown side of their board, and have them say the letter's name as they trace the shape.
   ▸ If students name a letter correctly twice, point to the letter and tell them its name. Have students touch the letter and say its name.

Objectives

- Identify letters of the alphabet.
- Identify beginning sounds in words.
- Identify individual sounds within words.
- Identify a word when given the onset and rime.
- Blend sounds to create words.

Signal Beginning Sounds

Use a special signal to help students identify **beginning sounds** in words.

1. **Say:** I'm going to tell you a special sound, and then I'll say some words. Repeat each word I say and make a special signal to tell me where the special sound is. If the special sound is at the beginning of the word, tug your ear. If the special sound is **not** at the beginning of the word, just smile at me. For example,

   ▸ If I ask you to listen for the sound /t/ and I say the word *table*, you'll repeat the word *table* and tug your ear because *table* has the sound /t/ at the beginning.

   ▸ If I say the word *pop*, you'll repeat the word *pop* and smile at me because *pop* has the sound /p/, not /t/, at the beginning.

2. Say each sound and group of words. Have students make the special signal to identify the beginning sound.

   ▸ /t/: *table, dinner, Tom, peas, time* tug ear: *table, Tom, time*
   ▸ /s/: *sand, start, zoom, yellow, some* tug ear: *sand, start, some*
   ▸ /ă/: *over, add, apple, under, after* tug ear: *add, apple, after*
   ▸ /m/: *mommy, number, more, taste, monster* tug ear: *mommy, more, monster*

TIP If students can't identify the beginning sound of each word, say the word again and emphasize the beginning sound by repeating it three times (for example, *taste* /t/ /t/ /t/). You can also draw out the beginning sound when you say the word (for example, *mmmustard*). If necessary, have students look at your mouth while you repeat the sounds.

Onset and Rime

In a word, the part of the syllable before the first vowel sound is the **onset**. The part of the syllable after the first vowel sound is the **rime**. For example, in *house*, /h/ is the onset and *ouse* is the rime. Help students put together words that are broken down into parts by onset and rime.

1. **Say:** I'm going to break a word into two parts. Your job is to put the parts together and say the word. If the first part of a word is /h/ and the last part of the word is *ouse*, then the whole word is *house*: /h/ . . . *ouse* . . . *house*.

2. Say the following pairs of word parts. Have students tell you the word that each pair forms.

   ▸ /s/ . . . *ick* sick
   ▸ /b/ . . . *ug* bug
   ▸ /m/ . . . *ost* most

Learn

Introduce Letters for Sounds

To help students learn the lowercase letters *a, m, s,* and *t,* have them practice identifying and naming the letters from the sounds.

1. Place the following letter tiles on students' whiteboard: *a, m, s,* and *t.*

2. **Say:** Let's learn letters for sounds. When we see the letter *a,* we say the sound /ă/. When we see the letter *m,* we say the sound /m/. When we see the letter *s,* we say the sound /s/. When we see the letter *t,* we say the sound /t/.

3. Have students

   ▸ Touch the letter *a* and say /ă/.
   ▸ Touch the letter *m* and say /m/.
   ▸ Touch the letter *s* and say /s/.
   ▸ Touch the letter *t* and say /t/.

4. **Say:** Let's practice these sounds and letters.

5. Say the sounds /ă/, /m/, /s/, and /t/ one at a time. Have students repeat each sound and touch the letter for each sound. It is important for students to touch the letter while they say the sound.

6. Redirect students if they name the letter and not the sound.

   Say: You're right that the name of the letter is [letter]. We want the sound for this letter. What is the sound?

7. Redirect students if they name the sound incorrectly.

   Say: That's the sound of another letter. The sound for this letter is [target sound]. Touch the letter and say the sound.

8. Help students. If they touch the wrong letter, point to the correct letter.

   Say: This is the letter for the sound [target sound]. Touch and say its sound.

Objectives

- Identify the letter, given the sound /ă/.
- Identify the sound, given the letter *a.*
- Identify the letter, given the sound /m/.
- Identify the sound, given the letter *m.*
- Identify the letter, given the sound /s/.
- Identify the sound, given the letter *s.*
- Identify the letter, given the sound /t/.
- Identify the sound, given the letter *t.*
- Identify individual sounds in words.
- Blend sounds to create words.
- Identify the new word when one sound is changed in a word.

Build Words

Help students use letters and sounds to build words.

1. Place the following letter tiles at the top of students' whiteboard: *a, m, s,* and *t.*

2. Draw three horizontal lines across the middle of students' whiteboard to represent the sounds in a word.

3. **Say:** Let's use letters and sounds to build the word *sat.*

4. Have students finger stretch the sounds in *sat.*

5. Have students

   ▸ Identify the first, next, and last sounds in *sat.*
   ▸ Choose the corresponding letter for each sound.
   ▸ Move the letters to the correct lines on their whiteboard.

6. Guide students with these questions:
   ▸ What is the first sound in *sat*? /s/
     Which line does the letter for that sound go on? the first one
   ▸ What is the next sound in *sat*? /ă/
     Which line does the letter for that sound go on? the second one
   ▸ What's the last sound in *sat*? /t/
     Which line does the letter for that sound go on? the last one

7. Have students touch and say the word.

8. Redirect students if they select the incorrect letter.

   Say: That sound is in the word [word], and it is the [first, second, third] sound. We want the sound [target sound].

   Continue until students select the correct letter.

9. Repeat the activity to build the word *mat*. /m/ /ă/ /t/

Word Chains
Have students build words by adding and changing letters to help them recognize and use individual sounds in words.

1. Place the following lowercase letter tiles at the top of students' whiteboard: *a, m, s,* and *t*.

2. **Say:** I am going to build the first word in a chain. The word is *at*.
   ▸ I will pull down the letters for the sounds /ă/ and /t/ to spell the word *at*.
   ▸ I will touch and say *at*. To change *at* to *mat*, I will think about which sound changes from the word *at* to *mat*. I will need to place the letter *m* in front of the letters *at*.
   ▸ Touch and say the word *mat*. Now it's your turn to change *mat* to *sat*. You can spell *sat* by making only one change. Touch and say the new word.

3. If needed, show students that the sound /m/ changes to /s/ when *mat* changes to *sat*, so the letter *m* must change to the letter *s*.

4. Redirect students if they select the incorrect letter for any sound.

   Say: That letter is for the sound [incorrect sound]. We want the letter for the sound [target sound]. What letter makes that sound? Answers wiill vary.

5. Redirect students if they name the sound incorrectly.

   Say: To change the word [first word] to [target word], we need the letter for the sound [target sound].

   Show students how to make the change. Have them touch and say the new word after they move the letters.

6. Follow this procedure to make the following words: *Sam* and *am*.

7. For every new word, have students add, replace, or remove only one letter.

TIP If students struggle, review the sounds and letters that are confusing them.

Try It ....

Reading Practice

Have students complete page PH 33 in *K¹² PhonicsWorks Basic Activity Book* for practice reading words with the letters *a, m, s,* and *t*. Have them touch and read each word aloud. Then they can color the picture.

[Online] ⓴ minutes

REVIEW: Sounds for Letters *a, m, s,* and *t*

Students will work online independently to

▸ Practice sounds for the letters *a, m, s,* and *t*.

Help students locate the online activities and provide support as needed.

___

Offline Alternative

No computer access? Have students name the letters that make the sounds /ă/, /m/, /s/, and /t/. Vice versa, have students name the sounds made by the letters *a, m, s,* and *t*. You might also ask students to spell simple words that contain just the letters *a, m, s,* and *t,* or ask them to think of words that begin with those letters.

Sounds for Letters *b* and *f*

Lesson Overview

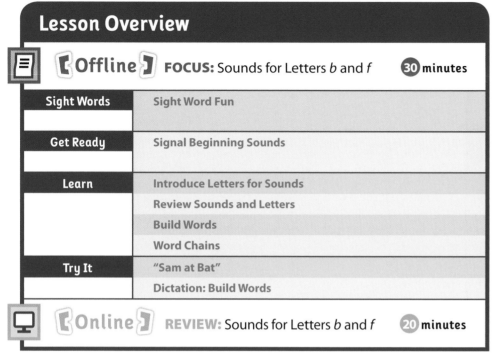

Offline FOCUS: Sounds for Letters *b* and *f*　**30** minutes

Sight Words	Sight Word Fun
Get Ready	Signal Beginning Sounds
Learn	Introduce Letters for Sounds
	Review Sounds and Letters
	Build Words
	Word Chains
Try It	"Sam at Bat"
	Dictation: Build Words

Online REVIEW: Sounds for Letters *b* and *f*　**20** minutes

[Materials]

Supplied
- *K¹² PhonicsWorks Readers Basic 1*, pp. 1–4
- whiteboard, Learning Coach
- whiteboard, student
- Tile Kit

Also Needed
- sight words box

 **30 minutes**

FOCUS: Sounds for Letters *b* and *f*

Work **together** with students to complete offline Sight Words, Get Ready, Learn, and Try It activities.

Sight Words

Sight Word Fun

Help students learn the sight words *the, and,* and *is,* and up to two additional sight words they have yet to master.

1. Gather the sight word cards *the, and,* and *is,* and up to two additional sight word cards.

2. Choose one sight word card to begin.

   Say: Look at this word and take a picture of it in your mind. When you think you can spell the word yourself, turn the card over and use your letter tiles to spell the word.

3. After students spell the word, have them check the card to see if they spelled the word correctly.

   Say: Read aloud the word you spelled with the letter tiles.

4. Repeat the activity with the remaining sight words.

 TIP Sight words can be very difficult for some students. Let students work at their own pace and really master these words.

> **Objectives**
> * Read sight words.
> * Spell sight words.

Get Ready

Signal Beginning Sounds

Use a special signal to help students identify **beginning sounds** in words.

1. **Say:** I'm going to tell you a special sound, and then I'll say some words. Repeat each word I say and make a special signal to tell me where the special sound is. If the special sound is at the beginning of the word, tug your ear. If the special sound is **not** at the beginning of the word, just smile at me. For example,
   * If I ask you to listen for the sound /m/ and I say the word *mat*, you'll repeat the word *mat* and tug your ear because *mat* has the sound /m/ at the beginning.
   * If I say the word *pop*, you'll repeat the word *pop* and smile at me because *pop* has the sound /p/, not /m/, at the beginning.

2. Say each sound and group of words. Have students make the special signal to identify the beginning sound.

   * /f/: *fish, lion, fun, fancy, tiger* tug ear: *fish, fun, fancy*
   * /b/: *day, bank, broom, bust, night* tug ear: *bank, broom, bust*
   * /ă/: *after, even, odd, ask, and* tug ear: *after, ask, and*

> **Objectives**
> * Identify beginning sounds in words.

TIP If students can't identify the beginning sound of each word, say the word again and emphasize the beginning sound by repeating it three times (for example, *taste* /t/ /t/ /t/). You can also draw out the beginning sound when you say the word (for example, *mmmustard*). If necessary, have students look at your mouth while you repeat the sounds.

Learn

Introduce Letters for Sounds

To help students learn the lowercase letters *b* and *f*, have them practice identifying and naming the letters from sounds.

1. Place the following letter tiles on students' whiteboard: *b* and *f*.

2. **Say:** Let's learn sounds for letters. When we see the letter *b*, we say the sound /b/. When we see the letter *f*, we say the sound /f/.

3. Have students
   ▸ Touch the letter *b* and say /b/.
   ▸ Touch the letter *f* and say /f/.

4. **Say:** Let's practice these sounds and letters.

5. Say the sounds /b/ and /f/ one at a time. Have students repeat each sound and touch the letter for each sound. It is important for students to touch the letter while they say the sound.

6. Redirect students if they name the letter and not the sound.

   Say: You're right that the name of the letter is [letter]. We want the sound for this letter. What is the sound?

7. Redirect students if they name the sound incorrectly.

   Say: That's the sound of another letter. The sound for this letter is [target sound]. Touch the letter and say the sound.

8. Help students. If they touch the wrong letter, point to the correct letter.

   Say: This is the letter for the sound [target sound]. Touch and say its sound.

Objectives

- Identify the letter, given the sound /b/.
- Identify the sound, given the letter *b*.
- Identify the letter, given the sound /f/.
- Identify the sound, given the letter *f*.
- Given the letter, identify the most common sound.
- Given the sound, identify the most common letter or letters.
- Identify individual sounds in words.
- Blend sounds to create words.
- Identify the new word when one sound is changed in a word.

Review Sounds and Letters

Help students review the sounds for the letters *a, b, f, m, s,* and *t,* plus any letters that are confusing for them.

1. Place the following letter tiles in random order on students' whiteboard: *a, b, f, m, s, and t,* plus any letters that are confusing.

2. **Say:** Let's go over some letters and sounds.

3. Point to each letter tile and have students say a sound that letter makes.

   ▸ *m* /m/
   ▸ *t* /t/
   ▸ *a* /ă/
   ▸ *s* /s/
   ▸ *b* /b/
   ▸ *f* /f/

4. Say each of the following sounds. Have students repeat the sound and touch the corresponding letter tile.

   ▸ /m/ *m*
   ▸ /t/ *t*
   ▸ /ă/ *a*
   ▸ /s/ *s*
   ▸ /b/ *b*
   ▸ /f/ *f*

5. As you do the activity, point to some letters two or three times so that students don't think they are finished with a sound after they have named it.

6. Redirect students if they say an incorrect sound when you point to a letter.

   Say: That's the sound of another letter. What is the sound for this letter?

7. Help students if they touch the wrong letter after they repeat a sound.

   Say: That letter goes with the sound [sound for incorrect letter]. We're looking for the letter that goes with the sound [target sound].

Build Words

Help students use letters and sounds to build words.

1. Place the following letter tiles at the top of students' whiteboard: *a, b, f,* and *t.*

2. Draw three horizontal lines across the middle of students' whiteboard to represent the sounds in a word.

3. **Say:** Let's use letters and sounds to build the word *bat.*

4. Have students finger stretch the sounds in *bat.*

5. Have students

   ▸ Identify the first, next, and last sounds in *bat.*
   ▸ Choose the corresponding letter for each sound.
   ▸ Move the letters to the correct lines on their whiteboard.

6. Guide students with these questions:

   ▸ What is the first sound in *bat*? /b/
     Which line does the letter for that sound go on? the first one
   ▸ What is the next sound in *bat*? /ă/
     Which line does the letter for that sound go on? the second one
   ▸ What's the last sound in *bat*? /t/
     Which line does the letter for that sound go on? the last one

7. Have students touch and say the word.

8. Redirect students if they select the incorrect letter.

   Say: That sound is in the word [word], and it is the [first, second, third] sound. We want the sound [target sound].

   Continue until students select the correct letter.

9. Repeat the activity to build the word *fat*. /f/ /ă/ /t/

Word Chains

Have students build words by adding and changing letters to help them recognize and use individual sounds in words.

1. Place the following letter tiles at the top of students' whiteboard: *a, b, f, m, s*, and *t*.

2. **Say:** I am going to build the first word in a chain. The word is *sat*.

   ▸ I will pull down the letters for the sounds /s/, /ă/, and /t/ to spell the word *sat*.

   ▸ I will touch and say *sat*. To change *sat* to *mat*, I will think about which sound changes from the word *sat* to *mat*. I will need to replace the letter *s* with the letter *m*.

   ▸ Touch and say the word *mat*. Now it's your turn to change *mat* to *at*. You can spell *at* by making only one change. Touch and say the new word.

3. Redirect students if they seelct the incorrect letter for any sound.

   Say: That letter is for the sound [incorrect sound]. We want the letter for the [target sound]. What letter makes that sound? Answers will vary.

4. Redirect students if they name the sound incorrectly.

   Say: To change the word [first word] to [target word], we need the letter for the sound [target sound].

   Show students how to make the change. Have them touch and say the new word after they move the letters.

5. Follow this procedure to make the following words: *fat, bat, sat, Sam, am, tam, tab*.

6. For every new word, have students add, replace, or remove only one letter.

TIP If students struggle, review the sounds and letters that are confusing them.

Try It

"Sam at Bat"

Have students read "Sam at Bat" on page 1 of *K¹² PhonicsWorks Readers Basic 1*.

   Students should read the story silently once or twice before reading the story aloud. When students miss a word that can be sounded out, point to it and give them three to six seconds to try the word again. If students still miss the word, tell them the word so the flow of the story isn't interrupted.

   After reading the story, make a list of all the words students missed, and go over those words with them. You may use letter tiles to show students how to read the words.

Dictation: Build Words

Have students build words that use the lowercase letters *a, b, f, m, s,* and *t,* and the uppercase letter *S.*

1. Place the following letters at the top of students' whiteboard: lowercase letters *a, b, f, m, s,* and *t,* and uppercase letter *S.*

2. Say the word *fat.* Then give these directions to students:

   ► Repeat the word.
   ► Finger stretch the sounds in the word.
   ► Spell the word with the letter tiles.
   ► Touch and say the word.

3. When students have finished, write the following word on your whiteboard: *fat.*

4. Have them compare their answer to your correct version.

5. Repeat this procedure with the words *tab, sat, mat,* and *Sam.*

   ► If students make an error and don't see it, help them correct their mistake by having them finger stretch the sounds in the word they missed.
   ► If students are having difficulty selecting the correct letters or sounds, review those letters or sounds that are confusing them.
   ► If students have difficulty with first, middle, and last sounds, have them finger stretch the sounds in words.

TIP Remind students that the word *Sam* is a proper name. Have them write the word with a beginning capital letter.

Objectives

- Read aloud grade-level text with appropriate automaticity, prosody, accuracy, and rate.
- Decode words by applying grade-level word analysis skills.
- Track text from left to right.
- Turn pages sequentially.
- Write words by applying grade-level phonics knowledge.
- Follow three-step directions.

 **minutes**

REVIEW: **Sounds for Letters *b* and *f***

Students will work online independently to

▶ Practice sounds for the letters *b* and *f*.

Help students locate the online activities and provide support as needed.

Offline Alternative

No computer access? Have students name the letters that make the sounds /b/ and /f/. Vice versa, have students name the sounds made by the letters *b* and *f*. You might also ask students to spell simple words that contain the letters *b*, *f*, and other letters students have learned, or ask them to think of words that begin with those letters.

Objectives

- Identify the letter, given the sound /b/.
- Identify the sound, given the letter *b*.
- Identify the letter, given the sound /f/.
- Identify the sound, given the letter *f*.
- Identify beginning sounds in words.
- Identify ending sounds in words.

Sounds for Letters *c* and *h*

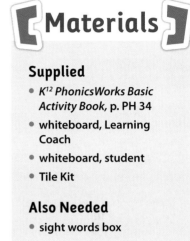

Lesson Overview

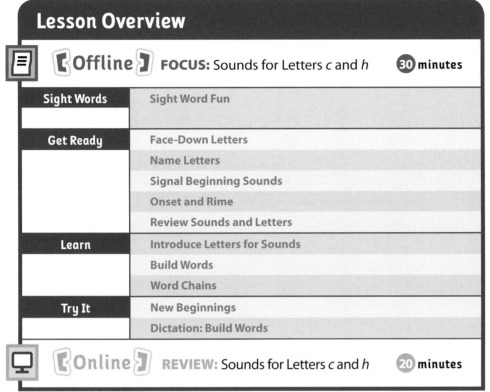

Offline FOCUS: Sounds for Letters *c* and *h* **30** minutes

Sight Words	Sight Word Fun
Get Ready	Face-Down Letters
	Name Letters
	Signal Beginning Sounds
	Onset and Rime
	Review Sounds and Letters
Learn	Introduce Letters for Sounds
	Build Words
	Word Chains
Try It	New Beginnings
	Dictation: Build Words

Online REVIEW: Sounds for Letters *c* and *h* **20** minutes

Materials

Supplied
- *K¹² PhonicsWorks Basic Activity Book,* p. PH 34
- whiteboard, Learning Coach
- whiteboard, student
- Tile Kit

Also Needed
- sight words box

Advance Preparation

Place lowercase letter tiles in alphabetical order on your whiteboard.

 **30 minutes**

FOCUS: Sounds for Letters *c* and *h*

Work **together** with students to complete offline Sight Words, Get Ready, Learn, and Try It activities.

Sight Words

Sight Word Fun

Help students learn the sight words *the, and,* and *is*.

1. Gather the sight word cards *the, and,* and *is*.

2. Choose one sight word card to begin.

   Say: Look at this word and take a picture of it in your mind. When you think you can spell the word yourself, turn the card over and use your letter tiles to spell the word.

3. After students spell the word, have them check the card to see if they spelled the word correctly.

   Say: Read aloud the word you spelled with the letter tiles.

4. Repeat the activity with the remaining sight words.

 Sight words can be very difficult for some students. Let students work at their own pace and really master these words.

> **Objectives**
> - Read sight words.
> - Spell sight words.

Get Ready

Face-Down Letters

To help students learn to recognize the letters of the alphabet, have them practice identifying and naming letters. Grab your whiteboard with letters placed in alphabetical order.

1. Lay your whiteboard down on a flat surface and flip over the following letter tiles so they are face down on the whiteboard: *b, f, k,* and *n*.

2. **Say:** These letters are face down. We are looking at the back of them. Name each letter, and then turn it over to see if you were right.

 If students miss any letters, have them turn over the missed ones and try again.

> **Objectives**
> - Identify letters of the alphabet.
> - Identify beginning sounds in words.
> - Identify a word when given the onset and rime.
> - Blend sounds to create words.
> - Identify individual sounds in words.
> - Given the letter, identify the most common sound.
> - Given the sound, identify the most common letter or letters.

Name Letters

To help students learn the alphabet, have them practice identifying and naming letters. Grab your whiteboard with letters placed in alphabetical order.

1. **Say:** Let's practice naming letters.

2. Have students touch the last letter in each row and say the letter's name.

3. Have students touch the third letter in each row and say the letter's name. Repeat the actions and mix up the order.

- ► If students name a letter incorrectly, name the letter they missed. Have students touch the letter and say its name. Have them trace the shape of the letter with their finger on the brown side of their board, and have them say the letter's name as they trace the shape.
- ► If students name a letter incorrectly twice, point to the letter and tell them its name. Have students touch the letter and say its name.
- ► If students continue to struggle with a letter, review that letter with them daily until understanding is achieved.

TIP To help students remember what a row is, run your finger from left to right along a row of letters. Have students do the same. Have them show you another row.

Signal Beginning Sounds

Use a special signal to help students identify **beginning sounds** in words.

1. **Say:** I'm going to tell you a special sound, and then I'll say some words. Repeat each word I say and make a special signal to tell me where the special sound is. If the special sound is at the beginning of the word, tug your ear. If the special sound is **not** at the beginning of the word, just smile at me. For example,

- ► If I ask you to listen for the sound /k/ and I say the word *kite*, you'll repeat the word *kite* and tug your ear because *kite* has the sound /k/ at the beginning.
- ► If I say the word *pop*, you'll repeat the word *pop* and smile at me because *pop* has the sound /p/, not /k/, at the beginning.

2. Say each sound and group of words. Have students make the special signal to identify the beginning sound.

- ► /k/: *come, cry, wall, gate, cave* tug ear: *come, cry, cave*
- ► /h/: *hit, gas, hunt, hall, laugh* tug ear: *hit, hunt, hall*
- ► /t/: *time, sap, chain, trip, tambourine* tug ear: *time, trip, tambourine*
- ► /b/: *basket, bag, peg, pebble, basketball* tug ear: *basket, bag, basketball*

TIP If students can't identify the beginning sound of each word, say the word again and emphasize the beginning sound by repeating it three times (for example, *taste* /t/ /t/ /t/). You can also draw out the beginning sound when you say the word (for example, *mmmustard*). If necessary, have students look at your mouth while you repeat the sounds.

Onset and Rime

In a word, the part of the syllable before the first vowel sound is the **onset**. The part of the syllable after the first vowel sound is the **rime**. For example, in *dog*, /d/ is the onset and *og* is the rime. Help students put together words that are broken down into parts by onset and rime.

1. **Say:** I'm going to break a word into two parts. Your job is to put the parts together and say the word. If the first part of a word is /b/ and the last part of the word is *ag*, then the whole word is *bag*: /b/ . . . *ag* . . . *bag*.

2. Say the following pairs of word parts. Have students tell you the word that each pair forms.

  ▸ /k/ ... *ick* *kick*
  ▸ /k/ ... *omb* *comb*
  ▸ /h/ ... *ike* *hike*
  ▸ /k/ ... *at* *cat*
  ▸ /h/ ... *at* *hat*

Review Sounds and Letters

Help students review sounds for the letters *a, b, f, m, s,* and *t,* plus any letters that are confusing for students.

1. Place the following letter tiles in random order on students' whiteboard: *a, b, f, m, s,* and *t,* plus any letters that are confusing.

2. **Say:** Let's go over some letters and sounds.

3. Point to each letter tile and have students say a sound that letter makes.

  ▸ *a* /ă/
  ▸ *m* /m/
  ▸ *s* /s/
  ▸ *t* /t/
  ▸ *b* /b/
  ▸ *f* /f/

4. Say each of the following sounds. Have students repeat the sound and touch the corresponding letter tile.

  ▸ /ă/ *a*
  ▸ /m/ *m*
  ▸ /s/ *s*
  ▸ /t/ *t*
  ▸ /b/ *b*
  ▸ /f/ *f*

5. As you do the activity, point to some letter tiles two or three times so that students don't think they are finished with a sound after they have named it.

6. Redirect students if they say an incorrect sound when you point to a letter tile.

  Say: That's the sound of another letter. What is the sound for this letter?

7. Help students if they touch the wrong letter tile after they repeat a sound.

  Say: That letter tile goes with the sound [sound for incorrect letter tile]. We're looking for the letter tile that goes with the sound [target sound].

Learn

Introduce Letters for Sounds

To help students learn the lowercase letters *c* and *h*, have them practice identifying and naming the letters from sounds.

1. Place the following letter tiles on students' whiteboard: *c* and *h*.

2. **Say:** Let's learn sounds for letters. When we see the letter *c*, we sometimes say the sound /k/. When we see the letter *h*, we say the sound /h/.

3. Have students
   ▸ Touch the letter *c* and say /k/.
   ▸ Touch the letter *h* and say /h/.

4. **Say:** Let's practice these sounds and letters.

5. Say the sounds /k/ and /h/ one at a time. Have students repeat each sound and touch the letter for each sound. It is important for students to touch the letter while they say the sound.

6. Redirect students if they name the letter and not the sound.

   Say: You're right that the name of the letter is [letter]. We want the sound for this letter. What is the sound?

7. Redirect students if they name the sound incorrectly.

   Say: That's the sound of another letter. The sound for this letter is [target sound]. Touch the letter and say the sound.

8. Help students. If they touch the wrong letter, point to the correct letter.

   Say: This is the letter for the sound [target sound]. Touch and say its sound.

Objectives

- Identify the letters, given the sound /k/.
- Identify the sound, given the letter *c*.
- Identify the letter, given the sound /h/.
- Identify the sound, given the letter *h*.
- Blend sounds to create words.
- Given the letter, identify the most common sound.
- Given the sound, identify the most common letter or letters.
- Identify individual sounds in words.
- Identify the new word when one sound is changed in a word.

Build Words

Help students use letters and sounds to build words.

1. Place the following letter tiles at the top of students' whiteboard: *a, b, c, h,* and *m*.

2. Draw three horizontal lines across the middle of students' whiteboard to represent the sounds in a word.

3. **Say:** Let's use letters and sounds to build the word *cab*.

4. Have students finger stretch the sounds in *cab*.

5. Have students
   ▸ Identify the first, next, and last sounds in *cab*.
   ▸ Choose the corresponding letter for each sound.
   ▸ Move the letters to the correct lines on their whiteboard.

6. Guide students with these questions:

 ▸ What is the first sound in *cab*? /k/
   Which line does the letter for that sound go on? the first one
 ▸ What is the next sound in *cab*? /ă/
   Which line does the letter for that sound go on? the second one
 ▸ What's the last sound in *cab*? /b/
   Which line does the letter for that sound go on? the last one

7. Have students touch and say the word.

8. Redirect students if they select the incorrect letter.

   Say: That sound is in the word [word], and it is the [first, second, third] sound. We want the sound [target sound].

   Continue until students select the correct letter.

9. Repeat the activity to build the word *ham.* /h/ /ă/ /m/

Word Chains
Have students build words by adding and changing letters to help them recognize and use individual sounds in words.

1. Place the following letter tiles at the top of students' whiteboard: *a, b, c, h, m,* and *t.*

2. **Say:** I am going to build the first word in a chain. The word is *ham.*

 ▸ I will pull down the letters for the sounds /h/, /ă/, and /m/ to spell the word *ham.*
 ▸ I will touch and say *ham.* To change *ham* to *hat,* I will think about which sound changes from the word *ham* to *hat.* I will need to replace the letter *m* with the letter *t.*
 ▸ Touch and say the word *hat.* Now it's your turn to change *hat* to *at.* You can spell *at* by making only one change. Touch and say the new word.

3. Redirect students if they select the incorrect letter for any sound.

   Say: That letter is for the sound [incorrect sound]. We want the letter for the sound [target sound]. What letter makes that sound? Answers will vary.

4. Redirect students if they name the sound incorrectly.

   Say: To change the word [first word] to [target word], we need the letter for the sound [target sound].

   Show students how to make the changes. Have them touch and say the new word after they move the letters.

5. Follow this procedure to make the following words: *cat* and *cab.*

6. For every new word, have students add, replace, or remove only one letter.

TIP If students struggle, review the sounds and letters that are confusing them.

Try It

New Beginnings

Have students complete page PH 34 in *K¹² PhonicsWorks Basic Activity Book* for more practice with beginning sounds. Have them say the name of each picture. Then have them circle the beginning letter of the picture name and write the letter. Have students read the word aloud.

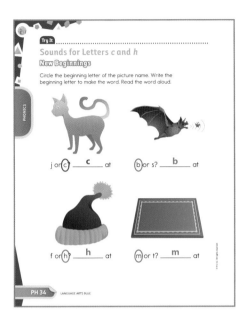

> **Objectives**
> - Identify beginning sounds in words.
> - Write words by applying grade-level phonics knowledge.
> - Follow three-step directions.

Dictation: Build Words

Have students build words that use the letters *a, b, c, h, m,* and *t.*

1. Place the following letters at the top of students' whiteboard: *a, b, c, h, m,* and *t.*

2. Say the word *ham.* Then give these directions to students:

   ▶ Repeat the word.
   ▶ Finger stretch the sounds in the word.
   ▶ Spell the word with the letter tiles.
   ▶ Touch and say the word.

3. When students have finished, write the following word on your whiteboard: *ham.*

4. Have them compare their answer to your correct version.

5. Repeat this procedure with the words *cat* and *bat.*

   ▶ If students make an error and don't see it, help them correct their mistake by having them finger stretch the sounds in the word they missed.
   ▶ If students are having difficulty selecting the correct letters or sounds, review those letters or sounds that are confusing them.
   ▶ If students have difficulty with first, middle, and last sounds, have them finger stretch the sounds in words.

 **20 minutes**

REVIEW: **Sounds for Letters *c* and *h***

Students will work online independently to

- ▸ Practice sounds for the letters *c* and *h*.
- ▸ Practice decoding text by reading sentences.

Help students locate the online activities and provide support as needed.

Offline Alternative

No computer access? Have students name the letters that make the sounds /k/ and /h/. Vice versa, have students name the sounds made by the letters *c* and *h*. You might also ask students to spell simple words that contain the letters *c*, *h*, and other letters students have learned, or ask them to think of words that begin with those letters.

Objectives

- Identify the letter, given the sound /k/.
- Identify the sound, given the letter *c*.
- Identify the letter, given the sound /h/.
- Identify the sound, given the letter *h*.
- Identify beginning sounds in words.
- Read aloud grade-level text with appropriate automaticity, prosody, accuracy, and rate.
- Decode words by applying grade-level word analysis skills.

Sound for Letter *j*

Lesson Overview

Materials

Supplied
- *K¹² PhonicsWorks Readers Basic 1*, pp. 5–10
- whiteboard, Learning Coach
- whiteboard, student
- Tile Kit

Also Needed
- sight words box

Offline FOCUS: Sound for Letter *j*   **30** minutes

Sight Words	Sight Word Fun
Get Ready	Signal Beginning Sounds
	Head, Waist, Toes
	Review Sounds and Letters
Learn	Introduce Letters for Sounds
	Build Words
	Word Chains
Try It	"Cam the Cat"
	Dictation: Build Words

Online REVIEW: Sound for Letter *j*   **20** minutes

Advance Preparation

Place lowercase letter tiles in alphabetical order on your whiteboard.

 **Offline** **30** minutes

FOCUS: Sound for Letter *j*

Work **together** with students to complete offline Sight Words, Get Ready, Learn, and Try It activities.

Sight Words ....

Sight Word Fun

Help students learn the sight words *the*, *and*, and *is*, and up to two additional sight words they have yet to master.

1. Gather the sight word cards *the*, *and*, and *is*, and up to two additional sight word cards.

2. Choose one sight word card to begin.

   Say: Look at this word and take a picture of it in your mind. When you think you can spell the word yourself, turn the card over and use your letter tiles to spell the word.

3. After students spell the word, have them check the card to see if they spelled the word correctly.

   Say: Read aloud the word you spelled with the letter tiles.

4. Repeat the activity with the remaining sight words.

   TIP Sight words can be very difficult for some students. Let students work at their own pace and really master these words.

Objectives
- Read sight words.
- Spell sight words.

Get Ready ....

Signal Beginning Sounds

Use a special signal to help students identify **beginning sounds** in words.

1. **Say:** I'm going to tell you a special sound, and then I'll say some words. Repeat each word I say and make a special signal to tell me where the special sound is. If the special sound is at the beginning of the word, pat your cheek. If the special sound is **not** at the beginning of the word, just smile at me. For example,

   ▶ If I ask you to listen for the sound /j/ and I say the word *June*, you'll repeat the word *June* and pat your cheek because *June* has the sound /j/ at the beginning.
   ▶ If I say the word *bat*, you'll repeat the word *bat* and smile at me because *bat* has the sound /b/, not /j/, at the beginning.

2. Say each sound and group of words. Have students make the special signal to identify the beginning sound.

   ▶ /j/: *June, climb, Jeff, jam, tray* pat cheek: *June, Jeff, jam*
   ▶ /k/: *cap, candle, sat, clay, axis* pat cheek: *cap, candle, clay*
   ▶ /ă/: *Abigail, anteater, apple, umbrella, island* pat cheek: *Abigail, anteater, apple*
   ▶ /h/: *fort, hornet, helmet, anchor, hot dog* pat cheek: *hornet, helmet, hot dog*

Objectives
- Identify beginning sounds in words.
- Identify individual sounds in words.
- Given the letter, identify the most common sound.
- Given the sound, identify the most common letter or letters.

TIP If students can't identify the beginning sound of each word, say the word again and emphasize the beginning sound by repeating it three times (for example, *taste* /t/ /t/ /t/). You can also draw out the beginning sound when you say the word (for example, *mmmommy*). If necessary, have students look at your mouth while you repeat the sounds.

Head, Waist, Toes

Help students practice identifying the sounds in words.

1. **Say:** Let's identify sounds in words by touching parts of our body as we say each sound. For example, I'll say *mat*, which has three sounds, and you'll repeat the word. Do these steps with me:

   ▸ The first sound in *mat* is /m/, so I touch my head as I say /m/.
   ▸ The middle sound is /ă/, so I touch my waist as I say /ă/.
   ▸ The last sound is /t/, so I touch my toes as I say /t/.

2. Say the words below. Have students repeat each word and then touch their head, waist, and toes as they say each sound in the word. After they say the sounds in each word, ask them the question for that word.

   ▸ *can* /k/ /ă/ /n/   What is the middle sound? /ă/
   ▸ *map* /m/ /ă/ /p/   What is the middle sound? /ă/
   ▸ *cab* /k/ /ă/ /b/   What is the first sound? /k/
   ▸ *had* /h/ /ă/ /d/   What is the last sound? /d/
   ▸ *tag* /t/ /ă/ /g/   What is the last sound? /g/
   ▸ *fat* /f/ /ă/ /t/   What is the first sound? /f/
   ▸ *Sam* /s/ /ă/ /m/   What is the last sound? /m/

TIP If students have difficulty with this activity, be sure they can identify beginning, middle, and ending. If students still have difficulty with this activity, try finger stretching the words instead.

Review Sounds and Letters

Help students review sounds for the letters *a, b, f, h, m, s,* and *t,* plus any additional letters that are confusing for them.

1. Place the following letter tiles in random order on students' whiteboard: *a, b, f, h, m, s,* and *t,* plus any letters that are confusing.

2. **Say:** Let's go over some letters and sounds.

3. Point to each letter tile and have students say a sound that letter makes.

   ▸ *a* /ă/   ▸ *b* /b/
   ▸ *m* /m/   ▸ *f* /f/
   ▸ *s* /s/   ▸ *c* /k/
   ▸ *t* /t/   ▸ *h* /h/

4. Say each of the following sounds. Have students repeat the sound and touch the corresponding letter tile.

- ► /ă/ *a*
- ► /m/ *m*
- ► /s/ *s*
- ► /t/ *t*

- ► /b/ *b*
- ► /f/ *f*
- ► /k/ *c*
- ► /h/ *h*

5. As you do the activity, point to some letters two or three times so that students don't think they are finished with a sound after they have named it.

6. Redirect students if they say an incorrect sound when you point to a letter.

Say: That's the sound of another letter. What is the sound for this letter?

7. Help students if they touch the wrong letter after they repeat a sound.

Say: That letter goes with the sound [sound for incorrect letter]. We're looking for the letter that goes with the sound [target sound].

Learn

Introduce Letters for Sounds

To help students learn the lowercase letter *j*, have them practice identifying and naming the letter.

1. Place the following letter tile on students' whiteboard: *j*.

2. **Say:** Let's learn the sound for this letter. When we see the letter *j*, we say the sound /j/.

3. Have students touch the letter *j* and say /j/.

4. **Say:** Let's practice this sound and letter.

5. Say the sound /j/. Have students repeat the sound and touch the letter for it. It is important for students to touch the letter while they say the sound.

6. Redirect students if they name the letter and not the sound.

Say: You're right that the name of the letter is *j*. We want the sound for this letter. What is the sound?

7. Redirect students if they name the sound incorrectly.

Say: That's the sound of another letter. The sound for this letter is /j/. Touch the letter and say the sound.

Objectives
- Identify the letter, given the sound /j/.
- Identify the sound, given the letter *j*.
- Given the letter, identify the most common sound.
- Given the sound, identify the most common letter or letters.
- Identify individual sounds in words.
- Blend sounds to create words.
- Identify the new word when one sound is changed in a word.

Build Words

Help students use letters and sounds to build words.

1. Place the following letter tiles at the top of students' whiteboard: *a, b, j,* and *m*.

2. Draw three horizontal lines across the middle of students' whiteboard to represent the sounds in a word.

3. **Say:** Let's use letters and sounds to build the word *jam*.

4. Have students finger stretch the sounds in *jam*.

5. Have students

   ▸ Identify the first, next, and last sounds in *jam*.
   ▸ Choose the corresponding letter for each sound.
   ▸ Move the letters to the correct lines on their whiteboard.

6. Guide students with these questions:

   ▸ What is the first sound in *jam*? /j/
     Which line does the letter for that sound go on? the first one
   ▸ What is the next sound in *jam*? /ă/
     Which line does the letter for that sound go on? the second one
   ▸ What's the last sound in *jam*? /m/
     Which line does the letter for that sound go on? the last one

7. Have students touch and say the word.

8. Redirect students if they select the incorrect letter.

   Say: That sound is in the word [word], and it is the [first, second, third] sound. We want the sound [target sound].

   Continue until students select the correct letter.

9. Repeat the activity to build the word *jab*. /j/ /ă/ /b/

Word Chains

Have students build words by adding and changing letters to help them recognize and use individual sounds in words.

1. Place the following letter tiles at the top of students' whiteboard: lowercase letters *a, b, c, h, j, m,* and *t,* and uppercase letter *S*.

2. **Say:** I am going to build the first word in a chain. The word is *ham*.

   ▸ I will pull down the letters for the sounds /h/, /ă/, and /m/ to spell the word *ham*.
   ▸ I will touch and say *ham*. To change *ham* to *Sam*, I will think about which sound changes from the word *ham* to *Sam*. I will need to replace the letter *h* with letter *S*.
   ▸ Touch and say the word *Sam*. Now it's your turn to change *Sam* to *jam*. You can spell *jam* by making only one change. Touch and say the new word.

3. Redirect students if they select the incorrect letter for any sound.

   Say: That letter is for the sound [incorrect sound]. We want the letter for the sound [target sound]. What letter makes that sound? Answers will vary.

4. Redirect students if they name the sound incorrectly.

   Say: To change the word [first word] to [target word], we need the letter for the sound [target sound].

   Show students how to make the change. Have them touch and say the new word after they move the letter.

5. Follow this procedure to make the following words: *jab, cab, tab.*

6. For every new word, have students add, replace, or remove only one letter.

TIP If students struggle, review the sounds and letters that are confusing them.

Try It

"Cam the Cat"
Have students read "Cam the Cat" on page 5 of *K¹² PhonicsWorks Readers Basic 1.*
   Students should read the story silently once or twice before reading the story aloud. When students miss a word that can be sounded out, point to it and give them three to six seconds to try the word again. If students still miss the word, tell them the word so the flow of the story isn't interrupted.
   After reading the story, make a list of all the words students missed, and go over those words with them. You may use letter tiles to show students how to read the words.

Objectives
- Read aloud grade-level text with appropriate automaticity, prosody, accuracy, and rate.
- Decode words by applying grade-level word analysis skills.
- Track text from left to right.
- Turn pages sequentially.
- Write words by applying grade-level phonics knowledge.
- Follow three-step directions.

Dictation: Build Words
Have students build words with the letters *a, b, h, j, m,* and *t.*

1. Place the following letters at the top of students' whiteboard: *a, b, h, j, m,* and *t.*

2. Say the word *jab.* Then give these directions to students:
   ▸ Repeat the word.
   ▸ Finger stretch the sounds in the word.
   ▸ Spell the word with the letter tiles.
   ▸ Touch and say the word.

3. When students have finished, write the following word on you whiteboard: *jab.*

4. Have them compare their answer to your correct version.

5. Repeat this procedure with the words *ham* and *mat.*
   ▸ If students make an error and don't see it, help them correct their mistake by having them finger stretch the sounds in the word they missed.
   ▸ If students are having difficulty selecting the correct letters or sounds, review those letters or sounds that are confusing them.
   ▸ If students have difficulty with first, middle, and last sounds, have them finger stretch the sounds in words.

 **20 minutes**

REVIEW: Sound for Letter *j*

Students will work online independently to

▸ Practice the sound for the letter *j*.

Help students locate the online activities and provide support as needed.

Offline Alternative

No computer access? Have students name the letter that makes the sound /j/. Vice versa, have students name the sound made by the letter *j*. You might also ask students to spell simple words that contain the letter *j* and other letters students have learned, or ask them to think of words that begin with those letters.

Objectives
- Identify the letter, given the sound /j/.
- Identify the sound, given the letter *j*.
- Identify individual sounds in words.

Unit Checkpoint

Lesson Overview

【Online】	**REVIEW:** Sounds for Letters *a, m, s, t, b, f, c, h,* and *j*	**20** minutes
【Offline】	**UNIT CHECKPOINT:** Sounds for Letters *a, m, s, t, b, f, c, h,* and *j*	**30** minutes

【Materials】

Supplied
- *K¹² PhonicsWorks Basic Assessments,* pp. PH 43–48

★ Objectives

- Identify the letter, given the sound /ă/.
- Identify the letter, given the sound /m/.
- Identify the letter, given the sound /s/.
- Identify the letter, given the sound /t/.
- Identify the letter, given the sound /b/.
- Identify the letter, given the sound /f/.
- Identify the letter, given the sound /k/.
- Identify the letter, given the sound /h/.
- Identify the letter, given the sound /j/.
- Identify the sound, given the letter *a.*
- Identify the sound, given the letter *m.*
- Identify the sound, given the letter *s.*
- Identify the sound, given the letter *t.*
- Identify the sound, given the letter *b.*
- Identify the sound, given the letter *f.*
- Identify the sound, given the letter *c.*
- Identify the sound, given the letter *h.*
- Identify the sound, given the letter *j.*
- Identify letters of the alphabet.
- Identify individual sounds in words.
- Given the letter, identify the most common sound.
- Given the sound, identify the most common letter or letters.
- Read instructional-level text with 90% accuracy.
- Read aloud grade-level text with appropriate automaticity, prosody, accuracy, and rate.
- Read sight words.

【Online】 **20** minutes

REVIEW: **Sounds for Letters *a, m, s, t, b, f, c, h,* and *j***

Students will review the sounds for *a, m, s, t, b, f, c, h,* and *j* to prepare for the Unit Checkpoint. Help students locate the online activities and provide support as needed.

 **30 minutes**

UNIT CHECKPOINT: Sounds for Letters *a, m, s, t, b, f, c, h,* and *j*

Explain that students are going to show what they have learned about letters, sounds, and words.

1. Give students the Unit Checkpoint pages for the Sounds for Letters *a, m, s, t, b, f, c, h,* and *j* unit and print the Unit Checkpoint Answer Key, if you'd like.

2. Use the instructions below to help administer the Checkpoint to students. On the Answer Key or another sheet of paper, note student answers to oral response questions to help with scoring the Checkpoint later.

3. Use the Answer Key to score the Checkpoint, and then enter the results online.

Part 1. Say Sounds Have students read across each row from left to right and say the sound of each letter. Note any sounds they say incorrectly.

Part 2. Word Dissection For each word, say the sound students should identify. Have them read the word aloud and circle the letter or groups of letters that spell the sound.

21. *beginning sound*

22. *ending sound*

23. *middle sound*

24. *ending sound*

25. *middle sound*

Part 3. Finger Stretching Say each word to students. Have them say each word aloud and finger stretch the sounds. Note any words they finger stretch incorrectly.

26. *cat*	29. *Sam*
27. *am*	30. *fat*
28. *bat*	31. *jam*

Part 4. Circle the Letter Say each sound and have students circle the letter that makes the sound.

32. /t/	37. /h/
33. /b/	38. /m/
34. /s/	39. /f/
35. /ă/	40. /k/
36. /j/	

Part 5. Read Aloud Listen to students read the sentences aloud. Count and note the number of words they read correctly.

Part 6. Say Letters Say each sound. Have students say the letter that makes that sound. Note any incorrect responses.

42. /ă/

43. /b/

44. /k/

45. /m/

46. /s/

47. /t/

48. /f/

49. /h/

50. /j/

51. /b/

52. /k/

53. /s/

54. /ă/

55. /t/

56. /j/

57. /h/

58. /m/

59. /f/

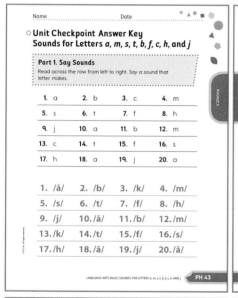

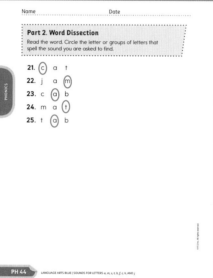

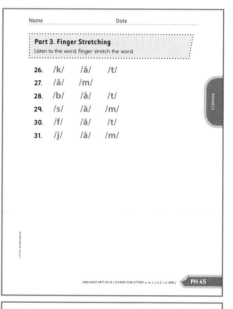

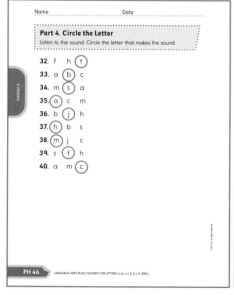

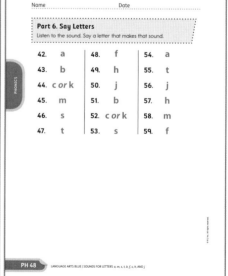

Sounds for Letters *l* and *n*

Unit Overview

In this unit, students will
- ► Identify the letters and sounds in the alphabet.
- ► Identify the sounds for the letters *l*, *n*, *p*, and *r*.
- ► Review vowels and vowels sounds.
- ► Identify individual sounds in words.
- ► Blend sounds to build words.
- ► Learn the sight words *on*, *to*, and *in*.

Materials

Supplied
- *K¹² PhonicsWorks Basic Activity Book,* p. PH 35
- whiteboard, Learning Coach
- whiteboard, student
- Tile Kit

Also Needed
- sight words box
- crayons

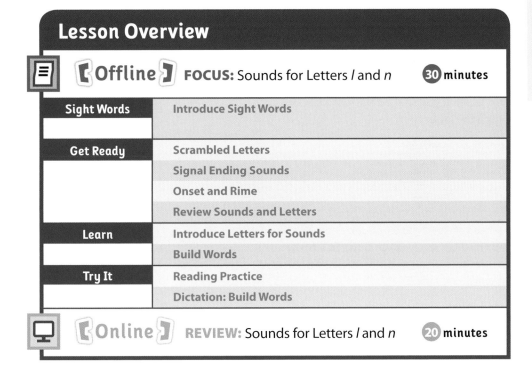

Lesson Overview

Offline FOCUS: Sounds for Letters *l* and *n*   **30** minutes

Sight Words	Introduce Sight Words
Get Ready	Scrambled Letters
	Signal Ending Sounds
	Onset and Rime
	Review Sounds and Letters
Learn	Introduce Letters for Sounds
	Build Words
Try It	Reading Practice
	Dictation: Build Words

Online REVIEW: Sounds for Letters *l* and *n*   **20** minutes

 **30 minutes**

FOCUS: Sounds for Letters *l* and *n*

Work **together** with students to complete offline Sight Words, Get Ready, Learn, and Try It activities.

Sight Words

Introduce Sight Words

Help students learn the sight words *on*, *to*, and *in*.

1. Gather the sight word cards *on*, *to*, and *in*.

2. Show students the *on* card.

3. **Say:** This is the word *on*. We see this word so often that we want to be able to read and spell it quickly without thinking about it. Look closely at the word *on*. Spell the word *on* aloud. Take a picture of the word *on* in your mind. When you think you can spell *on* yourself, turn the card over and use your letter tiles to spell the word *on*. Check the card to see if you spelled the word *on* correctly. Read aloud the word you spelled with the letter tiles.

4. Repeat the activity with the remaining sight words.

5. Chart students' progress on the back of each card.

   ▸ Divide the back of the card into two columns.
   ▸ Label the first column "Read" and the second column "Spell."
   ▸ Record the dates that students read or spell the word correctly. When students can read and spell the word correctly three times in a row, they have mastered the word. You may want to put a star or sticker on the card when they have mastered that word.

6. Add the cards to students' sight words box.

 Sight words can be very difficult for some students. Let students work at their own pace and really master these words, as they occur frequently in reading and writing.

Get Ready ....

Scrambled Letters

To help students master the alphabet, have them practice identifying and naming letters.

1. Place the following letter tiles on students' whiteboard: *b, k, m,* and *z.*

2. Have students arrange the letters in alphabetical order.

TIP Students may find this activity easier if they slowly sing "The Alphabet Song" to themselves as they work.

Signal Ending Sounds

Use a special signal to help students identify **ending sounds** in words.

1. **Say:** I'm going to tell you a special sound, and then I'll say some words. Repeat each word I say and make a special signal to tell me where the special sound is. If the special sound is at the end of the word, touch your nose. If the special sound is **not** at the end of the word, just smile at me. For example,

   ▸ If I ask you to listen for the sound /l/ and I say the word *pail,* you'll repeat the word *pail* and touch your nose because *pail* has the sound /l/ at the end.

   ▸ If I say the word *tan,* you'll repeat the word *tan* and smile at me because *tan* has the sound /n/, not /l/, at the end.

2. Say each sound and group of words. Have students make the special signal to identify the ending sound.

   ▸ /l/: *pail, tan, pull, swirl, call* touch nose: *pail, pull, swirl, call*
   ▸ /s/: *boss, lets, girl, Smith, kiss* touch nose: *boss, lets, kiss*
   ▸ /b/: *stamp, lid, crab, cob, clap, bib* touch nose: *crab, cob, bib*
   ▸ /f/: *rough, stuff, pin, laugh, math* touch nose: *rough, stuff, laugh*
   ▸ /t/: *ton, plant, land, smart, fit, fib* touch nose: *plant, smart, fit*
   ▸ /m/: *team, mist, Tim, swim, stop, Jim* touch nose: *team, Tim, swim, Jim*
   ▸ /k/: *pie, kick, Jack, lip, crack, quack* touch nose: *kick, Jack, crack, quack*

TIP If students can't identify the ending sound of each word, say the word again and emphasize the ending sound by repeating it three times (for example, *sit* /t/ /t/ /t/). You can also draw out the ending sound when you say the word (for example, *kisssss*). If necessary, have students look at your mouth while you repeat the sounds.

Objectives

- Identify letters of the alphabet.
- Identify ending sounds in words.
- Identify a word when given the onset and rime.
- Blend sounds to create words.
- Identify individual sounds in words.
- Given the letter, identify the most common sound.
- Given the sound, identify the most common letter or letters.

Onset and Rime

In a word, the part of the syllable before the first vowel sound is the **onset**. The part of the syllable after the first vowel sound is the **rime**. For example, in *nap*, /n/ is the onset and *ap* is the rime. Help students put together words that are broken down into parts by onset and rime.

1. **Say:** I'm going to break a word into two parts. Your job is to put the parts together and say the word. If the first part of a word is /r/ and the last part of the word is *ack*, then the whole word is *rack*: /r/ . . . *ack* . . . *rack*.

2. Say the following pairs of word parts. Have students tell you the word that each pair forms.

   ▸ /p/ . . . *an pan*
   ▸ /s/ . . . *and sand*

Review Sounds and Letters

Help students review sounds for the letters *a, b, c, f, h, j, m, s,* and *t,* plus any letters that are confusing for them.

1. Place the following letter tiles in random order on students' whiteboard: *a, b, c, f, h, j, m, s,* and *t,* plus any letters that are confusing.

2. **Say:** Let's go over some letters and sounds.

3. Point to each letter tile and have students say a sound that letter makes.

   ▸ *m* /m/   ▸ *b* /b/
   ▸ *t* /t/   ▸ *c* /k/
   ▸ *a* /ă/   ▸ *f* /f/
   ▸ *s* /s/   ▸ *h* /h/
   ▸ *j* /j/

4. Say each of the following sounds. Have students repeat the sound and touch the corresponding letter tile.

   ▸ /m/ *m*   ▸ /b/ *b*
   ▸ /t/ *t*   ▸ /k/ *c*
   ▸ /ă/ *a*   ▸ /f/ *f*
   ▸ /s/ *s*   ▸ /h/ *h*
   ▸ /j/ *j*

5. As you do the activity, point to some letter tiles two or three times so that students don't think they are finished with a sound after they have named it.

6. Redirect students if they say an incorrect sound when you point to a letter tile.

   Say: That's the sound of another letter. What is the sound for this letter?

7. Help students if they touch the wrong letter tile after they repeat a sound.

   Say: That letter goes with the sound [sound for incorrect letter]. We're looking for the letter that goes with the sound [target sound].

Learn

Introduce Letters for Sounds

To help students learn the lowercase letters *l* and *n*, have them practice identifying and naming the letters from their sounds.

1. Place the following letter tiles on students' whiteboard: *l* and *n*.

2. **Say:** Let's learn sounds for letters. When we see the letter *l*, we say the sound /l/. When we see the letter *n*, we say the sound /n/.

3. Have students

   ▸ Touch the letter *l* and say /l/.
   ▸ Touch the letter *n* and say /n/.

4. **Say:** Let's practice these sounds and letters.

5. Say the sounds /l/ and /n/ one at a time. Have students repeat each sound and touch the letter for each sound. It is important for students to touch the letter while they say the sound.

6. Redirect students if they name the letter and not the sound.

   Say: You're right that the name of the letter is [letter]. We want the sound for this letter. What is the sound?

7. Redirect students if they name the sound incorrectly.

   Say: That's the sound of another letter. The sound for this letter is [target sound]. Touch the letter and say the sound.

8. Help students. If they touch the wrong letter, point to the correct letter.

   Say: This is the letter for the sound [target sound]. Touch and say its sound.

Objectives

- Identify the letter, given the sound /l/.
- Identify the sound, given the letter *l*.
- Identify the letter, given the sound /n/.
- Identify the sound, given the letter *n*.
- Identify individual sounds in words.
- Blend sounds to create words.
- Given the letter, identify the most common sound.
- Given the sound, identify the most common letter or letters.

Build Words

Help students use letters and sounds to build words.

1. Place the following letter tiles at the top of students' whiteboard: *a*, *b*, *l*, *n*, and *s*.

2. Draw three horizontal lines across the middle of students' whiteboard to represent the sounds in a word.

3. **Say:** Let's use letters and sounds to build the word *nab*.

4. Have students finger stretch the sounds in *nab*.

5. Have students

   ▸ Identify the first, next, and last sounds in *nab*.
   ▸ Choose the corresponding letter for each sound.
   ▸ Move the letters to the correct lines on their whiteboard.

6. Guide students with these questions:

  ▶ What is the first sound in *nab*? /n/
    Which line does the letter for that sound go on? the first one
  ▶ What is the next sound in *nab*? /ă/
    Which line does the letter for that sound go on? the second one
  ▶ What's the last sound in *nab*? /b/
    Which line does the letter for that sound go on? the last one

7. Have students touch and say the word.

8. Redirect students if they select the incorrect letter.

   Say: That sound is in the word [word], and it is the [first, second, third] sound. We want the sound [target sound].

   Continue until students select the correct letter.

9. Repeat the activity to build the following words:

  ▶ *man* /m/ /ă/ /n/
  ▶ *lab* /l/ /ă/ /b/

Try It

Reading Practice

Have students complete page PH 35 in *K¹² PhonicsWorks Basic Activity Book* for practice reading words with the letters *l* and *n*. Have them touch and read each word aloud. Then they can color the picture.

Dictation: Build Words

Have students build words with the letters *a, b, c, l, m,* and *n.*

1. Place the following letters at the top of students' whiteboard: *a, b, c, l, m,* and *n.*

2. Say the word *can.* Then give these directions to students:

   ▸ Repeat the word.
   ▸ Finger stretch the sounds in the word.
   ▸ Spell the word with the letter tiles.
   ▸ Touch and say the word.

3. When students have finished, write the following word on your whiteboard: *can.*

4. Have them compare their answer to your correct version.

5. Repeat this procedure with the words *lab* and *man.*

   ▸ If students make an error and don't see it, help them correct their mistake by having them finger stretch the sounds in the word they missed.
   ▸ If students are having difficulty selecting the correct letters or sounds, review those letters or sounds that are confusing them.
   ▸ If students have difficulty with first, middle, and last sounds, have them finger stretch the sounds in words.

 **20 minutes**

REVIEW: **Sounds for Letters *l* and *n***

Students will work online independently to

▸ Practice the sounds for the letters *l* and *n.*
▸ Practice decoding text by reading sentences.

Help students locate the online activities and provide support as needed.

Offline Alternative

No computer access? Have students name the letters that make the sounds /l/ and /n/. Vice versa, have students name the sounds made by the letters *l* and *n.* You might also ask students to spell simple words that contain the letters *l, n,* and other letters students have learned, or ask them to think of words that begin with those letters.

Objectives

- Identify the letter, given the sound /l/.
- Identify the sound, given the letter *l.*
- Identify the letter, given the sound /n/.
- Identify the sound, given the letter *n.*
- Identify beginning sounds in words.
- Identify ending sounds in words.
- Read aloud grade-level text with appropriate automaticity, prosody, accuracy, and rate.
- Decode words by applying grade-level word analysis skills.

Sounds for Letters *p* and *r*

Lesson Overview

Offline FOCUS: Sounds for Letters *p* and *r* — **30** minutes

Sight Words	Sight Word Fun
Get Ready	Head, Waist, Toes
	Onset and Rime
	Review Sounds and Letters
Learn	Introduce Letters for Sounds
	Word Chains
Try It	"Pam"

Online REVIEW: Sounds for Letters *p* and *r* — **20** minutes

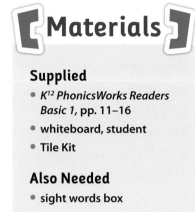

Materials

Supplied
- *K¹² PhonicsWorks Readers Basic 1*, pp. 11–16
- whiteboard, student
- Tile Kit

Also Needed
- sight words box

 **Offline** 🕙 **minutes**

FOCUS: Sounds for Letters *p* and *r*

Work **together** with students to complete offline Sight Words, Get Ready, Learn, and Try It activities.

Sight Words ●

Sight Word Fun

Help students learn the sight words *on, to,* and *in,* and up to two additional sight words they have yet to master.

1. Gather the sight word cards *on, to,* and *in,* plus up to two additional sight word cards.

2. Choose one sight word card to begin.

   Say: Look at this word and take a picture of it in your mind. When you think you can spell the word yourself, turn the card over and use your letter tiles to spell the word.

3. After students spell the word, have them check the card to see if they spelled the word correctly.

   Say: Read aloud the word you spelled with the letter tiles.

4. Repeat the activity with the remaining sight words.

 Sight words can be very difficult for some students. Let students work at their own pace and really master these words.

Objectives
- Read sight words.
- Spell sight words.

Get Ready ●

Head, Waist, Toes

Help students practice identifying the sounds in words.

1. **Say:** Let's identify sounds in words by touching parts of our body as we say each sound. For example, I'll say *lap,* which has three sounds, and you'll repeat the word. Do these steps with me:

   ▸ The first sound in *lap* is /l/, so I touch my head as I say /l/.
   ▸ The middle sound is /ă/, so I touch my waist as I say /ă/.
   ▸ The last sound is /p/, so I touch my toes as I say /p/.

2. Say the words below. Have students repeat each word and then touch their head, waist, and toes as they say each sound in the word. After they say the sounds in each word, ask them the question for that word.

   ▸ rat /r/ /ă/ /t/   What is the first sound? /r/
   ▸ jab /j/ /ă/ /b/   What is the middle sound? /ă/
   ▸ sad /s/ /ă/ /d/   What is the first sound? /s/
   ▸ bag /b/ /ă/ /g/   What is the last sound? /g/
   ▸ bat /b/ /ă/ /t/   What is the first sound? /b/
   ▸ Sal /s/ /ă/ /l/   What is the last sound? /l/

 Objectives
- Identify individual sounds in words.
- Identify a word when given the onset and rime.
- Blend sounds to create words.
- Given the letter, identify the most common sound.
- Given the sound, identify the most common letter or letters.

TIP If students have difficulty with this activity, be sure they can identify beginning, middle, and ending. If students still have difficulty with this activity, try finger stretching the words instead.

Onset and Rime

In a word, the part of the syllable before the first vowel sound is the **onset**. The part of the syllable after the first vowel sound is the **rime**. For example, in *house*, /h/ is the onset and *ouse* is the rime. Help students put together words that are broken down into parts by onset and rime.

1. **Say:** I'm going to break a word into two parts. Your job is to put the parts together and say the word. If the first part of a word is /b/ and the last part of the word is *ag*, then the whole word is *bag*: /b/ . . . *ag* . . . *bag*.

2. Say the following pairs of word parts. Have students tell you the word that each pair forms.

   ► /t/ . . . *ap* tap
   ► /kr/ . . . *ab* crab
   ► /l/ . . . *amp* lamp
   ► /h/ . . . *and* hand
   ► /n/ . . . *est* nest
   ► /j/ . . . *ump* jump

Review Sounds and Letters

Help students review sounds for the letters *a, c, f, h, j, l,* and *n,* plus any letters that are confusing for them.

1. Place the following letter tiles in random order on students' whiteboard: *a, c, f, h, j, l,* and *n,* plus any letters that are confusing.

2. **Say:** Let's go over some letters and sounds.

3. Point to each letter tile and have students say a sound that letter makes.

   ► *a* /ă/
   ► *j* /j/
   ► *c* /k/
   ► *f* /f/
   ► *h* /h/
   ► *l* /l/
   ► *n* /n/

4. Say each of the following sounds. Have students repeat the sound and touch the corresponding letter tile.

   ▸ /ă/ *a*
   ▸ /j/ *j*
   ▸ /k/ *c*
   ▸ /f/ *f*
   ▸ /h/ *h*
   ▸ /l/ *l*
   ▸ /n/ *n*

5. As you do the activity, point to some letter tiles two or three times so that students don't think they are finished with a sound after they have named it.

6. Redirect students if they say an incorrect sound when you point to a letter tile.

   Say: That's the sound of another letter. What is the sound for this letter?

7. Help students if they touch the wrong letter tile after they repeat a sound.

   Say: That letter goes with the sound [sound for incorrect letter tile]. We're looking for the letter that goes with the sound [target sound].

Learn

Introduce Letters for Sounds

To help students learn the lowercase letters *p* and *r*, have them practice identifying and naming the letters from sounds.

1. Place the following letter tiles on students' whiteboard: *p* and *r*.

2. **Say:** Let's learn sounds for letters. When we see the letter *p*, we say the sound /p/. When we see the letter *r*, we say the sound /r/.

3. Have students

   ▸ Touch the letter *p* and say /p/.
   ▸ Touch the letter *r* and say /r/.

4. **Say:** Let's practice these sounds and letters.

5. Say the sounds /p/ and /r/ one at a time. Have students repeat each sound and touch the letter for each sound. It is important for students to touch the letter while they say the sound.

6. Redirect students if they name the letter and not the sound.

   Say: You're right that the name of the letter is [letter]. We want the sound for this letter. What is the sound?

7. Redirect students if they name the sound incorrectly.

   Say: That's the sound of another letter. The sound for this letter is [target sound]. Touch the letter and say the sound.

8. Help students. If they touch the wrong letter, point to the correct letter.

   Say: This is the letter for the sound [target sound]. Touch and say its sound.

Objectives

- Identify the letter, given the sound /p/.
- Identify the sound, given the letter *p*.
- Identify the letter, given the sound /r/.
- Identify the sound, given the letter *r*.
- Given the letter, identify the most common sound.
- Given the sound, identify the most common letter or letters.
- Identify the new word when one sound is changed in a word.
- Identify individual sounds in words.

Word Chains

Have students build words by adding and changing letters to help them recognize and use individual sounds in words.

1. Place the following letters at the top of students' whiteboard: *a, b, c, n, p, r,* and *t.*

2. **Say:** I am going to build the first word in a chain. The word is *cab.*

   ▶ I will pull down the letters for the sounds /k/, /ă/, and /b/ to spell the word *cab.*

   ▶ I will touch and say *cab.* To change *cab* to *cap,* I will think about which sound changes from the word *cab* to *cap.* I will need to replace the letter *b* with the letter *p.*

   ▶ Touch and say the word *cap.* Now it's your turn to change *cap* to *rap.* You can spell *rap* by making only one change. Touch and say the new word.

3. Redirect students if they select the incorrect letter for any sound.

   Say: That letter is for the sound [incorrect letter]. We want the sound for [target sound]. What letter makes that sound? Answers will vary.

4. Redirect students if they name the sound incorrectly.

   Say: To change the word [first word] to [target word], we need the letter for the sound [target sound].

   Show students how to make the change. Have them touch and say the new word after they move the letters.

5. Follow this procedure to make the following words: *rat, ran, pan, tan.*

6. For every new word, have students add, replace, or remove only one letter.

   TIP If students struggle, review the sounds and letters that are confusing them.

Try It ••

"Pam"

Have students read "Pam" on page 11 of *K¹² PhonicsWorks Readers Basic 1.*

Students should read the story silently once or twice before reading the story aloud. When students miss a word that can be sounded out, point to it and give them three to six seconds to try the word again. If students still miss the word, tell them the word so the flow of the story isn't interrupted.

After reading the story, make a list of all the words students missed, and go over those words with them. You may use letter tiles to show students how to read the words.

Objectives

- Read aloud grade-level text with appropriate automaticity, prosody, accuracy, and rate.
- Decode words by applying grade-level word analysis skills.
- Track text from left to right.
- Turn pages sequentially.

 **20 minutes**

REVIEW: Sounds for Letters *p* and *r*

Students will work online independently to

▶ Practice the sounds for the letters *p* and *r*.

Help students locate the online activities and provide support as needed.

Offline Alternative

No computer access? Have students name the letters that make the sounds /p/ and /r/. Vice versa, have students name the sounds made by the letters *p* and *r*. You might also ask students to spell simple words that contain the letters *p*, *r*, and other letters students have learned, or ask them to think of words that begin with those letters.

Objectives

- Identify the letter, given the sound /p/.
- Identify the sound, given the letter *p*.
- Identify the letter, given the sound /r/.
- Identify the sound, given the letter *r*.
- Identify beginning sounds in words.
- Identify ending sounds in words.

Review Sounds for Letters

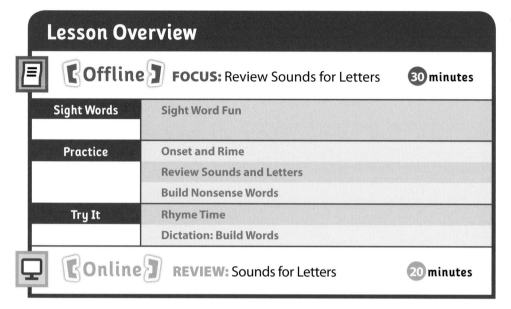

Lesson Overview

[Offline] **FOCUS:** Review Sounds for Letters **30** minutes

Sight Words	Sight Word Fun
Practice	Onset and Rime
	Review Sounds and Letters
	Build Nonsense Words
Try It	Rhyme Time
	Dictation: Build Words

[Online] **REVIEW:** Sounds for Letters **20** minutes

Materials

Supplied
- *K¹² PhonicsWorks Basic Activity Book*, p. PH 36
- whiteboard, Learning Coach
- whiteboard, student
- Tile Kit

Also Needed
- sight words box

 **30 minutes**

FOCUS: Review Sounds for Letters

Work **together** with students to complete offline Sight Words, Practice, and Try It activities.

Sight Words

Sight Word Fun

Help students learn the sight words *on, to,* and *in,* and up to two additional sight words they have yet to master.

1. Gather the sight word cards *on, to,* and *in,* and up to two additional sight word cards.

2. Choose one sight word card to begin.

   Say: Look at this word and take a picture of it in your mind. When you think you can spell the word yourself, turn the card over and use your letter tiles to spell the word.

3. After students spell the word, have them check the card to see if they spelled the word correctly.

   Say: Read aloud the word you spelled with the letter tiles.

4. Repeat the activity with the remaining sight words.

   TIP Sight words can be very difficult for some students. Let students work at their own pace and really master these words.

> **Objectives**
> • Read sight words.
> • Spell sight words.

Practice

Onset and Rime

In a word, the part of the syllable before the first vowel sound is the **onset**. The part of the syllable after the first vowel sound is the **rime**. For example, in *dog,* /d/ is the onset and *og* is the rime. Help students put together words that are broken down into parts by onset and rime.

1. **Say:** I'm going to break a word into two parts. Your job is to put the parts together and say the word. If the first part of a word is /r/ and the last part of the word is *ag,* then the whole word is *rag:* /r/ . . . *ag* . . . *rag.*

2. Say the following pairs of word parts. Have students tell you the word that each pair forms.

   ► /p/ . . . *ants pants*
   ► /l/ . . . *ast last*
   ► /k/ . . . *ab cab*

> **Objectives**
> • Identify individual sounds in words.
> • Identify a word when given the onset and rime.
> • Blend sounds to create words.
> • Given the letter, identify the most common sound.
> • Given the sound, identify the most common letter or letters.

Review Sounds and Letters

Help students review sounds for the letters *a, c, f, h, j, l, n, p,* and *r,* plus any letters that are confusing for students.

1. Place the following letter tiles in random order on students' whiteboard: *c, f, h, j, l, n, p,* and *r,* plus any letters that are confusing.

2. **Say:** Let's go over some letters and sounds.

3. Point to each letter tile and have students say a sound that letter makes.

   - *a* /ă/
   - *j* /j/
   - *c* /k/
   - *f* /f/
   - *h* /h/

   - *l* /l/
   - *n* /n/
   - *p* /p/
   - *r* /r/

4. Say each of the following sounds. Have students repeat the sound and touch the corresponding letter tile.

   - /ă/ *a*
   - /j/ *j*
   - /k/ *c*
   - /f/ *f*
   - /h/ *h*

   - /l/ *l*
   - /n/ *n*
   - /p/ *p*
   - /r/ *r*

5. As you do the activity, point to some letter tiles two or three times so that students don't think they are finished with a sound after they have named it.

6. Redirect students if they say an incorrect sound when you point to a letter tile.

   Say: That's the sound of another letter. What is the sound for this letter?

7. Help students if they touch the wrong letter tile after they repeat a sound.

   Say: That letter goes with the sound [sound for incorrect letter tile]. We're looking for the letter tile that goes with the sound [target sound].

Build Nonsense Words

Help students use letters and sounds to build nonsense words.

1. Place the following letter tiles at the top of students' whiteboard: *a, b, f, l, m, p,* and *t.*

2. Draw three horizontal lines across the middle of students' whiteboard to represent the sounds in a word.

3. **Say:** Some words don't have any meaning. We call these **nonsense words**. Even though we don't know what a word means, we can still read it. Nonsense words will be very important when we read longer words. When we break longer words into parts, sometimes the parts are nonsense words.

4. **Say:** Let's use letters and sounds to build the nonsense word *mab.*

5. Have students finger stretch the sounds in *mab.*

6. Have students

   ▸ Identify the first, next, and last sounds in *mab*.
   ▸ Choose the corresponding letter for each sound.
   ▸ Move the letters to the correct lines on their whiteboard.

7. Guide students with these questions:

   ▸ What is the first sound in *mab*? /m/
     Which line does the letter for that sound go on? the first one
   ▸ What is the next sound in *mab*? /ă/
     Which line does the letter for that sound go on? the second one
   ▸ What's the last sound in *mab*? /b/
     Which line does the letter for that sound go on? the last one

8. Have students touch and say the word.

9. Redirect students if they select the incorrect letter.

   Say: That sound is in the word [word], and it is the [first, second, third] sound. We want the sound [target sound].

   Continue until students select the correct letter.

10. Repeat the activity to build the following nonsense words:

    ▸ *paf* /p/ /ă/ /f /
    ▸ *tal* /t/ /ă/ /l/

Try It

Rhyme Time

Have students complete page PH 36 in *K¹² PhonicsWorks Basic Activity Book* for practice with words that rhyme. First have students read each sentence aloud and circle the word that rhymes with the underlined word. Then have them write the word and read the sentence aloud again.

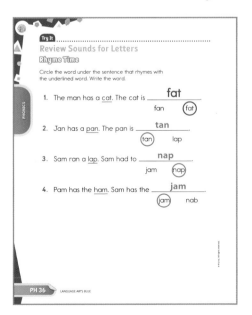

Objectives

• Identify words that rhyme.
• Identify individual sounds in words.
• Write words by applying grade-level phonics knowledge.
• Follow three-step directions.

Dictation: Build Words
Have students build words with the letters *a, b, f,* and *s.*

1. Place the following letters at the top of students' whiteboard: *a, b, f,* and *s.*

2. Say the word *baf.* Then give these directions to students:
   - ► Repeat the word.
   - ► Finger stretch the sounds in the word.
   - ► Spell the word with the letter tiles.
   - ► Touch and say the word.

3. When students have finished, write the following word on your whiteboard: *baf.*

4. Have them compare their answer to your correct version.

5. Repeat this procedure with the word *sab.*
   - ► If students make an error and don't see it, help them correct their mistake by having them finger stretch the sounds in the word they missed.
   - ► If students are having difficulty selecting the correct letters or sounds, review those letters or sounds that are confusing them.
   - ► If students have difficulty with first, middle, and last sounds, have them finger stretch the sounds in words.

 **20 minutes**

REVIEW: Sounds for Letters
Students will work online independently to

► Practice sounds for the letters *a, b, c, f, h, j, l, m, n, p, r, s,* and *t.*

Help students locate the online activities and provide support as needed.

Objectives
- Given the letter, identify the most common sound.
- Given the sound, identify the most common letter or letters.
- Identify beginning sounds in words.

Offline Alternative

No computer access? Have students name the letters that make the sounds /ă/, /b/, /k/, /f/, /h/, /j/, /l/, /m/, /n/, /p/, /r/, /s/, and /t/. Vice versa, have students name the sounds made by the letters *a, b, c, f, h, j, l, m, n, p, r, s,* and *t.* You might also ask students to spell simple words that contain those letters, or ask them to think of words that begin with those letters.

Vowels as Red Letters

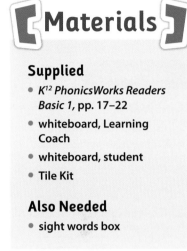

Lesson Overview

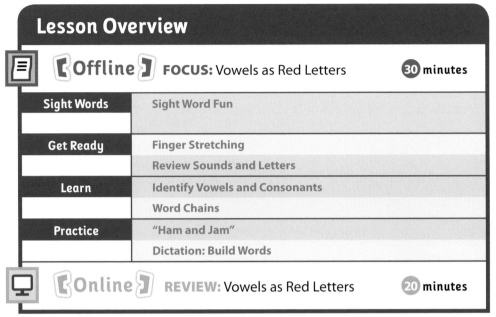

Offline	**FOCUS:** Vowels as Red Letters	**30** minutes
Sight Words	Sight Word Fun	
Get Ready	Finger Stretching	
	Review Sounds and Letters	
Learn	Identify Vowels and Consonants	
	Word Chains	
Practice	"Ham and Jam"	
	Dictation: Build Words	
Online	**REVIEW:** Vowels as Red Letters	**20** minutes

Materials

Supplied
- *K¹² PhonicsWorks Readers Basic 1*, pp. 17–22
- whiteboard, Learning Coach
- whiteboard, student
- Tile Kit

Also Needed
- sight words box

Advance Preparation

Place lowercase letter tiles in alphabetical order on your whiteboard.

 30 minutes

FOCUS: Vowels as Red Letters

Work **together** with students to complete offline Sight Words, Get Ready, Learn, and Try It activities.

Sight Words

Sight Word Fun

Help students learn the sight words *on, to,* and *in,* and up to two additional sight words they have yet to master.

1. Gather the sight word cards *on, to,* and *in,* and up to two additional sight word cards.

2. Choose one sight word card to begin.

   Say: Look at this word and take a picture of it in your mind. When you think you can spell the word yourself, turn the card over and use your letter tiles to spell the word.

3. After students spell the word, have them check the card to see if they spelled the word correctly.

   Say: Read aloud the word you spelled with the letter tiles.

4. Repeat the activity with the remaining sight words.

 Sight words can be very difficult for some students. Let students work at their own pace and really master these words.

Objectives
- Read sight words.
- Spell sight words.

Get Ready

Finger Stretching

Use finger stretching to help students identify individual sounds in words.

1. **Say:** Let's review finger stretching. In the word *fan,* the first sound is /f/, the middle sound is /ă/, and the last sound is /n/. I will finger stretch each sound as I say it. Then I'll say the word while pulling my fist toward my body.

2. Finger stretch the word *fan* for students.

3. **Say:** I'm going to say words with several sounds in them. You'll say the word and then finger stretch it while you say each sound in the word.

Objectives
- Identify individual sounds in words.
- Given the letter, identify the most common sound.
- Given the sound, identify the most common letter or letters.

4. Say the following words and have students finger stretch them. After they finger stretch each word, ask them the question for that word.

- *pal* /p/ /ă/ /l/   What is the first sound? /p/
- *sat* /s/ /ă/ /t/   What is the first sound? /s/
- *ran* /r/ /ă/ /n/   What is the last sound? /n/
- *bat* /b/ /ă/ /t/   What is the middle sound? /ă/
- *jam* /j/ /ă/ /m/   What is the first sound? /j/
- *Sam* /s/ /ă/ /m/   What is the middle sound? /ă/

 Refer to the *K¹² PhonicsWorks* video for a demonstration of finger stretching.

Review Sounds and Letters
Help students review sounds for the letters *a, b, h, j, l, m, n, p,* and *r,* plus any letters that are confusing for them.

1. Place the following letter tiles in random order on students' whiteboard: *a, b, h, j, l, m, n, p,* and *r,* plus any letters that are confusing.

2. **Say:** Let's go over some letters and sounds.

3. Point to each letter tile and have students say a sound that letter makes.

- *a* /ă/
- *m* /m/
- *b* /b/
- *j* /j/
- *h* /h/
- *l* /l/
- *n* /n/
- *p* /p/
- *r* /r/

4. Say each of the following sounds. Have students repeat the sound and touch the corresponding letter tile.

- /ă/ *a*
- /m/ *m*
- /b/ *b*
- /j/ *j*
- /h/ *h*
- /l/ *l*
- /n/ *n*
- /p/ *p*
- /r/ *r*

5. As you do the activity, point to some letter tiles two or three times so that students don't think they are finished with a sound after they have named it.

6. Redirect students if they say an incorrect sound when you point to a letter tile.

   Say: That's the sound of another letter. What is the sound for this letter?

7. Help students if they touch the wrong letter tile after they repeat a sound.

   Say: That letter goes with the sound [sound for incorrect letter tile]. We're looking for the letter tile that goes with the sound [target sound].

Learn

Identify Vowels and Consonants

Help students identify vowels and consonants. Grab your whiteboard with letters.

1. **Say:** All the red letters on my whiteboard are called **vowels**. Every syllable in every word has at least one vowel in it.

2. **Say:** Let's name the vowels and point to them as we name them.

   ▸ What is the first vowel? *a*
   ▸ What is the next vowel? *e*
   ▸ What is the next vowel? *i*
   ▸ What is the next vowel? *o*
   ▸ What is the last vowel? *u*

3. **Say:** Let's look at some words and figure out what the vowel is.

4. Write these words on students' whiteboard:

   ▸ *cat*
   ▸ *red*
   ▸ *lip*
   ▸ *hot*
   ▸ *pun*

5. Have students read each word aloud.

6. Have students say the letter for the vowel and its sound in each word.

   ▸ *cat* a, /ă/
   ▸ *red* e, /ĕ/
   ▸ *lip* i, /ĭ/
   ▸ *hot* o, /ŏ/
   ▸ *pun* u, /ŭ/

7. **Say:** All the black letters on my whiteboard are called **consonants**.

8. **Say:** Let's name some consonants and point to them as we name them.

   Point to several consonants on your whiteboard, and have students say the name of each letter.

9. Point to the following letters. Have students say the name of each letter and say whether it is a vowel or a consonant.

   ▸ *v* consonant
   ▸ *x* consonant
   ▸ *b* consonant
   ▸ *a* vowel
   ▸ *e* vowel
   ▸ *s* consonant

   ▸ *f* consonant
   ▸ *o* vowel
   ▸ *t* consonant
   ▸ *l* consonant
   ▸ *u* vowel
   ▸ *m* consonant

Objectives
- Identify and distinguish between consonants and vowels.
- Identify and use vowels and vowel sounds.
- Identify short vowel sounds.
- Identify individual sounds in words.
- Identify the new word when one sound is changed in a word.

Word Chains

Have students build words by adding and changing letters to help them recognize and use individual sounds in words.

1. Place the following letters at the top of students' whiteboard: *a, b, c, f, n,* and *t.*

2. **Say:** I am going to build the first word in a chain. The word is *cab.*

    ▸ I will pull down the letters for the sounds /k/, /ă/, and /b/ to spell the word *cab.*

    ▸ I will touch and say *cab.* To change *cab* to *can,* I will think about which sound changes from the word *cab* to *can.* I will need to replace the letter *b* with the letter *n.*

    ▸ Touch and say the word *can.* Now it's your turn to change *can* to *fan.* You can spell *fan* by making only one change. Touch and say the new word.

3. Redirect students if they select the incorrect for any sound.

    Say: That letter is for the sound [incorrect sound]. We want the letter for the sound [target sound]. What letter makes that sound? Answers will vary.

4. Redirect students if they name the sound incorrectly.

    Say: To change the word [first word] to [target word], we need the letter for the sound [target sound].

    Show students how to make the change. Have them touch and say the new word after they move the letters.

5. Follow this procedure to make the following words: *fat, cat, bat, ban, tan.*

6. For every new word, have students add, replace, or remove only one letter.

TIP If students struggle, review the sounds and letters that are confusing them.

Try It
· ·

"Ham and Jam"

Have students read "Ham and Jam" on page 17 of *K¹² PhonicsWorks Readers Basic 1.*

Students should read the story silently once or twice before reading the story aloud. When students miss a word that can be sounded out, point to it and give them three to six seconds to try the word again. If students still miss the word, tell them the word so the flow of the story isn't interrupted.

After reading the story, make a list of all the words students missed, and go over those words with them. You may use letter tiles to show students how to read the words.

Objectives

- Read aloud grade-level text with appropriate automaticity, prosody, accuracy, and rate.
- Decode words by applying grade-level word analysis skills.
- Track text from left to right.
- Turn pages sequentially.
- Write words by applying grade-level phonics knowledge.
- Follow three-step directions.

Dictation: Build Words

Have students build words with the letters *a, b, h, j, m,* and *t.*

1. Place the following letters at the top of students' whiteboard: *a, b, h, j, m,* and *t.*

2. Say the word *jab.* Then give these directions to students:

   ▸ Repeat the word.
   ▸ Finger stretch the sounds in the word.
   ▸ Spell the word with the letter tiles.
   ▸ Touch and say the word.

3. When students have finished, write the following word on the whiteboard: *jab.*

4. Have them compare their answer to your correct version.

5. Repeat this procedure with the words *ham* and *mat.*

   ▸ If students make an error and don't see it, help them correct their mistake by having them finger stretch the sounds in the word they missed.
   ▸ If students are having difficulty selecting the correct letters or sounds, review those letters or sounds that are confusing them.
   ▸ If students have difficulty with first, middle, and last sounds, have them finger stretch the sounds in words.

 **minutes**

REVIEW: Vowels as Red Letters

Students will work online independently to

▸ Practice identifying vowels and consonants.

Help students locate the online activities and provide support as needed.

Offline Alternative

No computer access? Have students point out vowels and consonants in words that they see and say what sound each letter makes.

> **Objectives**
> • Identify and use vowels and vowel sounds.
> • Identify individual sounds in words.
> • Identify and distinguish between consonants and vowels.

Unit Checkpoint

Lesson Overview

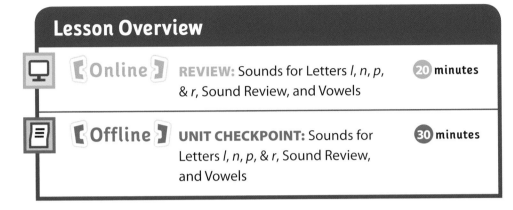

🖥️	**【Online】**	**REVIEW:** Sounds for Letters *l*, *n*, *p*, & *r*, Sound Review, and Vowels	**20** minutes
📄	**【Offline】**	**UNIT CHECKPOINT:** Sounds for Letters *l*, *n*, *p*, & *r*, Sound Review, and Vowels	**30** minutes

【Materials】

Supplied
- *K¹² PhonicsWorks Basic Assessments*, pp. PH 49–54

⭐ Objectives

- Identify the letter, given the sound /l/.
- Identify the letter, given the sound /n/.
- Identify the letter, given the sound /p/.
- Identify the letter, given the sound /r/.
- Identify the sound, given the letter *l*.
- Identify the sound, given the letter *n*.
- Identify the sound, given the letter *p*.
- Identify the sound, given the letter *r*.
- Identify beginning sounds in words.
- Identify letters of the alphabet.
- Identify individual sounds in words.
- Given the letter, identify the most common sound.
- Given the sound, identify the most common letter or letters.
- Read sight words.
- Read instructional-level text with 90% accuracy.
- Read aloud grade-level text with appropriate automaticity, prosody, accuracy, and rate.

 **20** minutes

REVIEW: **Sounds for Letters *l*, *n*, *p*, & *r*, Sound Review, and Vowels**

Students will review the letters *l*, *n*, *p*, and *r* and their sounds, and vowels to prepare for the Unit Checkpoint. Help students locate the online activities and provide support as needed.

 **30 minutes**

UNIT CHECKPOINT: Sounds for Letters *l, n, p, & r*, Sound Review, and Vowels

Explain that students are going to show what they have learned about letters and sounds.

1. Give students the Unit Checkpoint pages for the Sounds for Letters *l, n, p, & r*, Sound Review, and Vowels unit and print the Unit Checkpoint Answer Key, if you'd like.

2. Use the instructions below to help administer the Checkpoint to students. On the Answer Key or another sheet of paper, note student answers to oral response questions to help with scoring the Checkpoint later.

3. Use the Answer Key to score the Checkpoint, and then enter the results online.

Part 1. Say Sounds Have students read across the rows from left to right and say a sound that each letter makes. Note any sounds they say incorrectly.

Part 2. Word Dissection For each word, say the sound students should identify. Have them read the word aloud and circle the letter or groups of letters that spell the sound.

21. *beginning sound*

22. *ending sound*

23. *middle sound*

24. *ending sound*

25. *middle sound*

Part 3. Finger Stretching Say each word to students. Have them say each word aloud and finger stretch the sounds. Note any words they finger stretch incorrectly.

26. *ran*   29. *pan*

27. *can*   30. *man*

28. *map*   31. *nap*

Part 4. Circle the Letter Say each sound and have students circle the letter that makes the sound.

32. /l/   36. /p/

33. /r/   37. /b/

34. /n/   38. /ă/

35. /ă/   39. /h/

Part 5. Read Aloud Listen to students read the sentences aloud. Count and note the number of words they read correctly.

Part 6. Say Letters Say each sound. Have students say the letter that makes that sound. Note any incorrect responses.

41. /ă/
42. /l/
43. /n/
44. /p/
45. /r/
46. /ă/
47. /n/
48. /p/
49. /r/

50. /l/
51. /s/
52. /b/
53. /h/
54. /f/
55. /m/
56. /j/
57. /t/
58. /k/

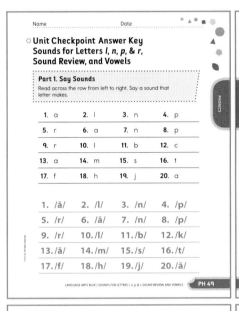

Name _____ Date _____

Unit Checkpoint Answer Key
Sounds for Letters *l, n, p,* & *r,*
Sound Review, and Vowels

Part 1. Say Sounds
Read across the row from left to right. Say a sound that letter makes.

1. a	2. l	3. n	4. p
5. r	6. a	7. n	8. p
9. r	10. l	11. b	12. c
13. a	14. m	15. s	16. t
17. f	18. h	19. j	20. a

1. /ă/	2. /l/	3. /n/	4. /p/
5. /r/	6. /ă/	7. /n/	8. /p/
9. /r/	10. /l/	11. /b/	12. /k/
13. /ă/	14. /m/	15. /s/	16. /t/
17. /f/	18. /h/	19. /j/	20. /ă/

LANGUAGE ARTS BLUE | SOUNDS FOR LETTERS *l, n, p,* & *r,* SOUND REVIEW, AND VOWELS   **PH 49**

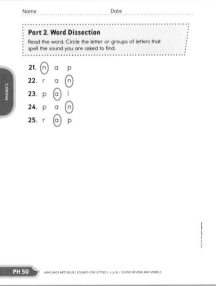

PH 50   LANGUAGE ARTS BLUE | SOUNDS FOR LETTERS *l, n, p,* & *r,* SOUND REVIEW, AND VOWELS

Name _____ Date _____

Part 2. Word Dissection
Read the word. Circle the letter or groups of letters that spell the sound you are asked to find.

21. (n) a   p
22. r   a   (n)
23. p   (a)   l
24. p   a   (n)
25. r   (a)   p

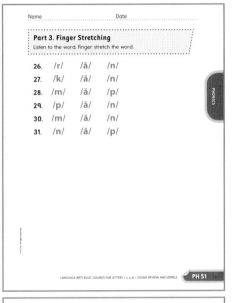

Name _____ Date _____

Part 3. Finger Stretching
Listen to the word. Finger stretch the word.

26. /r/   /ă/   /n/
27. /k/   /ă/   /n/
28. /m/   /ă/   /p/
29. /p/   /ă/   /n/
30. /m/   /ă/   /n/
31. /n/   /ă/   /p/

LANGUAGE ARTS BLUE | SOUNDS FOR LETTERS *l, n, p,* & *r,* SOUND REVIEW, AND VOWELS   **PH 51**

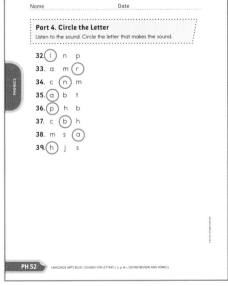

Name _____ Date _____

Part 4. Circle the Letter
Listen to the sound. Circle the letter that makes the sound.

32. (l)   n   p
33. a   m   (r)
34. c   (n)   m
35. (a)   b   t
36. (p)   h   b
37. c   (b)   h
38. m   s   (a)
39. (h)   j   s

PH 52   LANGUAGE ARTS BLUE | SOUNDS FOR LETTERS *l, n, p,* & *r,* SOUND REVIEW, AND VOWELS

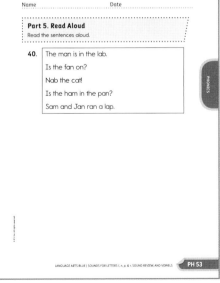

Name _____ Date _____

Part 5. Read Aloud
Read the sentences aloud.

40.
> The man is in the lab.
> Is the fan on?
> Nab the cat!
> Is the ham in the pan?
> Sam and Jan ran a lap.

LANGUAGE ARTS BLUE | SOUNDS FOR LETTERS *l, n, p,* & *r,* SOUND REVIEW, AND VOWELS   **PH 53**

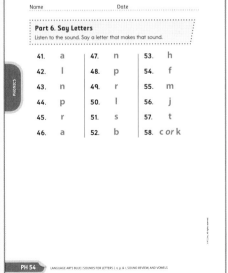

Name _____ Date _____

Part 6. Say Letters
Listen to the sound. Say a letter that makes that sound.

41. a	47. n	53. h
42. l	48. p	54. f
43. n	49. r	55. m
44. p	50. l	56. j
45. r	51. s	57. t
46. a	52. b	58. c or k

PH 54   LANGUAGE ARTS BLUE | SOUNDS FOR LETTERS *l, n, p,* & *r,* SOUND REVIEW, AND VOWELS

Sound for Letter *o*

Unit Overview

In this unit, students will
- ▶ Learn the sight words *it*, *he*, and *was*.
- ▶ Identify the letters and sounds in the alphabet.
- ▶ Identify the sounds for the letters *o*, *d*, *g*, and *k*.
- ▶ Identify beginning and ending sounds in words.
- ▶ Build words.

Lesson Overview

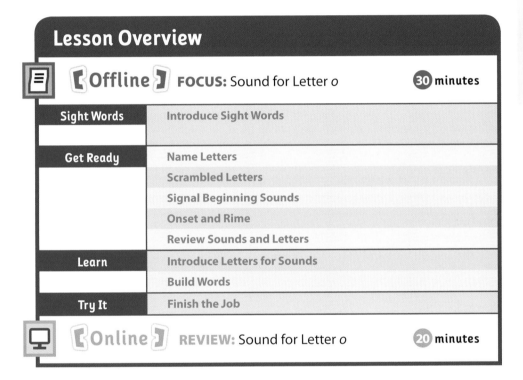

📄 **Offline** FOCUS: Sound for Letter *o* **30** minutes

Sight Words	Introduce Sight Words
Get Ready	Name Letters
	Scrambled Letters
	Signal Beginning Sounds
	Onset and Rime
	Review Sounds and Letters
Learn	Introduce Letters for Sounds
	Build Words
Try It	Finish the Job

🖥 **Online** REVIEW: Sound for Letter *o* **20** minutes

Advance Preparation

Place lowercase letter tiles in alphabetical order on your whiteboard.

 **Offline** **30** minutes

FOCUS: Sound for Letter *o*

Work **together** with students to complete offline Sight Words, Get Ready, Learn, and Try It activities.

Sight Words ....

Introduce Sight Words

Help students learn the sight words *it*, *he*, and *was*.

1. Gather the sight word cards *it*, *he*, and *was*.

2. Show students the *it* card.

   Say: This is the word *it*. We see this word so often that we want to be able to read and spell *it* quickly without thinking about it. Look closely at the word *it*. Spell the word *it* aloud. Take a picture of the word *it* in your mind. When you think you can spell *it* yourself, turn the card over and use your letter tiles to spell the word *it*. Check blue card to see if you spelled the word *it* correctly. Read aloud the word you spelled with the letter tiles.

3. Repeat the activity with the remaining sight words.

4. Chart students' progress on the back of each card.

   ▸ Divide the back of the card into two columns.
   ▸ Label the first column "Read" and the second column "Spell."
   ▸ Record the dates that students read or spell the word correctly. When students can read and spell the word correctly three times in a row, they have mastered the word. You may want to put a star or sticker on the card when they have mastered that word.

5. Add the cards to students' sight words box.

TIP Sight words can be very difficult for some students. Let students work at their own pace and really master these words, as they occur frequently in reading and writing.

Objectives
- Read sight words.
- Spell sight words.

Get Ready

Name Letters

To help students master the alphabet, have them practice identifying and naming letters. Grab your whiteboard with letters placed in alphabetical order.

1. **Say:** Let's practice naming letters.

2. Have students touch the last letter in each row on your whiteboard and say the letter's name.

3. Have students touch the third letter in each row and say the letter's name. Repeat the actions and mix up the order.

   ▸ If students name a letter incorrectly, name the letter students missed. Have students touch the letter and say its name. Have them trace the shape of the letter with their finger on the brown side of their board and have them say the letter's name as they trace the shape.

   ▸ If students name a letter incorrectly twice, point to the letter and tell them its name. Have students touch the letter and say its name.

   ▸ If students continue to struggle with a letter, review that letter with them daily until understanding is achieved.

TIP To help students remember what a row is, run your finger from left to right along a row of letters. Have students do the same. Have them show you another row.

Objectives

- Identify letters of the alphabet.
- Identify beginning sounds in words.
- Identify individual sounds in words.
- Given the letter, identify the most common sound.
- Given the sound, identify the most common letter or letters.
- Identify a word when given the onset and rime.
- Blend sounds to create words.

Scrambled Letters

To help students master the alphabet, have them practice identifying and naming letters.

1. Place the following letter tiles in random order on students' whiteboard: *b*, *k*, *m*, and *z*.

2. Have students arrange the letters in alphabetical order.

TIP Students may find this activity easier if they slowly sing "The Alphabet Song" to themselves as they work.

Signal Beginning Sounds

Use a special signal to help students identify **beginning sounds** in words.

1. **Say:** I'm going to tell you a special sound, and then I'll say some words. Repeat each word I say and make a special signal to tell me where the special sound is. If the special sound is at the beginning of the word, touch your ear. If the special sound is **not** at the beginning of the word, just smile at me. For example,

   ▸ If I ask you to listen for the sound /ŏ/ and I say the word *often*, you'll repeat the word *often* and touch your ear because *often* has the sound /ŏ/ at the beginning.

   ▸ If I say the word *dig*, you'll repeat the word *dig* and smile at me because *dig* has the sound /d/, not /ŏ/, at the beginning.

2. Say each sound and group of words. Have students make the special signal to identify the beginning sound.

- ► /ŏ/: *often, Oscar, after, wish, odd* touch ear: *often, Oscar, odd*
- ► /k/: *clock, cup, cast, scar* touch ear: *clock, cup, cast*
- ► /v/: *fun, very, vine, Vincent, five* touch ear: *very, vine, Vincent*
- ► /p/: *pretty, phone, plus, party, blast* touch ear: *pretty, plus, party*

TIP If students can't identify the beginning sound of each word, say the word again and emphasize the beginning sound by repeating it three times (for example, /t/ /t/ /t/ *taste*). You can also draw out the beginning sound when you say the word (for example, *mmmommy*). If necessary, have students look at you mouth while you repeat the sounds.

Onset and Rime

In a word, the part of the syllable before the first vowel sound is the **onset**. The part of the syllable after the first vowel sound is the **rime**. For example, in *first*, /f/ is the onset and *irst* is the rime. Help students put together words that are broken down into parts by onset and rime.

1. **Say:** I'm going to break a word into two parts. Your job is to put the parts together and say the word. If the first part of a word is /f/ and the last part of the word is *irst*, then the whole word is *first*: /f/ . . . *irst* . . . *first*.

2. Say the following pairs of word parts. Have students tell you the word that each pair forms.

- ► /h/ . . . *elp* help
- ► /k/ . . . *ar* car
- ► /b/ . . . *ond* bond

Review Sounds and Letters

Help students review sounds for the letters *a, b, c, f, h, j, l, m, n, p, r, s,* and *t,* plus any letters that are confusing for them.

1. Place the following letter tiles in random order on students' whiteboard: *a, b, c, f, h, j, l, m, n, p, r, s,* and *t,* plus any other letters that are confusing.

2. **Say:** Let's go over some letters and sounds.

3. Point to each letter tile and have students say the sound for that letter.

- ► *a* /ă/
- ► *m* /m/
- ► *s* /s/
- ► *t* /t/
- ► *b* /b/
- ► *f* /f/
- ► *c* /k/

- ► *h* /h/
- ► *j* /j/
- ► *l* /l/
- ► *n* /n/
- ► *p* /p/
- ► *r* /r/

4. Say each of the following sounds. Have students repeat the sound and touch the corresponding letter tile.

- ▸ /ă/ *a*
- ▸ /m/ *m*
- ▸ /s/ *s*
- ▸ /t/ *t*
- ▸ /b/ *b*
- ▸ /f/ *f*
- ▸ /k/ *c*

- ▸ /h/ *h*
- ▸ /j/ *j*
- ▸ /l/ *l*
- ▸ /n/ *n*
- ▸ /p/ *p*
- ▸ /r/ *r*

5. As you do the activity, point to some letter tiles two or three times so that students don't think they are finished with a sound after they have named it.

6. Redirect students if they say an incorrect sound when you point to a letter tile.

   Say: That's the sound of another letter. What is the sound for this letter?

7. Help students if they touch the wrong letter tile after they repeat a sound.

   Say: That letter goes with the sound [sound for incorrect letter tile]. We're looking for the letter tile that goes with the sound [target sound].

Learn

Introduce Letters for Sounds

To help students learn the lowercase letter *o*, have them practice identifying and naming the letter from the sound.

1. Place the following letter tile on students' whiteboard: *o*.

2. **Say:** Let's learn a sound for the letter *o*. When we see the letter *o*, we sometimes say the sound /ŏ/.

3. Have students touch the letter *o* and say /ŏ/.

4. **Say:** Let's practice this sound and letter.

5. Say the sound /ŏ/. Have students repeat the sound and touch the letter. It is important for students to touch the letter while they say the sound.

6. Redirect students if they name the letter and not the sound.

   Say: You're right that the name of the letter is [letter]. We want the sound for this letter. What is the sound?

7. Redirect students if they name the sound incorrectly.

   Say: That's the sound of another letter. The sound for this letter is [target sound]. Touch the letter and say the sound.

Objectives
- Identify the letter, given the sound /ŏ/.
- Identify the sound, given the letter *o*.
- Identify and use the sound /ŏ/.
- Identify individual sounds in words.
- Blend sounds to create words.

Build Words

Help students use letters and sounds to build words.

1. Place the following letter tiles at the top of students' whiteboard: *b, c, j, o, p,* and *t*.

2. Draw three horizontal lines across the middle of students' whiteboard to represent the sounds in a word.

3. **Say:** Let's use letters and sounds to build the word *cot*.

4. Have students finger stretch the sounds in *cot*.

5. Have students

   ► Identify the first, next, and last sounds in *cot*.
   ► Choose the corresponding letter for each of the sounds.
   ► Move the letters to the correct lines on their whiteboard.

6. Guide students with these questions:

   ► What is the first sound in *cot*? /k/
   Which line does the letter for that sound go on? the first one
   ► What is the next sound in *cot*? /ŏ/
   Which line does the letter for that sound go on? the second one
   ► What's the last sound in *cot*? /t/
   Which line does the letter for that sound go on? the last one

7. Have students touch and say the word.

8. Redirect students if they select the incorrect letter.

   Say: That sound is in the word [word], and it is the [first, second, third] sound. We want the sound [target sound].

   Continue until students select the correct letter.

9. Repeat the activity to build the following words:

   ► *job* /j/ /ŏ/ /b/
   ► *pot* /p/ /ŏ/ /t/

Try It

Finish the Job

Have students complete page PH 37 in *K¹² PhonicsWorks Basic Activity Book* for more practice with the sound /ŏ/. Have them choose a word from the box that best completes the sentence and write the word. Have them read the sentence aloud.

Objectives
- Read sight words.
- Identify and use the sound /ŏ/.

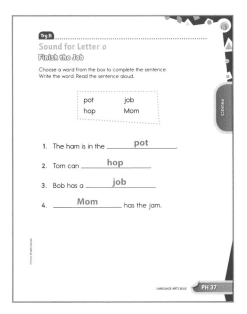

Online · 20 minutes

REVIEW: Sound for Letter *o*

Students will work online independently to

▸ Practice the sound /ŏ/ for the letter *o*.
▸ Practice decoding text by reading a story.

Help students locate the online activities and provide support as needed.

Offline Alternative

No computer access? Have students point out and name things that contain the sound /ŏ/ for the letter *o* (for example, *pot* and *ostrich*). You might also ask students to spell words that contain the sound /ŏ/.

Objectives
- Identify the letter, given the sound /ŏ/.
- Identify the sound, given the letter *o*.
- Identify and use the sound /ŏ/.
- Identify individual sounds in words.
- Read aloud grade-level text with appropriate automaticity, prosody, accuracy, and rate.
- Decode words by applying grade-level word analysis skills.

Sounds for Letters *d* and *g*

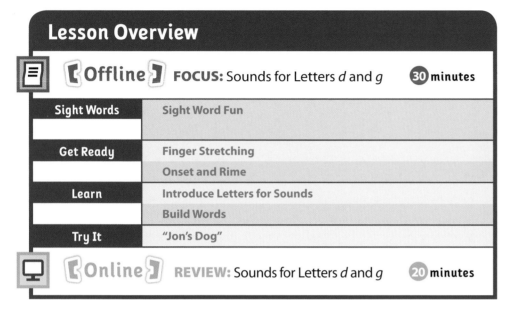

Lesson Overview

Offline FOCUS: Sounds for Letters *d* and *g* **30** minutes

Sight Words	Sight Word Fun
Get Ready	Finger Stretching
	Onset and Rime
Learn	Introduce Letters for Sounds
	Build Words
Try It	"Jon's Dog"

Online REVIEW: Sounds for Letters *d* and *g* **20** minutes

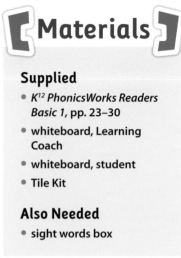

Materials

Supplied
- *K¹² PhonicsWorks Readers Basic 1*, pp. 23–30
- whiteboard, Learning Coach
- whiteboard, student
- Tile Kit

Also Needed
- sight words box

 **Offline** 30 minutes

FOCUS: Sounds for Letters *d* and *g*

Work **together** with students to complete offline Sight Words, Get Ready, Learn, and Try It activities.

Sight Words

Sight Word Fun

Help students learn the sight words *it*, *he*, and *was*, and up to two additional sight words they have yet to master.

1. Gather the sight word cards *it*, *he*, and *was*, and up to two additional sight word cards.

2. Choose one sight word card to begin.

   Say: Look at this word and take a picture of it in your mind. When you think you can spell the word yourself, turn the card over and use your letter tiles to spell the word.

3. After students spell the word, have them check the card to see if they spelled the word correctly.

   Say: Read aloud the word you spelled with the letter tiles.

4. Repeat the activity with the remaining sight words.

TIP Sight words can be very difficult for some students. Let students work at their own pace and really master these words.

> **Objectives**
> * Read sight words.
> * Spell sight words.

Get Ready

Finger Stretching

Use finger stretching to help students identify individual sounds in words.

1. **Say:** Let's review finger stretching. In the word *hop*, the first sound is /h/, the next sound is /ŏ/, and the last sound is /p/. I will finger stretch each sound as I say it. Then I'll say the word, while pulling my fist toward my body.

2. Finger stretch the word *hop* for students.

3. **Say:** I'm going to say words with several sounds in them. You'll say the word and then finger stretch it while you say each sound in the word.

4. Say the following words and have students finger stretch them. After they finger stretch each word, ask them the question for that word.

   ▸ *pot* /p/ /ŏ/ /t/   What is the middle sound? /ŏ/
   ▸ *dog* /d/ /ŏ/ /g/   What is the first sound? /d/
   ▸ *tan* /t/ /ă/ /n/   What is the last sound? /n/
   ▸ *fog* /f/ /ŏ/ /g/   What is the middle sound? /ŏ/
   ▸ *cap* /k/ /ă/ /p/   What is the first sound? /k/
   ▸ *got* /g/ /ŏ/ /t/   What is the middle sound? /ŏ/

TIP Refer to the *K¹² PhonicsWorks* video for a demonstration of finger stretching.

> **Objectives**
> * Identify individual sounds in words.
> * Identify a word when given the onset and rime.
> * Blend sounds to create words.

Onset and Rime

In a word, the part of the syllable before the first vowel sound is the **onset**. The part of the syllable after the first vowel sound is the **rime**. For example, in *dog*, /d/ is the onset and *og* is the rime. Help students put together words that are broken down into parts by onset and rime.

1. **Say:** I'm going to break a word into two parts. Your job is to put the parts together and say the word. If the first part of a word is /k/ and the last part of the word is *ab*, then the whole word is *cab*: /k/. . . *ab* . . . *cab*.

2. Say the following pairs of word parts. Have students tell you the word that each pair forms.

   ▸ /r/ . . . *ob* rob
   ▸ /j/ . . . *og* jog
   ▸ /p/ . . . *ot* pot
   ▸ /k/ . . . *ap* cap
   ▸ /b/ . . . *op* bop

Learn

Introduce Letters for Sounds

To help students learn the lowercase letters *d* and *g*, have them practice identifying and naming the letters from the sounds.

1. Place the following letter tiles on students' whiteboard: *d* and *g*.

2. **Say:** Let's learn sounds for letters. When we see the letter *d*, we say the sound /d/. When we see the letter *g*, we sometimes say the sound /g/.

3. Have students

   ▸ Touch the letter *d* and say /d/.
   ▸ Touch the letter *g* and say /g/.

4. **Say:** Let's practice these sounds and letters.

5. Say the sounds /d/ and /g/ one at a time. Have students repeat each sound and touch the letter for each sound. It is important for students to touch the letter while they say the sound.

6. Redirect students if they name the letter and not the sound.

   Say: You're right that the name of the letter is [letter]. We want the sound for this letter. What is the sound?

7. Redirect students if they name the sound incorrectly.

   Say: That's the sound of another letter. The sound for this letter is [target sound]. Touch the letter and say the sound.

8. Help students. If they touch the wrong letter, point to the correct letter.

   Say: This is the letter for the sound [target sound]. Touch and say its sound.

Objectives

- Identify the sound, given the letter *d*.
- Identify the letter, given the sound /d/.
- Identify and use the sound /d/.
- Identify the sound, given the letter *g*.
- Identify the letter, given the sound /g/.
- Identify and use the sound /g/.
- Blend sounds to create words.
- Identify individual sounds in words.
- Given the letter, identify the most common sound.
- Given the sound, identify the most common letter or letters.

Build Words

Help students use letters and sounds to build words.

1. Place the following letter tiles at the top of students' whiteboard: *d, g, o,* and *t.*

2. Draw three horizontal lines across the middle of students' whiteboard to represent the sounds in a word.

3. **Say:** Let's use letters and sounds to build the word *got.*

4. Have students finger stretch the sounds in *got.*

5. Have students

    ▸ Identify the first, next, and last sounds in *got.*
    ▸ Choose the corresponding letter for each of the sounds.
    ▸ Move the letters to the correct lines on their whiteboard.

6. Guide students with these questions:

    ▸ What is the first sound in *got?* /g/
      Which line does the letter for that sound go on? the first one
    ▸ What is the next sound in *got?* /ŏ/
      Which line does the letter for that sound go on? the second one
    ▸ What's the last sound in *got?* /t/
      Which line does the letter for that sound go on? the last one

7. Have students touch and say the word.

8. Redirect students if they select the incorrect letter.

    Say: That sound is in the word [word], and it is the [first, second, third] sound. We want the sound [target sound].

    Continue until students select the correct letter.

9. Repeat the activity to build the word *dog.* /d/ /ŏ/ /g/

Try It ....

"Jon's Dog"

Have students read "Jon's Dog" on page 23 of *K¹² PhonicsWorks Readers Basic 1.*

Students should read the story silently once or twice before reading the story aloud. When they miss a word that can be sounded out, point to it and give them three to six seconds to try the word again. If students still miss the word, tell them the word so the flow of the story isn't interrupted.

After reading the story, make a list of all the words students missed, and go over those words with them. You may use letter tiles to show them how to read the words.

Objectives

- Read aloud grade-level text with appropriate automaticity, prosody, accuracy, and rate.
- Decode words by applying grade-level word analysis skills.
- Track text from left to right.
- Turn pages sequentially.

 **minutes**

REVIEW: Sounds for Letters *d* and *g*

Students will work online independently to

▶ Practice sounds for the letters *d* and *g*.

Help students locate the online activities and provide support as needed.

Offline Alternative

No computer access? Have students point out and name things that begin with the sounds for the letters *d* and *g* (for example, *dog* and *gap*). You might also ask students to spell words that contain the sounds /d/ and /g/.

Objectives

- Identify the letter, given the sound /d/.
- Identify the sound, given the letter *d*.
- Identify and use the sound /d/.
- Identify the letter, given the sound /g/.
- Identify the sound, given the letter *g*.
- Identify and use the sound /g/.
- Identify beginning sounds in words.

Sounds for Letters *k* and *v*

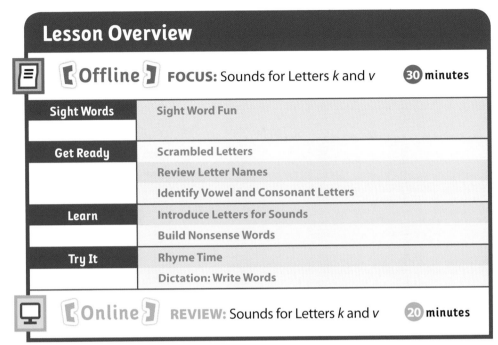

Lesson Overview

Offline FOCUS: Sounds for Letters *k* and *v* **30** minutes

Sight Words	Sight Word Fun
Get Ready	Scrambled Letters
	Review Letter Names
	Identify Vowel and Consonant Letters
Learn	Introduce Letters for Sounds
	Build Nonsense Words
Try It	Rhyme Time
	Dictation: Write Words

Online REVIEW: Sounds for Letters *k* and *v* **20** minutes

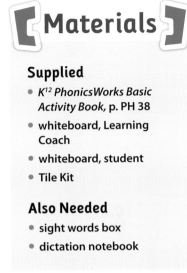

Materials

Supplied
- *K¹² PhonicsWorks Basic Activity Book*, p. PH 38
- whiteboard, Learning Coach
- whiteboard, student
- Tile Kit

Also Needed
- sight words box
- dictation notebook

Advance Preparation

Place lowercase letter tiles in alphabetical order on your whiteboard.

Big Ideas

Decoding nonsense words allows early readers to rely on letter-sound knowledge only.

 **Offline** 🕤 minutes

FOCUS: Sounds for Letters *k* and *v*

Work **together** with students to complete offline Sight Words, Get Ready, Learn, and Try It activities.

Sight Words ●

Sight Word Fun

Help students learn the sight words *it*, *he*, and *was*, and up to two additional sight words they have yet to master.

Objectives
- Read sight words.
- Spell sight words.

1. Gather the sight word cards *it*, *he*, and *was*, and up to two additional sight word cards.

2. Choose one sight word card to begin.

   Say: Look at this word and take a picture of it in your mind. When you think you can spell the word yourself, turn the card over and use your letter tiles to spell the word.

3. After students spell the word, have them check the card to see if they spelled the word correctly.

   Say: Read aloud the word you spelled with the letter tiles.

4. Repeat the activity with the remaining sight words.

   TIP Sight words can be very difficult for some students. Let students work at their own pace and really master these words.

Get Ready ●

Scrambled Letters

To help students master the alphabet, have them practice identifying and naming letters.

Objectives
- Identify letters of the alphabet.
- Given the letter, identify the most common sound.
- Given the sound, identify the most common letter or letters.
- Identify and use vowels and vowel sounds.

1. Place the following lowercase letters in random order on students' whiteboard: *c, d, e, f, g, k, o,* and *v*.

2. Have students arrange the letters in alphabetical order.

   TIP Students may find this activity easier if they slowly sing "The Alphabet Song" to themselves as they work.

Review Letter Names

To help students master the alphabet, have them practice identifying and naming the letters *c*, *h*, *p*, *s*, and *y*. Grab your whiteboard with letters.

1. Point to each letter, and have students touch and name each one.

   c   h   p   s   y

2. Say the name of each letter. After each one, have students repeat the name and touch the tile.

   c   h   p   s   y

3. Redirect students if they name a letter incorrectly.

   ▸ Name the letter students missed.
   ▸ Have them touch the letter and say its name.
   ▸ Have students trace the shape of the letter with their finger on the brown side of their board, and have them say the letter's name as they trace the shape.
   ▸ If students name a letter incorrectly twice, point to the letter and tell them its name. Have students touch the letter and say its name.

Identify Vowel and Consonant Letters

Help students identify vowels and consonants. Grab your whiteboard with letters.

1. **Say:** Let's name the vowels and consonants. I will point to a letter. Say the name of the letter, and then tell me if it is a vowel or a consonant.

2. Point to the following letters. Have students say the name of each letter and say whether it is a vowel or a consonant.

   ▸ *a* vowel
   ▸ *l* consonant
   ▸ *m* consonant
   ▸ *o* vowel
   ▸ *p* consonant
   ▸ *a* vowel
   ▸ *j* consonant
   ▸ *o* vowel
   ▸ *d* consonant
   ▸ *h* consonant

Learn

Introduce Letters for Sounds

To help students learn the lowercase letters for the sounds /k/ and /v/, have them practice identifying and naming the letters from the sounds.

1. Place the following letter tiles on students' whiteboard: *k* and *v*.

2. **Say:** Let's learn sounds for letters. When we see the letter *k*, we often say the sound /k/. When we see the letter *v*, we say the sound /v/.

3. Have students
   - ▸ Touch the letter *k* and say /k/.
   - ▸ Touch the letter *v* and say /v/.

4. **Say:** Let's practice these sounds and letters.

5. Say the sounds /k/ and /v/ one at a time. Have students repeat each sound and touch the letter for each sound. It is important for students to touch the letter while they say the sound.

6. Redirect students if they name the letter and not the sound.

   Say: You're right that the name of the letter is [letter]. We want the sound for this letter. What is the sound?

7. Redirect students if they name the sound incorrectly.

   Say: That's the sound of another letter. The sound for this letter is [target sound]. Touch the letter and say the sound.

8. Help students. If they touch the wrong letter, point to the correct letter.

   Say: This is the letter for the sound [target sound]. Touch and say its sound.

Objectives
- Identify the sound, given the letter *k*.
- Identify the letter or letters, given the sound /k/.
- Identify and use the sound /k/.
- Identify the sound, given the letter *v*.
- Identify the letter, given the sound /v/.
- Identify and use the sound /v/.
- Blend sounds to create words.

Build Nonsense Words

Help students use letters and sounds to build nonsense words.

1. Place the following letter tiles at the top of students' whiteboard: *b*, *k*, *o*, *s*, and *v*.

2. Draw three horizontal lines across the middle of students' whiteboard to represent the sounds in a word.

3. **Say:** Some words don't have any meaning. We call these **nonsense words**. Even though we don't know what a word means, we can still read it. Nonsense words will be very important when we read longer words. When we break longer words into parts, sometimes the parts are nonsense words.

4. **Say:** Let's use letters and sounds to build the nonsense word *vob*.

5. Have students finger stretch the sounds in *vob*.

6. Have students
   ▸ Identify the first, next, and last sounds in *vob*.
   ▸ Choose the corresponding letter for each of the sounds.
   ▸ Move the letters to the correct lines on their whiteboard.

7. Guide students with these questions:
   ▸ What is the first sound in *vob*? /v/
     Which line does the letter for that sound go on? the first one
   ▸ What is the next sound in *vob*? /ŏ/
     Which line does the letter for that sound go on? the second one
   ▸ What's the last sound in *vob*? /b/
     Which line does the letter for that sound go on? the last one

8. Redirect students if they select the incorrect letter.

   Say: That sound is in the word [word], and it is the [first, second, third] sound. We want the sound [target sound].

   Continue until students select the correct letter.

9. Have students touch and say the word.

10. Have them say the word as they use a dry-erase marker to write the word on the whiteboard.

11. Repeat the activity to build the word *kos*. /k/ /ŏ/ /s/

Try It

Rhyme Time
Have students complete page PH 38 in *K¹² PhonicsWorks Basic Activity Book* for more practice with the sounds /k/ and /v/, and words that rhyme. First have students read each sentence aloud and circle the word that rhymes with the underlined word. Then have them write the word and read the sentence aloud again.

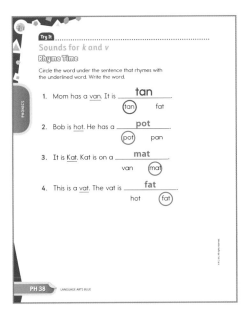

Objectives
- Identify words that rhyme.
- Identify and use the sound /k/.
- Identify and use the sound /v/.
- Write words by applying grade-level phonics knowledge.
- Follow three-step directions.

Dictation: Write Words

Have students practice identifying sounds and writing words.

1. Gather a pencil and the dictation notebook. Say the word *van*. Then give these directions to students:

    ▸ Repeat the word.
    ▸ Write the word in your notebook.
    ▸ Read the word aloud.

2. When students have finished, write the following word on your whiteboard: *van*.

3. Have them compare their answer to your correct version.

4. Repeat this procedure with the word *gap*.

    ▸ If students make an error and don't see it, help them correct their mistake by having them finger stretch the sounds in the word they missed.
    ▸ If students are having difficulty selecting the correct letters or sounds, review those letters or sounds that are confusing them.
    ▸ If students have difficulty with first, middle, and last sounds, have them finger stretch the sounds in words.

 ⏱ **minutes**

REVIEW: **Sounds for Letters *k* and *v***

Students will work online independently to

▸ Practice sounds for the letters *k* and *v*.
▸ Practice decoding text by reading a story.

Help students locate the online activities and provide support as needed.

Offline Alternative

No computer access? Have students name things that begin with the sounds for *k* and *v* (for example, *kite* and *vine*). You might also ask students to spell words that begin with the sounds /k/ and /v/.

 Objectives

*   Identify and use the sound /k/.
*   Identify the letter or letters, given the sound /k/.
*   Identify and use the sound /v/.
*   Identify the letter, given the sound /v/.
*   Identify beginning sounds in words.
*   Read aloud grade-level text with appropriate automaticity, prosody, accuracy, and rate.
*   Decode words by applying grade-level word analysis skills.

PHONICS

Review Sounds for Letters *o, d, g, k,* and *v*

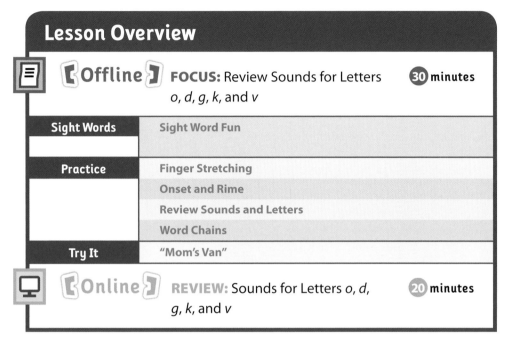

Lesson Overview

Offline — **FOCUS:** Review Sounds for Letters *o, d, g, k,* and *v* — **30** minutes

Sight Words	Sight Word Fun
Practice	Finger Stretching
	Onset and Rime
	Review Sounds and Letters
	Word Chains
Try It	"Mom's Van"

Online — **REVIEW:** Sounds for Letters *o, d, g, k,* and *v* — **20** minutes

Materials

Supplied
- *K¹² PhonicsWorks Readers Basic 1,* pp. 31–36
- whiteboard, student
- Tile Kit

Also Needed
- sight words box

Offline 30 minutes

FOCUS: Review Sounds for Letters *o*, *d*, *g*, *k*, and *v*

Work **together** with students to complete offline Sight Words, Practice, and Try It activities.

Sight Words

Sight Word Fun

Help students learn the sight words *it*, *he*, and *was*, and up to two additional sight words they have yet to master.

1. Gather the sight word cards for *it*, *he*, and *was*, and up to two additional sight word cards.

2. Choose one sight word card to begin.

    Say: Look at this word and take a picture of it in your mind. When you think you can spell the word yourself, turn the card over and use your letter tiles to spell the word.

3. After students spell the word, have them check the card to see if they spelled the word correctly.

    Say: Read aloud the word you spelled with the letter tiles.

4. Repeat the activity with the remaining sight words.

TIP Sight words can be very difficult for some students. Let students work at their own pace and really master these words.

Objectives

- Read sight words.
- Spell sight words.

Practice •

Finger Stretching

Use finger stretching to help students identify individual sounds in words.

1. **Say:** Let's review finger stretching. In the word *van*, the first sound is /v/, the middle sound is /ă/, and the last sound is /n/. I will finger stretch each sound as I say it. Then I'll say the word, while pulling my fist toward my body.

2. Finger stretch the word *van* for students.

3. **Say:** I'm going to say words with several sounds in them. You'll say the word and then finger stretch it while you say each sound in the word.

4. Say the following words and have students finger stretch them. After they finger stretch each word, ask them the question for that word.

   ▸ *tag* /t/ /ă/ /g/   What is the middle sound? /ă/
   ▸ *cot* /k/ /ŏ/ /t/   What is the first sound? /k/
   ▸ *log* /l/ /ŏ/ /g/   What is the last sound? /g/
   ▸ *mad* /m/ /ă/ /d/   What is the middle sound? /ă/
   ▸ *mat* /m/ /ă/ /t/   What is the first sound? /m/
   ▸ *mop* /m/ /ŏ/ /p/   What is the middle sound? /ŏ/

 Refer to the *K¹² PhonicsWorks* video for a demonstration of finger stretching.

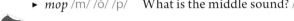

Onset and Rime

In a word, the part of the syllable before the first vowel sound is the **onset**. The part of the syllable after the first vowel sound is the **rime**. For example, in *pack*, /p/ is the onset and *ack* is the rime. Help students put together words that are broken down into parts by onset and rime.

1. **Say:** I'm going to break a word into two parts. Your job is to put the parts together and say the word. If the first part of a word is /p/ and the last part of the word is *ack*, then the whole word is *pack*: /p/ . . . *ack* . . . *pack*.

2. Say the following pairs of word parts. Have students tell you the word that each pair forms.

   ▸ /d/ . . . *ot* dot
   ▸ /f/ . . . *og* fog
   ▸ /r/ . . . *ob* rob
   ▸ /s/ . . . *op* sop
   ▸ /k/ . . . *an* can

Objectives
- Identify individual sounds in words.
- Identify a word when given the onset and rime.
- Blend sounds to create words.
- Given the letter, identify the most common sound.
- Given the sound, identify the most common letter or letters.
- Identify and use the sound /ŏ/.
- Identify and use the sound /d/.
- Identify and use the sound /g/.
- Identify and use the sound /k/.
- Identify and use the sound /v/.
- Identify the new word when one sound is changed in a word.

Review Sounds and Letters

Help students review sounds for the letters *a, d, g, h, k, l, o, p, r,* and *v,* plus any letters that are confusing for them.

1. Place the following letter tiles in random order on students' whiteboard: *a, d, g, h, k, l, o, p, r,* and *v,* plus any letters that are confusing.

2. **Say:** Let's go over some letters and sounds.

3. Point to each letter tile and have students say a sound that letter makes.

   - *k* /k/
   - *o* /ŏ/
   - *g* /g/
   - *d* /d/
   - *v* /v/

   - *a* /ă/
   - *p* /p/
   - *r* /r/
   - *l* /l/
   - *h* /h/

4. Say each of the following sounds. Have students repeat the sound and touch the corresponding letter tile.

   - /k/ *k*
   - /ŏ/ *o*
   - /g/ *g*
   - /d/ *d*
   - /v/ *v*

   - /ă/ *a*
   - /p/ *p*
   - /r/ *r*
   - /l/ *l*
   - /h/ *h*

5. As you do the activity, point to some letter tiles two or three times so that students don't think they are finished with a sound after they have named it.

6. Redirect students if they say an incorrect sound when you point to a letter tile.

   Say: That's the sound of another letter. What is the sound for this letter?

7. Help students if they touch the wrong letter tile after they repeat a sound.

   Say: That letter tile goes with the sound [sound for incorrect letter tile]. We're looking for the letter tile that goes with the sound [target sound].

Word Chains

Have students build words by adding and changing letters to help them recognize and use individual sounds in words.

1. Place the following letters at the top of students' whiteboard: *b, d, f, g, h, l,* and *o.*

2. **Say:** I am going to build the first word in a chain. The word is *dog.*

   - I will pull down the letters for the sounds /d/, /ŏ/, and /g/ to spell the word *dog.*
   - I will touch and say *dog.* To change *dog* to *log,* I will think about which sound changes from the word *dog* to *log.* I will need to replace the letter *d* with the letter *l.*
   - Touch and say the word *log.* Now it's your turn to change *log* to *hog.* You can spell *hog* by making only one change. Touch and say the new word.

3. Redirect students if they select the incorrect letter for any sound.

   Say: That letter is for the sound [incorrect sound]. We want the letter for the sound [target sound]. What letter makes that sound? Answers will vary.

4. Redirect students if they name the sound incorrectly.

   Say: That's the sound of another letter. The sound for this letter is [target sound].

   Touch the letter tile and say the sound.

5. Follow this procedure to make the following words: *fog* and *bog*.

6. For every new word, have students add, replace, or remove only one letter.

 TIP If students struggle, review the sounds and letters that are confusing them.

"Mom's Van"

Have students read "Mom's Van" on page 31 of *K¹² PhonicsWorks Readers Basic 1.*

Students should read the story silently once or twice before reading the story aloud. When they miss a word that can be sounded out, point to it and give them three to six seconds to try the word again. If students still miss the word, tell them the word so the flow of the story isn't interrupted.

After reading the story, make a list of all the words students missed, and go over those words with them. You may use letter tiles to show them how to read the words.

Objectives
- Read aloud grade-level text with appropriate automaticity, prosody, accuracy, and rate.
- Decode words by applying grade-level word analysis skills.
- Track text from left to right.
- Turn pages sequentially.

[Online] ⏱ **20** minutes

REVIEW: **Sounds for Letters *o*, *d*, *g*, *k*, and *v***

Students will work online independently to

▶ Practice sounds for the letters *o*, *d*, *g*, *k*, and *v*.

Help students locate the online activities and provide support as needed.

Offline Alternative

No computer access? Have students name things that begin with the sounds for the letters *o*, *d*, *g*, *k*, and *v* (for example, *ostrich*, *dog*, *gap*, *kite*, and *vine*).

Objectives
- Identify and use the sound /ŏ/.
- Identify the letter, given the sound /ŏ/.
- Identify and use the sound /d/.
- Identify the letter, given the sound /d/.
- Identify and use the sound /g/.
- Identify the letter, given the sound /g/.
- Identify and use the sound /k/.
- Identify the letter or letters, given the sound /k/.
- Identify and use the sound /v/.
- Identify the letter, given the sound /v/.
- Identify individual sounds in words.

Unit Checkpoint

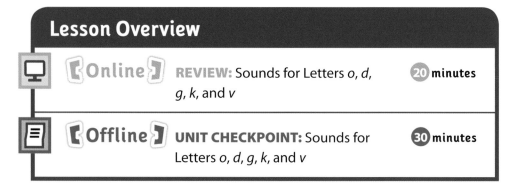

Lesson Overview

[Online] **REVIEW:** Sounds for Letters *o, d, g, k,* and *v* — **20** minutes

[Offline] **UNIT CHECKPOINT:** Sounds for Letters *o, d, g, k,* and *v* — **30** minutes

Materials

Supplied
- *K¹² PhonicsWorks Basic Assessments,* pp. PH 55–60

⭐ Objectives
- Identify the letter, given the sound /ŏ/.
- Identify the letter, given the sound /d/.
- Identify the letter, given the sound /g/.
- Identify the letter or letters, given the sound /k/.
- Identify the letter, given the sound /v/.
- Identify the sound, given the letter *o*.
- Identify the sound, given the letter *d*.
- Identify the sound, given the letter *g*.
- Identify the sound, given the letter *k*.
- Identify the sound, given the letter *v*.
- Identify letters of the alphabet.
- Identify individual sounds in words.
- Given the letter, identify the most common sound.
- Given the sound, identify the most common letter or letters.
- Read sight words.
- Read instructional-level text with 90% accuracy.
- Read aloud grade-level text with appropriate automaticity, prosody, accuracy, and rate.

 **20** minutes

REVIEW: **Sounds for Letters *o, d, g, k,* and *v***

Students will review sounds for the letters *o, d, g, k,* and *v* to prepare for the Unit Checkpoint. Help students locate the online activities and provide support as needed.

 **30 minutes**

UNIT CHECKPOINT: Sounds for Letters *o*, *d*, *g*, *k*, and *v*

Explain that students are going to show what they have learned about letters and sounds.

1. Give students the Unit Checkpoint pages for the Sounds for Letters *o*, *d*, *g*, *k*, and *v* unit and print the Unit Checkpoint Answer Key, if you'd like.

2. Use the instructions below to help administer the Checkpoint to students. On the Answer Key or another sheet of paper, note student answers to oral response questions to help with scoring the Checkpoint later.

3. Use the answer key to score the Checkpoint, and then enter the results online.

Part 1. Say Sounds Have students read across the row from left to right and say a sound that each letter makes. Note any sounds they say incorrectly.

Part 2. Word Dissection For each word, say the sound students should identify. Have them read the word aloud and circle the letter or groups of letters that spell the sound.

21. *middle sound*
22. *ending sound*
23. *beginning sound*
24. *ending sound*
25. *middle sound*

Part 3. Finger Stretching Say each word to students. Have them say each word and finger stretch the sounds. Note any words they finger stretch incorrectly.

26. *job*   29. *top*
27. *dog*   30. *pot*
28. *log*   31. *rod*

Part 4. Circle the Letter Say the sound and have students circle the letter that makes the sound.

32. /g/   36. /v/
33. /ă/   37. /ŏ/
34. /k/   38. /l/
35. /d/   39. /r/

Part 5. Read Aloud Listen to students read the sentences aloud. Count and note the number of words they read correctly.

Part 6. Say Letters Say each sound. Have students say the letter that makes that sound. Note any incorrect responses.

41. /ŏ/   50. /l/

42. /ă/   51. /s/

43. /d/   52. /b/

44. /g/   53. /h/

45. /k/   54. /f/

46. /v/   55. /m/

47. /n/   56. /j/

48. /p/   57. /t/

49. /r/   58. /k/

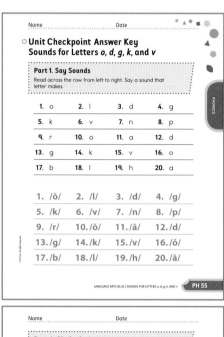

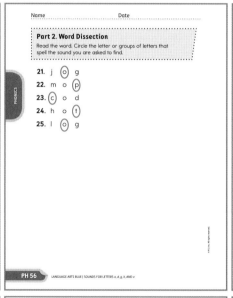

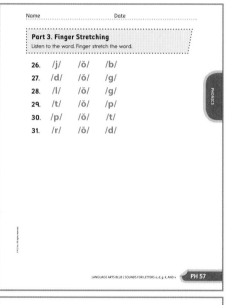

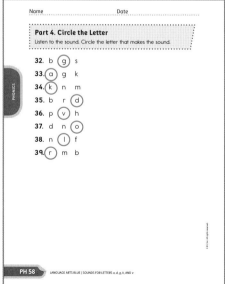

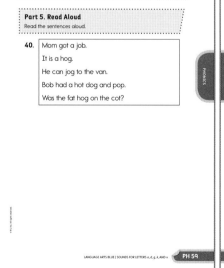

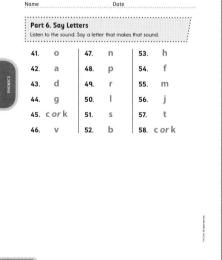

Getting Stronger: Sounds /ă/ and /ŏ/ (A)

Unit Overview

In this unit, students will
- ▸ Review sight words.
- ▸ Identify the letters and sounds in the alphabet.
- ▸ Review the sounds /ă/ and /ŏ/.
- ▸ Identify beginning and ending sounds in words.
- ▸ Build words.

Lesson Overview

【Offline】 FOCUS: Getting Stronger: Sounds /ă/ and /ŏ/ — **30** minutes

Sight Words	Review Sight Words
Practice	Face-Down Letters
	Match Uppercase and Lowercase Letters
	Finger Stretching
	Review Sounds and Letters
	Word Fun
Try It	Go Fish!

【Online】 REVIEW: Sounds /ă/ and /ŏ/ — **20** minutes

Advance Preparation

Place lowercase letter tiles in alphabetical order on your whiteboard.

For Word Fun, print words on index cards of ten items that may be located nearby, using one card per word, such as *hat, cat, dog, pot, top, can, map, pan, mat,* and *cap.*

 30 minutes

FOCUS: Getting Stronger: Sounds /ă/ and /ŏ/

Work **together** with students to complete offline Sight Words, Practice, and Try It activities.

Sight Words

Review Sight Words

Help students learn to recognize sight words.

Objectives
- Read sight words.
- Spell sight words.
- Write sight words.

1. Gather all the sight word cards students have yet to master from their sight words box. Stack the cards on the table face down.

2. Have students pick up a word and read it to you.

3. If they read it quickly and correctly, put the card in one stack. If they hesitate or do not read the word correctly, put it in another stack. The second stack should have words that they will review again.

4. Take the stack of words that students read correctly and dictate each word to them. They may choose to either write the word or spell it aloud.

5. If students spell the word correctly, put the card in the first stack because they have mastered the word. If they misspell the word, add it to the stack of cards to review again.

6. Chart students' progress on the back of each card.
   - ▶ Divide the back of the card into two columns.
   - ▶ Label the first column "Read" and the second column "Spell."
   - ▶ Record the dates that students read or spell the word correctly. When students can read and spell the word correctly three times in a row, they have mastered the word. You may want to put a star or sticker on their card when they have mastered that word.

TIP Even if students can read and spell all the words correctly, it is still beneficial for them to review sight words. Choose as many additional words as you would like for each subsequent activity.

Practice

Face-Down Letters

To help students learn to recognize the letters of the alphabet, have them practice identifying and naming letters. Grab your whiteboard with letters placed in alphabetical order.

1. Lay your whiteboard down on a flat surface and flip over the following letter tiles so they are face down on the whiteboard: *c*, *g*, *l*, *p*, *s*, and *v*.

2. **Say:** These letters are face down. We are looking at the back of them. Name each letter and then turn it over to see if you were right.

TIP If students miss any of the letters, have them turn over the missed ones and try again.

Match Uppercase and Lowercase Letters

To help students learn to recognize the difference between lowercase and uppercase letters of the alphabet, have them practice identifying and naming letters. Grab your whiteboard with letters.

1. Place the following uppercase letters on students' whiteboard in a row: *D*, *F*, *Q*, and *R*.

2. Point to a letter and have students name it.

3. Have students select the matching lowercase letter from your whiteboard.

4. Have students place the lowercase letter under the uppercase letter to make a pair.

TIP If students have difficulty with this activity, have them practice naming the letters in the alphabet. When they can name all the letters in the correct order, have them touch and name the lowercase and uppercase letters for each letter.

Finger Stretching

Use finger stretching to help students identify individual sounds in words.

1. **Say:** Let's review finger stretching. In the word *fog*, the first sound is /f/, the next sound is /ŏ/, and the last sound is /g/. I will finger stretch each sound as I say it. Then I'll say the word while pulling my fist toward my body.

2. Finger stretch the word *fog* for students.

3. **Say:** I'm going to say words with several sounds in them. You'll say each word and then finger stretch it while you say each sound in the word.

Objectives

- Identify letters of the alphabet.
- Match capital letters to lowercase letters.
- Identify individual sounds in words.
- Identify and use the sound /ă/.
- Identify and use the sound /ŏ/.
- Given the letter, identify the most common sound.
- Given the sound, identify the most common letter or letters.

4. Say the following words and have students finger stretch them. After they finger stretch each word, ask them the question for that word.

- *pat* /p/ /ă/ /t/   What is the middle sound? /ă/
- *bad* /b/ /ă/ /d/   What is the first sound? /b/
- *cab* /k/ /ă/ /b/   What is the last sound? /b/
- *top* /t/ /ŏ/ /p/   What is the middle sound? /ŏ/
- *lap* /l/ /ă/ /p/   What is the first sound? /l/
- *cob* /k/ /ŏ/ /b/   What is the middle sound? /ŏ/

 TIP Refer to the *K¹² PhonicsWorks* video for a demonstration of finger stretching.

Review Sounds and Letters

Help students review sounds for the letters *a, c, d, j, l, o, r, t,* and *v,* plus any letters that are confusing for them.

1. Place the following letter tiles in random order on students' whiteboard: *a, c, d, j, l, o, r, t,* and *v,* plus any letters that are confusing.

2. **Say:** Let's go over some letters and sounds.

3. Point to each letter tile and have students say a sound that letter makes.

- *o* /ŏ/
- *c* /k/
- *d* /d/
- *r* /r/
- *a* /ă/

- *v* /v/
- *t* /t/
- *j* /j/
- *l* /l/

4. Say each of the following sounds. Have students repeat the sound and touch the corresponding letter tile.

- /ŏ/ *o*
- /k/ *c*
- /d/ *d*
- /r/ *r*
- /ă/ *a*

- /v/ *v*
- /t/ *t*
- /j/ *j*
- /l/ *l*

5. As you do the activity, point to some letter tiles two or three times so that students don't think they are finished with a sound after they have named it.

6. Redirect students if they say an incorrect sound when you point to a letter tile.

   Say: That's the sound of another letter. What is the sound for this letter?

7. Help students if they touch the wrong letter tile after they repeat a sound.

   Say: That letter goes with the sound [sound for incorrect letter tile]. We're looking for the letter tile that goes with the sound [target sound].

Word Fun

Have students practice reading words and identifying names of common objects.

1. Gather the index cards you prepared and place them face down in one pile.

2. **Say:** You are going to practice reading and writing some words.

   ▸ You will choose a card from the pile and read the word on it.
   ▸ Then you are going to flip the card over and write the word on the backside of the card.
   ▸ I'll try first.

3. Choose a card from the pile, and say and write the word.

   Say: Now it's your turn. Choose a card and read it to me.

4. If time permits, have students choose two words and draw a picture of those words on the back of the card.

   TIP If students stumble over any words, have them touch and say the words. Touch and say these words along with them.

Try It •

Go Fish!

Have students complete page PH 39 in *K¹² PhonicsWorks Basic Activity Book* for more practice with the sounds /ă/ and /ŏ/. Have students read the word aloud and color the fish yellow for words that contain the sound /ŏ/, and pink for words that contain the sound /ă/.

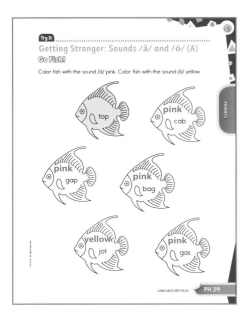

Objectives

- Read aloud grade-level text with appropriate automaticity, prosody, accuracy, and rate.
- Identify and use the sound /ŏ/.
- Identify and use the sound /ă/.

 **minutes**

REVIEW: **Sounds /ă/ and /ŏ/**

Students will work online independently to

- ▸ Practice the sounds /ă/ and /ŏ/.
- ▸ Practice decoding text by reading a story.

Help students locate the online activities and provide support as needed.

Offline Alternative

No computer access? Have students name the letters that make the sounds /ă/ and /ŏ/. Vice versa, have students name the sounds made by the letters *a* and *o*. You might also ask students to spell simple words that contain the letters *a*, *o*, and other letters students have learned, or ask them to think of words that begin with those letters.

Objectives

- Identify the letter, given the sound /ă/.
- Identify the sound, given the letter *a*.
- Identify and use the sound /ă/.
- Identify the letter, given the sound /ŏ/.
- Identify the sound, given the letter *o*.
- Identify and use the sound /ŏ/.
- Identify individual sounds in words.
- Read aloud grade-level text with appropriate automaticity, prosody, accuracy, and rate.
- Decode words by applying grade-level word analysis skills.

Getting Stronger: Sounds /ă/ and /ŏ/ (B)

Lesson Overview

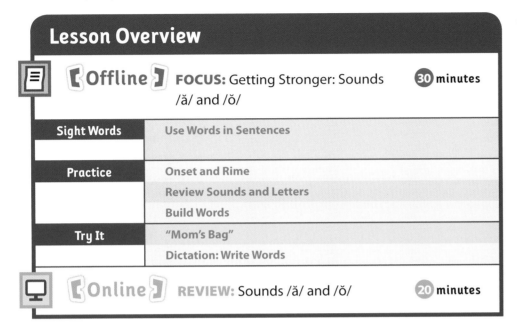

Offline	**FOCUS:** Getting Stronger: Sounds /ă/ and /ŏ/	**30** minutes

Sight Words	Use Words in Sentences
Practice	Onset and Rime
	Review Sounds and Letters
	Build Words
Try It	"Mom's Bag"
	Dictation: Write Words

Online	**REVIEW:** Sounds /ă/ and /ŏ/	**20** minutes

Materials

Supplied
- *K12 PhonicsWorks Readers Basic 2*, pp. 1–6
- whiteboard, Learning Coach
- whiteboard, student
- Tile Kit

Also Needed
- sight words box
- dictation notebook

 **30 minutes**

FOCUS: Getting Stronger: Sounds /ă/ and /ŏ/

Work **together** with students to complete offline Sight Words, Practice, and Try It activities.

Sight Words

Use Words in Sentences

Help students use sight words in sentences.

1. Gather all the sight word cards students have yet to master from their sight words box. Spread the sight word cards on the table.

2. **Say:** Let's use sight words in sentences.

3. Have students

   ▸ Touch each card and read the word on it.
   ▸ Make up a sentence using the word.
   ▸ Put the card in a pile after using the word in a sentence.
   ▸ Go through the pile of cards and read each sight word again.
   ▸ Spell each word.

TIP If students have difficulty with any of the sight words, place those cards in a pile to review again.

> **Objectives**
> • Read sight words.
> • Spell sight words.

Practice

Onset and Rime

In a word, the part of the syllable before the first vowel sound is the **onset**. The part of the syllable after the first vowel sound is the **rime**. For example, in *first*, /f/ is the onset and *irst* is the rime. Help students put together words that are broken down into parts by onset and rime.

1. **Say:** I'm going to break a word into two parts. Your job is to put the parts together and say the word. If the first part of a word is /b/ and the last part of the word is *ag*, then the whole word is *bag*: /b/ . . . *ag* . . . *bag*.

2. Say the following pairs of word parts. Have students tell you the word that each pair forms.

   ▸ /d/ . . . *og* dog
   ▸ /t/ . . . *om* Tom
   ▸ /f/ . . . *og* fog
   ▸ /k/ . . . *at* cat
   ▸ /h/ . . . *ot* hot

> **Objectives**
> • Identify a word when given the onset and rime.
> • Blend sounds to create words.
> • Given the letter, identify the most common sound.
> • Given the sound, identify the most common letter or letters.
> • Identify individual sounds in words.

Review Sounds and Letters

Help students review sounds for the letters *a, b, c, g, m, o, p,* and *s,* plus any letters that are confusing for them.

1. Place the following letter tiles in random order on students' whiteboard: *a, b, c, g, m, o, p,* and *s,* plus any letters that are confusing.

2. **Say:** Let's go over some letters and sounds.

3. Point to each letter tile and have students say a sound that letter makes.

   - ▸ *b* /b/
   - ▸ *g* /g/
   - ▸ *a* /ă/
   - ▸ *c* /k/

   - ▸ *m* /m/
   - ▸ *p* /p/
   - ▸ *o* /ŏ/
   - ▸ *s* /s/

4. Say each of the following sounds. Have students repeat the sound and touch the corresponding letter tile.

   - ▸ /b/ *b*
   - ▸ /g/ *g*
   - ▸ /ă/ *a*
   - ▸ /k/ *c*

   - ▸ /m/ *m*
   - ▸ /p/ *p*
   - ▸ /ŏ/ *o*
   - ▸ /s/ *s*

5. As you do the activity, point to some letter tiles two or three times so that students don't think they are finished with a sound after they have named it.

6. Redirect students if they say an incorrect sound when you point to a letter tile.

   Say: That's the sound of another letter. What is the sound for this letter?

7. Help students if they touch the wrong letter tile after they repeat a sound.

   Say: That letter tile goes with the sound [sound for incorrect letter tile]. We're looking for the letter tile that goes with the sound [target sound].

Build Words

Help students use letters and sounds to build words.

1. Place the following letter tiles at the top of students' whiteboard: *a, b, c, h,* and *m.*

2. Draw three horizontal lines across the middle of students' whiteboard to represent the sounds in a word.

3. **Say:** Let's use letters and sounds to build the word *cab.*

4. Have students finger stretch the sounds in *cab.*

5. Have students

   - ▸ Identify the first, next, and last sounds in *cab.*
   - ▸ Choose the corresponding letter for each of the sounds.
   - ▸ Move the letters to the correct lines on their whiteboard.

6. Guide students with these questions:

   ▶ What is the first sound in *cab*? /k/
   Which line does the letter for that sound go on? the first one
   ▶ What is the next sound in *cab*? /ă/
   Which line does the letter for that sound go on? the second one
   ▶ What's the last sound in *cab*? /b/
   Which line does the letter for that sound go on? the last one

7. Have students touch and say the word.

8. Redirect students if they select the incorrect letter.

   Say: That sound is in the word [word], and it is the [first, second, third] sound. We want the sound [target sound].

   Continue until students select the correct letter.

9. Repeat the activity to build the word *ham*. /h/ /ă/ /m/

Try It

"Mom's Bag"
Have students read "Mom's Bag" on page 1 of *K¹² PhonicsWorks Readers Basic 2*.
   Students should read the story silently once or twice before reading the story aloud. When they miss a word that can be sounded out, point to it and give them three to six seconds to try the word again. If students still miss the word, tell them the word so the flow of the story isn't interrupted.
   After reading the story, make a list of all the words students missed, and go over those words with them. You may use tiles to show students how to read the words.

Dictation: Write Words
Have students practice identifying sounds and writing words.

1. Gather a pencil and the dictation notebook. Say the word *cab*. Then give these directions to students:

   ▶ Repeat the word.
   ▶ Write the word in your notebook.
   ▶ Read the word aloud.

2. When students have finished, write the following word on your whiteboard: *cab*.

3. Have them compare their answer to your correct version.

4. Repeat this procedure with the words *pot* and *pan*.

   ▶ If students make an error and don't see it, help them correct their mistake by having them finger stretch the sounds in the word they missed.
   ▶ If students are having difficulty selecting the correct letters or sounds, review those letters or sounds that are confusing them.
   ▶ If students have difficulty with first, middle, and last sounds, have them finger stretch the sounds in words.

Objectives
- Read aloud grade-level text with appropriate automaticity, prosody, accuracy, and rate.
- Decode words by applying grade-level word analysis skills.
- Track text from left to right.
- Turn pages sequentially.
- Write words by applying grade-level phonics knowledge.
- Follow three-step directions.

 **20 minutes**

REVIEW: **Sounds /ă/ and /ŏ/**

Students will work online independently to

▶ Practice the sounds /ă/ and /ŏ/.

Help students locate the online activities and provide support as needed.

Offline Alternative

No computer access? Have students name the letters that make the sounds /ă/ and /ŏ/. Vice versa, have students name the sounds made by the letters *a* and *o*. You might also ask students to spell simple words that contain the letters *a*, *o*, and other letters students have learned, or ask them to think of words that begin with those letters.

Objectives

- Identify the letter, given the sound /ă/.
- Identify the sound, given the letter *a*.
- Identify and use the sound /ă/.
- Identify the letter, given the sound /ŏ/.
- Identify and use the sound /ŏ/.
- Identify the sound, given the letter *o*.
- Identify individual sounds in words.

Getting Stronger: Sounds /ă/ and /ŏ/ (C)

Lesson Overview

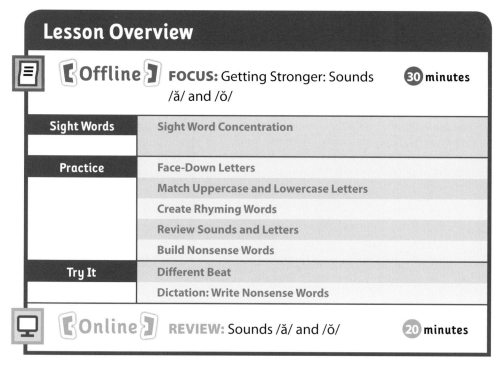

[Offline] FOCUS: Getting Stronger: Sounds /ă/ and /ŏ/ — **30** minutes

Sight Words	Sight Word Concentration
Practice	Face-Down Letters
	Match Uppercase and Lowercase Letters
	Create Rhyming Words
	Review Sounds and Letters
	Build Nonsense Words
Try It	Different Beat
	Dictation: Write Nonsense Words

[Online] REVIEW: Sounds /ă/ and /ŏ/ — **20** minutes

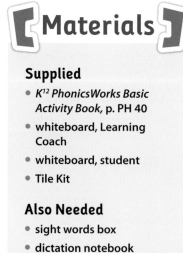

[Materials]

Supplied
- *K¹² PhonicsWorks Basic Activity Book*, p. PH 40
- whiteboard, Learning Coach
- whiteboard, student
- Tile Kit

Also Needed
- sight words box
- dictation notebook

Advance Preparation

Gather two sets of all the sight word cards you have used to date.

Place lowercase letter tiles in alphabetical order on your whiteboard.

 **Offline** ⏱ **30** minutes

FOCUS: Getting Stronger: Sounds /ă/ and /ŏ/

Work **together** with students to complete offline Sight Words, Practice, and Try It activities.

Sight Words ···

Sight Word Concentration

Help students review sight words.

1. Gather two sets of all sight word cards.

2. Scramble both sets of sight word cards and place them face down on the table or floor.

3. Have students turn over two cards at a time; take turns with students. If the cards match, the person turning over the matching cards reads the word and uses it in a sentence. If the cards don't match, the person turns them back over.

4. Remove and save the matching cards.

5. Continue the activity until all the cards are paired.

6. Have students read all the words.

7. Take the stack of words that students read correctly and dictate each word to them.

8. Have students write each word or spell it aloud.

TIP If students have difficulty with any of the sight words, let them work at their own pace to really master these words.

> **Objectives**
> - Read sight words.
> - Spell sight words.
> - Write sight words.

Practice ···

Face-Down Letters

To help students learn to recognize the letters of the alphabet, have them practice identifying and naming letters. Grab your whiteboard with letters placed in alphabetical order.

1. Lay your whiteboard down on a flat surface and flip over the following letter tiles so they are face down on the whiteboard: *b*, *f*, *h*, *n*, and *t*.

2. **Say:** These letters are face down. We are looking at the back of them. Name each letter and then turn it over to see if you were right.

TIP If students miss any of the letters, have them turn over the missed ones and try again.

> **Objectives**
> - Identify letters of the alphabet.
> - Match capital letters to lowercase letters.
> - Identify words that rhyme.
> - Given the letter, identify the most common sound.
> - Given the sound, identify the most common letter or letters.
> - Blend sounds to create words.
> - Identify individual sounds in words.

Match Uppercase and Lowercase Letters

To help students learn to recognize the difference between lowercase and uppercase letters of the alphabet, have them practice identifying and naming letters. Grab your whiteboard with letters.

1. Place the following uppercase letters on students' whiteboard in a row: *B, G, L, N, V,* and *Y.*

2. Point to a letter and have students name it.

3. Have students select the matching lowercase letter from your whiteboard.

4. Have students place the lowercase letter under the uppercase letter to make a pair.

TIP If students have difficulty with this activity, have them practice naming the letters in the alphabet. When they can name all the letters in the correct order, have them touch and name the lowercase and uppercase letters for each letter.

Create Rhyming Words

Have students combine word parts and make words that rhyme.

1. **Say:** I'm going to break a word into two parts. Your job is to put the parts back together and say the word.

   ▸ For example, if the first part of the word is /j/ and the last part is /ŏb/, then you'll say *job*: /j/ . . . /ŏb/ . . . *job.*
   ▸ Next you'll add a new **beginning sound** to make a word that rhymes. For example, you'll use the same last part, /ŏb/, and add a new first sound, like /k/. The rhyming word is /k/ . . . /ŏb/ . . . *cob.*

2. **Say:** Now it's your turn: /r/ . . . /ăm/.

   ▸ What's the word? *ram*
   ▸ Now use the same last part, /ăm/, but add a new sound, /h/, at the beginning. What word did you make? *ham*

3. Have students add a new beginning sound to the last part of the word and make a rhyming word.

   ▸ /h/ . . . /ăm/ *ham*; Possible rhyming words: *Pam, Sam*
   ▸ /l/ . . . /ŏt/ *lot*; Possible rhyming words: *pot, hot, got*

Review Sounds and Letters

Help students review sounds for the letters *b, f, h, n,* and *t,* plus any letters that are confusing for them.

1. Place the following letter tiles in random order on students' whiteboard: *b, f, h, n,* and *t,* plus any letters that are confusing.

2. **Say:** Let's go over some letters and sounds.

3. Point to each letter tile and have students say a sound that letter makes.

   - *b* /b/
   - *f* /f/
   - *h* /h/
   - *n* /n/
   - *t* /t/

4. Say each of the following sounds. Have students repeat the sound and touch the corresponding letter tile.

   - /b/ *b*
   - /f/ *f*
   - /h/ *h*
   - /n/ *n*
   - /t/ *t*

5. As you do the activity, point to some letter tiles two or three times so that students don't think they are finished with a sound after they have named it.

6. Redirect students if they say an incorrect sound when you point to a letter tile.

   Say: That's the sound of another letter. What is the sound for this letter?

7. Help students if they touch the wrong letter tile after they repeat a sound.

   Say: That letter tile goes with the sound [sound for incorrect letter tile]. We're looking for the letter tile that goes with the sound [target sound].

Build Nonsense Words

Help students use letters and sounds to build nonsense words.

1. Place the following letter tiles at the top of students' whiteboard: *a, b, g, k, o, p, t,* and *v*.

2. Draw three horizontal lines across the middle of students' whiteboard to represent the sounds in a word.

3. **Say:** Some words don't have any meaning. We call these **nonsense words**. Even though we don't know what a word means, we can still read it. Nonsense words will be very important when we read longer words. When we break longer words into parts, sometimes the parts are nonsense words.

4. **Say:** Let's use letters and sounds to build the nonsense word *kov*.

5. Have students finger stretch the sounds in *kov*.

6. Have students

   - Identify the first, next, and last sounds in *kov*.
   - Choose the corresponding letter for each of the sounds.
   - Move the letters to the correct lines on their whiteboard.

7. Guide students with these questions:
   - ▶ What is the first sound in *kov*? /k/
     Which line does the letter for that sound go on? the first one
   - ▶ What is the next sound in *kov*? /ŏ/
     Which line does the letter for that sound go on? the second one
   - ▶ What's the last sound in *kov*? /v/
     Which line does the letter for that sound go on? the last one

8. Redirect students if they select the incorrect letter.

   Say That sound is in the word [word], and it is the [first, second, third] sound. We want the sound [target sound].

   Continue until students select the correct letter.

9. Have students touch and say the word.

10. Repeat the activity to build the following words:
    - ▶ *pag* /p/ /ă/ /g/
    - ▶ *tob* /t/ /ŏ/ /b/

Try It

Different Beat

Have students complete page PH 40 in *K¹² PhonicsWorks Basic Activity Book* for more practice with the sounds /ă/ and /ŏ/. Have them read each word in the row aloud and circle the word that does **not** rhyme.

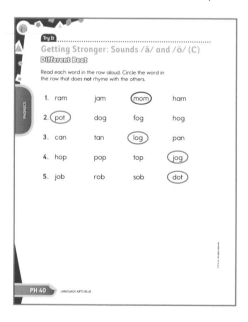

Objectives
- Identify words that rhyme.
- Identify and use the sound /ă/.
- Identify and use the sound /ŏ/.
- Read aloud grade-level text with appropriate automaticity, prosody, accuracy, and rate.
- Write words by applying grade-level phonics knowledge.
- Follow three-step directions.

Dictation: Write Nonsense Words

Have students practice identifying sounds and writing words.

1. Gather a pencil and the dictation notebook.

2. **Say:** Today's dictation words will be **nonsense words**. Even though we don't know what the word means, we can still read and write it.

3. Say the nonsense word *kov*. Give these directions to students:

   ▸ Repeat the nonsense word.
   ▸ Write the word in your notebook.
   ▸ Read the word aloud.

4. When students have finished, write the following nonsense word on your whiteboard: *kov*.

5. Have them compare their answer to your correct version.

6. Repeat this procedure with the words *saf* and *rom*.

   ▸ If students make an error and don't see it, help them correct their mistake by having them finger stretch the sounds in the word they missed.
   ▸ If students are having difficulty selecting the correct letters or sounds, review those letters or sounds that are confusing them.
   ▸ If students have difficulty with first, middle, and last sounds, have them finger stretch the sounds in words.

 **20 minutes**

REVIEW: Sounds /ă/ and /ŏ/

Students will work online independently to

▸ Practice the sounds /ă/ and /ŏ/.
▸ Practice decoding text by reading a story.

Help students locate the online activities and provide support as needed.

Offline Alternative

No computer access? Have students name the letters that make the sounds /ă/ and /ŏ/. Vice versa, have students name the sounds made by the letters *a* and *o*. You might also ask students to spell simple words that contain the letters *a*, *o*, and other letters students have learned, or ask them to think of words that begin with those letters.

Objectives

- Identify the letter, given the sound /ă/.
- Identify the sound, given the letter *a*.
- Identify and use the sound /ă/.
- Identify the letter, given the sound /ŏ/.
- Identify the sound, given the letter *o*.
- Identify and use the sound /ŏ/.
- Identify individual sounds in words.
- Read aloud grade-level text with appropriate automaticity, prosody, accuracy, and rate.
- Decode words by applying grade-level word analysis skills.

Getting Stronger: Sounds /ă/ and /ŏ/ (D)

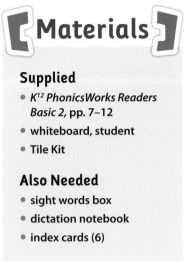

PHONICS

Lesson Overview

⌷ Offline ⌷	**FOCUS:** Getting Stronger: Sounds /ă/ and /ŏ/	**30** minutes

Sight Words	Pick a Pair
Practice	Finger Stretching
	Review Sounds and Letters
	Make Up a Sentence
Try It	"Dad's Job"

⌷ Online ⌷	**REVIEW:** Sounds /ă/ and /ŏ/	**20** minutes

⌷ Materials ⌷

Supplied
- *K¹² PhonicsWorks Readers Basic 2*, pp. 7–12
- whiteboard, student
- Tile Kit

Also Needed
- sight words box
- dictation notebook
- index cards (6)

Advance Preparation

For Make Up a Sentence, print the following words on index cards, using one card per word: *dog, cat, man, sap, Sam,* and *hop.*

 **30 minutes**

FOCUS: Getting Stronger: Sounds /ă/ and /ŏ/

Work **together** with students to complete offline Sight Words, Practice, and Try It activities.

Sight Words

Pick a Pair

Play a card game with students for more practice with sight words.

1. Gather the sight word cards that students are reviewing. Choose two words and place the cards on the table.

2. Ask questions to help students identify each word. For example, if the words are *in* and *he*, you could ask, "Which word means *a boy*?" If the words are *on* and *is*, you could ask, "Which word is the opposite of *off*?"

3. Continue the activity until students identify all the words.

4. Take the stack of words that students read correctly and dictate each word to them.

5. Have students write each word or spell it aloud.

Objectives
- Read sight words.
- Spell sight words.
- Write sight words.

Practice

Finger Stretching

Use finger stretching to help students identify individual sounds in words.

1. **Say:** Let's review finger stretching. In the word *lot*, the first sound is /l/, the next sound is /ŏ/, and the last sound is /t/. I will finger stretch each sound as I say it. Then I'll say the word, while pulling my fist toward my body.

2. Finger stretch the word *lot* for students.

3. **Say:** I'm going to say words with several sounds in them. You'll say each word and then finger stretch it while you say each sound in the word.

4. Say the following words and have students finger stretch them. After they finger stretch each word, ask them the question for that word.

   ▸ *hop* /h/ /ŏ/ /p/   What is the middle sound? /ŏ/
   ▸ *can* /k/ /ă/ /n/   What is the first sound? /k/
   ▸ *pop* /p/ /ŏ/ /p/   What is the last sound? /p/
   ▸ *sag* /s/ /ă/ /g/   What is the middle sound? /ă/
   ▸ *fan* /f/ /ă/ /n/   What is the first sound? /f/
   ▸ *tot* /t/ /ŏ/ /t/   What is the middle sound? /ŏ/

Objectives
- Identify individual sounds in words.
- Given the letter, identify the most common sound.
- Given the sound, identify the most common letter or letters.
- Read aloud grade-level text with appropriate automaticity, prosody, accuracy, and rate.
- Decode words by applying grade-level word analysis skills.

Review Sounds and Letters

Help students review sounds for the letters *a, b, c, d, f, o, r, s,* and *v,* plus any letters that are confusing for students.

1. Place the following letter tiles in random order on students' whiteboard: *a, b, c, d, f, o, r, s,* and *v,* plus any letters that are confusing.

2. **Say:** Let's go over some letters and sounds.

3. Point to each letter tile and have students say a sound that letter makes.

   - *o* /ŏ/
   - *b* /b/
   - *s* /s/
   - *a* /ă/
   - *d* /d/

   - *c* /k/
   - *f* /f/
   - *v* /v/
   - *r* /r/

4. Say each of the following sounds. Have students repeat the sound and touch the corresponding letter tile.

   - /ŏ/ *o*
   - /b/ *b*
   - /s/ *s*
   - /ă/ *a*
   - /d/ *d*

   - /k/ *c*
   - /f/ *f*
   - /v/ *v*
   - /r/ *r*

5. As you do the activity, point to some letter tiles two or three times so that students don't think they are finished with a sound after they have named it.

6. Redirect students if they say an incorrect sound when you point to a letter tile.

   Say: That's the sound of another letter. What is the sound for this letter?

7. Help students if they touch the wrong letter tile after they repeat a sound.

   Say: That letter tile goes with the sound [sound for incorrect letter tile]. We're looking for the letter tile that goes with the sound [target sound].

Make Up a Sentence

Help students use words to make sentences.

1. Gather the index cards you prepared.

2. Place the index cards face down in one pile.

3. Have students

   - Select a card.
   - Read the word.
   - Use the word in an interesting, fun, or silly sentence.

TIP If students read a word incorrectly, have them finger stretch the sounds in the word.

Try It ....

"Dad's Job"

Have students read "Dad's Job" on page 7 of *K¹² PhonicsWorks Readers Basic 2*.

Students should read the story silently once or twice before reading the story aloud. When they miss a word that can be sounded out, point to it and give them three to six seconds to try the word again. If students still miss the word, tell them the word so the flow of the story isn't interrupted.

After reading the story, make a list of all the words students missed, and go over those words with them. You may use tiles to show them how to read the words.

Objectives

- Read aloud grade-level text with appropriate automaticity, prosody, accuracy, and rate.
- Decode words by applying grade-level word analysis skills.
- Track text from left to right.
- Turn pages sequentially.

 **20 minutes**

REVIEW: Sounds /ă/ and /ŏ/

Students will work online independently to

▸ Practice the sounds /ă/ and /ŏ/.

Help students locate the online activities and provide support as needed.

Objectives

- Identify the letter, given the sound /ă/.
- Identify the sound, given the letter *a*.
- Identify and use the sound /ă/.
- Identify the letter, given the sound /ŏ/.
- Identify the sound, given the letter *o*.
- Identify and use the sound /ŏ/.
- Identify individual sounds in words.

Offline Alternative

No computer access? Have students name the letters that make the sounds /ă/ and /ŏ/. Vice versa, have students name the sounds made by the letters *a* and *o*. You might also ask students to spell simple words that contain the letters *a*, *o*, and other letters students have learned, or ask them to think of words that begin with those letters.

Unit Checkpoint

Lesson Overview

🖥	**[Online]**	**REVIEW:** Sounds /ă/ and /ŏ/	**20** minutes
📄	**[Offline]**	**UNIT CHECKPOINT:** Getting Stronger: Sounds /ă/ and /ŏ/	**30** minutes

Materials

Supplied
- *K¹² PhonicsWorks Basic Assessments*, pp. PH 61–66

Objectives
- Identify the letter, given the sound /ă/.
- Identify the letter, given the sound /ŏ/.
- Identify the sound, given the letter *a*.
- Identify the sound, given the letter *o*.
- Identify letters of the alphabet.
- Identify individual sounds in words.
- Given the letter, identify the most common sound.
- Given the sound, identify the most common letter or letters.
- Read sight words.
- Spell sight words.
- Read instructional-level text with 90% accuracy.
- Read aloud grade-level text with appropriate automaticity, prosody, accuracy, and rate.

[Online] **20** minutes

REVIEW: **Sounds /ă/ and /ŏ/**

Students will review the sounds /ă/ and /ŏ/ to prepare for the Unit Checkpoint.
Help students locate the online activities and provide support as needed.

 **30 minutes**

UNIT CHECKPOINT: Getting Stronger: Sounds /ă/ and /ŏ/

Explain that students are going to show what they have learned about letters and sounds.

1. Give students the Unit Checkpoint pages for the Getting Stronger: Sounds /ă/ and /ŏ/ unit and print the Unit Checkpoint Answer Key, if you'd like.

2. Use the instructions below to help administer the Checkpoint to students. On the Answer Key or another sheet of paper, note student answers to oral response questions to help with scoring the Checkpoint later.

3. Use the Answer Key to score the Checkpoint, and then enter the results online.

Part 1. Say Sounds Have students read across the rows from left to right and say a sound that each letter makes. Note any sounds they say incorrectly.

Part 2. Word Dissection For each word, say the sound students should identify. Have them read the word aloud and circle the letter or groups of letters that spell the requested sound.

21. *middle sound*

22. *ending sound*

23. *beginning sound*

24. *ending sound*

25. *middle sound*

Part 3. Finger Stretching Say each word to students. Have them say each word and finger stretch the sounds. Note any words they finger stretch incorrectly.

26. *got*   28. *cab*

27. *mad*   29. *rob*

Part 4. Circle and Write Say the sound and have students circle the letter that makes the sound. Then have them write the letter.

30. /l/   32. /f/

31. /n/   33. /v/

Part 5. Read Aloud Listen to students read the sentences aloud. Count and note the number of words they read correctly.

Part 6. Say Letters Say each sound. Have students say a letter that makes that sound. Note any incorrect responses.

35. /ŏ/	44. /p/
36. /ă/	45. /b/
37. /g/	46. /s/
38. /v/	47. /d/
39. /k/	48. /f/
40. /r/	49. /ŏ/
41. /v/	50. /j/
42. /n/	51. /t/
43. /l/	52. /ă/

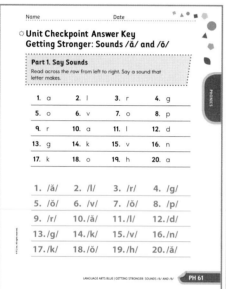

Name _____ Date _____

Unit Checkpoint Answer Key
Getting Stronger: Sounds /ă/ and /ŏ/

Part 1. Say Sounds
Read across the row from left to right. Say a sound that letter makes.

1. a	2. l	3. r	4. g
5. o	6. v	7. o	8. p
9. r	10. a	11. l	12. d
13. g	14. k	15. v	16. n
17. k	18. o	19. h	20. a

1. /ă/	2. /l/	3. /r/	4. /g/
5. /ŏ/	6. /v/	7. /ŏ/	8. /p/
9. /r/	10. /ă/	11. /l/	12. /d/
13. /g/	14. /k/	15. /v/	16. /n/
17. /k/	18. /ŏ/	19. /h/	20. /ă/

LANGUAGE ARTS BLUE | GETTING STRONGER: SOUNDS /ă/ AND /ŏ/ PH 61

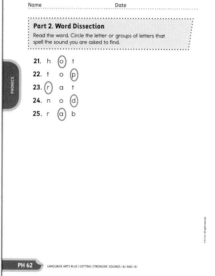

Name _____ Date _____

Part 2. Word Dissection
Read the word. Circle the letter or groups of letters that spell the sound you are asked to find.

21. h (o) t
22. t o (p)
23. (r) a t
24. n o (d)
25. r (a) b

PH 62 LANGUAGE ARTS BLUE | GETTING STRONGER: SOUNDS /ă/ AND /ŏ/

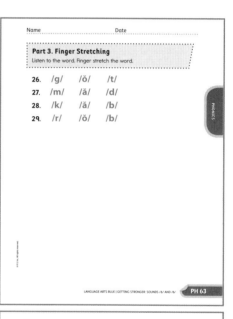

Name _____ Date _____

Part 3. Finger Stretching
Listen to the word. Finger stretch the word.

26.	/g/	/ŏ/	/t/
27.	/m/	/ă/	/d/
28.	/k/	/ă/	/b/
29.	/r/	/ŏ/	/b/

LANGUAGE ARTS BLUE | GETTING STRONGER: SOUNDS /ă/ AND /ŏ/ PH 63

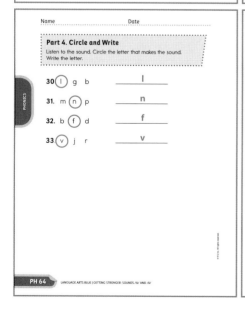

Name _____ Date _____

Part 4. Circle and Write
Listen to the sound. Circle the letter that makes the sound. Write the letter.

30. (l) g b   _____ l
31. m (n) p   _____ n
32. b (f) d   _____ f
33. (v) j r   _____ v

PH 64 LANGUAGE ARTS BLUE | GETTING STRONGER: SOUNDS /ă/ AND /ŏ/

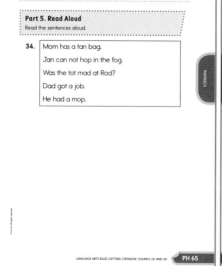

Name _____ Date _____

Part 5. Read Aloud
Read the sentences aloud.

34. Mom has a tan bag.
Jan can not hop in the fog.
Was the tot mad at Rod?
Dad got a job.
He had a mop.

LANGUAGE ARTS BLUE | GETTING STRONGER: SOUNDS /ă/ AND /ŏ/ PH 65

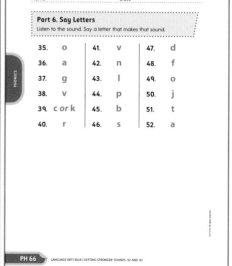

Name _____ Date _____

Part 6. Say Letters
Listen to the sound. Say a letter that makes that sound.

35.	o	41.	v	47.	d
36.	a	42.	n	48.	f
37.	g	43.	l	49.	o
38.	v	44.	p	50.	j
39.	c or k	45.	b	51.	t
40.	r	46.	s	52.	a

PH 66 LANGUAGE ARTS BLUE | GETTING STRONGER: SOUNDS /ă/ AND /ŏ/

Introduce Sounds for Letters *i*, *qu*, and *z*

Unit Overview

In this unit, students will
- ► Learn the sight words *says*, *have*, and *with*.
- ► Identify the letters and sounds in the alphabet.
- ► Learn the sounds for letters *i*, *qu*, and *z*.
- ► Identify individual sounds in words.
- ► Blend sounds to build words.

Materials

Supplied
- *K¹² PhonicsWorks Basic Activity Book*, p. PH 41
- whiteboard, Learning Coach
- whiteboard, student
- Tile Kit

Also Needed
- sight words box
- crayons

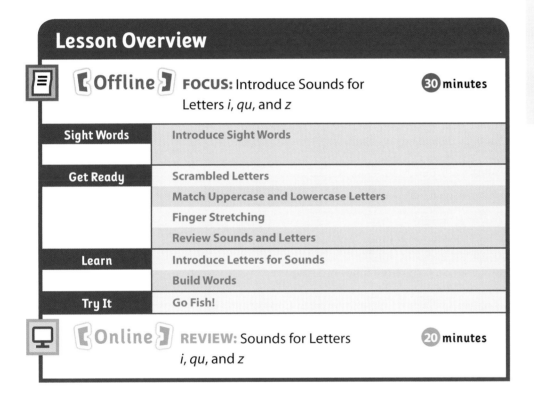

Lesson Overview

Offline **FOCUS:** Introduce Sounds for Letters *i*, *qu*, and *z* — **30** minutes

Sight Words	Introduce Sight Words
Get Ready	Scrambled Letters
	Match Uppercase and Lowercase Letters
	Finger Stretching
	Review Sounds and Letters
Learn	Introduce Letters for Sounds
	Build Words
Try It	Go Fish!

Online **REVIEW:** Sounds for Letters *i*, *qu*, and *z* — **20** minutes

Advance Preparation

Place lowercase letter tiles in alphabetical order on your whiteboard.

 **Offline** **30** minutes

FOCUS: Introduce Sounds for Letters *i*, *qu*, and *z*

Work **together** with students to complete offline Sight Words, Get Ready, Learn, and Try It activities.

Sight Words

Introduce Sight Words

Help students learn the sight words *says*, *have*, and *with*.

1. Gather the sight word cards *says*, *have*, and *with*.

2. Show students the *says* card.

3. **Say:** This is the word *says*. We see this word so often that we want to be able to read and spell it quickly without thinking about it. Look closely at the word *says*. Spell the word *says* aloud. Take a picture of the word *says* in your mind. When you think you can spell *says* yourself, turn the card over and use your letter tiles to spell the word *says*. Check the card to see if you spelled the word *says* correctly. Read aloud the word you spelled with the letter tiles.

4. Repeat the activity with the remaining sight words.

5. Chart students' progress on the back of each card.

   ► Divide the back of the card into two columns.
   ► Label the first column "Read" and the second column "Spell."
   ► Record the dates that students read or spell the word correctly. When students can read and spell the word correctly three times in a row, they have mastered the word. You may want to put a star or sticker on the card when they have mastered that word.

6. Add the cards to students' sight words box.

 TIP Sight words can be very difficult for some students. Let students work at their own pace and really master these words, as they occur frequently in reading and writing.

> **Objectives**
> • Read sight words.
> • Spell sight words.

Get Ready

Scrambled Letters

To help students master the alphabet, have them practice identifying and naming the letters.

1. Place the following letter tiles in random order on students' whiteboard: *c, j, l, m, o, r,* and *t.*

2. Have students arrange the letters in alphabetical order.

TIP Students may find this activity easier if they slowly sing "The Alphabet Song" to themselves as they work.

Match Uppercase and Lowercase Letters

To help students learn to recognize the difference between lowercase and uppercase letters of the alphabet, have them practice identifying and naming letters. Grab your whiteboard with letters.

1. Place the following uppercase letters on students' whiteboard in a horizontal row: *A, D, H, I, J,* and *P.*

2. Point to a letter and have students name it.

3. Have students select the matching lowercase letter from your whiteboard.

4. Have them place the lowercase letter under the uppercase letter to make a pair.

TIP If students have difficulty with this activity, have them practice naming the letters in the alphabet. When they can name all the letters in the correct order, have them touch and name the lowercase and uppercase letters for each letter.

Finger Stretching

Use finger stretching to help students identify individual sounds in words.

1. **Say:** Let's review finger stretching. In the word *pot,* the first sound is /p/, the next sound is /ŏ/, and the last sound is /t/. I will finger stretch each sound as I say it. Then I'll say the word while pulling my fist toward my body.

2. Finger stretch the word *pot* for students.

3. **Say:** I'm going to say words with several sounds in them. You'll say each word and then finger stretch it while you say each sound in the word.

4. Say the following words and have students finger stretch them. After they finger stretch each word, ask them the question for that word.

   ▸ *pig* /p/ /ĭ/ /g/   What is the middle sound? /ĭ/
   ▸ *sip* /s/ /ĭ/ /p/   What is the first sound? /s/
   ▸ *kin* /k/ /ĭ/ /n/   What is the last sound? /n/
   ▸ *fit* /f/ /ĭ/ /t/   What is the middle sound? /ĭ/
   ▸ *got* /g/ /ŏ/ /t/   What is the first sound? /g/
   ▸ *lap* /l/ /ă/ /p/   What is the middle sound? /ă/

TIP Refer to the K¹² *PhonicsWorks* video for a demonstration of finger stretching.

Objectives

- Identify letters of the alphabet.
- Match capital letters to lowercase letters.
- Identify individual sounds in words.
- Given the letter, identify the most common sound.
- Given the sound, identify the most common letter or letters.

Review Sounds and Letters

Help students review sounds for the letters *a*, *b*, *k*, *o*, *p*, *s*, and *t*, plus any letters that are confusing for them.

1. Place the following letter tiles in random order on students' whiteboard: *a*, *b*, *k*, *o*, *p*, *s*, and *t*, plus any letters that are confusing.

2. **Say:** Let's go over some letters and sounds.

3. Point to each letter tile and have students say a sound that letter makes.

   - *k* /k/
   - *a* /ă/
   - *t* /t/
   - *s* /s/
   - *o* /ŏ/
   - *b* /b/
   - *p* /p/

4. Say each of the following sounds. Have students repeat the sound and touch the corresponding letter tile.

   - /k/ *k*
   - /ă/ *a*
   - /t/ *t*
   - /s/ *s*
   - /ŏ/ *o*
   - /b/ *b*
   - /p/ *p*

5. As you do the activity, point to some letter tiles two or three times so that students don't think they are finished with a sound after they have named it.

6. Redirect students if they say an incorrect sound when you point to a letter tile.

   Say: That's the sound of another letter. What is the sound for this letter?

7. Help students if they touch the wrong letter tile after they repeat a sound.

   Say: That letter goes with the sound [sound for incorrect letter tile]. We're looking for the letter that goes with the sound [target sound].

Learn

Introduce Letters for Sounds

To help students learn the lowercase letters *i*, *qu*, and *z*, have them practice identifying and naming the letters from the sounds.

1. Place the following letter tiles on students' whiteboard: *i*, *qu*, and *z*.

2. **Say:** Let's learn sounds for letters. When we see the letter *i*, we can say the sound /ĭ/. When we see the letters *qu*, we say the sound /kw/. When we see the letter *z*, we say the sound /z/.

3. Have students
   - ▸ Touch the letter *i* and say /ĭ/.
   - ▸ Touch the letters *qu* and say /kw/.
   - ▸ Touch the letter *z* and say /z/.

4. **Say:** Let's practice these sounds and letters.

5. Say the sounds /ĭ/, /kw/, and /z/ one at a time. Have students repeat each sound and touch the letter for each sound. It is important for them to touch the letter while they say the sound.

6. Redirect students if they name the letter and not the sound.

   Say: You're right that the name of the letter is [letter]. We want the sound for this letter. What is the sound?

7. Redirect students if they name the sound incorrectly.

   Say: That's the sound of another letter. The sound for this letter is [target sound]. Touch the letter and say the sound.

Build Words

Help students use letters and sounds to build words.

1. Place the following letter tiles at the top of students' whiteboard: *i*, *n*, *p*, *qu*, *t*, and *z*.

2. Draw three horizontal lines across the middle of students' whiteboard to represent the sounds in a word.

3. **Say:** Let's use letters and sounds to build the word *pin*.

4. Have students finger stretch the sounds in *pin*.

5. Have students
   - ▸ Identify the first, next, and last sounds in *pin*.
   - ▸ Choose the corresponding letter for each of the sounds.
   - ▸ Move the letters to the correct lines on their whiteboards.

Objectives

- Identify the letter, given the sound /ĭ/.
- Identify the sound, given the letter *i*.
- Identify the letters, given the sound /kw/.
- Identify the sound, given the letters *qu*.
- Identify the letter, given the sound /z/.
- Identify the sound, given the letter *z*.
- Blend sounds to create words.
- Identify individual sounds in words.

6. Guide students with these questions:

   ▶ What is the first sound in *pin*? /p/
   Which line does the letter for that sound go on? the first one
   ▶ What is the next sound in *pin*? /ĭ/
   Which line does the letter for that sound go on? the second one
   ▶ What's the last sound in *pin*? /n/
   Which line does the letter for that sound go on? the last one

7. Have students touch and say the word.

8. Redirect students if they select the incorrect letter.

   Say: That sound is in the word [word], and it is the [first, second, third] sound.
   We want the sound [target sound].

   Continue until students select the correct letter.

9. Repeat the activity to build the following words:

   ▶ *quit* /kw/ /ĭ/ /t/
   ▶ *zip* /z/ /ĭ/ /p/

Try It •

Go Fish!

Have students complete page PH 41 in *K¹² PhonicsWorks Basic Activity Book* for more practice with the sounds /ĭ/ and /ŏ/. Have students read the word aloud and color the fish pink for words that contain the sound /ĭ/ and yellow for words that contain the sound /ŏ/.

Objectives

● Read aloud grade-level text with appropriate automaticity, prosody, accuracy, and rate.

● Identify and use the sound /ŏ/.

● Identify and use the sound /ĭ/.

● Identify individual sounds in words.

 **20 minutes**

REVIEW: Sounds for Letters *i*, *qu*, and *z*

Students will work online independently to

- ▶ Practice the sounds for letters *i*, *qu*, and *z*.
- ▶ Practice decoding text by reading story.

Help students locate the online activities and provide support as needed.

Offline Alternative

No computer access? Have students point out and name things that contain the sounds /i/, /kw/, and /z/ (for example, *lip* and *quiz*). You might also ask students to spell simple words that contain the letters *i*, *qu*, *z*, and other letters students have learned, or ask them to think of words that begin with those letters.

Objectives

- Identify the letter, given the sound /i/.
- Identify the sound, given the letter *i*.
- Identify the letters, given the sound /kw/.
- Identify the sound, given the letters *qu*.
- Identify the letter, given the sound /z/.
- Identify the sound, given the letter *z*.
- Identify individual sounds in words.
- Read aloud grade-level text with appropriate automaticity, prosody, accuracy, and rate.
- Decode words by applying grade-level word analysis skills.

Practice Sounds for Letters *i, qu,* and *z* (A)

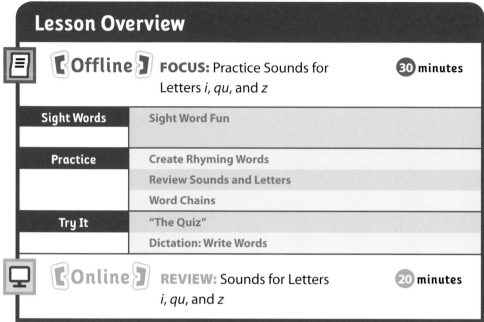

Lesson Overview

⊟ 〔Offline〕 FOCUS: Practice Sounds for Letters *i, qu,* and *z*		**30** minutes

Sight Words	Sight Word Fun
Practice	Create Rhyming Words
	Review Sounds and Letters
	Word Chains
Try It	"The Quiz"
	Dictation: Write Words

▢ 〔Online〕 REVIEW: Sounds for Letters *i, qu,* and *z*		**20** minutes

〔Materials〕

Supplied
- *K¹² PhonicsWorks Readers Basic 2,* pp. 13–18
- whiteboard, Learning Coach
- whiteboard, student
- Tile Kit

Also Needed
- sight words box
- dictation notebook

 **Offline** ⏱ **30 minutes**

FOCUS: Practice Sounds for Letters *i*, *qu*, and *z*

Work **together** with students to complete offline Sight Words, Practice, and Try It activities.

Sight Words ....

Sight Word Fun

Help students learn the sight words *says, have,* and *with,* and up to two additional sight words they have yet to master.

1. Gather the sight word cards *says, have,* and *with,* and up to two additional sight word cards.

2. Choose one sight word card to begin.

   Say: Look at this word and take a picture of it in your mind. When you think you can spell the word yourself, turn the card over and use your letter tiles to spell the word.

3. After students spell the word, have them check the card to see if they spelled the word correctly.

   Say: Read aloud the word you spelled with the letter tiles.

4. Repeat the activity with the remaining sight words.

   TIP Sight words can be very difficult for some students. Let them work at their own pace and really master these words.

> **Objectives**
> - Read sight words.
> - Spell sight words.

Practice ....

Create Rhyming Words

Have students combine word parts and make words that rhyme.

1. **Say:** I'm going to break a word into two parts. Your job is to put the parts back together and say the word.

   ▸ For example, if the first part of the word is /t/ and the last part is /ĭp/, then you'll say *tip.*

   ▸ Next you'll add a new **beginning sound** to make a word that rhymes. For example, you'll use the same last part, /ĭp/, and add a new first sound, like /n/. The rhyming word is *nip.*

2. **Say:** Now it's your turn: /n/ . . . /ĭp/.

   ▸ What's the word? *nip*
   ▸ Now use the same last part, /ĭp/, but add a new sound, /h/, at the beginning. What word did you make? *hip*

> **Objectives**
> - Identify words that rhyme.
> - Given the letter, identify the most common sound.
> - Given the sound, identify the most common letter or letters.
> - Identify individual sounds in words.
> - Blend sounds to create words.

3. Have students add a new beginning sound to the last part of the word below to make rhyming words.

   ▸ /h/ . . . /ĭp/ *hip; Possible rhyming words: sip, lip*
   ▸ /j/ . . . /ĭg/ *jig; Possible rhyming words: rig, pig, fig*

Review Sounds and Letters

Help students review sounds for the letters *a, b, f, i, m, o, qu,* and *z,* plus any letters that are confusing for them.

1. Place the following letter tiles in random order on students' whiteboard: *a, b, f, i, m, o, qu,* and *z,* plus any letters that are confusing.

2. **Say:** Let's go over some letters and sounds.

3. Point to each letter tile and have students say a sound that letter or letters make.

   ▸ *i* /ĭ/
   ▸ *o* /ŏ/
   ▸ *a* /ă/
   ▸ *qu* /kw/
   ▸ *f* /f/
   ▸ *m* /m/
   ▸ *b* /b/
   ▸ *z* /z/

4. Say each of the following sounds. Have students repeat the sound and touch the corresponding letter tile.

   ▸ /ĭ/ *i*
   ▸ /ŏ/ *o*
   ▸ /ă/ *a*
   ▸ /kw/ *qu*
   ▸ /f/ *f*
   ▸ /m/ *m*
   ▸ /b/ *b*
   ▸ /z/ *z*

5. As you do the activity, point to some letter tiles two or three times so that students don't think they are finished with a sound after they have named it.

6. Redirect students if they say an incorrect sound when you point to a letter tile.

   Say: That's the sound of another letter. What is the sound for this letter?

7. Help students if they touch the wrong letter tile after they repeat a sound.

   Say: That letter tile goes with the sound [sound for incorrect letter tile]. We're looking for the letter that goes with the sound [target sound].

Word Chains

Have students build words by adding and changing letters to help them recognize and use individual sounds in words.

1. Place the following letter tiles on students' whiteboard: *a, b, f, h, i, o, p, qu, s,* and *t.*

2. **Say:** I am going to build the first word in a chain. The word is *fat.*

   ▸ I will pull down the letters for the sounds /f/, /ă/, and /t/ to spell the word *fat.*

   ▸ Next I will touch and say *fat.* To change *fat* to *fit,* I will think about what sound is changed from the word *fat* to *fit.* I will need to change the letter *a* to the letter *i* in the middle of the word to make the word *fit.*

   ▸ Touch and say the word *fit.* Now it's your turn to change *fit* to *bit.* You can spell *bit* by making only one change. Touch and say the new word.

3. Redirect students if they select the incorrect letter for any sound.

   Say: That letter is for the sound [incorrect sound]. We want the letter for the sound [target sound]. What letter makes that sound? Answers will vary.

4. Redirect students if they name the sound incorrectly.

   Say: To change the word [first word] to [target word], we need the letter for the sound [target sound].

   Show students how to make the change. Have them touch and say the new word after they move the letters.

5. Follow this procedure to make the following words: *quit, quip, sip, sap, sop, hop, hip.*

6. For every new word, have students add, replace, or remove only one letter tile.

   TIP If students struggle, review the sounds and letters that are confusing them.

Try It

"The Quiz"

Have students read "The Quiz" on page 13 of *K¹² PhonicsWorks Readers Basic 2.*

Students should read the story silently once or twice before reading the story aloud. When students miss a word that can be sounded out, point to it and give them three to six seconds to try the word again. If students still miss the word, tell them the word so the flow of the story isn't interrupted.

After reading the story, make a list of all the words students missed, and go over those words with them. You may use tiles to show them how to read the words.

Objectives

- Read aloud grade-level text with appropriate automaticity, prosody, accuracy, and rate.
- Decode words by applying grade-level word analysis skills.
- Track text from left to right.
- Turn pages sequentially.
- Write words by applying grade-level phonics knowledge.
- Follow three-step directions.

Dictation: Write Words

Have students practice identifying sounds and writing words.

1. Gather a pencil and the dictation notebook. Say the word *lip*. Then give these directions to students:

   ▶ Repeat the word.
   ▶ Write the word in your notebook.
   ▶ Read the word aloud.

2. When students have finished, write the the following word on your whiteboard: *lip*.

3. Have them compare their answer to your correct version.

4. Repeat this procedure with the words *zap* and *quiz*.

   ▶ If students make an error and don't see it, help them correct their mistake by having them finger stretch the sounds in the word they missed.
   ▶ If students are having difficulty selecting the correct letters or sounds, review those letters or sounds that are confusing them.
   ▶ If students have difficulty with first, middle, and last sounds, have them finger stretch the sounds in words.

 **20 minutes**

REVIEW: **Sounds for Letters *i*, *qu*, and *z***

Students will work online independently to

▶ Practice sounds for the letters *i*, *qu*, and *z*.

Help students locate the online activities and provide support as needed.

Offline Alternative

No computer access? Have students point out and name things that contain the sounds /i/, /kw/, and /z/ (for example, *rib*, *quit*, and *zig*). You might also ask students to spell simple words that contain the letters *i*, *qu*, *z*, and other letters students have learned, or ask them to think of words that begin with those letters.

Objectives

- Identify the letter, given the sound /i/.
- Identify the sound, given the letter *i*.
- Identify the letters, given the sound /kw/.
- Identify the sound, given the letters *qu*.
- Identify the letter, given the sound /z/.
- Identify the sound, given the letter *z*.
- Identify individual sounds in words.

Practice Sounds for Letters *i*, *qu*, and *z* (B)

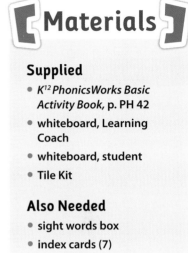

Lesson Overview

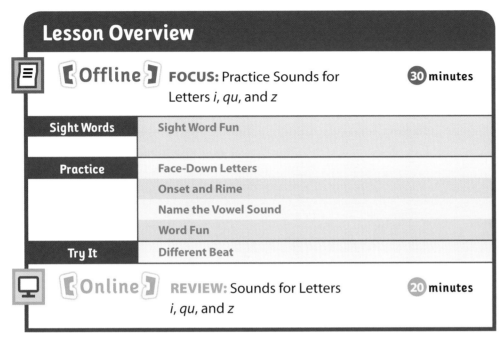

Offline FOCUS: Practice Sounds for Letters *i*, *qu*, and *z*		**30** minutes
Sight Words	Sight Word Fun	
Practice	Face-Down Letters	
	Onset and Rime	
	Name the Vowel Sound	
	Word Fun	
Try It	Different Beat	
Online REVIEW: Sounds for Letters *i*, *qu*, and *z*		**20** minutes

Materials

Supplied

- *K¹² PhonicsWorks Basic Activity Book*, p. PH 42
- whiteboard, Learning Coach
- whiteboard, student
- Tile Kit

Also Needed

- sight words box
- index cards (7)

Advance Preparation

Place lowercase letter tiles in alphabetical order on your whiteboard.

For Word Fun, print each of the following words on index cards, using one card per word: *mop, fan, pan, lip, pot, can,* and *top*.

 **30 minutes**

FOCUS: Practice Sounds for Letters *i*, *qu*, and *z*

Work **together** with students to complete offline Sight Words, Practice, and Try It activities.

Sight Words

Sight Word Fun

Help students learn the sight words *says*, *have*, and *with*, and up to two additional sight words they have yet to master.

1. Gather the sight word cards *says*, *have*, and *with*, and up to two additional sight word cards.

2. Choose one sight word card to begin.

   Say: Look at this word and take a picture of it in your mind. When you think you can spell the word yourself, turn the card over and use your letter tiles to spell the word.

3. After students spell the word, have them check the card to see if they spelled the word correctly.

   Say: Read aloud the word you spelled with the letter tiles.

4. Repeat the activity with the remaining sight words.

TIP Sight words can be very difficult for some students. Let them work at their own pace and really master these words.

Objectives
- Read sight words.
- Spell sight words.

Practice

Face-Down Letters

To help students master the letters of the alphabet, have them practice identifying and naming letters. Grab your whiteboard with letters placed in alphabetical order.

1. Lay your whiteboard down on a flat surface and flip over the following letter tiles so they are face down on the whiteboard: *c*, *g*, *k*, *l*, *o*, *r*, *v*, and *z*.

2. **Say:** These letters are face down. We are looking at the back of them. Name each letter and then turn it over to see if you were right.

3. Place the following letters on students' whiteboard in random order: *b*, *e*, *h*, *i*, *n*, *p*, *s*, *u*, and *w*. Have students arrange the letters in alphabetical order.

Objectives
- Identify letters of the alphabet.
- Identify and use vowels and vowel sounds.
- Identify a word when given the onset and rime.
- Blend sounds to create words.
- Identify individual sounds in words.
- Read aloud grade-level text with appropriate automaticity, prosody, accuracy, and rate.

Onset and Rime

In a word, the part of the syllable before the first vowel sound is the **onset**. The part of the syllable after the first vowel sound is the **rime**. For example, in *ad*, /ă/ is the onset and *d* is the rime. Help students put together words that are broken down into parts by onset and rime.

1. **Say:** I'm going to break a word into two parts. Your job is to put the parts together and say the word. If the first part of a word is /ă/ and the last part of the word is *d*, then the whole word is *ad*: /ă/ . . . *d* . . . *ad*.

2. Say the following pairs of word parts. Have students tell you the word that each pair forms.

   ▸ /ŏ/ . . . *ff off*
   ▸ /ĭ/ . . . *f if*
   ▸ /ĭ/ . . . *tch itch*
   ▸ /ă/ . . . *sk ask*
   ▸ /ŏ/ . . . *dd odd*

Name the Vowel Sound

To help students learn vowel sounds, have them practice identifying and naming the letters *a*, *i*, and *o*.

1. Place the following letter tiles in the order shown on students' whiteboard: *a*, *i*, and *o*, plus any other letters that are confusing to them.

2. **Say:** I am going to point to each letter. Tell me a sound for that letter.

3. **Say:** Now I am going to say each sound. Repeat the sound and touch its letter.

4. Redirect students if they name the letter and not its sound.

   Say: You are right that the name of the letter is [letter]. What is a sound for this letter?

5. Redirect students if they name the sound incorrectly.

   Say: That is the sound of another letter.

6. Provide additional guidance if students touch the wrong letter tile during the review.

   Say: That is the letter tile for the sound [sound of incorrect letter tile]. We are looking for the letter tile for the sound [target sound].

7. If students touch the wrong letter tile again, point to the correct letter tile.

   Say: This is the letter tile for the sound [target sound]. Touch this letter tile and say its sound.

Word Fun

Have students practice reading words and identifying names of common objects.

1. Gather the index cards you prepared and place them face down in one pile.

2. **Say:** You are going to practice reading and writing some words.

   ▸ You will choose a card from the pile and read the word on it.
   ▸ Then you are going to flip the card over, and write the word on the back of the card.
   ▸ I'll try first.

3. Choose a card from the pile, and say and write the word.

   Say: Now it's your turn. Choose a card and read it to me.

4. If time permits, have students choose two words and draw a picture of those words on the back of the card.

TIP If students stumble over any words, have them touch and say the words. Touch and say these words along with them.

Try It

Different Beat

Have students complete page PH 42 in *K¹² PhonicsWorks Basic Activity Book* for more practice with the sounds /ĭ/, /kw/, and /z/. Have students read each word in the row aloud and circle the word that does **not** rhyme.

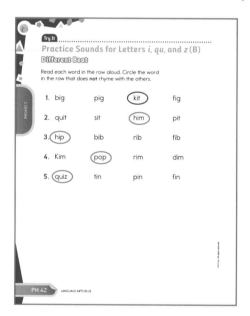

Objectives

- Read aloud grade-level text with appropriate automaticity, prosody, accuracy, and rate.
- Identify words that rhyme.
- Identify and use the sound /ĭ/.
- Identify and use the sound /kw/.
- Identify and use the sound /z/.

 **20** minutes

REVIEW: Sounds for Letters *i*, *qu*, and *z*

Students will work online independently to

▸ Practice sounds for the letters *i*, *qu*, and *z*.
▸ Practice decoding text by reading a story.

Help students locate the online activities and provide support as needed.

Offline Alternative

No computer access? Have students point out and name things that contain the sounds /i/, /kw/, and /z/ (for example, *hit, quip,* and *zag*). You might also ask students to spell simple words that contain the letters *i, qu, z,* and other letters students have learned, or ask them to think of words that contain those letters.

Objectives

- Identify the letter, given the sound /i/.
- Identify the sound, given the letter *i*.
- Identify the letters, given the sound /kw/.
- Identify the sound, given the letters *qu*.
- Identify the letter, given the sound /z/.
- Identify the sound, given the letter *z*.
- Identify individual sounds in words.
- Read aloud grade-level text with appropriate automaticity, prosody, accuracy, and rate.
- Decode words by applying grade-level word analysis skills.

Practice Sounds for Letters *i, qu,* and *z* (C)

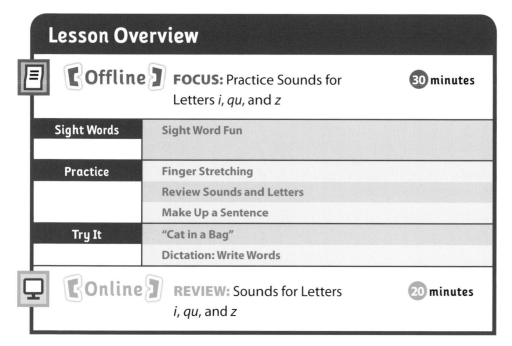

Lesson Overview

Offline FOCUS: Practice Sounds for Letters *i, qu,* and *z*		**30** minutes
Sight Words	Sight Word Fun	
Practice	Finger Stretching	
	Review Sounds and Letters	
	Make Up a Sentence	
Try It	"Cat in a Bag"	
	Dictation: Write Words	
Online REVIEW: Sounds for Letters *i, qu,* and *z*		**20** minutes

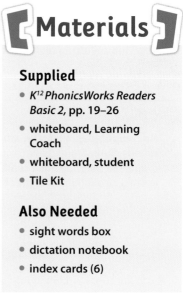

Materials

Supplied
- *K¹² PhonicsWorks Readers Basic 2*, pp. 19–26
- whiteboard, Learning Coach
- whiteboard, student
- Tile Kit

Also Needed
- sight words box
- dictation notebook
- index cards (6)

Advance Preparation

For Make Up a Sentence, print each of the following words on index cards, using one card per word: *mat, lip, quit, fin, Jim,* and *cot.*

 **30 minutes**

FOCUS: Practice Sounds for Letters *i*, *qu*, and *z*

Work **together** with students to complete offline Sight Words, Practice, and Try It activities.

Sight Words

Sight Word Fun

Help students learn the sight words *says*, *have*, and *with*, and up to two additional sight words they have yet to master.

Objectives
- Read sight words.
- Spell sight words.

1. Gather the sight word cards *says*, *have*, and *with*, and up to two additional sight word cards.

2. Choose one sight word card to begin.

   Say: Look at this word and take a picture of it in your mind. When you think you can spell the word yourself, turn the card over and use your letter tiles to spell the word.

3. After students spell the word, have them check the card to see if they spelled the word correctly.

   Say: Read aloud the word you spelled with the letter tiles.

4. Repeat the activity with the remaining sight words.

TIP Sight words can be very difficult for some students. Let them work at their own pace and really master these words.

Practice

Finger Stretching

Use finger stretching to help students identify individual sounds in words.

Objectives
- Identify individual sounds in words.
- Given the letter, identify the most common sound.
- Given the sound, identify the most common letter or letters.
- Read aloud grade-level text with appropriate automaticity, prosody, accuracy, and rate.
- Decode words by applying grade-level word analysis skills.

1. **Say:** Let's review finger stretching. In the word *lip*, the first sound is /l/, the next sound is /ĭ/, and the last sound is /p/. I will finger stretch each sound as I say it. Then I'll say the word while pulling my fist toward my body.

2. Finger stretch the word *lip* for students.

3. **Say:** I'm going to say words with several sounds in them. You'll say each word and then finger stretch it while you say each sound in the word.

4. Say the following words and have students finger stretch them. After they finger stretch each word, ask them the question for that word.

   ▸ *fin* /f/ /ĭ/ /n/   What is the middle sound? /ĭ/
   ▸ *itch* /ĭ/ /ch/   What is the first sound? /ĭ/
   ▸ *fib* /f/ /ĭ/ /b/   What is the last sound? /b/
   ▸ *sit* /s/ /ĭ/ /t/   What is the middle sound? /ĭ/
   ▸ *gap* /g/ /ă/ /p/   What is the first sound? /g/
   ▸ *sod* /s/ /ŏ/ /d/   What is the middle sound? /ŏ/

TIP Refer to the *K¹² PhonicsWorks* video for a demonstration of finger stretching.

Review Sounds and Letters
Help students review sounds for the letters *a, d, g, i, l, o, p, qu,* and *z,* plus any letters that are confusing for them.

1. Place the following letter tiles in random order on students' whiteboards: *a, d, i, g, l, p, qu, l, o,* and *z,* plus any letters that are confusing.

2. **Say:** Let's go over some letters and sounds.

3. Point to each letter tile and have students say a sound that letter or letters make.

    -   *i* /ĭ/
    -   *o* /ŏ/
    -   *a* /ă/
    -   *qu* /kw/
    -   *p* /p/

    -   *d* /d/
    -   *g* /g/
    -   *l* /l/
    -   *z* /z/

4. Say each of the following sounds. Have students repeat the sound and touch the corresponding letter tile.

    -   /ĭ/ *i*
    -   /ŏ/ *o*
    -   /ă/ *a*
    -   /kw/ *qu*
    -   /p/ *p*

    -   /d/ *d*
    -   /g/ *g*
    -   /l/ *l*
    -   /z/ *z*

5. As you do the activity, point to some letter tiles two or three times so that students don't think they are finished with a sound after they have named it.

6. Redirect students if they say an incorrect sound when you point to a letter tile.

    Say: That's the sound of another letter. What is the sound for this letter?

7. Help students if they touch the wrong letter tile after they repeat a sound.

    Say: That letter tile goes with the sound [sound for incorrect letter tile]. We're looking for the letter that goes with the sound [target sound].

Make Up a Sentence
Help students use words to make sentences.

1. Gather the word cards you prepared and place them face down on the table in one pile.

2. Have students

    -   Select a card.
    -   Read the word.
    -   Use the word in an interesting, fun, or silly sentence.

TIP If students read a word incorrectly, have them finger stretch the sounds in the word.

Try It

"Cat in a Bag"

Have students read the "Cat in a Bag" story on page 19 of *K¹² PhonicsWorks Readers Basic 2*.

Students should read the story silently once or twice before reading the story aloud. When students miss a word that can be sounded out, point to it and give them three to six seconds to try the word again. If students still miss the word, tell them the word so the flow of the story isn't interrupted.

After reading the story, make a list of all the words students missed, and go over those words with them. You may use tiles to show them how to read the words.

Dictation: Write Words

Have students practice identifying sounds and writing words.

1. Gather a pencil and the dictation notebook. Say the word *zip*. Then give these directions to students:

   ▸ Repeat the word.
   ▸ Write the word in your notebook.
   ▸ Read the word aloud.

2. When students have finished, write the following word on your whiteboard: *zip*.

3. Have them compare their answer to your correct version.

4. Repeat this procedure with the words *quip* and *hog*.

   ▸ If students make an error and don't see it, help them correct their mistake by having them finger stretch the sounds in the word they missed.
   ▸ If students are having difficulty selecting the correct letters or sounds, review those letters or sounds that are confusing them.
   ▸ If students have difficulty with first, middle, and last sounds, have them finger stretch the sounds in words.

Objectives

- Read aloud grade-level text with appropriate automaticity, prosody, accuracy, and rate.
- Decode words by applying grade-level word analysis skills.
- Track text from left to right.
- Turn pages sequentially.
- Write words by applying grade-level phonics knowledge.
- Follow three-step directions.

 **20 minutes**

REVIEW: Sounds for Letters *i*, *qu*, and *z*

Students will work online independently to

▶ Practice with the sounds letters *i*, *qu*, and *z* for the sounds /ĭ/, /kw/, and /z/.

Help students locate the online activities and provide support as needed.

Offline Alternative

No computer access? Have students point out and name things that contain the sounds /ĭ/, /kw/, and /z/ (for example, *fin, quit,* and *zip).* You might also ask students to spell simple words that contain the letters *i, qu, z,* and other letters students have learned, or ask them to think of words that begin with those letters.

Objectives
- Identify the letter, given the sound /ĭ/.
- Identify the sound, given the letter *i*.
- Identify the letters, given the sound /kw/.
- Identify the sound, given the letters *qu*.
- Identify the letter, given the sound /z/.
- Identify the sound, given the letter *z*.
- Identify individual sounds in words.

Unit Checkpoint

Lesson Overview

  [Online] **REVIEW:** Sounds for Letters *i*, *qu*, and *z* **20** minutes

[Offline] **UNIT CHECKPOINT:** Sounds for Letters *i*, *qu*, and *z* **30** minutes

Materials

Supplied

- *K¹² PhonicsWorks Basic Assessments*, pp. PH 67–72

Objectives

- Identify and use the sound /ĭ/.
- Identify and use the sound /kw/.
- Identify and use the sound /z/.
- Identify individual sounds in words.
- Given the letter, identify the most common sound.
- Given the sound, identify the most common letter or letters.
- Read sight words.
- Read instructional-level text with 90% accuracy.
- Read aloud grade-level text with appropriate automaticity, prosody, accuracy, and rate.

[Online] **20** minutes

REVIEW: Sounds for Letters *i*, *qu*, and *z*

Students will review the sounds /ĭ/, /kw/, and /z/ made by the letters *i*, *qu*, and *z* to prepare for the Unit Checkpoint. Help students locate the online activities and provide support as needed.

 **30 minutes**

UNIT CHECKPOINT: Sounds for Letters *i*, *qu*, and *z*

Explain that students are going to show what they have learned about letters and sounds.

1. Give students the Unit Checkpoint pages for the Sounds for Letters *i*, *qu*, and *z* unit and print the Unit Checkpoint Answer Key, if you'd like.

2. Use the instructions below to help administer the Checkpoint to students. On the Answer Key or another sheet of paper, note student answers to oral response questions to help with scoring the Checkpoint later.

3. Use the Answer Key to score the Checkpoint, and then enter the results online.

Part 1. Say Sounds Have students read across the rows from left to right and say a sound that each letter or letters make. Note any sounds they say incorrectly.

Part 2. Word Dissection For each word, say the sound students should identify. Have them read the word aloud and circle the letter or group of letters that spells the requested sound. Note any incorrect responses.

21. *middle sound*

22. *ending sound*

23. *beginning sound*

24. *ending sound*

25. *middle sound*

Part 3. Finger Stretching Say each word to students. Have them say each word aloud and finger stretch the sounds. Note any words they finger stretch incorrectly.

26. *quit*

27. *quiz*

28. *dig*

29. *zip*

Part 4. Circle and Write Say each sound and have students circle the letter or letters that make the sound. Have them write the letter or letters.

30. /z/

31. /ĭ/

32. /kw/

33. /g/

Part 5. Read Aloud Listen to students read the sentences aloud. Count and note the number of words they read correctly.

Part 6. Say Letters Say each sound. Have students say the letter or letters that make that sound. Note any incorrect responses.

35. /ĭ/

36. /ă/

37. /ŏ/

38. /z/

39. /k/

40. /r/

41. /kw/

42. /j/

43. /l/

44. /ă/

45. /kw/

46. /z/

47. /ĭ/

48. /k/

49. /ŏ/

50. /p/

51. /r/

52. /ĭ/

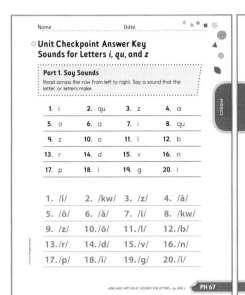

Name _____ Date _____

Unit Checkpoint Answer Key
Sounds for Letters *i*, *qu*, and *z*

Part 1. Say Sounds
Read across the row from left to right. Say a sound that the letter or letters make.

1. i	2. qu	3. z	4. a
5. o	6. a	7. i	8. qu
9. z	10. o	11. l	12. b
13. r	14. d	15. v	16. n
17. p	18. i	19. g	20. i

1. /ĭ/	2. /kw/	3. /z/	4. /ă/
5. /ŏ/	6. /ă/	7. /ĭ/	8. /kw/
9. /z/	10. /ŏ/	11. /l/	12. /b/
13. /r/	14. /d/	15. /v/	16. /n/
17. /p/	18. /ĭ/	19. /g/	20. /ĭ/

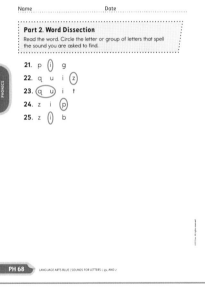

Name _____ Date _____

Part 2. Word Dissection
Read the word. Circle the letter or group of letters that spell the sound you are asked to find.

21. p (i) g

22. q u i (z)

23. (q u) i t

24. z i (p)

25. z (i) b

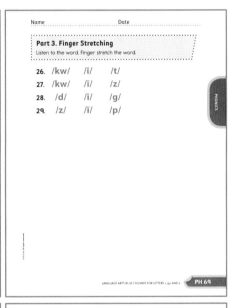

Name _____ Date _____

Part 3. Finger Stretching
Listen to the word. Finger stretch the word.

26. /kw/ /ĭ/ /t/

27. /kw/ /ĭ/ /z/

28. /d/ /ĭ/ /g/

29. /z/ /ĭ/ /p/

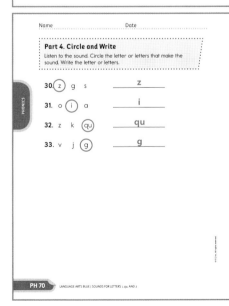

Name _____ Date _____

Part 4. Circle and Write
Listen to the sound. Circle the letter or letters that make the sound. Write the letter or letters.

30. (z) g s _____ z

31. o (i) a _____ i

32. z k (qu) _____ qu

33. v j (g) _____ g

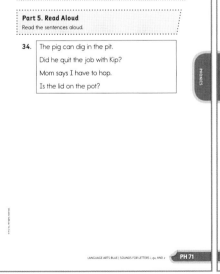

Name _____ Date _____

Part 5. Read Aloud
Read the sentences aloud.

34. The pig can dig in the pit.
Did he quit the job with Kip?
Mom says I have to hop.
Is the lid on the pot?

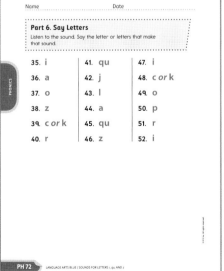

Name _____ Date _____

Part 6. Say Letters
Listen to the sound. Say the letter or letters that make that sound.

35. i	41. qu	47. i
36. a	42. j	48. c or k
37. o	43. l	49. o
38. z	44. a	50. p
39. c or k	45. qu	51. r
40. r	46. z	52. i

Getting Stronger: Sounds /ă/, /ĭ/, and /ŏ/ (A)

Unit Overview

In this unit, students will
- ▸ Review sight words.
- ▸ Identify the letters and sounds in the alphabet.
- ▸ Practice the sounds /ă/, /ĭ/, and /ŏ/.
- ▸ Identify individual sounds in words.
- ▸ Blend sounds to build words.

Materials

Supplied
- *K¹² PhonicsWorks Basic Activity Book*, p. PH 43
- whiteboard, Learning Coach
- whiteboard, student
- Tile Kit

Also Needed
- sight words box
- index cards (6)

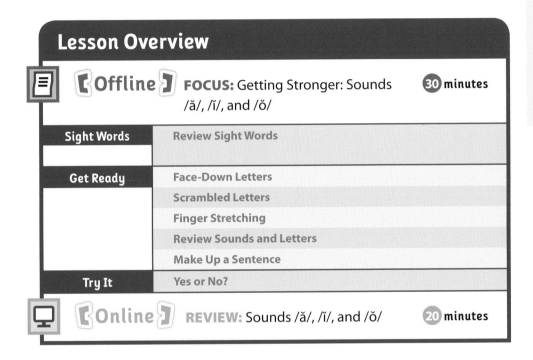

Lesson Overview

	Offline FOCUS: Getting Stronger: Sounds /ă/, /ĭ/, and /ŏ/	30 minutes
Sight Words	Review Sight Words	
Get Ready	Face-Down Letters	
	Scrambled Letters	
	Finger Stretching	
	Review Sounds and Letters	
	Make Up a Sentence	
Try It	Yes or No?	
	Online REVIEW: Sounds /ă/, /ĭ/, and /ŏ/	20 minutes

Advance Preparation

Place lowercase letter tiles in alphabetical order on your whiteboard.

For Make Up a Sentence, print each of the following words on index cards, using one card per word: *man, tap, nip, fit, cop,* and *pot.*

 **30 minutes**

FOCUS: Getting Stronger: Sounds /ă/, /ĭ/, and /ŏ/

Work **together** with students to complete offline Sight Words, Practice, and Try It activities.

Sight Words

Review Sight Words

Help students learn to recognize sight words.

1. Gather all the sight word cards students have yet to master from their sight words box. Stack the cards on the table face down.

2. Have students pick up a word and read it to you.

3. If they read it quickly and correctly, put the card in one stack. If they hesitate or do not read the word correctly, put it in another stack. The second stack should have words that they will review again.

4. Take the stack of words that students read correctly and dictate each word to them. They may choose to either write the word or spell it aloud.

5. If students spell the word correctly, they have mastered the word. If they misspell the word, add it to the stack of cards to review again.

6. Chart students' progress on the back of each card.

   ▶ Divide the back of the card into two columns.
   ▶ Label the first column "Read" and the second column "Spell."
   ▶ Record the dates that students read or spell the word correctly. When students can read and spell the word correctly three times in a row, they have mastered the word. You may want to put a star or sticker on their card when they have mastered that word.

TIP Even if students can read and spell all the words correctly, it is still beneficial for them to review sight words. Choose as many additional words as you would like for each subsequent activity.

Objectives
- Read sight words.
- Spell sight words.
- Write sight words.

Practice ....

Face-Down Letters

To help students master the letters of the alphabet, have them practice identifying and naming letters. Grab your whiteboard with letters placed in alphabetical order.

1. Lay your whiteboard down on a flat surface and flip over the following letter tiles so they are face down on the whiteboard: *b, f, i, o, r, w,* and *z.*

2. **Say:** These letters are face down. We are looking at the back of them. Name each letter and then turn it over to see if you were right.

TIP If students miss any of the letters, have them turn over the missed ones and try again.

Scrambled Letters

To help students master the alphabet, have them practice identifying and naming letters.

1. Place the following letter tiles in random order on students' whiteboard: *b, r,* and *z.*

2. Have students arrange the letters in alphabetical order.

TIP Students may find this activity easier if they slowly sing "The Alphabet Song" to themselves as they work.

Finger Stretching

Use finger stretching to help students identify individual sounds in words.

1. **Say:** Let's review finger stretching. In the word *and*, the first sound is /ă/, the next sound is /n/, and the last sound is /d/. I will finger stretch each sound as I say it. Then I'll say the word while pulling my fist toward my body.

2. Finger stretch the word *and* for students.

3. **Say:** I'm going to say words with several sounds in them. You'll say each word and then finger stretch it while you say each sound in the word.

4. Say the following words and have students finger stretch them. After they finger stretch each word, ask them the question for that word.

   ▶ *hop* /h/ /ŏ/ /p/   What is the first sound? /h/
   ▶ *hot* /h/ /ŏ/ /t/   What is the middle sound? /ŏ/
   ▶ *its* /ĭ/ /t/ /s/   What is the first sound? /ĭ/
   ▶ *cab* /k/ /ă/ /b/   What is the last sound? /b/
   ▶ *tip* /t/ /ĭ/ /p/   What is the middle sound? /ĭ/
   ▶ *fat* /f/ /ă/ /t/   What is the first sound? /f/
   ▶ *pod* /p/ /ŏ/ /d/   What is the middle sound? /ŏ/

TIP Refer to the *K¹² PhonicsWorks* video for a demonstration of finger stretching.

Objectives

- Identify letters of the alphabet.
- Identify individual sounds in words.
- Given the letter, identify the most common sound.
- Given the sound, identify the most common letter or letters.
- Identify the letter, given the sound /ĭ/.
- Identify the sound, given the letter *i.*
- Identify and use the sound /ĭ/.
- Identify the letter, given the sound /ă/.
- Identify the sound, given the letter *a.*
- Identify and use the sound /ă/.
- Identify the letter, given the sound /ŏ/.
- Identify the sound, given the letter *o.*
- Identify and use the sound /ŏ/.
- Read aloud grade-level text with appropriate automaticity, prosody, accuracy, and rate.
- Decode words by applying grade-level word analysis skills.

Review Sounds and Letters

Help students review sounds for the letters *a, b, h, i, l, m, p, r,* and *v,* plus any letters that are confusing for them.

1. Place the following letter tiles in random order on students' whiteboard: *a, b, h, i, l, m, p, r,* and *v,* plus any letters that are confusing.

2. **Say:** Let's go over some letters and sounds.

3. Point to each letter tile and have students say a sound that letter makes.

   - *a* /ă/   - *m* /m/
   - *b* /b/   - *p* /p/
   - *h* /h/   - *r* /r/
   - *i* /ĭ/   - *v* /v/
   - *l* /l/

4. Say each of the following sounds. Have students repeat the sound and touch the corresponding letter tile.

   - /ă/ *a*   - /m/ *m*
   - /b/ *b*   - /p/ *p*
   - /h/ *h*   - /r/ *r*
   - /ĭ/ *i*   - /v/ *v*
   - /l/ *l*

5. As you do the activity, point to some letter tiles two or three times so that students don't think they are finished with a sound after they have named it.

6. Redirect students if they say an incorrect sound when you point to a letter tile.

   Say: That's the sound of another letter. What is the sound for this letter?

7. Help students if they touch the wrong letter tile after they repeat a sound.

   Say: That letter tile goes with the sound [sound for incorrect letter tile]. We're looking for the letter that goes with the sound [target sound].

Make Up a Sentence

Help students use words to make sentences.

1. Gather the index cards you prepared and place them face down on the table in one pile.

2. Have students

   ▸ Select a card.
   ▸ Read the word.
   ▸ Use the word in an interesting, fun, or silly sentence.

TIP If students read a word incorrectly, have them finger stretch the sounds in the word.

Try It

Yes or No?

Have students complete page PH 43 in *K¹² PhonicsWorks Basic Activity Book* for more practice with the sounds /ă/, /ĭ/, and /ŏ/. Have students look at the picture and read the question aloud. Have them answer the question by writing *Yes* or *No* on the line.

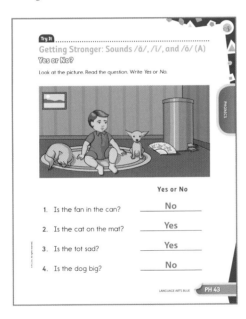

Objectives

- Read aloud grade-level text with appropriate automaticity, prosody, accuracy, and rate.
- Identify and use the sound /ă/.
- Identify and use the sound /ĭ/.
- Identify and use the sound /ŏ/.
- Identify individual sounds in words.

 20 minutes

REVIEW: Sounds /ă/, /ĭ/, and /ŏ/

Students will work online independently to

▸ Practice the sounds /ă/, /ĭ/, and /ŏ/ made by the letters *a*, *i*, and *o*.

▸ Practice decoding text by reading a story.

Help students locate the online activities and provide support as needed.

Offline Alternative

No computer access? Have students point out and name things that contain the sounds /ă/, /ĭ/, and /ŏ/ (for example, *dad*, *hip*, and *pop*). You might also ask students to spell simple words that contain the letters *a*, *i*, and *o*.

Objectives

- Identify the letter, given the sound /ĭ/.
- Identify the sound, given the letter *i*.
- Identify the letter, given the sound /ă/.
- Identify the sound, given the letter *a*.
- Identify the letter, given the sound /ŏ/.
- Identify the sound, given the letter *o*.
- Identify individual sounds in words.
- Read aloud grade-level text with appropriate automaticity, prosody, accuracy, and rate.
- Decode words by applying grade-level word analysis skills.

Getting Stronger: Sounds /ă/, /ĭ/, and /ŏ/ (B)

Lesson Overview

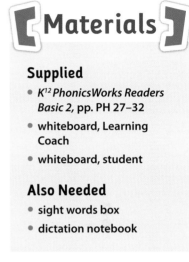

[Materials]

Supplied
- *K¹² PhonicsWorks Readers Basic 2*, pp. PH 27–32
- whiteboard, Learning Coach
- whiteboard, student

Also Needed
- sight words box
- dictation notebook

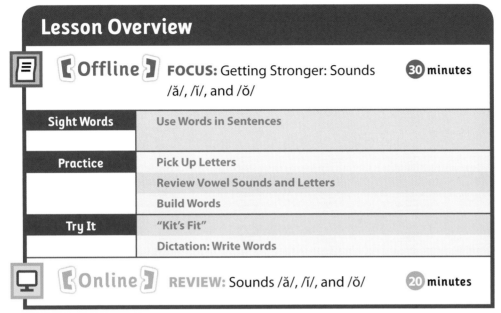

[Offline] **FOCUS:** Getting Stronger: Sounds /ă/, /ĭ/, and /ŏ/ — **30** minutes

Sight Words	Use Words in Sentences
Practice	Pick Up Letters
	Review Vowel Sounds and Letters
	Build Words
Try It	"Kit's Fit"
	Dictation: Write Words

[Online] **REVIEW:** Sounds /ă/, /ĭ/, and /ŏ/ — **20** minutes

[Offline] 30 minutes

FOCUS: Getting Stronger: Sounds /ă/, /ĭ/, and /ŏ/

Work **together** with students to complete offline Sight Words, Practice, and Try It activities.

Sight Words

Use Words in Sentences

Help students use sight words in sentences.

1. Gather all the sight word cards students have yet to master from their sight words box. Spread the sight word cards on the table.

2. **Say:** Let's use sight words in sentences.

3. Have students

   ▸ Touch each card and read the word on it.
   ▸ Make up a sentence using the word.
   ▸ Put the card in a pile after using the word in a sentence.
   ▸ Go through the pile of cards and read each sight word again.
   ▸ Spell each word.

TIP If students have difficulty with any of the sight words, place those word cards in a pile to review later in the week.

> **Objectives**
> • Read sight words.
> • Spell sight words.

Practice

Pick Up Letters

Help students use letters and sounds to make words and sentences.

1. Place the following letter tiles on students' whiteboard: *b, c, f, i, n, o,* and *qu.*

2. **Say:** Let's play a game with these letters.

3. Pick up the letter tile for *b.*

4. **Say:** I chose the letter *b.* The sound is /b/. A word that starts with the sound /b/ is *black.* A sentence using that word is, "My favorite kitty is black." Now it's your turn.

5. Continue taking turns until all the letter tiles have been chosen.

6. Have students answer the following questions for each letter or group of letters:

   ▸ What is (are) the letter(s)?
   ▸ What is the sound?
   ▸ What is a word that starts with that sound?
   ▸ What sentence can you make with that word?

> **Objectives**
> • Given the letter, identify the most common sound.
> • Given the sound, identify the most common letter or letters.
> • Identify and use vowels and vowel sounds.
> • Identify and use the sound /ă/.
> • Identify and use the sound /ĭ/.
> • Identify and use the sound /ŏ/.
> • Identify individual sounds in words.
> • Blend sounds to create words.

7. Redirect students if they name a word that starts with the sound but not the letter (such as *knob*).

   Say: That is a word that doesn't follow the rules that we know for spelling. Try another word.

8. Prompt students if they have trouble matching the sounds with words. For example,

   Say: That's /j/, as in *jelly*. Can you think of another word that starts with that sound?

Review Vowel Sounds and Letters

Help students review vowel sounds and letters.

1. Place the following letter tiles on students' whiteboard: *a*, *i*, and *o*, plus any letters that are confusing for them.

2. **Say:** I am going to point to each letter. Tell me a sound for that letter.

3. **Say:** I am going to say each sound. Repeat the sound and touch its letter.

4. Point to some letters two or three times, so students don't think that once they have named a sound they are finished with it.

5. Redirect students if they name the letter and not its sound.

   Say: You are right that the name of the letter is [letter]. We want the sound for this letter. What is the sound?

6. Redirect students if they name the sound incorrectly.

   Say: That is the sound of another letter.

7. Provide additional guidance if students touch the wrong letter tile during the review.

   Say: That is the letter for the sound [sound of incorrect letter tile]. We are looking for the letter for the sound [target sound].

8. If students touch the wrong letter again, point to the correct letter.

   Say: This is the letter for the sound [target sound]. Touch this letter tile and say its sound.

Build Words

Help students use letters and sounds to build words.

1. Place the following letter tiles at the top of students' whiteboard: *a, f, i, l, n, o, p, s,* and *t.*

2. Draw three horizontal lines across the middle of students' whiteboard to represent the sounds in a word.

3. **Say:** Let's use letters and sounds to build the word *lot.*

4. Have students finger stretch the sounds in *lot.*

5. Have students

   ▸ Identify the first, next, and last sounds in *lot*.
   ▸ Choose the corresponding letter for each of the sounds.
   ▸ Move the letters to the correct lines on their whiteboard.

6. Guide students with these questions:

   ▸ What is the first sound in *lot*? /l/
     Which line does the letter for that sound go on? the first one
   ▸ What is the next sound in *lot*? /ŏ/
     Which line does the letter for that sound go on? the second one
   ▸ What's the last sound in *lot*? /t/
     Which line does the letter for that sound go on? the last one

7. Have students touch and say the word.

8. Redirect students if they select the incorrect letter.

   Say: That sound is in the word [word], and it is the [first, second, third] sound. We want the sound [target sound].

   Continue until students select the correct letter.

9. Repeat the activity to build the following words:

   ▸ *tan* /t/ /ă/ /n/
   ▸ *fin* /f/ /ĭ/ /n/
   ▸ *sap* /s/ /ă/ /p/

Try It

"Kit's Fit"

Have students read "Kit's Fit" on page 27 of *K¹² PhonicsWorks Readers Basic 2*.

Students should read the story silently once or twice before reading the story aloud. When students miss a word that can be sounded out, point to it and give them three to six seconds to try the word again. If students still miss the word, tell them the word so the flow of the story isn't interrupted.

After reading the story, make a list of all the words students missed, and go over those words with them. You may use tiles to show them how to read the words.

Objectives

- Read aloud grade-level text with appropriate automaticity, prosody, accuracy, and rate.
- Decode words by applying grade-level word analysis skills.
- Track text from left to right.
- Turn pages sequentially.
- Write words by applying grade-level phonics knowledge.
- Follow three-step directions.

Dictation: Write Words

Have students practice identifying sounds and writing words.

1. Gather a pencil and the dictation notebook. Say the word *sap*. Then give these directions to students:

   ▶ Repeat the word.
   ▶ Write the word in your notebook.
   ▶ Read the word aloud.

2. When students have finished, write the following word on your whiteboard: *sap*.

3. Have them compare their answer to your correct version.

4. Repeat this procedure with the words *fin* and *lot*.

   ▶ If students make an error and don't see it, help them correct their mistake by asking them to finger stretch the sounds in the word they missed.
   ▶ If students are having difficulty selecting the correct letters or sounds, review those letters or sounds that are confusing them.
   ▶ If students have difficulty with first, middle, and last sounds, have them finger stretch the sounds in words.

 **minutes**

REVIEW: Sounds /ă/, /ĭ/, and /ŏ/

Students will work online independently to

▶ Practice the sounds /ă/, /ĭ/, and /ŏ/ made by the letters *a*, *i*, and *o*.

Help students locate the online activities and provide support as needed.

Offline Alternative

No computer access? Have students point out and name things that contain the sounds /ă/, /ĭ/, and /ŏ/ (for example, *dad*, *hip*, and *pop*). You might also ask students to spell simple words that contain the letters *a*, *i*, and *o*.

Objectives
- Identify the letter, given the sound /ĭ/.
- Identify the sound, given the letter *i*.
- Identify the letter, given the sound /ă/.
- Identify the sound, given the letter *a*.
- Identify the letter, given the sound /ŏ/.
- Identify the sound, given the letter *o*.
- Identify individual sounds in words.

Getting Stronger: Sounds /ă/, /ĭ/, and /ŏ/ (C)

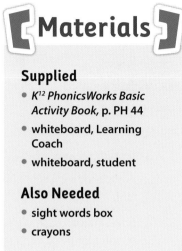

Lesson Overview

[Offline] **FOCUS:** Getting Stronger: Sounds /ă/, /ĭ/, and /ŏ/   **30** minutes

Sight Words	Sight Word Concentration
Practice	Match Uppercase and Lowercase Letters
	Signal Beginning Sounds
	Review Sounds and Letters
Try It	To the Rescue

[Online] **REVIEW:** Sounds /ă/, /ĭ/, and /ŏ/   **20** minutes

[Materials]

Supplied

- *K¹² PhonicsWorks Basic Activity Book*, p. PH 44
- whiteboard, Learning Coach
- whiteboard, student

Also Needed

- sight words box
- crayons

Advance Preparation

Gather two sets of all the sight word cards you have used to date.

Place lowercase letter tiles in alphabetical order on your whiteboard.

 **30 minutes**

FOCUS: Getting Stronger: Sounds /ă/, /ĭ/, and /ŏ/

Work **together** with students to complete offline Sight Words, Practice, and Try It activities.

Sight Words

Sight Word Concentration

Help students review sight words.

Objectives
- Read sight words.
- Spell sight words.
- Write sight words.

1. Gather the two sets of sight word cards.

2. Scramble both sets of sight word cards and place them face down on the floor or a table.

3. Turn over two cards at a time; take turns with students. If the cards match, the person turning over the matching cards reads the word and uses it in a sentence. If the cards don't match, the person turns them back over.

4. Remove and save the matching cards.

5. Continue the activity until all the word cards are paired.

6. Have students read all the words.

7. Take the stack of words that students read correctly and dictate each word to them.

8. Have students write each word or spell it aloud.

TIP If students have difficulty with any of the sight words, let them work at their own pace and really master these words.

Practice ••

Match Uppercase and Lowercase Letters

To help students master the difference between lowercase and uppercase letters of the alphabet, have them practice identifying and naming letters. Grab your whiteboard with letters.

1. Arrange the following uppercase letters on students' whiteboard in a horizontal row: *A, F, M, R, T,* and *W.*

2. Point to a letter and have students name it.

3. Have students select the matching lowercase letter from your whiteboard.

4. Have students place the lowercase letter under the uppercase letter to make a pair.

TIP If students have difficulty with this activity, have them practice naming the letters in the alphabet. When they can name all the letters in the correct order, have them touch and name the lowercase and uppercase letters for each letter.

Signal Beginning Sounds

Use a special signal to help students identify **beginning sounds** in words.

1. **Say:** I'm going to tell you a special sound, and then I'll say some words. Repeat each word I say and make a special signal to tell me where the special sound is. If the special sound is at the beginning of the word, pat your cheek. If the special sound is **not** at the beginning of the word, just smile at me. For example,

   ▸ If I ask you to listen for the sound /ă/ and I say the word *at,* you'll repeat the word *at* and pat your cheek because *at* has the sound /ă/ at the beginning.
   ▸ If I say the word *pop,* you'll repeat the word *pop* and smile at me because *pop* has the sound /p/, not /ă/, at the beginning.

2. Say each sound and group of words. Have students make the special signal to identify the beginning sound.

   ▸ /ă/: *at, up, accident, ant, on* pat cheek: *at, accident, ant*
   ▸ /ch/: *chair, can, shop, cheese* pat cheek: *chair, cheese*
   ▸ /ŏ/: *apple, onto, offer, after, Oliver* pat cheek: *onto, offer, Oliver*
   ▸ /ĭ/: *Indian, isn't, operation, itch, if* pat cheek: *Indian, isn't, itch, if*

TIP If students enjoy this activity, you can add to the lists as they think of more words with those beginning sounds.

Objectives

- Match capital letters to lowercase letters.
- Identify capital and lowercase letters.
- Identify letters of the alphabet.
- Identify beginning sounds in words.
- Identify and use the sound /ă/.
- Identify and use the sound /ĭ/.
- Identify and use the sound /ŏ/.
- Given the letter, identify the most common sound.
- Given the sound, identify the most common letter or letters.

Review Sounds and Letters

Help students review sounds for the letters *d, i, m, n, o, qu, s,* and *w,* plus any letters that are confusing for them.

1. Place the following letter tiles in random order on students' whiteboard: *d, i, m, n, o, qu, s,* and *w,* plus any letters that are confusing.

2. **Say:** Let's go over some letters and sounds.

3. Point to each letter tile and have students say a sound that letter or letters make.

   ▶ *m* /m/
   ▶ *d* /d/
   ▶ *i* /ĭ/
   ▶ *n* /n/
   ▶ *o* /ŏ/
   ▶ *qu* /kw/
   ▶ *s* /s/
   ▶ *w* /w/

4. Say each of the following sounds. Have students repeat the sound and touch the corresponding letter tile.

   ▶ /m/ *m*
   ▶ /d/ *d*
   ▶ /ĭ/ *i*
   ▶ /n/ *n*
   ▶ /ŏ/ *o*
   ▶ /kw/ *qu*
   ▶ /s/ *s*
   ▶ /w/ *w*

5. As you do the activity, point to some letter tiles two or three times so that students don't think they are finished with a sound after they have named it.

6. Redirect students if they say an incorrect sound when you point to a letter tile.

   Say: That's the sound of another letter. What is the sound for this letter?

7. Help students if they touch the wrong letter tile after they repeat a sound.

   Say: That letter tile goes with the sound [sound for incorrect letter tile]. We're looking for the letter that goes with the sound [target sound].

Try It

To the Rescue

Have students complete page PH 44 in *K¹² PhonicsWorks Basic Activity Book* for more practice with the sounds /ă/, /ĭ/, and /ŏ/. Have them read each word and color the boxes that name real words to help the rabbit find the path to the log.

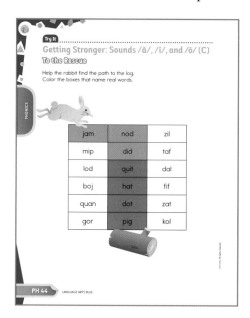

 **20 minutes**

REVIEW: **Sounds /ă/, /ĭ/, and /ŏ/**

Students will work online independently to

▶ Practice the sounds /ă/, /ĭ/, and /ŏ/ made by the letters *a*, *i*, and *o*.
▶ Practice decoding text by reading a story.

Help students locate the online activities and provide support as needed.

Offline Alternative

No computer access? Have students point out and name things that contain the sounds /ă/, /ĭ/, and /ŏ/ (for example, *gap*, *pit*, and *dog*). You might also ask students to spell simple words that contain the letters *a*, *i*, and *o*.

Objectives

- Identify the letter, given the sound /ĭ/.
- Identify the sound, given the letter *i*.
- Identify the letter, given the sound /ă/.
- Identify the sound, given the letter *a*.
- Identify the letter, given the sound /ŏ/.
- Identify the sound, given the letter *o*.
- Identify individual sounds in words.
- Read aloud grade-level text with appropriate automaticity, prosody, accuracy, and rate.
- Decode words by applying grade-level word analysis skills.

Getting Stronger: Sounds /ă/, /ĭ/, and /ŏ/ (D)

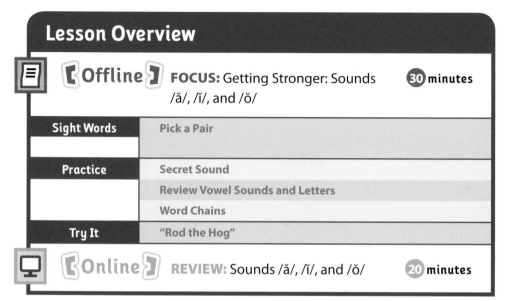

Lesson Overview

Offline FOCUS: Getting Stronger: Sounds /ă/, /ĭ/, and /ŏ/   **30** minutes

Sight Words	Pick a Pair
Practice	Secret Sound
	Review Vowel Sounds and Letters
	Word Chains
Try It	"Rod the Hog"

Online REVIEW: Sounds /ă/, /ĭ/, and /ŏ/   **20** minutes

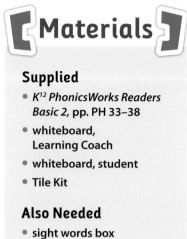

Materials

Supplied
- *K¹² PhonicsWorks Readers Basic 2*, pp. PH 33–38
- whiteboard, Learning Coach
- whiteboard, student
- Tile Kit

Also Needed
- sight words box

 **Offline** ⏳ **30 minutes**

FOCUS: Getting Stronger: Sounds /ă/, /ĭ/, and /ŏ/

Work **together** with students to complete offline Sight Words, Practice, and Try It activities.

Sight Words •••

Pick a Pair

Play a card game with students for more practice with sight words.

1. Gather the sight word cards that students are reviewing. Choose two words and place the cards on the table.

2. Ask questions to help students identify each word. For example, if the words are *or* and *one*, you could ask, "Which word names a number?" If the words are *on* and *but*, you could ask, "Which word is the opposite of *off*?"

3. Continue the activity until students identify all the words.

4. Take the stack of words that students read correctly and dictate each word to them.

5. Have students write each word or spell it aloud.

 Objectives
- Read sight words.
- Spell sight words.
- Write sight words.

Practice •••

Secret Sound

Say groups of words that have the same sound to help students recognize **middle sounds** in words.

1. **Say:** I am going to say some groups of words. Listen for a secret sound at the middle of each word. Then tell me what sound you hear at the middle of each group of words.

2. Say each of the following groups of words. Have students identify the secret sound in each group.

   ▸ *top, not, cob, sock* /ŏ/
   ▸ *tab, fan, sat, lad* /ă/
   ▸ *win, tip, sick, pit* /ĭ/

   TIP If students can't identify the secret sound, have them listen while you say each word again and then have them repeat each word. Have them say the sound they hear in the middle of each word.

 Objectives
- Identify middle sounds in words.
- Identify and use the sound /ă/.
- Identify and use the sound /ĭ/.
- Identify and use the sound /ŏ/.
- Identify and use vowels andvowel sounds.
- Identify the new word when one sound is changed in a word.
- Identify individual sounds in words.

Review Vowel Sounds and Letters

Help students review vowel sounds and letters.

1. Place the following letter tiles in random order on students' whiteboard: *a*, *i*, and *o*, plus any letters that are confusing for them.

2. **Say:** I am going to point to each letter. Tell me a sound for that letter.

3. **Say:** I am going to say each sound. Repeat the sound and touch its letter.

4. Point to some letters two or three times, so students don't think that once they have named a sound they are finished with it.

5. Redirect students if they name the letter and not its sound.

   Say: You are right that the name of the letter is [letter]. We want the sound for this letter. What is the sound?

6. Redirect students if they name the sound incorrectly.

   Say: That is the sound of another letter.

7. Provide additional guidance if students touch the wrong letter tile during the review.

   Say: That is the letter for the sound [sound of incorrect letter tile]. We are looking for the letter for the sound [target sound].

8. If students touch the wrong letter again, point to the correct letter.

   Say: This is the letter for the sound [target sound]. Touch this letter and say its sound.

Word Chains

Have students build words by adding and changing letters to help them recognize and use individual sounds in words.

1. Place the following letters on students' whiteboard: *a*, *b*, *h*, *i*, *o*, *p*, *s*, and *t*.

2. **Say:** I am going to build the first word in a chain. The word is *hat*.

   ▸ I will pull down the letters for the sounds /h/, /ă/, and /t/ to spell the word *hat*.

   ▸ I will touch and say *hat*. To change *hat* to *pat*, I will think about what sound is changed from the word *hat* to *pat*. I will need to change the the letter *h* to the letter *p* at the beginning of the word to make the word *pat*.

   ▸ Touch and say the word *pat*. Now it's your turn to change *pat* to *pot*. You can spell *pot* by making only one change. Touch and say the new word.

3. Redirect students if they select the incorrect letter for any sound.

   Say: That letter is for the sound [incorrect sound]. We want the letter for the sound [target sound]. What letter makes that sound? Answers will vary.

4. Redirect students if they name the sound incorrectly.

   Say: To change the word [first word] to [target word], we need the letter for the sound [target sound].

   Show students how to make the change. Have them touch and say the new word after they move the letters.

5. Follow this procedure to make the following words: *hot, hit, hip, hop, top, tap, tip, sip.*

6. For every new word, have students add, replace, or remove only one letter.

 If students struggle, review the sounds and letters that are confusing them.

 Try It •••

"Rod the Hog"
Have students read "Rod the Hog" on page 33 of *K¹² PhonicsWorks Readers Basic 2.*

Students should read the story silently once or twice before reading the story aloud. When students miss a word that can be sounded out, point to it and give them three to six seconds to try the word again. If students still miss the word, tell them the word so the flow of the story isn't interrupted.

After reading the story, make a list of all the words the student missed, and go over those words with them. You may use tiles to show them how to read the words.

 Objectives
- Read aloud grade-level text with appropriate automaticity, prosody, accuracy, and rate.
- Decode words by applying grade-level word analysis skills.
- Track text from left to right.
- Turn pages sequentially.

Online **20 minutes**

REVIEW: Sounds /ă/, /ĭ/, and /ŏ/
Students will work online independently to

▶ Practice the sounds /ă/, /ĭ/, and /ŏ/ made by the letters *a, i,* and *o.*

Help students locate the online activities and provide support as needed.

Offline Alternative

No computer access? Have students point out and name things that contain the sounds /ă/, /ĭ/, and /ŏ/ (for example, *pan, sit,* and *job*). You might also ask students to spell simple words that contain the letters *a, i,* and *o.*

 Objectives
- Identify the letter, given the sound /ĭ/.
- Identify the sound, given the letter *i.*
- Identify the letter, given the sound /ă/.
- Identify the sound, given the letter *a.*
- Identify the sound, given the letter *o.*
- Identify the sound, given the letter *o.*
- Identify individual sounds in words.

Unit Checkpoint

Lesson Overview

 [Online] **REVIEW:** Sounds /ă/, /ĭ/, and /ŏ/   **20** minutes

[Offline] **UNIT CHECKPOINT:** Getting Stronger: Sounds /ă/, /ĭ/, and /ŏ/   **30** minutes

[Materials]

Supplied
- *K¹² PhonicsWorks Basic Assessments,* pp. PH 73–78

Objectives
- Identify the letter, given the sound /ă/.
- Identify the letter, given the sound /ĭ/.
- Identify the letter, given the sound /ŏ/.
- Identify the sound, given the letter *a*.
- Identify the sound, given the letter *i*.
- Identify the sound, given the letter *o*.
- Identify individual sounds in words.
- Given the letter, identify the most common sound.
- Given the sound, identify the most common letter or letters.
- Identify letters of the alphabet.
- Read sight words.
- Read instructional-level text with 90% accuracy.
- Read aloud grade-level text with appropriate automaticity, prosody, accuracy, and rate.

 **20** minutes

REVIEW: **Sounds /ă/, /ĭ/, and /ŏ/**
Students will review the sounds /ă/, /ĭ/, and /ŏ/ made by the letters *a*, *i*, and *o* to prepare for the Unit Checkpoint. Help students locate the online activities and provide support as needed.

 **Offline** ⏱ **minutes**

UNIT CHECKPOINT: Getting Stronger: Sounds /ă/, /ĭ/, and /ŏ/

Explain that students are going to show what they have learned about letters and sounds.

1. Give students the Unit Checkpoint pages for the Getting Stronger: Sounds /ă/, /ĭ/, and /ŏ/ unit and print the Unit Checkpoint Answer Key, if you'd like.

2. Use the instructions below to help administer the Checkpoint to students. On the Answer Key or another sheet of paper, note student answers to oral response questions to help with scoring the Checkpoint later.

3. Use the Answer Key to score the Checkpoint, and then enter the results online.

Part 1. Say Sounds Have students read across the rows from left to right and say the sound of each letter or letters aloud. Note any sounds they say incorrectly.

Part 2. Word Dissection For each word, say the sound students should identify. Have them read the word aloud and circle the letter or group of letters that spells the requested sound.

21. *middle sound*

22. *ending sound*

23. *middle sound*

24. *ending sound*

25. *middle sound*

Part 3. Finger Stretching Say each word to students. Have them say each word aloud and finger stretch the sounds. Note any words they finger stretch incorrectly.

26. *hot*   28. *quiz*

27. *cab*   29. *pin*

Part 4. Circle and Write Say each sound and have students circle the letter or letters that make the sound. Have them write the letter or letters.

30. /ĭ/   32. /kw/

31. /z/   33. /ŏ/

Part 5. Read Aloud Listen to students read the sentences aloud. Count and note the number of words they read correctly.

Part 6. Say Letters Say each sound. Have students say the letter or letters that make that sound. Note any incorrect responses.

35. /ă/

36. /ŏ/

37. /ĭ/

38. /d/

39. /m/

40. /b/

41. /f/

42. /l/

43. /kw/

44. /f/

45. /kw/

46. /b/

47. /ŏ/

48. /l/

49. /d/

50. /ĭ/

51. /ă/

52. /m/

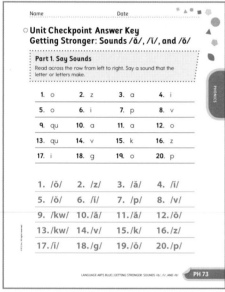

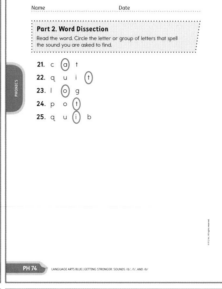

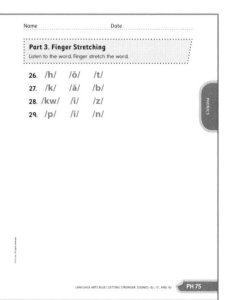

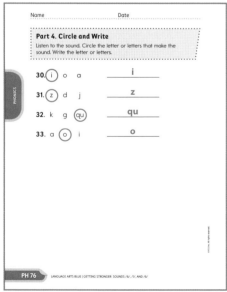

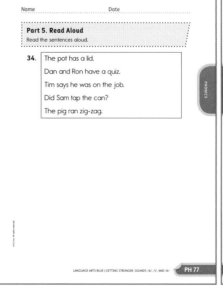

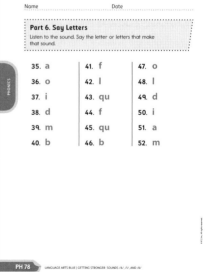

Introduce Sounds for Letters *u*, *w*, and *x*

Unit Overview

In this unit, students will
- ▸ Learn the sight words *where*, *from*, and *there*.
- ▸ Identify letters and sounds in the alphabet.
- ▸ Learn the letters *u*, *w*, and *x* for the sounds /ŭ/, /w/, and /ks/.
- ▸ Identify beginning and ending sounds in words.
- ▸ Build words.

[Materials]

Supplied
- K¹² *PhonicsWorks Basic Activity Book*, p. PH 45
- whiteboard, Learning Coach
- whiteboard, student
- Tile Kit

Also Needed
- sight words box

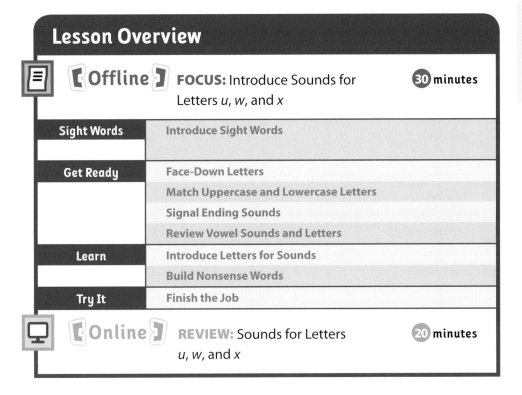

Lesson Overview

📄 **[Offline]** FOCUS: Introduce Sounds for Letters *u*, *w*, and *x*		**30** minutes
Sight Words	Introduce Sight Words	
Get Ready	Face-Down Letters	
	Match Uppercase and Lowercase Letters	
	Signal Ending Sounds	
	Review Vowel Sounds and Letters	
Learn	Introduce Letters for Sounds	
	Build Nonsense Words	
Try It	Finish the Job	
🖥 **[Online]** REVIEW: Sounds for Letters *u*, *w*, and *x*		**20** minutes

Advance Preparation

Place lowercase letter tiles in alphabetical order on your whiteboard.

 **30 minutes**

FOCUS: Introduce Sounds for Letters *u*, *w*, and *x*

Work **together** with students to complete offline Sight Words, Get Ready, Learn, and Try It activities.

Sight Words

Introduce Sight Words

Help students learn the sight words *where*, *from*, and *there*.

1. Gather the sight word cards *where*, *from*, and *there*.

2. Show students the *where* card.

   Say: This is the word *where*. We see this word so often that we want to be able to read and spell *where* quickly without thinking about it. Look closely at the word *where*. Spell the word *where* aloud. Take a picture of the word *where* in your mind. When you think you can spell *where* yourself, turn the card over and use your letter tiles to spell the word *where*. Check the card to see if you spelled the word *where* correctly. Read aloud the word you spelled with the letter tiles.

3. Repeat the activity with the remaining sight words.

4. Chart students' progress on the back of each card.

   ▸ Divide the back of the card into two columns.
   ▸ Label the first column "Read" and the second column "Spell."
   ▸ Record the dates that students read or spell the word correctly. When students can read and spell the word correctly three times in a row, they have mastered the word. You may want to put a star or sticker on the card when they have mastered that word.

5. Add the cards to students' sight words box.

TIP Sight words can be very difficult for some students. Let students work at their own pace and really master these words, as they occur frequently in reading and writing.

 Objectives
- Read sight words.
- Spell sight words.

Get Ready

Face-Down Letters

To help students master the letters of the alphabet, have them practice identifying and naming letters. Grab your whiteboard with letters placed in alphabetical order.

1. Lay your whiteboard down on a flat surface and flip over the following letter tiles so they are face down on the whiteboard: *a, c, f, j, m, t, u,* and *x*.

2. **Say:** These letters are face down. We are looking at the back of them. Name each letter and then turn it over to see if you were right.

TIP If students miss any of the letters, have them turn over the missed ones and try again.

Objectives
- Identify letters of the alphabet.
- Match capital letters to lowercase letters.
- Identify ending sounds in words.
- Identify short vowel sounds.
- Identify and use vowels and vowel sounds.

Match Uppercase and Lowercase Letters

To help students learn to recognize the difference between lowercase and uppercase letters of the alphabet, have them practice identifying and naming letters. Grab your whiteboard with letters.

1. Place the following uppercase letters on students' whiteboard in a horizontal row: *F, I, M, R, T, U, X,* and *W*.

2. Point to a letter and have students name it.

3. Have students select the matching lowercase letter from your whiteboard.

4. Have students place the lowercase letter under the uppercase letter to make a pair.

TIP If students have difficulty with this activity, have them practice naming the letters in the alphabet. When they can name all the letters in the correct order, have them touch and name the lowercase and uppercase letters for each letter.

Signal Ending Sounds

Use a special signal to help students identify **ending sounds** in words.

1. **Say:** I'm going to tell you a special sound, and then I'll say some words. Repeat each word I say and make a special signal to tell me where the special sound is. If the special sound is at the end of the word, pull your ear. If the special sound is **not** at the end of the word, just smile at me. For example,

   ▸ If I ask you to listen for the sound /l/ and I say the word *call*, you'll repeat the word *call* and pull your ear because *call* has the sound /l/ at the end.

   ▸ If I say the word *flip*, you'll repeat the word *flip* and smile at me because *flip* has the sound /p/, not /l/, at the end.

2. Say each sound and group of words. Have students make the special signal to identify the ending sound.

> ▶ /f/: *cuff, lips, stiff, tough, fun* pull ear: *cuff, stiff, tough*
> ▶ /k/: *cane, cake, back, tap, clack* pull ear: *cake, back, clack*
> ▶ /ks/: *wax, hits, ax, mask, tax, ox* pull ear: *wax, ax, tax, ox*
> ▶ /v/: *five, off, stuff, give, hive, Dave* pull ear: *five, give, hive, Dave*
> ▶ /d/: *suds, mud, sad, punt, Dad,calf* pull ear: *mud, sad, Dad*
> ▶ /p/: *pie, pump, lot, jump, pick, strip* pull ear: *pump, jump, strip*

TIP If students can't identify the ending sound of each word, say the word again and emphasize the ending sound by repeating it three times (for example, *sit* /t/ /t/ /t/). You can also draw out the ending sound when you say the word (for example, *kisssss*). If necessary, have students look at your mouth while you repeat the sounds.

Review Vowel Sounds and Letters
Help students review vowel sounds and letters.

1. Place the following letter tiles on students' whiteboards: *a*, *i*, and *o*, plus any letters that are confusing for them.

2. **Say:** I am going to point to each letter. Tell me a sound for that letter.

3. **Say:** I am going to say a sound. Repeat the sound and touch its letter.

4. Point to some letters two or three times, so students don't think that once they have named a sound they are finished with it.

5. Redirect students if they name the letter and not its sound.

   Say: You are right that the name of the letter is [letter]. We want the sound for this letter. What is the sound?

6. Redirect students if they name the sound incorrectly.

   Say: That is the sound of another letter.

7. Provide additional guidance if students touch the wrong letter tile during the review.

   Say: That is the letter tile for the sound [sound of incorrect letter tile]. We are looking for the letter tile for the sound [target sound].

8. If students touch the wrong letter again, point to the correct letter.

   Say: This is the letter tile for the sound [target sound]. Touch this letter tile and say its sound.

Learn

Introduce Letters for Sounds

To help students learn the lowercase letters *u*, *w* and *x*, have them practice identifying and naming the letters from the sounds.

1. Place the following letter tiles on students' whiteboard: *u*, *w*, and *x*.

2. **Say:** Let's learn sounds for letters. When we see the letter *u*, we can say the sound /ŭ/. When we see the letter *w*, we say the sound /w/. When we see the letter *x*, we can say the sound /ks/.

3. Have students
   - ▸ Touch the letter *u* and say /ŭ/.
   - ▸ Touch the letter *w* and say /w/.
   - ▸ Touch the letter *x* and say /ks/.

4. **Say:** Let's practice these sounds and letters.

5. Say the sounds /ŭ/, /w/, and /ks/ one at a time. Have students repeat each sound and touch the letter for each sound. It is important for students to touch the letter while they say the sound.

6. Redirect students if they name the letter and not the sound.

   Say: You're right that the name of the letter is [letter]. We want the sound for this letter. What is the sound?

7. Redirect students if they name the sound incorrectly.

   Say: That's the sound of another letter. The sound for this letter is [sound]. Touch the letter and say the sound.

8. Help students. If they touch the wrong letter, point to the correct letter.

   Say: This is the letter for the sound [target sound]. Touch and say its sound.

Objectives

- Identify the letter, given the sound /ŭ/.
- Identify the sound, given the letter *u*.
- Identify the letter, given the sound /w/.
- Identify the sound, given the letter *w*.
- Identify the letter, given the sound /ks/.
- Identify the sound, given the letter *x*.
- Identify individual sounds in words.
- Blend sounds to create words.

Build Nonsense Words

Help students use letters and sounds to build nonsense words.

1. Place the following letter tiles at the top of students' whiteboard: *b*, *m*, *u*, *w*, and *x*.

2. Draw three horizontal lines across the middle of students' whiteboard to represent the sounds in a word.

3. **Say:** Some words don't have any meaning. We call these **nonsense words**. Even though we don't know what a word means, we can still read it. Nonsense words will be very important when we read longer words. When we break longer words into parts, sometimes the parts are nonsense words.

4. **Say:** Let's use letters and sounds to build the nonsense word *wub*.

5. Have students finger stretch the sounds in *wub*.

6. Have students

   ▸ Identify the first, next, and last sounds in *wub*.
   ▸ Choose the corresponding letter for each of the sounds.
   ▸ Move the letters to the correct lines on their whiteboard.

7. Guide students with these questions:

   ▸ What is the first sound in *wub*? /w/
     Which line does the letter for that sound go on? the first one
   ▸ What is the next sound in *wub*? /ŭ/
     Which line does the letter for that sound go on? the second one
   ▸ What's the last sound in *wub*? /b/
     Which line does the letter for that sound go on? the last one

8. Have students touch and say the word.

9. Redirect students if they select the incorrect letter.

   Say: That sound is in the word [word], and it is the [first, second, third] sound.
   We want the sound [target sound].

   Continue until students select the correct letter.

10. Repeat the activity to build the following words:

    ▸ *mux* /m/ /ŭ/ /ks/
    ▸ *bux* /b/ /ŭ/ /ks/

Try It

Finish the Job
Have students complete page PH 45 in *K¹² PhonicsWorks Basic Activity Book* for more practice with the sounds /ŭ/, /w/, and /ks/. Have students choose a word from the box that best completes the sentence and write the word. Have them read the sentence aloud.

Objectives
- Read aloud grade-level text with appropriate automaticity, prosody, accuracy, and rate.
- Write words by applying grade-level phonics knowledge.
- Identify and use the sound /ŭ/.
- Identify and use the sound /w/.
- Identify and use the sound /ks/.

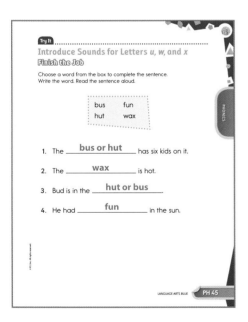

 **minutes**

REVIEW: **Sounds for Letters *u*, *w*, and *x***

Students will work online independently to

▶ Practice sounds for the letters *u*, *w*, and *x*.

▶ Practice decoding text by reading a story.

Help students locate the online activities and provide support as needed.

Offline Alternative

No computer access? Have students name the letters that make the sounds /ŭ/, /w/, and /ks/. Vice versa, have students name the sounds made by the letters *u*, *w*, and *x*. You might also ask students to spell simple words that contain the letters *u*, *w*, and *x* and other letters they have learned, or ask them to think of words that contain those letters.

Objectives

- Identify the letter, given the sound /ŭ/.
- Identify the sound, given the letter *u*.
- Identify and use the sound /ŭ/.
- Identify the letter, given the sound /w/.
- Identify the sound, given the letter *w*.
- Identify and use the sound /w/.
- Identify the letter, given the sound /ks/.
- Identify the sound, given the letter *x*.
- Identify and use the sound /ks/.
- Identify individual sounds in words.
- Read aloud grade-level text with appropriate automaticity, prosody, accuracy, and rate.
- Decode words by applying grade-level word analysis skills.

Practice Sounds for Letters *u*, *w*, and *x* (A)

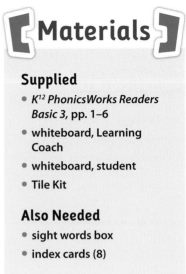

Lesson Overview

[Offline] FOCUS: Practice Sounds for Letters *u*, *w*, and *x*		**30** minutes

Sight Words	Sight Word Fun
Practice	Signal Beginning Short Vowel Sounds
	Review Sounds and Letters
	Word Fun
Try It	"Kim's Pup"

[Online] REVIEW: Sounds for Letters *u*, *w*, and *x*		**20** minutes

[Materials]

Supplied
- *K¹² PhonicsWorks Readers Basic 3*, pp. 1–6
- whiteboard, Learning Coach
- whiteboard, student
- Tile Kit

Also Needed
- sight words box
- index cards (8)

Advance Preparation

For Word Fun, print the following words on index cards, using one index card per word: *sun*, *cup*, *bug*, *gum*, *bun*, *bus*, *mug*, and *mud*.

 **30 minutes**

FOCUS: Practice Sounds for Letters *u*, *w*, and *x*

Work **together** with students to complete offline Sight Words, Practice, and Try It activities.

Sight Words

Sight Word Fun

Help students learn the sight words *where, from,* and *there,* and up to two additional sight words they have yet to master.

1. Gather the sight word cards *where, from,* and *there,* and up to two additional sight word cards.

2. Choose one sight word card to begin.

   Say: Look at this word and take a picture of it in your mind. When you think you can spell the word yourself, turn the card over and use your letter tiles to spell the word.

3. After students spell the word, have them check the card to see if they spelled the word correctly.

   Say: Read aloud the word you spelled with the letter tiles.

4. Repeat the activity with the remaining sight words.

TIP Sight words can be very difficult for some students. Let students work at their own pace and really master these words.

Objectives
- Read sight words.
- Spell sight words.

Practice

Signal Beginning Short Vowel Sounds

Use a special signal to help students identify **beginning short vowel sounds** in words.

1. **Say:** I'm going to tell you a special sound, and then I'll say some words. Repeat each word I say and make a special signal to tell me where the special sound is. If the special sound is at the beginning of the word, pinch your cheeks. If the special sound is **not** at the beginning of the word, just smile at me. For example,

   ▸ If I ask you to listen for the sound /ă/ and I say the word *apple*, you'll repeat the word *apple* and pinch your cheeks because *apple* has the short vowel sound /ă/ the at the beginning.

   ▸ If I say the word *bed*, you'll repeat the word *bed* and smile at me because *bed* has the sound /b/, not /ă/, at the beginning.

2. Say each sound and group of words. Have students make the special signal to identify the beginning sound.

   ▸ /ŭ/: *umbrella, elephant, itch, under* pinch cheeks: *umbrella, under*
   ▸ /ă/: *igloo, otter, alligator, anteater* pinch cheeks: *alligator, anteater*
   ▸ /ŏ/: *operator, apple, up, oddball* pinch cheeks: *operator, oddball*
   ▸ /ĭ/: *inch, igloo, elf, ugly, icky* pinch cheeks: *inch, igloo, icky*

TIP If students can't identify the beginning sound of each word, say the word again and emphasize the beginning sound by repeating it three times (for example, /t/ /t/ /t/ *taste*). You can also draw out the beginning sound when you say the word (for example, *mmommy*). If necessary, have students look at your mouth while you repeat the sounds.

Review Sounds and Letters

Help students review sounds for the letters *a, c, f, g, i, m, o, u,* and *x,* plus any letters that are confusing for them.

1. Place the following letter tiles in random order on students' whiteboard: *a, c, f, g, i, m, o, u,* and *x,* plus any letters that are confusing.

2. **Say:** Let's go over some letters and sounds.

3. Point to each letter tile and have students say a sound that letter makes.

   ▸ *u* /ŭ/
   ▸ *x* /ks/
   ▸ *i* /ĭ/
   ▸ *m* /m/
   ▸ *c* /k/

   ▸ *a* /ă/
   ▸ *o* /ŏ/
   ▸ *f* /f/
   ▸ *g* /g/
   ▸ *w* /w/

Objectives
- Identify beginning sounds in words.
- Identify short vowel sounds.
- Given the letter, identify the most common sound.
- Given the sound, identify the most common letter or letters.
- Identify the letter, given the sound /ŭ/.
- Identify the sound, given the letter *u*.
- Identify the letter, given the sound /w/.
- Identify the sound, given the letter *w*.
- Identify the letter, given the sound /ks/.
- Identify the sound, given the letter *x*.
- Identify individual sounds in words.
- Identify and use the sound /ŭ/.

4. Say each of the following sounds. Have students repeat the sound and touch the corresponding letter tile.

   - ► /ŭ/ *u*
   - ► /ks/ *x*
   - ► /ĭ/ *i*
   - ► /m/ *m*
   - ► /k/ *c*

   - ► /ă/ *a*
   - ► /ŏ/ *o*
   - ► /f/ *f*
   - ► /g/ *g*
   - ► /w/ *w*

5. As you do the activity, point to some letter tiles two or three times so that students don't think they are finished with a sound after they have named it.

6. Redirect students if they say an incorrect sound when you point to a letter tile.

   Say: That's the sound of another letter. What is the sound for this letter?

7. Help students if they touch the wrong letter tile after they repeat a sound.

   Say: That letter tile goes with the sound [sound for incorrect letter tile]. We're looking for the letter that goes with the sound [target sound].

Word Fun

Have students practice reading words.

1. Gather the index cards you prepared and place them face down in one pile.

2. **Say:** You are going to practice reading and writing some words.

   - ► You will choose a card from the pile and read the word on it.
   - ► Then you are going to flip the card over and write the word on the backside of the card.
   - ► I'll try first.

3. Choose a card from the pile and say and write the word.

   Say: Now it's your turn. Choose a card and read it to me.

TIP If students stumble over any words, have them touch and say the words. Touch and say these words along with them.

Try It •

"Kim's Pup"

Have students read "Kim's Pup" on page 1 of *K¹² PhonicsWorks Readers Basic 3*.

Students should read the story silently once or twice before reading the story aloud. When students miss a word that can be sounded out, point to it and give them three to six seconds to try the word again. If students still miss the word, tell them the word so the flow of the story isn't interrupted.

After reading the story, make a list of all the words students missed, and go over those words with them. You may use letter tiles to show students how to read the words.

Objectives

- Read aloud grade-level text with appropriate automaticity, prosody, accuracy, and rate.
- Decode words by applying grade-level word analysis skills.
- Track text from left to right.
- Turn pages sequentially.

 **20 minutes**

REVIEW: Sounds for Letters *u*, *w*, and *x*

Students will work online independently to

▸ Practice sounds for the letters *u*, *w*, and *x*.

Help students locate the online activities and provide support as needed.

Objectives

- Identify the letter, given the sound /ŭ/.
- Identify the sound, given the letter *u*.
- Identify and use the sound /ŭ/.
- Identify the letter, given the sound /w/.
- Identify the sound, given the letter *w*.
- Identify and use the sound /w/.
- Identify the letter, given the sound /ks/.
- Identify the sound, given the letter *x*.
- Identify and use the sound /ks/.
- Identify individual sounds in words.

Offline Alternative

No computer access? Have students name the letters that make the sounds /ŭ/, /w/, and /ks/. Vice versa, have students name the sounds made by the letters *u*, *w*, and *x*. You might also ask students to spell simple words that contain the letters *u*, *w*, and *x* and other letters they have learned, or ask them to think of words that contain those letters.

Practice Sounds for Letters *u*, *w*, and *x* (B)

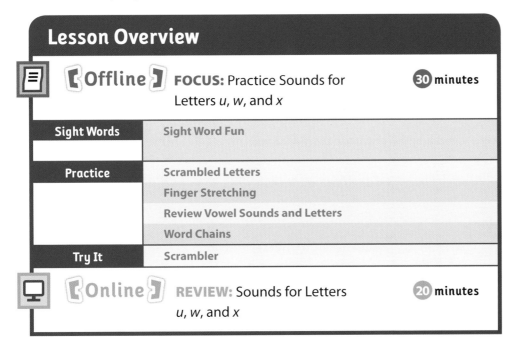

Lesson Overview

Offline FOCUS: Practice Sounds for Letters *u*, *w*, and *x* **30** minutes

Sight Words	Sight Word Fun
Practice	Scrambled Letters
	Finger Stretching
	Review Vowel Sounds and Letters
	Word Chains
Try It	Scrambler

Online REVIEW: Sounds for Letters *u*, *w*, and *x* **20** minutes

Materials

Supplied
- *K¹² PhonicsWorks Basic Activity Book*, p. PH 46
- whiteboard, student
- Tile Kit

Also Needed
- sight words box

 **30** minutes

FOCUS: Practice Sounds for Letters *u, w,* and *x*

Work **together** with students to complete offline Sight Words, Practice, and Try It activities.

Sight Words

Sight Word Fun

Help students learn the sight words *where, from,* and *there,* and up to two additional sight words they have yet to master.

1. Gather the sight word cards *where, from,* and *there,* and up to two additional sight word cards.

2. Choose one sight word card to begin.

   Say: Look at this word and take a picture of it in your mind. When you think you can spell the word yourself, turn the card over and use your letter tiles to spell the word.

3. After students spell the word, have them check the card to see if they spelled the word correctly.

   Say: Read aloud the word you spelled with the letter tiles.

4. Repeat the activity with the remaining sight words.

   TIP Sight words can be very difficult for some students. Let students work at their own pace and really master these words.

> **Objectives**
> • Read sight words.
> • Spell sight words.

Practice

Scrambled Letters

To help students master the alphabet, have them practice identifying and naming letters.

1. Place the following letter tiles in random order on students' whiteboard: *c, h, l, o, qu, s, u, w, x,* and *y.*

2. Have students arrange the letters in alphabetical order.

   TIP Students may find this activity easier if they slowly sing "The Alphabet Song" to themselves as they work.

Finger Stretching

Use finger stretching to help students identify individual sounds in words.

1. **Say:** Let's review finger stretching. In the word *wig,* the first sound is /w/, the next sound is /ĭ/, and the last sound is /g/. I will finger stretch each sound as I say it. Then I'll say the word while pulling my fist toward my body.

> **Objectives**
> • Identify letters of the alphabet.
> • Identify individual sounds in words.
> • Identify and use vowels and vowel sounds.
> • Identify short vowel sounds.
> • Given the letter, identify the most common sound.
> • Given the sound, identify the most common letter or letters.
> • Identify the new word when one sound is changed in a word.

2. Finger stretch the word *wig* for students.

3. **Say:** I'm going to say words with several sounds in them. You'll say each word and then finger stretch it while you say each sound in the word.

4. Say the following words and have students finger stretch them. After they finger stretch each word, ask them the question for that word.

   ▸ *gum* /g/ /ŭ/ /m/   What is the middle sound? /ŭ/
   ▸ *cut* /k/ /ŭ/ /t/   What is the first sound? /k/
   ▸ *wax* /w/ /ă/ /ks/   What is the last sound? /ks/
   ▸ *hot* /h/ /ŏ/ /t/   What is the middle sound? /ŏ/
   ▸ *well* /w/ /ĕ/ /l/   What is the first sound? /w/
   ▸ *cub* /k/ /ŭ/ /b/   What is the middle sound? /ŭ/
   ▸ *Sam* /s/ /ă/ /m/   What is the middle sound? /ă/

 Refer to the *K¹² PhonicsWorks* video for a demonstration of finger stretching.

Review Vowel Sounds and Letters

Help students review vowel sounds and letters.

1. Place the following letter tiles on students' whiteboard: *a, l, o,* and *u,* plus any letters that are confusing for them.

2. **Say:** I am going to point to each letter. Tell me a sound for that letter.

3. **Say:** I am going to say a sound. Repeat the sound and touch its letter.

4. Point to some letters two or three times, so students don't think that once they have named a sound they are finished with it.

5. Redirect students if they name the letter and not its sound.

   Say: You are right that the name of the letter is [letter]. We want the sound for this letter. What is the sound?

6. Redirect students if they name the sound incorrectly.

   Say: That is the sound of another letter.

7. Provide additional guidance if students touch the wrong letter tile during the review.

   Say: That is the letter tile for the sound [sound of incorrect letter tile]. We are looking for the letter tile for the sound [target sound].

8. If students touch the wrong letter again, point to the correct letter.

   Say: This is the letter tile for the sound [target sound]. Touch this letter tile and say its sound.

Word Chains

Have students build words by adding and changing letters to help them recognize and use individual sounds in words.

1. Place the following letters on students' whiteboard: *a, b, c, f, g, n, o, r, s,* and *u.*

2. **Say:** I am going to build the first word in a chain. The word is *gab.*

   ▸ I will pull down the letters for the sounds /g/, /ă/, and /b/ to spell the word *gab.*

   ▸ Next I will touch and say *gab.* To change *gab* to *cab,* I will think about what sound is changed from the word *gab* to *cab.* I will need to replace the letter *g* with the letter *c.*

   ▸ Touch and say the word *cab.* Now it's your turn to change *cab* to *cub.* You can spell *cub* by making only one change. Touch and say the new word.

3. Redirect students if they select the incorrect letter for any sound.

   Say: That letter is for the sound [incorrect sound]. We want the letter for the sound [target sound]. What letter makes that sound? Answers will vary.

4. Redirect students if they name the sound incorrectly.

   Say: To change the word [first word] to [target word], we need the letter for the sound [target sound].

   Show students how to make the change. Have them touch and say the new word after they move the letters.

5. Follow this procedure to make the following words: *cob, con, can, fan, ran, rag, rug.*

6. For every new word, have students replace only one letter.

   TIP If students struggle, review the sounds and letters that are confusing them.

Try It •

Scrambler

Have students complete page PH 46 in *K¹² PhonicsWorks Basic Activity Book* for more practice with the sounds /ŭ/, /w/, and /ks/. Have students unscramble the letters to create a word. Have them write the word and read the word aloud.

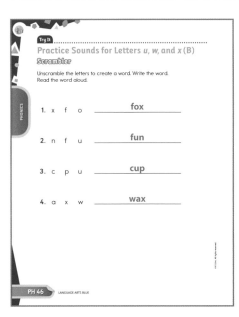

Objectives

- Read aloud grade-level text with appropriate automaticity, prosody, accuracy, and rate.
- Write words by applying grade-level phonics knowledge.
- Identify and use the sound /ŭ/.
- Identify and use the sound /w/.
- Identify and use the sound /ks/.

 **minutes**

REVIEW: **Sounds for Letters *u*, *w*, and *x***

Students will work online independently to

- ▸ Practice sounds for the letters *u*, *w*, and *x*.
- ▸ Practice decoding text by reading a story.

Help students locate the online activities and provide support as needed.

Offline Alternative

No computer access? Have students name the letters that make the sounds /ŭ/, /w/, and /ks/. Vice versa, have students name the sounds made by the letters *u*, *w*, and *x*. You might also ask students to spell simple words that contain the letters *u*, *w*, and *x* and other letters they have learned, or ask them to think of words that contain those letters.

Objectives

- Identify the letter, given the sound /ŭ/.
- Identify the sound, given the letter *u*.
- Identify and use the sound /ŭ/.
- Identify the letter, given the sound /w/.
- Identify the sound, given the letter *w*.
- Identify and use the sound /w/.
- Identify the letter, given the sound /ks/.
- Identify the sound, given the letter *x*.
- Identify and use the sound /ks/.
- Identify individual sounds in words.
- Read aloud grade-level text with appropriate automaticity, prosody, accuracy, and rate.
- Decode words by applying grade-level word analysis skills.

Practice Sounds for Letters *u*, *w*, and *x* (C)

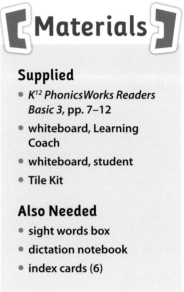

Lesson Overview

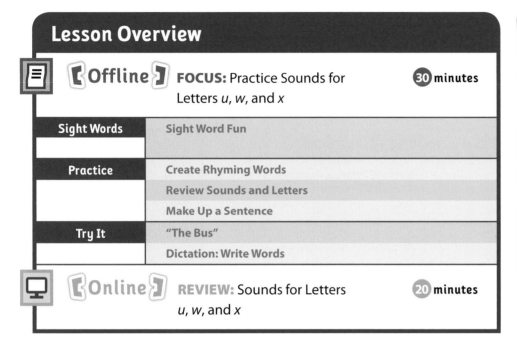

Offline **FOCUS:** Practice Sounds for Letters *u*, *w*, and *x*   **30** minutes

Sight Words	Sight Word Fun
Practice	**Create Rhyming Words**
	Review Sounds and Letters
	Make Up a Sentence
Try It	"The Bus"
	Dictation: Write Words

Online **REVIEW:** Sounds for Letters *u*, *w*, and *x*   **20** minutes

Materials

Supplied
- *K¹² PhonicsWorks Readers Basic 3*, pp. 7–12
- whiteboard, Learning Coach
- whiteboard, student
- Tile Kit

Also Needed
- sight words box
- dictation notebook
- index cards (6)

Advance Preparation

For Make Up a Sentence, print the following words on index cards, using one index card per word: *gum, hot, bus, tub, ax,* and *wig*.

 **30 minutes**

FOCUS: Practice Sounds for Letters *u*, *w*, and *x*

Work **together** with students to complete offline Sight Words, Practice, and Try It activities.

Sight Words

Sight Word Fun

Help students learn the sight words *where, from,* and *there,* and up to two additional sight words they have yet to master.

1. Gather the sight word cards *where, from,* and *there,* and up to two additional sight word cards.

2. Choose one sight word card to begin.

   Say: Look at this word and take a picture of it in your mind. When you think you can spell the word yourself, turn the card over and use your letter tiles to spell the word.

3. After students spell the word, have them check the card to see if they spelled the word correctly.

   Say: Read aloud the word you spelled with the letter tiles.

4. Repeat the activity with the remaining sight words.

   TIP Sight words can be very difficult for some students. Let students work at their own pace and really master these words.

Objectives
- Read sight words.
- Spell sight words.

Practice

Create Rhyming Words

Have students combine word parts and make words that rhyme.

1. **Say:** I'm going to break a word into two parts. Your job is to put the parts back together and say the word.

   ▸ For example, if the first part of the word is /m/ and the last part is /ăks/, then you'll say *Max*: /m/ . . . /ăks/ . . . *Max*.
   ▸ Next you'll add a new **beginning sound** to make a word that rhymes. For example, you'll use the same last part, /ăks/, and add a new first sound, like /f/. The rhyming word is /f/. . . /ăks/ . . . *fax*.

2. **Say:** Now it's your turn: /w/ . . . /ăks/.

   ▸ What's the word? *wax*
   ▸ Now use the same last part, /ăks/, but add a new sound, /l/, at the beginning. What word did you make? *lax*

3. Have students add a new beginning sound to the last part of each word below to make a rhyming word. Continue this procedure until students have made all the rhyming words.

   ▸ /l/ . . . /ăks/ *lax;* Possible rhyming words: *tax*
   ▸ /r/ . . . /ŭn/ *run;* Possible rhyming words: *sun, fun*

<table>
<tr><td>

Objectives
- Identify words that rhyme.
- Identify individual sounds in words.
- Identify the letter, given the sound /ŭ/.
- Identify the sound, given the letter *u*.
- Identify the letter, given the sound /w/.
- Identify the sound, given the letter *w*.
- Identify the letter, given the sound /ks/.
- Identify the sound, given the letter *x*.
- Given the letter, identify the most common sound.
- Given the sound, identify the most common letter or letters.

</td></tr>
</table>

Review Sounds and Letters

Help students review sounds for the letters *a, b, d, l, o, qu, t, u, w,* and *z,* plus any letters that are confusing for them.

1. Place the following letter tiles in random order on students' whiteboard: *a, b, d, l, o, qu, t, u, w,* and *z,* plus any letters that are confusing.

2. **Say:** Let's go over some letters and sounds.

3. Point to each letter tile and have students say a sound that letter or letters make.

   ▸ *b* /b/   ▸ *t* /t/
   ▸ *d* /d/   ▸ *u* /ŭ/
   ▸ *l* /l/   ▸ *z* /z/
   ▸ *o* /ŏ/   ▸ *qu* /kw/
   ▸ *w* /w/   ▸ *a* /ă/

4. Say each of the following sounds. Have students repeat the sound and touch the corresponding letter tile.

   ▸ /b/ *b*   ▸ /t/ *t*
   ▸ /d/ *d*   ▸ /ŭ/ *u*
   ▸ /l/ *l*   ▸ /z/ *z*
   ▸ /ŏ/ *o*   ▸ /kw/ *qu*
   ▸ /w/ *w*   ▸ /ă/ *a*

5. As you do the activity, point to some letter tiles two or three times so that students don't think they are finished with a sound after they have named it.

6. Redirect students if they say an incorrect sound when you point to a letter tile.

   Say: That's the sound of another letter. What is the sound for this letter?

7. Help students if they touch the wrong letter tile after they repeat a sound.

   Say: That letter goes with the sound [sound for incorrect letter tile]. We're looking for the letter that goes with the sound [target sound].

Make Up a Sentence
Help students use words to make sentences.

1. Gather the index cards you prepared and place them face down in one pile.

2. Have students
   - ▸ Select a card.
   - ▸ Read the word.
   - ▸ Use the word in an interesting, fun, or silly sentence.

(TIP) If students read a word incorrectly, have them finger stretch the sounds in the word.

Try It

"The Bus"
Have students read "The Bus" on page 7 of *K¹² PhonicsWorks Readers Basic 3*.

Students should read the story silently once or twice before reading the story aloud. When students miss a word that can be sounded out, point to it and give them three to six seconds to try the word again. If students still miss the word, tell them the word so the flow of the story isn't interrupted.

After reading the story, make a list of all the words students missed, and go over those words with them. You may use tiles to show students how to read the words.

Dictation: Write Words
Have students practice identifying sounds and writing words.

1. Gather a pencil and the dictation notebook. Say the word *cup*. Then give these directions to students:
   - ▸ Repeat the word.
   - ▸ Write the word in your notebook.
   - ▸ Read the word aloud.

Objectives
- Read aloud grade-level text with appropriate automaticity, prosody, accuracy, and rate.
- Decode words by applying grade-level word analysis skills.
- Track text from left to right.
- Turn pages sequentially.
- Write words by applying grade-level phonics knowledge.
- Write sight words.
- Follow three-step directions.
- Identify and use the sound /ŭ/.
- Identify and use the sound /w/.
- Identify and use the sound /ks/.

2. When students have finished, write the following word on your whiteboard: *cup*.

3. Have them compare their answer to your correct version.

4. Repeat this procedure with the words *wax* and *tub*.

   ► If students make an error and don't see it, help them correct their mistake by having them finger stretch the sounds in the word they missed.
   ► If students are having difficulty selecting the correct letters or sounds, review those letters or sounds that are confusing them.
   ► If students have difficulty with first, middle, and last sounds, have them finger stretch the sounds in words.

 **minutes**

REVIEW: Sounds for Letters *u*, *w*, and *x*

Students will work online independently to

► Practice the sounds for the letters *u*, *w*, and *x*.

Help students locate the online activities and provide support as needed.

Offline Alternative

No computer access? Have students name the letters that make the sounds /ŭ/, /w/, and /ks/. Vice versa, have students name the sounds made by the letters *u*, *w*, and *x*. You might also ask students to spell simple words that contain the letters *u*, *w*, and *x* and other letters they have learned, or ask them to think of words that contain those letters.

Objectives
- Identify the letter, given the sound /ŭ/.
- Identify the sound, given the letter *u*.
- Identify and use the sound /ŭ/.
- Identify the letter, given the sound /w/.
- Identify the sound, given the letter *w*.
- Identify and use the sound /w/.
- Identify the letter, given the sound /ks/.
- Identify the sound, given the letter *x*.
- Identify and use the sound /ks/.
- Identify individual sounds in words.

Unit Checkpoint

Lesson Overview

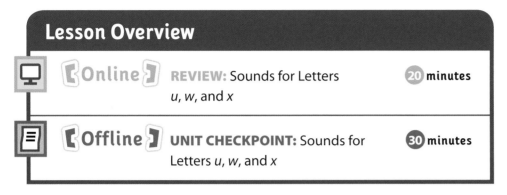

🖥	**[Online]**	**REVIEW:** Sounds for Letters *u, w,* and *x*	**20** minutes
📄	**[Offline]**	**UNIT CHECKPOINT:** Sounds for Letters *u, w,* and *x*	**30** minutes

[Materials]

Supplied
- *K¹² PhonicsWorks Basic Assessments,* pp. PH 79–84

⭐ Objectives
- Identify the letters, given the sound /ŭ/.
- Identify the sound, given the letter *u*.
- Identify the letters, given the sound /w/.
- Identify the sound, given the letter *w*.
- Identify the letters, given the sound /ks/.
- Identify the sound, given the letter *x*.
- Identify letters of the alphabet.
- Identify individual sounds in words.
- Given the letter, identify the most common sound.
- Given the sound, identify the most common letter or letters.
- Read sight words.
- Read instructional-level text with 90% accuracy.
- Read aloud grade-level text with appropriate automaticity, prosody, accuracy, and rate.
- Write words by applying grade-level phonics knowledge.

 **[Online]** **20** minutes

REVIEW: Sounds for Letters *u, w,* and *x*

Students will review sounds for the letters *u, w,* and *x* to prepare for the Unit Checkpoint. Help students locate the online activities and provide support as needed.

【Offline】 30 minutes

UNIT CHECKPOINT: Sounds for Letters *u*, *w*, and *x*

Explain that students are going to show what they have learned about letters, sounds, and words.

1. Give students the Unit Checkpoint pages for the Sounds for Letters *u*, *w*, and *x* unit and print the Unit Checkpoint Answer Key, if you'd like.

2. Use the instructions below to help administer the Checkpoint to students. On the Answer Key or another sheet of paper, note student answers to oral response questions to help with scoring the Checkpoint later.

3. Use the Answer Key to score the Checkpoint, and then enter the results online.

Part 1. Say Sounds Have students read across the rows from left to right and say a sound that each letter or letters make. Note any sounds they say incorrectly.

Part 2. Word Dissection For each word, say the sound students should identify. Have them read the word aloud and circle the letter or group of letters that spells the requested sound.

19. *middle sound*

20. *ending sound*

21. *beginning sound*

22. *ending sound*

23. *middle sound*

Part 3. Finger Stretching Say each word to students. Have them say each word and finger stretch the sounds. Note any words they finger stretch incorrectly.

24. *bus*   26. *six*

25. *cup*   27. *wax*

Part 4. Dictation Say each word to students. Have them repeat and write the word.

28. *fit*   30. *sun*

29. *us*   31. *box*

Part 5. Read Aloud Listen to students read the sentences aloud. Count and note the number of words they read correctly.

Part 6. Say Letters Say each sound. Have students say the letter or letters that make that sound. Note any incorrect responses.

33. /ŭ/

34. /ă/

35. /ŏ

36. /w/

37. /ks/

38. /r/

39. /ĭ/

40. /kw/

41. /z/

42. /ă/

43. /ŭ/

44. /z/

45. /ĭ/

46. /ks/

47. /ŏ/

48. /ŭ/

49. /kw/

50. /w/

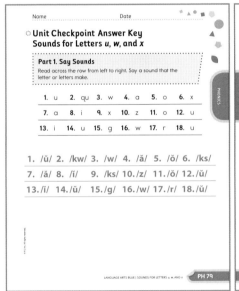

Name _____ Date _____

Unit Checkpoint Answer Key
Sounds for Letters u, w, and x

Part 1. Say Sounds
Read across the row from left to right. Say a sound that the letter or letters make.

1. u	2. qu	3. w	4. a	5. o	6. x
7. a	8. i	9. x	10. z	11. o	12. u
13. i	14. u	15. g	16. w	17. r	18. u

1. /ŭ/ 2. /kw/ 3. /w/ 4. /ă/ 5. /ŏ/ 6. /ks/
7. /ă/ 8. /ĭ/ 9. /ks/ 10./z/ 11./ŏ/ 12./ŭ/
13./ĭ/ 14./ŭ/ 15./g/ 16./w/ 17./r/ 18./ŭ/

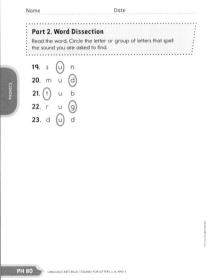

Name _____ Date _____

Part 2. Word Dissection
Read the word. Circle the letter or group of letters that spell the sound you are asked to find.

19. s (u) n
20. m u (d)
21. (t) u b
22. r u (g)
23. d (u) d

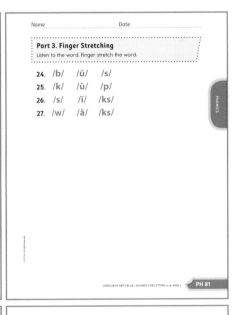

Name _____ Date _____

Part 3. Finger Stretching
Listen to the word. Finger stretch the word.

24. /b/ /ŭ/ /s/
25. /k/ /ŭ/ /p/
26. /s/ /ĭ/ /ks/
27. /w/ /ă/ /ks/

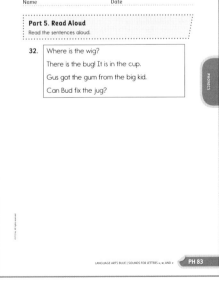

Name _____ Date _____

Part 4. Dictation
Listen to the word. Repeat the word, and then write it.

28. fit _____
29. us _____
30. sun _____
31. box _____

Name _____ Date _____

Part 5. Read Aloud
Read the sentences aloud.

32. Where is the wig?
There is the bug! It is in the cup.
Gus got the gum from the big kid.
Can Bud fix the jug?

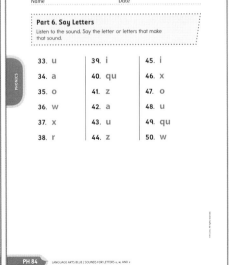

Name _____ Date _____

Part 6. Say Letters
Listen to the sound. Say the letter or letters that make that sound.

33. u	39. i	45. i
34. a	40. qu	46. x
35. o	41. z	47. o
36. w	42. a	48. u
37. x	43. u	49. qu
38. r	44. z	50. w

Getting Stronger: Sounds /ă/, /ĭ/, /ŏ/, and /ŭ/ (A)

Unit Overview

In this unit, students will
- ▶ Review sight words.
- ▶ Identify letters and sounds in the alphabet.
- ▶ Practice the sounds /ă/, /ĭ/, /ŏ/, and /ŭ/.
- ▶ Identify individual sounds in words.
- ▶ Build words.

[Materials]

Supplied
- *K¹² PhonicsWorks Basic Activity Book*, p. PH 47
- whiteboard, student
- Tile Kit

Also Needed
- sight words box

Lesson Overview

[Offline] FOCUS: Getting Stronger: Sounds /ă/, /ĭ/, /ŏ/, and /ŭ/		30 minutes
Sight Words	Review Sight Words	
Practice	Scrambled Letters	
	Signal Beginning Short Vowel Sounds	
	Review Vowel Sounds and Letters	
	Word Chains	
Try It	The Amazing Alphabet	
[Online] REVIEW: Sounds /ă/, /ĭ/, /ŏ/, and /ŭ/		20 minutes

 **30 minutes**

FOCUS: Getting Stronger: Sounds /ă/, /ĭ/, /ŏ/, and /ŭ/

Work **together** with students to complete offline Sight Words, Practice, and Try It activities.

Sight Words

Review Sight Words

Help students learn to recognize sight words.

1. Gather all the sight word cards students have yet to master from their sight words box. Stack the cards on the table face down.

2. Have students pick up a word and read it to you.

3. If they read it quickly and correctly, put the card in one stack. If they hesitate or do not read the word correctly, put it in another stack. The second stack should have words that they will review again.

4. Take the stack of words that students read correctly and dictate each word to them. They may choose to either write the word or spell it aloud.

5. If students spell the word correctly, put the card in the first stack because they have mastered the word. If they misspell the word, add it to the stack of cards to review again.

6. Chart students' progress on the back of each card.

   ▶ Divide the back of the card into two columns.
   ▶ Label the first column "Read" and the second column "Spell."
   ▶ Record the dates that students read or spell the word correctly. When students can read and spell the word correctly three times in a row, they have mastered the word. You may want to put a star or sticker on their card when they have mastered that word.

TIP Even if students can read and spell all the words correctly, it is still beneficial for them to review sight words. Choose as many additional words as you would like for each subsequent activity.

Objectives
- Read sight words.
- Spell sight words.
- Write sight words.

Practice ••

Scrambled Letters

To help students master the alphabet, have them practice identifying and
naming letters.

1. Place the following letter tiles in random order on students' whiteboard: *a, d, e,
   k, n, r, s,* and *v.*

2. Have students arrange the letters in alphabetical order.

TIP Students may find this activity easier if they slowly sing "The Alphabet Song"
to themselves as they work.

Signal Beginning Short Vowel Sounds

Use a special signal to help students identify **beginning short vowel sounds** in words.

1. **Say:** I'm going to tell you a special sound, and then I'll say some words. Repeat
   each word I say and make a special signal to tell me where the special sound
   is. If the special sound is at the beginning of the word, pat your cheek. If the
   special sound is **not** at the beginning of the word, just smile at me.
   For example,

   ▸ If I ask you to listen for the sound /ŏ/ and I say the word *on,* you'll repeat the
     word *on* and pat your cheek because *on* has the sound /ŏ/ at the beginning.

   ▸ If I say the word *apple,* you'll repeat the word *apple* and smile at me
     because *apple* has the sound /ă/, not /ŏ/, at the beginning.

2. Say each sound and group of words. Have students make the special signal to
   identify the beginning sound.

   ▸ /ŏ/: *Oliver, angle, under, opposite, on* pat cheek: *Oliver, opposite, on*
   ▸ /ŭ/: *echo, up, iron, under, ankle* pat cheek: *up, under*
   ▸ /ĭ/: *itchy, is, am, off, if, ox* pat cheek: *itchy, is, if*
   ▸ /ă/: *elf, ask, ant, ox, am, Dave* pat cheek: *ask, ant, am*

TIP If students can't identify the beginning sound of each word, say the word again
and emphasize the beginning sound by repeating it three times (for example, /t/
/t/ /t/, *taste*). You can also draw out the beginning sound when you say the word
(for example, *mmmommy*). If necessary, have students look at your mouth while you
repeat the sounds.

Review Vowel Sounds and Letters

Help students review vowel sounds and letters.

1. Place the following letter tiles on students' whiteboard: *a, i, o,* and *u,* plus any
   letters that are confusing for them.

2. **Say:** I am going to point to a letter. Tell me a sound for that letter.

3. **Say:** I am going to say a sound. Repeat the sound and touch its letter.

Objectives

- Identify letters of the alphabet.
- Identify beginning sounds in words.
- Identify and use vowels and vowel sounds.
- Identify short vowel sounds.
- Identify and use the sound /ă/.
- Identify and use the sound /ĭ/.
- Identify and use the sound /ŏ/.
- Identify and use the sound /ŭ/.
- Identify the new word when one sound is changed in a word.

4. Point to some letters two or three times, so students don't think that once they have named a sound they are finished with it.

5. Redirect students if they name the letter and not its sound.

    Say: You are right that the name of the letter is [letter]. We want the sound for this letter. What is the sound?

6. Redirect students if they name the sound incorrectly.

    Say: That is the sound of another letter.

7. Provide additional guidance if students touch the wrong letter tile during the review.

    Say: That is the letter tile for the sound [sound of incorrect letter tile]. We are looking for the letter tile for the sound [target sound].

8. If students touch the wrong letter again, point to the correct letter.

    Say: This is the letter tile for the sound [target sound]. Touch this letter tile and say its sound.

Word Chains

Have students build words by adding and changing letters to help them recognize and use individual sounds in words.

1. Place the following letter tiles at the top of students' whiteboard: *a, b, g, i, l, n, o, p, t,* and *u.*

2. **Say:** I am going to build the first word in a chain. The word is *nip.*

    ▸ I will pull down the letters for the sounds /n/, /ĭ/, and /p/ to spell the word *nip.*
    ▸ I will touch and say *nip.* To change *nip* to *lip,* I will think about what sound is changed from the word *nip* to *lip.* I will need to replace the letter *n* with the letter *l.*
    ▸ Touch and say the word *lip.* Now it's your turn to change *lip* to *lap.* You can spell *lap* by making only one change. Touch and say the new word.

3. Redirect students if they select the incorrect letter for any sound.

    Say: That letter is for the sound [incorrect sound]. We want the letter for the sound [target sound]. What letter makes that sound? Answers will vary.

4. Redirect students if they name the sound incorrectly.

    Say: To change the word [first word] to [target word], we need the letter for the sound [target sound].

    Show students how to make the change. Have them touch and say the new word after they move the letters.

5. Follow this procedure to make the following words: *lop, lot, lit, bit, big, bug.*

6. For every new word, have students add, replace, or remove only one letter.

    TIP If students struggle, review the sounds and letters that are confusing them.

Try It ●●

The Amazing Alphabet

Have students complete page PH 47 in *K¹² PhonicsWorks Basic Activity Book* for more practice with the sounds /ă/, /ĭ/, /ŏ/, and /ŭ/. Have students circle the letter that makes the vowel sound in the name of the picture and write the letter. Have them read the word aloud.

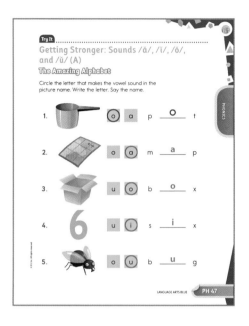

Objectives

- Read aloud grade-level text with appropriate automaticity, prosody, accuracy, and rate.
- Write words by applying grade-level phonics knowledge.
- Identify and use the sound /ă/.
- Identify and use the sound /ĭ/.
- Identify and use the sound /ŏ/.
- Identify and use the sound /ŭ/.
- Identify short vowel sounds.

⟦Online⟧ 🕒 20 minutes

REVIEW: Sounds /ă/, /ĭ/, /ŏ/, and /ŭ/

Students will work online independently to

- ▸ Practice the sounds /ă/, /ĭ/, /ŏ/, and /ŭ/ for the letters *a, i, o,* and *u.*
- ▸ Practice decoding text by reading sentences.

Help students locate the online activities and provide support as needed.

Objectives

- Identify and use the sound /ă/.
- Identify and use the sound /ĭ/.
- Identify and use the sound /ŏ/.
- Identify and use the sound /ŭ/.
- Identify short vowel sounds.
- Read aloud grade-level text with appropriate automaticity, prosody, accuracy, and rate.
- Decode words by applying grade-level word analysis skills.

Offline Alternative

No computer access? Have students name the letters that make the sounds /ă/, /ĭ/, /ŏ/, and /ŭ/. Vice versa, have students name the sounds made by the letters *a, i, o,* and *u.* You might also ask students to spell simple words that contain the letters *a, i, o,* and *u* and other letters they have learned.

Getting Stronger: Sounds /ă/, /ĭ/, /ŏ/, and /ŭ/ (B)

Lesson Overview

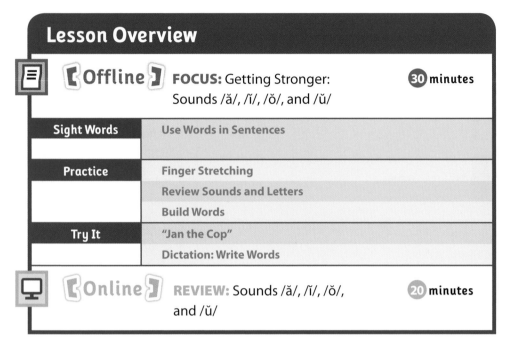

[Offline] **FOCUS:** Getting Stronger: Sounds /ă/, /ĭ/, /ŏ/, and /ŭ/   **30** minutes

Sight Words	Use Words in Sentences
Practice	Finger Stretching
	Review Sounds and Letters
	Build Words
Try It	"Jan the Cop"
	Dictation: Write Words

[Online] **REVIEW:** Sounds /ă/, /ĭ/, /ŏ/, and /ŭ/   **20** minutes

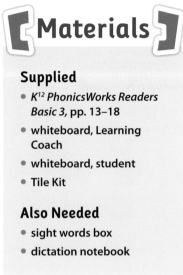

[Materials]

Supplied
- *K¹² PhonicsWorks Readers Basic 3*, pp. 13–18
- whiteboard, Learning Coach
- whiteboard, student
- Tile Kit

Also Needed
- sight words box
- dictation notebook

 **30 minutes**

FOCUS: Getting Stronger: Sounds /ă/, /ĭ/, /ŏ/, and /ŭ/

Work **together** with students to complete offline Sight Words, Practice, and Try It activities.

Sight Words

Use Words in Sentences

Help students use sight words in sentences.

1. Gather all the sight word cards students have yet to master from their sight words box. Spread the sight word cards on the table.

2. **Say:** Let's use sight words in sentences.

3. Have students

   ▶ Touch each card and read the word on it.
   ▶ Make up a sentence using the word.
   ▶ Put the card in a pile after using the word in a sentence.
   ▶ Go through the pile of cards and read each sight word again.
   ▶ Spell each word.

TIP If students have difficulty with any of the sight words, place those cards in a pile to review again.

> **Objectives**
> • Read sight words.
> • Spell sight words.

Practice

Finger Stretching

Use finger stretching to help students identify individual sounds in words.

1. **Say:** Let's review finger stretching. In the word *zip*, the first sound is /z/, the next sound is /ĭ/, and the last sound is /p/. I will finger stretch each sound as I say it. Then I'll say the word while pulling my fist toward my body.

2. Finger stretch the word *zip* for students.

3. **Say:** I'm going to say words with several sounds in them. You'll say each word and then finger stretch it while you say each sound in the word.

4. Say the following words and have students finger stretch them. After they finger stretch each word, ask them the question for that word.

   ▶ *zap* /z/ /ă/ /p/   What is the middle sound? /ă/
   ▶ *its* /ĭ/ /t/ /s/   What is the first sound? /ĭ/
   ▶ *cub* /k/ /ŭ/ /b/   What is the middle sound? /ŭ/
   ▶ *ant* /ă/ /n/ /t/   What is the first sound? /ă/
   ▶ *rod* /r/ /ŏ/ /d/   What is the last sound? /d/
   ▶ *rub* /r/ /ŭ/ /b/   What is the middle sound? /ŭ/

TIP Refer to the *K¹² PhonicsWorks* video for a demonstration of finger stretching.

> **Objectives**
> • Identify individual sounds in words.
> • Identify short vowel sounds.
> • Identify and use the sound /ă/.
> • Identify and use the sound /ĭ/.
> • Identify and use the sound /ŏ/.
> • Identify and use the sound /ŭ/.
> • Given the letter, identify the most common sound.
> • Given the sound, identify the most common letter or letters.
> • Blend sounds to create words.

Review Sounds and Letters

Help students review sounds for the letters *a, b, c, h, i, n, o, u,* and *w,* plus any letters that are confusing for them.

1. Place the following letter tiles in random order on students' whiteboard: *a, b, c, h, i, n, o, u,* and *w,* plus any letters that are confusing.

2. **Say:** Let's go over some letters and sounds.

3. Point to each letter tile and have students say a sound that letter makes.

   ▸ *n* /n/   ▸ *c* /k/
   ▸ *u* /ŭ/   ▸ *o* /ŏ/
   ▸ *w* /w/   ▸ *a* /ă/
   ▸ *i* /ĭ/   ▸ *h* /h/
   ▸ *b* /b/

4. Say each of the following sounds. Have students repeat the sound and touch the corresponding letter tile.

   ▸ /n/ *n*   ▸ /k/ *c*
   ▸ /ŭ/ *u*   ▸ /ŏ/ *o*
   ▸ /w/ *w*   ▸ /ă/ *a*
   ▸ /ĭ/ *i*   ▸ /h/ *h*
   ▸ /b/ *b*

5. As you do the activity, point to some letter tiles two or three times so that students don't think they are finished with a sound after they have named it.

6. Redirect students if they say an incorrect sound when you point to a letter tile.

   Say: That's the sound of another letter. What is the sound for this letter?

7. Help students if they touch the wrong letter tile after they repeat a sound.

   Say: That letter tile goes with the sound [sound for incorrect letter tile]. We're looking for the letter that goes with the sound [target sound].

Build Words

Help students use letters and sounds to build words.

1. Place the following letter tiles at the top of students' whiteboard: *a, d, d, h, i, n, p, r,* and *u.*

2. Draw three horizontal lines across the middle of students' whiteboard to represent the sounds in a word.

3. **Say:** Let's use letters and sounds to build the word *hip.*

4. Have students finger stretch the sounds in *hip.*

5. Have students

   ▸ Identify the first, next, and last sounds in *hip.*
   ▸ Choose the corresponding letter for each sound.
   ▸ Move the letters to the correct lines on their whiteboard.

6. Guide students with these questions:

   ▸ What is the first sound in *hip*? /h/
     Which line does the letter for that sound go on? the first one
   ▸ What is the next sound in *hip*? /ĭ/
     Which line does the letter for that sound go on? the second one
   ▸ What's the last sound in *hip*? /p/
     Which line does the letter for that sound go on? the last one

7. Have students touch and say the word.

8. Redirect students if they select the incorrect letter.

   Say: That sound is in the word [word], and it is the [first, second, third] sound. We want the sound [target sound].

   Continue until students select the correct letter.

9. Repeat the activity to build the following words:

   ▸ *dad* /d/ /ă/ /d/
   ▸ *run* /r/ /ŭ/ /n/

Try It

"Jan the Cop"
Have students read "Jan the Cop" on page 13 of *K¹² PhonicsWorks Readers Basic 3*.

Students should read the story silently once or twice before reading the story aloud. When students miss a word that can be sounded out, point to it and give them three to six seconds to try the word again. If students still miss the word, tell them the word so the flow of the story isn't interrupted.

After reading the story, make a list of all the words students missed, and go over those words with the student. You may use tiles to show students how to read the words.

_____

Dictation: Write Words
Have students practice identifying sounds and writing words.

1. Gather a pencil and the dictation notebook. Say the word *rug*. Then give these directions to students:

   ▸ Repeat the word.
   ▸ Write the word in your notebook.
   ▸ Read the word aloud.

2. When students have finished, write the following word on your whiteboard: *rug*.

3. Have them compare their answer to your correct version.

Objectives

- Read aloud grade-level text with appropriate automaticity, prosody, accuracy, and rate.
- Decode words by applying grade-level word analysis skills.
- Track text from left to right.
- Turn pages sequentially.
- Identify and use the sound /ĭ/.
- Identify and use the sound /ŏ/.
- Identify and use the sound /ŭ/.
- Write words by applying grade-level phonics knowledge.
- Follow three-step directions.

4. Repeat this procedure with the words *hot* and *Tim*.

   ▸ If students make an error and don't see it, help them correct their mistake by having them finger stretch the sounds in the word they missed.

   ▸ If students are having difficulty selecting the correct letters or sounds, review those letters or sounds that are confusing them.

   ▸ If students have difficulty with first, middle, and last sounds, have them finger stretch the sounds in words.

 **minutes**

REVIEW: **Sounds /ă/, /ĭ/, /ŏ/, and /ŭ/**

Students will work online independently to

▸ Practice the sounds /ă/, /ĭ/, /ŏ/, and /ŭ/ for the letters *a, i, o,* and *u*.

Help students locate the online activities and provide support as needed.

_____

Offline Alternative

No computer access? Have students name the letters that make the sounds /ă/, /ĭ/, /ŏ/, and /ŭ/. Vice versa, have students name the sounds made by the letters *a, i, o,* and *u*. You might also ask students to spell simple words that contain the letters *a, i, o,* and *u* and other letters students have learned.

Objectives
- Identify and use the sound /ă/.
- Identify and use the sound /ĭ/.
- Identify and use the sound /ŏ/.
- Identify and use the sound /ŭ/.
- Identify short vowel sounds.

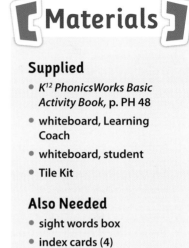

Getting Stronger: Sounds /ă/, /ĭ/, /ŏ/, and /ŭ/ (C)

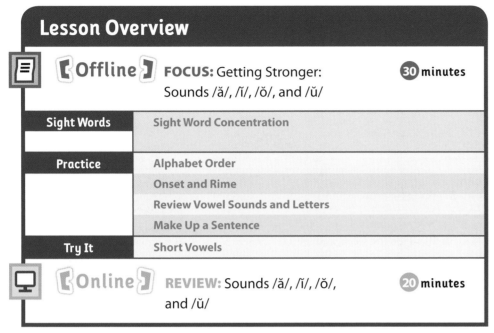

Lesson Overview

Offline FOCUS: Getting Stronger: Sounds /ă/, /ĭ/, /ŏ/, and /ŭ/		**30** minutes
Sight Words	Sight Word Concentration	
Practice	Alphabet Order	
	Onset and Rime	
	Review Vowel Sounds and Letters	
	Make Up a Sentence	
Try It	Short Vowels	
Online REVIEW: Sounds /ă/, /ĭ/, /ŏ/, and /ŭ/		**20** minutes

Materials

Supplied
- *K¹² PhonicsWorks Basic Activity Book,* p. PH 48
- whiteboard, Learning Coach
- whiteboard, student
- Tile Kit

Also Needed
- sight words box
- index cards (4)

Advance Preparation

Place lowercase letter tiles in alphabetical order on your whiteboard. Gather two sets of all the sight word cards you have used to date.

For Make Up a Sentence, print the following words on index cards, using one index card per word: *van, hum, quiz,* and *spot.*

 **Offline** **30** minutes

FOCUS: Getting Stronger: Sounds /ă/, /ĭ/, /ŏ/, and /ŭ/

Work **together** with students to complete offline Sight Words, Practice, and Try It activities.

Sight Words

Sight Word Concentration

Help students review sight words.

1. Gather the two sets of sight word cards.

2. Scramble both sets of sight word cards and place them face down on the table or floor.

3. Turn over two cards at a time; take turns with students. If the cards match, the person turning over the matching cards reads the word and uses it in a sentence. If the cards don't match, the person turns them back over.

4. Remove and save the matching cards.

5. Continue the activity until all the cards are paired.

6. Have students read all the words.

7. Take the stack of words that students read correctly and dictate each word to them.

8. Have students write each word or spell it aloud.

TIP If students have difficulty with any of the sight words, let them work at their own pace to really master these words.

 Objectives
- Read sight words.
- Spell sight words.
- Write sight words.

Practice •

Alphabet Order

Review alphabetic order with students. Place the lowercase letter tiles *a* through *z* in alphabetic order on students' whiteboard.

1. **Say:** Let's review the order of some letters in the alphabet.

2. Without looking at their whiteboards, have students

   ▸ Name the letter after *b*.
   ▸ Name the letter before *b*.
   ▸ Name any two letters that come after *m*.
   ▸ Name any two letters that come before *m*.

    If students hesitate, have them check the letters on the whiteboard.

Onset and Rime

In a word, the part of the syllable before the first vowel sound is the **onset**. The part of the syllable after the first vowel sound is the **rime**. For example, in *nap*, /n/ is the onset and *ap* is the rime. Help students put together words that are broken down into parts by onset and rime.

1. **Say:** I'm going to break a word into two parts. Your job is to put the parts together and say the word. If the first part of a word is /r/ and the last part of the word is *ut*, then the whole word is *rut*: /r/ . . . *ut* . . . *rut*.

2. Say the following pairs of word parts. Have students tell you the word that each pair forms.

   ▸ /n/ . . . *ut* nut
   ▸ /k/ . . . *ut* cut
   ▸ /w/ . . . *ax* wax
   ▸ /f/ . . . *ax* fax
   ▸ /s/ . . . *ip* sip
   ▸ /l/ . . . *ip* lip
   ▸ /r/ . . . *ip* rip
   ▸ /h/ . . . *og* hog
   ▸ /l/ . . . *og* log
   ▸ /d/ . . . *og* dog

Objectives

- Identify letters of the alphabet.
- Identify a word when given the onset and rime.
- Blend sounds to create words.
- Identify individual sounds in words.
- Identify and use vowels and vowel sounds.
- Identify short vowel sounds.
- Identify and use the sound /ă/.
- Identify and use the sound /ĭ/.
- Identify and use the sound /ŏ/.
- Identify and use the sound /ŭ/.

Review Vowel Sounds and Letters

Help students review vowel sounds and letters.

1. Place the following letter tiles on students' whiteboard: *a*, *i*, *o*, and *u*, plus any letters that are confusing for them.

2. **Say:** I am going to point to a letter. Tell me a sound for that letter.

3. **Say:** I am going to say a sound. Repeat the sound and touch its letter.

4. Point to some letters two or three times, so students don't think that once they have named a sound they are finished with it.

5. Redirect students if they name the letter and not its sound.

   Say: You are right that the name of the letter is [letter]. We want the sound for this letter. What is the sound?

6. Redirect students if they name the sound incorrectly.

   Say: That is the sound of another letter.

7. Provide additional guidance if students touch the wrong letter tile during the review.

   Say: That is the letter tile for the sound [sound of incorrect letter tile]. We are looking for the letter tile for the sound [target sound].

8. If students touch the wrong letter again, point to the correct letter.

   Say: This is the letter tile for the sound [target sound]. Touch this letter tile and say its sound.

Make Up a Sentence

Help students use words to make sentences.

1. Gather the index cards you prepared and place them face down in one pile.

2. Have students

   ▸ Select a card.
   ▸ Read the word.
   ▸ Use the word in an interesting, fun, or silly sentence.

TIP If students read a word incorrectly, have them finger stretch the sounds in the word.

Try It

Short Vowels

Have students complete page PH 48 in *K¹² PhonicsWorks Basic Activity Book* for more practice with the sounds /ă/, /ĭ/, /ŏ/, and /ŭ/. Have students read the word aloud and circle the vowel sound in the word. Have them read the sentence aloud.

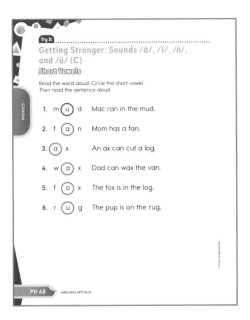

 Online ⏱ **20 minutes**

REVIEW: Sounds /ă/, /ĭ/, /ŏ/, and /ŭ/

Students will work online independently to

▶ Practice the sounds /ă/, /ĭ/, /ŏ/, and /ŭ/ for the letters *a*, *i*, *o*, and *u*.
▶ Practice decoding text by reading a story.

Help students locate the online activities and provide support as needed.

Offline Alternative

No computer access? Have students name the letters that make the sounds /ă/, /ĭ/, /ŏ/, and /ŭ/. Vice versa, have students name the sounds made by the letters *a*, *i*, *o*, and *u*. You might also ask students to spell simple words that contain the letters *a*, *i*, *o*, and *u* and other letters they have learned.

Getting Stronger: Sounds /ă/, /ĭ/, /ŏ/, and /ŭ/ (D)

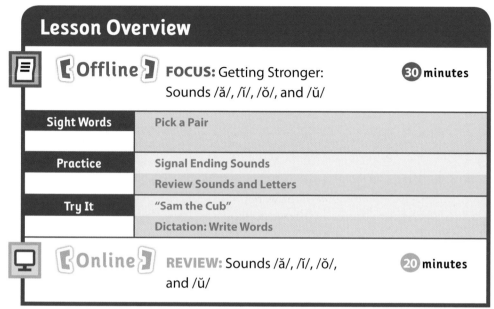

Lesson Overview

Offline FOCUS: Getting Stronger: Sounds /ă/, /ĭ/, /ŏ/, and /ŭ/ — **30** minutes

Sight Words	Pick a Pair
Practice	Signal Ending Sounds
	Review Sounds and Letters
Try It	"Sam the Cub"
	Dictation: Write Words

Online REVIEW: Sounds /ă/, /ĭ/, /ŏ/, and /ŭ/ — **20** minutes

Materials

Supplied
- *K¹² PhonicsWorks Readers Basic 3*, pp. 19–24
- Whiteboard, Learning Coach
- whiteboard, student
- Tile Kit

Also Needed
- sight words box
- dictation notebook

 **Offline** 🕙 **minutes**

FOCUS: Getting Stronger: Sounds /ă/, /ĭ/, /ŏ/, and /ŭ/

Work **together** with students to complete offline Sight Words, Practice, and Try It activities.

Sight Words

Pick a Pair

Play a card game with students for more practice with sight words.

1. Gather the sight word cards that students are reviewing. Choose two words and place the cards on the table.

2. Ask questions to help students identify each word. For example, if the words are *or* and *one*, you could ask, "Which word names a number?" If the words are *off* and *but*, you could ask, "Which word is the opposite of *off*?"

3. Continue the activity until students identify all the words.

4. Take the stack of words that students read correctly and dictate each word to them.

5. Have students write each word or spell it aloud.

 Objectives
- Read sight words.
- Spell sight words.
- Write sight words.

Practice

Signal Ending Sounds

Use a special signal to help students identify **ending sounds** in words.

1. **Say:** I'm going to tell you a special sound, and then I'll say some words. Repeat each word I say and make a special signal to tell me where the special sound is. If the special sound is at the end of the word, blink your eyes. If the special sound is **not** at the end of the word, just smile at me. For example,

   ▸ If I ask you to listen for the sound /t/ and I say the word *mat*, you'll repeat the word *mat* and blink your eyes because *mat* has the sound /t/ at the end.

   ▸ If I say the word *pop*, you'll repeat the word *pop* and smile at me because *pop* has the sound /p/, not /t/, at the end.

2. Say each sound and group of words. Have students make the special signal to identify the ending sound.

   ▸ /k/: *sick, pack, Kim, trip, think* blink: *sick, pack, think*
   ▸ /g/: *frog, pod, log, pig, girl, snip* blink: *frog, log, pig*
   ▸ /z/: *tin, zip, pins, buzz, fizz* blink: *pins, buzz, fizz*
   ▸ /v/: *love, laugh, like, five, gave* blink: *love, five, gave*
   ▸ /f/: *stop, stuff, sell, first, laugh* blink: *stuff, laugh*
   ▸ /b/: *bib, bake, cub, ball, crib* blink: *bib, cub, crib*

TIP If students can't identify the ending sound of each word, say the word again and emphasize the ending sound by repeating it three times (for example, *sit* /t/ /t/ /t/). You can also draw out the ending sound when you say the word (for example, *kisssss*). If necessary, have students look at your mouth while you repeat the sounds.

 Objectives
- Identify ending sounds in words.
- Identify short vowel sounds.
- Identify and use the sound /ă/.
- Identify and use the sound /ĭ/.
- Identify and use the sound /ŏ/.
- Identify and use the sound /ŭ/.
- Given the letter, identify the most common sound.
- Given the sound, identify the most common letter or letters.
- Read aloud grade-level text with appropriate automaticity, prosody, accuracy, and rate.
- Decode words by applying grade-level word analysis skills.

Review Sounds and Letters

Help students review sounds for the letters *a, d, g, i, j, o, p, s, u,* and *x,* plus any letters that are confusing for them.

1. Place the following letter tiles in random order on students' whiteboard: *a, d, g, i, j, o, p, s, u,* and *x,* plus any letters that are confusing.

2. **Say:** Let's go over some letters and sounds.

3. Point to each letter tile and have students say a sound that letter makes.

   ▸ *o* /ŏ/   ▸ *d* /d/
   ▸ *s* /s/   ▸ *x* /ks/
   ▸ *j* /j/   ▸ *u* /ŭ/
   ▸ *g* /g/   ▸ *i* /ĭ/
   ▸ *a* /ă/   ▸ *p* /p/

4. Say each of the following sounds. Have students repeat the sound and touch the corresponding letter tile.

   ▸ /ŏ/ *o*   ▸ /d/ *d*
   ▸ /s/ *s*   ▸ /ks/ *x*
   ▸ /j/ *j*   ▸ /ŭ/ *u*
   ▸ /g/ *g*   ▸ /ĭ/ *i*
   ▸ /ă/ *a*   ▸ /p/ *p*

5. As you do the activity, point to some letter tiles two or three times so that students don't think they are finished with a sound after they have named it.

6. Redirect students if they say an incorrect sound when you point to a letter tile.

   Say: That's the sound of another letter. What is the sound for this letter?

7. Help students if they touch the wrong letter tile after they repeat a sound.

   Say: That letter tile goes with the sound [sound for incorrect letter tile]. We're looking for the letter that goes with the sound [target sound].

Try It

"Sam the Cub"

Have students read "Sam the Cub" on page 19 of *K¹² PhonicsWorks Readers Basic 3*.

Students should read the story silently once or twice before reading the story aloud. When students miss a word that can be sounded out, point to it and give them three to six seconds to try the word again. If students still miss the word, tell them the word so the flow of the story isn't interrupted.

After reading the story, make a list of all the words students missed, and go over those words with them. You may use tiles to show students how to read the words.

Dictation: Write Words

Have students practice identifying sounds and writing words.

1. Gather a pencil and the dictation notebook. Say the word *lap*. Then give these directions to students:

   ▸ Repeat the word.
   ▸ Write the word in your notebook.
   ▸ Read the word aloud.

2. When students have finished, write the following word on your whiteboard: *lap*.

3. Have them compare their answer to your correct version.

4. Repeat this procedure with the words *sit, fun,* and *hot*.

   ▸ If students make an error and don't see it, help them correct their mistake by having them finger stretch the sounds in the word they missed.
   ▸ If students are having difficulty selecting the correct letters or sounds, review those letters or sounds that are confusing them.
   ▸ If students have difficulty with first, middle, and last sounds, have them finger stretch the sounds in words.

Objectives

- Read aloud grade-level text with appropriate automaticity, prosody, accuracy, and rate.
- Decode words by applying grade-level word analysis skills.
- Track text from left to right.
- Turn pages sequentially.
- Write words by applying grade-level phonics knowledge.
- Follow three-step directions.
- Identify short vowel sounds.
- Identify and use the sound /ă/.
- Identify and use the sound /ĭ/.
- Identify and use the sound /ŏ/.
- Identify and use the sound /ŭ/.

 **20 minutes**

REVIEW: **Sounds /ă/, /ĭ/, /ŏ/, and /ŭ/**

Students will work online independently to

▸ Practice the sounds for letters /ă/, /ĭ/, /ŏ/, and /ŭ/ for the letters *a*, *i*, *o*, and *u*.

Help students locate the online activities and provide support as needed.

Offline Alternative

No computer access? Have students name the letters that make the sounds /ă/, /ĭ/, /ŏ/, and /ŭ/. Vice versa, have students name the sounds made by the letters *a*, *i*, *o*, and *u*. You might also ask students to spell simple words that contain the letters *a*, *i*, *o*, and *u* and other letters they have learned.

Objectives
- Identify and use the sound /ă/.
- Identify and use the sound /ĭ/.
- Identify and use the sound /ŏ/.
- Identify and use the sound /ŭ/.
- Identify short vowel sounds.

Unit Checkpoint

Lesson Overview

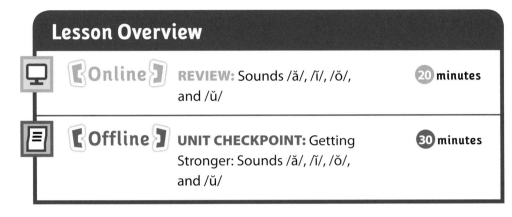

Online REVIEW: Sounds /ă/, /ĭ/, /ŏ/, and /ŭ/   **20** minutes

Offline UNIT CHECKPOINT: Getting Stronger: Sounds /ă/, /ĭ/, /ŏ/, and /ŭ/   **30** minutes

Materials

Supplied
- *K¹² PhonicsWorks Basic Assessments*, pp. PH 85–90

Objectives
- Identify and use the sound /ă/.
- Identify and use the sound /ĭ/.
- Identify and use the sound /ŏ/.
- Identify and use the sound /ŭ/.
- Identify letters of the alphabet.
- Identify individual sounds in words.
- Given the letter, identify the most common sound.
- Given the sound, identify the most common letter or letters.
- Read sight words.
- Read instructional-level text with 90% accuracy.
- Read aloud grade-level text with appropriate automaticity, prosody, accuracy, and rate.
- Write words by applying grade-level phonics knowledge.

 **20** minutes

REVIEW: Sounds /ă/, /ĭ/, /ŏ/, and /ŭ/

Students will review the sounds /ă/, /ĭ/, /ŏ/, and /ŭ/ for the letters *a, i, o,* and *u* to prepare for the Unit Checkpoint. Help students locate the online activities and provide support as needed.

 **30 minutes**

UNIT CHECKPOINT: Getting Stronger: Sounds /ă/, /ĭ/, /ŏ/, and /ŭ/

Explain that students are going to show what they have learned about letters, sounds, and words.

1. Give students the Unit Checkpoint pages for the Getting Stronger: Sounds /ă/, /ĭ/, /ŏ/, and /ŭ/ unit and print the Unit Checkpoint Answer Key, if you'd like.

2. Use the instructions below to help administer the Checkpoint to students. On the Answer Key or another sheet of paper, note student answers to oral response questions to help with scoring the Checkpoint later.

3. Use the Answer Key to score the Checkpoint, and then enter the results online.

Part 1. Say Sounds Have students read across the rows from left to right and say a sound that each letter or letters make. Note any sounds they say incorrectly.

Part 2. Word Dissection For each word, say the sound students should identify. Have them read the word aloud and circle the letter or group of letters that spells the requested sound.

19. *middle sound*

20. *ending sound*

21. *beginning sound*

22. *ending sound*

23. *middle sound*

Part 3. Finger Stretching Say each word to students. Have them say each word and finger stretch the sounds. Note any words they finger stretch incorrectly.

24. *cob*   26. *rap*

25. *rug*   27. *quit*

Part 4. Dictation Say each word to students. Have them repeat and write the word.

28. *bug*   30. *rat*

29. *six*   31. *box*

Part 5. Read Aloud Listen to students read the sentences aloud. Count and note the number of words they read correctly.

Part 6. Say Letters Say each sound. Have students say the letter or letters that make that sound. Note any incorrect responses.

33. /ŭ/	**42.** /ă/
34. /ă/	**43.** /ŭ/
35. /ŏ/	**44.** /b/
36. /w/	**45.** /ĭ/
37. /ks/	**46.** /d/
38. /r/	**47.** /ŏ/
39. /ĭ/	**48.** /k/
40. /kw/	**49.** /p/
41. /z/	**50.** /l/

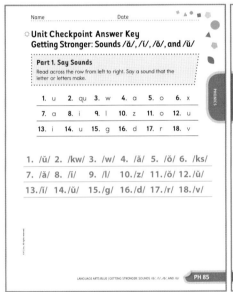

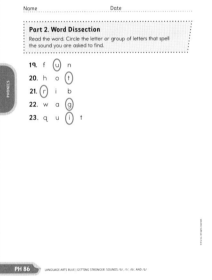

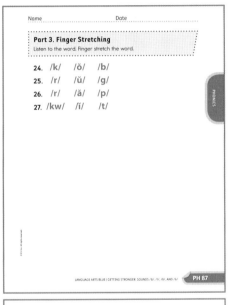

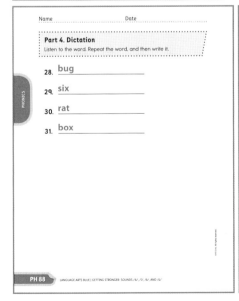

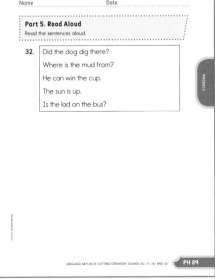

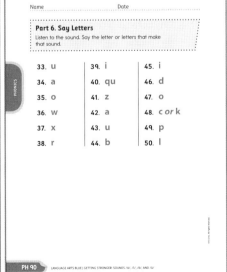

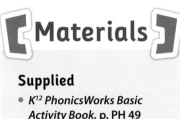

Introduce Sounds for Letters *e* and *y*

Unit Overview

In this unit, students will
- ▶ Learn the sight words *that*, *of*, and *put*.
- ▶ Identify the letters and sounds in the alphabet.
- ▶ Learn the sounds for the letters *e* and *y*.
- ▶ Identify beginning and ending sounds in words.
- ▶ Build words.

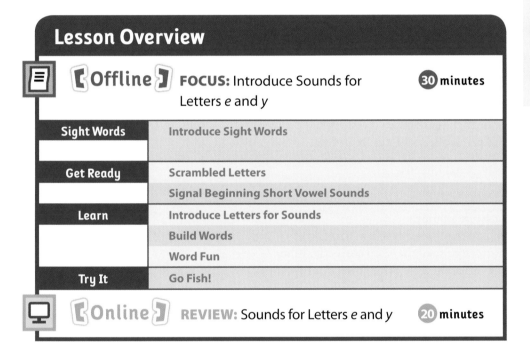

Lesson Overview

	[Offline] FOCUS: Introduce Sounds for Letters *e* and *y*	**30** minutes
Sight Words	Introduce Sight Words	
Get Ready	Scrambled Letters	
	Signal Beginning Short Vowel Sounds	
Learn	Introduce Letters for Sounds	
	Build Words	
	Word Fun	
Try It	Go Fish!	

[Online] REVIEW: Sounds for Letters *e* and *y*	**20** minutes

Advance Preparation

For Word Fun, print on the cards names of items that may be located nearby, using one card per word, such as *bin, cap, can, net, pin, peg, pen, lid, hat,* and *tap.*

 **30 minutes**

FOCUS: Introduce Sounds for Letters *e* and *y*

Work **together** with students to complete offline Sight Words, Get Ready, Learn, and Try It activities.

Sight Words

Introduce Sight Words

Help students learn the sight words *that*, *of*, and *put*.

1. Gather the sight word cards *that*, *of*, and *put*.

2. Show students the *that* card.

3. **Say:** This is the word *that*. We see this word so often that we want to be able to read and spell *that* quickly without thinking about it. Look closely at the word *that*. Spell the word *that* aloud. Take a picture of the word *that* in your mind. When you think you can spell *that* yourself, turn the card over and use your letter tiles to spell the word *that*. Check the card to see if you spelled the word *that* correctly. Read aloud the word you spelled with the letter tiles.

4. Repeat the activity with the remaining sight words.

5. Chart students' progress on the back of each card.
   - ► Divide the back of the card into two columns.
   - ► Label the first column "Read" and the second column "Spell."
   - ► Record the dates that students read or spell the word correctly. When students can read and spell the word correctly three times in a row, they have mastered the word. You may want to put a star or sticker on the card when they have mastered that word.

6. Add the cards to students' sight words box.

TIP Sight words can be very difficult for some students. Let students work at their own pace and really master these words, as they occur frequently in reading and writing.

Objectives
- Read sight words.
- Spell sight words.

Get Ready

Scrambled Letters
To help students master the alphabet, have them practice identifying and naming letters.

1. Place the following letter tiles in random order on students' whiteboard: *b, f, i, l, o, qu, u, w,* and *z.*
2. Have students arrange the letters in alphabetical order.

TIP Students may find this activity easier if they slowly sing "The Alphabet Song" to themselves as they work.

Signal Beginning Short Vowel Sounds
Use a special signal to help students identify **beginning short vowel sounds** in words.

1. **Say:** I'm going to tell you a special sound, and then I'll say some words. Repeat each word I say and make a special signal to tell me where the special sound is. If the special sound is at the beginning of the word, touch your nose. If the special sound is **not** at the beginning of the word, just smile at me. For example,

   ▸ If I ask you to listen for the sound /ă/ and I say the word *apple*, you'll repeat the word *apple* and touch your nose because *apple* has the sound /ă/ at the beginning.
   ▸ If I say the word *odd*, you'll repeat the word *odd* and smile at me because *odd* has the sound /ŏ/, not /ă/, at the beginning.

2. Say each sound and group of words. Have students make the special signal to identify the beginning sound.

   ▸ /ă/: *actor, elephant, aspirin, off, apple* touch nose: *actor, aspirin, apple*
   ▸ /ŭ/: *under, ankle, uncle, upper, into* touch nose: *under, uncle, upper*
   ▸ /ĭ/: *after, into, ill, is, over,* touch nose: *into, ill, is*
   ▸ /ŏ/: *five, use, operator, Ollie, onto, octopus* touch nose: *operator, Ollie, onto, octopus*

TIP If students can't identify the beginning sound of each word, say the word again and emphasize the beginning sound by repeating it three times (for example, /t/ /t/ /t/, *taste*). You can also draw out the beginning sound when you say the word (for example, *mmmommy*). If necessary, have students look at your mouth while you repeat the sounds.

Objectives
- Identify letters of the alphabet.
- Identify beginning sounds in words.
- Identify and use vowels and vowel sounds.
- Identify and use the sound /ă/.
- Identify and use the sound /ĭ/.
- Identify and use the sound /ŏ/.
- Identify and use the sound /ŭ/.

Learn

Introduce Letters for Sounds

To help students learn the lowercase letters *e* and *y*, have them practice identifying and naming the letters from the sounds.

1. Place the following letter tiles on students' whiteboard: *e* and *y*.

2. **Say:** Let's learn sounds for letters. When we see the letter *e*, we sometimes say the sound /ĕ/. When we see the letter *y*, we sometimes say the sound /y/.

3. Have students
   ▸ Touch the letter *e* and say /ĕ/.
   ▸ Touch the letter *y* and say /y/.

4. **Say:** Let's practice these sounds and letters.

5. Say the sounds /ĕ/ and /y/ one at a time. Have students repeat each sound and touch the letter for each sound. It is important for students to touch the letter while they say the sound.

6. Redirect students if they name the letter and not the sound.

   Say: You're right that the name of the letter is [letter]. We want the sound for this letter. What is the sound?

7. Redirect students if they name the sound incorrectly.

   Say: That's the sound of another letter. The sound for this letter is [target sound]. Touch the letter and say the sound.

8. Help students. If they touch the wrong letter, point to the correct letter.

   Say: This is the letter for the sound [target sound]. Touch and say its sound.

Objectives

- Identify the letter, given the sound /ĕ/.
- Identify the sound, given the letter *e*.
- Identify the letter, given the sound /y/.
- Identify the sound, given the letter *y*.
- Identify individual sounds in words.
- Blend sounds to create words.

Build Words

Help students use letters and sounds to build words.

1. Place the following letter tiles at the top of students' whiteboard: *b, d, e, g, t, T,* and *y*.

2. Draw three horizontal lines across the middle of students' whiteboard to represent the sounds in a word.

3. **Say:** Let's use letters and sounds to build the word *yet*.

4. Have students finger stretch the sounds in *yet*.

5. Have students
   ▸ Identify the first, next, and last sounds in *yet*.
   ▸ Choose the corresponding letter for each of the sounds.
   ▸ Move the letters to the correct lines on their whiteboard.

6. Guide students with these questions:

   ▸ What is the first sound in *yet*? /y/
   Which line does the letter for that sound go on? the first one
   ▸ What is the next sound in *yet*? /ĕ/
   Which line does the letter for that sound go on? the second one
   ▸ What's the last sound in *yet*? /t/
   Which line does the letter for that sound go on? the last one

7. Have students touch and say the word.

8. Redirect students if they select the incorrect letter.

   Say: That sound is in the word [word], and it is the [first, second, third] sound. We want the sound [target sound].

   Continue until students select the correct letter.

9. Repeat the activity to build the following words:

   ▸ *beg* /b/ /ĕ/ /g/
   ▸ *Ted* /t/ /ĕ/ /d/

Word Fun

Have students practice reading words and identifying names of common objects.

1. Gather the index cards you prepared and place them face down in one pile.

2. **Say:** You are going to practice reading and writing some words.

   ▸ You will choose a card from the pile and read the word on it.
   ▸ Then you are going to flip the card over and write the word on the backside of the card.
   ▸ I'll try first.

3. Choose a card from the pile and say and write the word.

   Say: Now it's your turn. Choose a card and read it to me.

4. If time permits, have students choose two words and draw a picture of those words on the back of the card.

   TIP If students stumble over any words, have them touch and say the words. Touch and say these words along with them.

Try It ....

Go Fish!

Have students complete page PH 49 in *K¹² PhonicsWorks Basic Activity Book* for more practice with the sounds /ĕ/ and /y/. Have students read the word aloud and color the fish yellow for words that contain the sound /ĕ/ and pink for words that contain the sound /y/.

Objectives

- Read aloud grade-level text with appropriate automaticity, prosody, accuracy, and rate.
- Identify and use the sound /ĕ/.
- Identify and use the sound /y/.

Online   20 minutes

REVIEW: Sounds for Letters *e* and *y*

Students will work online independently to

▶ Practice the sounds /ĕ/ and /y/ made by the letters *e* and *y*.
▶ Practice decoding text by reading sentences.

Help students locate the online activities and provide support as needed.

Offline Alternative

No computer access? Have students name the letters that make the sounds /ĕ/ and /y/. Vice versa, have students name the sounds made by the letters *e* and *y*. You might also ask students to spell simple words that contain the sounds /ĕ/ and /y/ made by the letters *e* and *y* and other letters students have learned, such as *pen*, *hen*, *yak*, and *yip*.

Objectives

- Identify the letter, given the sound /ĕ/.
- Identify the sound, given the letter *e*.
- Identify the letter, given the sound /y/.
- Identify the sound, given the letter *y*.
- Identify individual sounds in words.
- Read aloud grade-level text with appropriate automaticity, prosody, accuracy, and rate.
- Decode words by applying grade-level word analysis skills.

Practice Sounds for Letters
e and *y* (A)

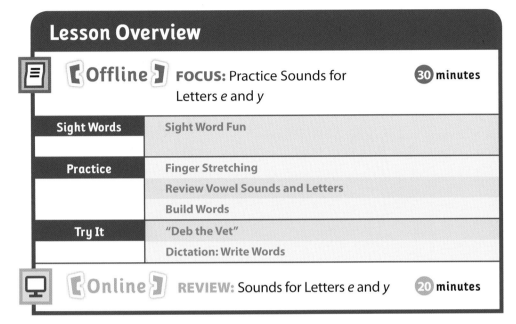

Lesson Overview

[Offline] **FOCUS:** Practice Sounds for Letters *e* and *y* **30** minutes

Sight Words	Sight Word Fun
Practice	Finger Stretching
	Review Vowel Sounds and Letters
	Build Words
Try It	"Deb the Vet"
	Dictation: Write Words

[Online] **REVIEW:** Sounds for Letters *e* and *y* **20** minutes

[Materials]

Supplied
- *K¹² PhonicsWorks Readers Basic 3*, pp. 25–30
- whiteboard, Learning Coach
- whiteboard, student
- Tile Kit

Also Needed
- sight words box
- dictation notebook

 **30 minutes**

FOCUS: Practice Sounds for Letters *e* and *y*

Work **together** with students to complete offline Sight Words, Practice, and Try It activities.

Sight Words

· ·

Sight Word Fun

Help students learn the sight words *that*, *of*, and *put*, and up to two additional sight words they have yet to master.

1. Gather the sight word cards *that*, *of*, and *put*, and up to two additional sight word cards.

2. Choose one sight word card to begin.

   Say: Look at this word and take a picture of it in your mind. When you think you can spell the word yourself, turn the card over and use your letter tiles to spell the word.

3. After students spell the word, have them check the card to see if they spelled the word correctly.

   Say: Read aloud the word you spelled with the letter tiles.

4. Repeat the activity with the remaining sight words.

 Sight words can be very difficult for some students. Let them work at their own pace and really master these words.

 Objectives

- Read sight words.
- Spell sight words.

Practice

· ·

Finger Stretching

Use finger stretching to help students identify individual sounds in words.

1. **Say:** Let's review finger stretching. In the word *fed*, the first sound is /f/, the next sound is /ĕ/, and the last sound is /d/. I will finger stretch each sound as I say it. Then I'll say the word while pulling my fist toward my body.

2. Finger stretch the word *fed* for students.

3. **Say:** I'm going to say words with several sounds in them. You'll say each word and then finger stretch it while you say each sound in the word.

Objectives

- Identify individual sounds in words.
- Identify and use vowels and vowel sounds.
- Blend sounds to create words.
- Identify the letter, given the sound /ĕ/.
- Identify the sound, given the letter *e*.
- Identify and use the sound /ĕ/.
- Identify the letter, given the sound /y/.
- Identify the sound, given the letter *y*.
- Identify and use the sound /y/.

4. Say the following words and have students finger stretch them. After they finger stretch each word, ask them the question for that word.

- *cop* /k/ /ŏ/ /p/   What is the middle sound? /ŏ/
- *set* /s/ /ĕ/ /t/   What is the first sound? /s/
- *peg* /p/ /ĕ/ /g/   What is the middle sound? /ĕ/
- *lap* /l/ /ă/ /p/   What is the first sound? /l/
- *yes* /y/ /ĕ/ /s/   What is the middle sound? /ĕ/
- *Ted* /t/ /ĕ/ /d/   What is the middle sound? /ĕ/

 Refer to the *K¹² PhonicsWorks* video for a demonstration of finger stretching.

Review Vowel Sounds and Letters

Help students review vowel sounds and letters.

1. Place the following letter tiles on students' whiteboard: *a, e, i, o,* and *u,* plus any letters that are confusing for them.

2. **Say:** I am going to point to each letter. Tell me a sound for that letter.

3. **Say:** I am going to say a sound. Repeat the sound and touch its letter.

4. Point to some letters two or three times, so students don't think that once they have named a sound they are finished with it.

5. Redirect students if they name the letter and not its sound.

   Say: You are right that the name of the letter is [letter]. We want the sound for this letter. What is the sound?

6. Redirect students if they name the sound incorrectly.

   Say: That is the sound of another letter.

7. Provide additional guidance if students touch the wrong letter during the review.

   Say: That is the letter for the sound [sound of incorrect letter]. We are looking for the letter for the sound [target sound].

8. If students touch the wrong letter again, point to the correct letter.

   Say: This is the letter for the sound [target sound]. Touch this letter and say its sound.

Build Words

Help students use letters and sounds to build words.

1. Place the following letter tiles at the top of students' whiteboard: *d, e, f, j, s, t, w,* and *y.*

2. Draw three horizontal lines across the middle of students' whiteboard to represent the sounds in a word.

3. **Say:** Let's use letters and sounds to build the word *yet*.

4. Have students finger stretch the sounds in *yet*.

5. Have students

   ▸ Identify the first, next, and last sounds in *yet*.
   ▸ Choose the corresponding letter for each of the sounds.
   ▸ Move the letters to the correct lines on their whiteboard.

6. Guide students with these questions:
   ▸ What is the first sound in *yet*? /y/
      Which line does the letter for that sound go on? the first one
   ▸ What is the next sound in *yet*? /ĕ/
      Which line does the letter for that sound go on? the second one
   ▸ What's the last sound in *yet*? /t/
      Which line does the letter for that sound go on? the last one

7. Have students touch and say the word.

8. Redirect students if they select the incorrect letter.

   Say: That sound is in the word [word], and it is the [first, second, third] sound.
   We want the sound [target sound]. Continue until students select the correct
   letter.

9. Repeat the activity to build the following words:

   ▸ *wet* /w/ /ĕ/ /t/
   ▸ *yes* /y/ /ĕ/ /s/
   ▸ *fed* /f/ /ĕ/ /d/
   ▸ *jet* /j/ /ĕ/ /t/

Try It

"Deb the Vet"
Have students read "Deb the Vet" on page 25 of *K¹² PhonicsWorks Readers Basic 3*.
   Students should read the story silently once or twice before reading the story
aloud. When students miss a word that can be sounded out, point to it and give them
three to six seconds to try the word again. If students still miss the word, tell them the
word so the flow of the story isn't interrupted.
   After reading the story, make a list of all the words students missed, and go over
those words with them. You may use tiles to show students how to read the words.

Objectives
- Read aloud grade-level text with appropriate automaticity, prosody, accuracy, and rate.
- Decode words by applying grade-level word analysis skills.
- Track text from left to right.
- Turn pages sequentially.
- Write words by applying grade-level phonics knowledge.
- Follow three-step directions.

Dictation: Write Words

Have students practice identifying sounds and writing words.

1. Gather a pencil and the dictation notebook. Say the word *yes*. Then give these directions to students:

   ▸ Repeat the word.
   ▸ Write the word in your notebook.
   ▸ Read the word aloud.

2. When students have finished, write the following word on your whiteboard: *yes*.

3. Have them compare their answer to your correct version.

4. Repeat this procedure with the words *yet* and *met*.

   ▸ If students make an error and don't see it, help them correct their mistake by having them finger stretch the sounds in the word they missed.
   ▸ If students are having difficulty selecting the correct letters or sounds, review those letters or sounds that are confusing them.
   ▸ If students have difficulty with first, middle, and last sounds, have them finger stretch the sounds in words.

 **20 minutes**

REVIEW: **Sounds for Letters *e* and *y***

Students will work online independently to

▸ Practice the sounds /ĕ/ and /y/ made by the letters *e* and *y*.

Help students locate the online activities and provide support as needed.

Offline Alternative

No computer access? Have students name the letters that make the sounds /ĕ/ and /y/. Vice versa, have students name the sounds made by the letters *e* and *y*. You might also ask students to spell simple words that contain the sounds /ĕ/ and /y/ made by the letters *e* and *y* and other letters students have learned, such as *pen*, *hen*, *yak*, and *yip*.

 Objectives

- Identify the letter, given the sound /ĕ/.
- Identify the sound, given the letter *e*.
- Identify and use the sound /ĕ/.
- Identify the letter, given the sound /y/.
- Identify the sound, given the letter *y*.
- Identify and use the sound /y/.
- Identify individual sounds in words.

Practice Sounds for Letters
e and *y* (B)

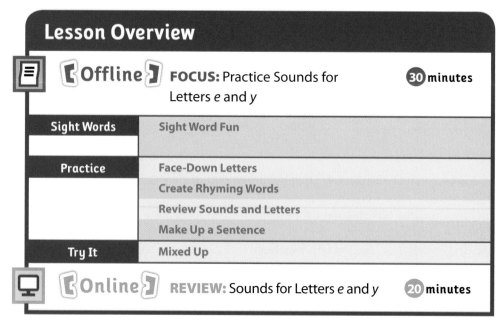

Lesson Overview		
Offline FOCUS: Practice Sounds for Letters *e* and *y*		**30** minutes
Sight Words	Sight Word Fun	
Practice	Face-Down Letters	
	Create Rhyming Words	
	Review Sounds and Letters	
	Make Up a Sentence	
Try It	Mixed Up	
Online REVIEW: Sounds for Letters *e* and *y*		**20** minutes

Materials

Supplied
- *K¹² PhonicsWorks Basic Activity Book*, p. PH 50
- whiteboard, Learning Coach
- whiteboard, student
- Tile Kit

Also Needed
- sight words box

Advance Preparation

Place lowercase letter tiles in alphabetical order on your whiteboard.

 **30** minutes

FOCUS: Practice Sounds for Letters *e* and *y*
Work **together** with students to complete offline Sight Words, Practice, and
Try It activities.

Sight Words

Sight Word Fun
Help students learn the sight words *that*, *of*, and *put*, and up to two additional sight
words they have yet to master.

1. Gather the sight word cards *that*, *of*, and *put*, and up to two additional sight
   word cards.

2. Choose one sight word card to begin.

   Say: Look at this word and take a picture of it in your mind. When you think
   you can spell the word yourself, turn the card over and use your letter tiles to
   spell the word.

3. After students spell the word, have them check the card to see if they spelled
   the word correctly.

   Say: Read aloud the word you spelled with the letter tiles.

4. Repeat the activity with the remaining sight words.

    Sight words can be very difficult for some students. Let them work at their own
   pace and really master these words.

> **Objectives**
> • Read sight words.
> • Spell sight words.

Practice

Face-Down Letters
To help students master the letters of the alphabet, have them practice identifying
and naming letters. Grab your whiteboard with letters placed in alphabetical order.

1. Lay your whiteboard down on a flat surface and flip over the following letter
   tiles so they are face down on the whiteboard: *d, e, i, j, m, o, r, t* and *x*.

2. **Say:** These letters are face down. We are looking at the back of them. Name
   each letter and then turn it over to see if you were right.

    If students miss any of the letters, have them turn over the missed ones and
   try again.

> **Objectives**
> • Identify letters of the alphabet.
> • Identify individual sounds in words.
> • Identify words that rhyme.
> • Given the letter, identify the most common sound.
> • Given the sound, identify the most common letter or letters.
> • Read aloud grade-level text with appropriate automaticity, prosody, accuracy, and rate.
> • Decode words by applying grade-level word analysis skills.

Create Rhyming Words

Have students combine word parts and make words that rhyme.

1. **Say:** I'm going to break a word into two parts. Your job is to put the parts back together and say the word.

   ▸ For example, if the first part of the word is /j/ and the last part is /ŏb/, then you'll say *job*: /j/ . . . /ŏb/ . . . *job*.
   ▸ Next you'll add a new **beginning sound** to make a word that rhymes. For example, you'll use the same last part, /ŏb/, and add a new first sound, like /k/. The rhyming word is /k/ . . . /ŏb/ . . . *cob*.

2. **Say:** Now it's your turn: /r/ . . . /ĕd/.

   ▸ What's the word? *red*
   ▸ Now use the same last part, /ĕd/, but add a new sound, /f/, at the beginning. What word did you make? *fed*

3. Have students add a new beginning sound to the last part of each word to make rhyming words.

   ▸ /f/ . . . /ĕd/ *fed*; Possible rhyming words: *bed, led, said*
   ▸ /k/ . . . /ŭt/ *cut*; Possible rhyming words: *rut, nut, but*
   ▸ /j/ . . . /ĕt/ *jet*; Possible rhyming words: *met, set, pet*

Review Sounds and Letters

Help students review sounds for the letters *a, b, c, e, f, h, i, o, n, u,* and *y*, plus any letters that are confusing for them.

1. Place the following letter tiles in random order on students' whiteboard: *a, b, c, e, f, h, i, o, n, u,* and *y*, plus any letters that are confusing.

2. **Say:** Let's go over some letters and sounds.

3. Point to each letter tile and have students say a sound that letter makes.

   ▸ *u* /ŭ/
   ▸ *b* /b/
   ▸ *c* /k/
   ▸ *e* /ĕ/
   ▸ *o* /ŏ/
   ▸ *i* /ĭ/
   ▸ *f* /f/
   ▸ *n* /n/
   ▸ *a* /ă/
   ▸ *y* /y/
   ▸ *h* /h/

4. Say each of the following sounds. Have students repeat the sound and touch the corresponding letter tile.

   ▸ /ŭ/ *u*
   ▸ /b/ *b*
   ▸ /k/ *c*
   ▸ /ĕ/ *e*
   ▸ /ŏ/ *o*
   ▸ /ĭ/ *i*
   ▸ /f/ *f*
   ▸ /n/ *n*
   ▸ /ă/ *a*
   ▸ /y/ *y*
   ▸ /h/ *h*

5. As you do the activity, point to some letter tiles two or three times so that students don't think they are finished with a sound after they have named it.

6. Redirect students if they say an incorrect sound when you point to a letter tile.

   Say: That's the sound of another letter. What is the sound for this letter?

7. Help students if they touch the wrong letter tile after they repeat a sound.

   Say: That letter goes with the sound [sound for incorrect letter tile]. We're looking for the letter that goes with the sound [target sound].

Make Up a Sentence
Help students use words to make sentences.

1. Write the following words on students' whiteboard: *bed, ten, set, pen*.

2. Have students read a word and use the word in an interesting, fun, or silly sentence. Repeat until they have named and used each word in a sentence.

TIP If students read a word incorrectly, have them finger stretch the sounds in the word.

Try It

Mixed Up
Have students complete page PH 50 in *K¹² PhonicsWorks Basic Activity Book* for more practice with the sounds /ĕ/ and /y/. Have students read each row of mixed-up words aloud. Have them unscramble the words and write a sentence.

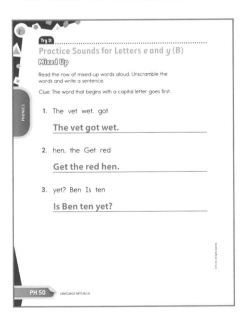

Objectives

- Read aloud grade-level text with appropriate automaticity, prosody, accuracy, and rate.
- Decode words by applying grade-level word analysis skills.
- Track text from left to right.
- Identify and use the sound /ĕ/.
- Identify and use the sound /y/.

 **20 minutes**

REVIEW: **Sounds for Letters *e* and *y***

Students will work online independently to

► Practice the sounds /ĕ/ and /y/ made by the letters *e* and *y*.
► Practice decoding text by reading a story.

Help students locate the online activities and provide support as needed.

Offline Alternative

No computer access? Have students name the letters that make the sounds /ĕ/ and /y/. Vice versa, have students name the sounds made by the letters *e* and *y*. You might also ask students to spell simple words that contain the sounds /ĕ/ and /y/ made by the letters *e* and *y* and other letters students have learned, such as *bed*, *den*, *yes*, and *yet*.

Objectives
- Identify the letter, given the sound /ĕ/.
- Identify the sound, given the letter *e*.
- Identify the letter, given the sound /y/.
- Identify the sound, given the letter *y*.
- Identify individual sounds in words.
- Read aloud grade-level text with appropriate automaticity, prosody, accuracy, and rate.
- Decode words by applying grade-level word analysis skills.

Practice Sounds for Letters
e and *y* (C)

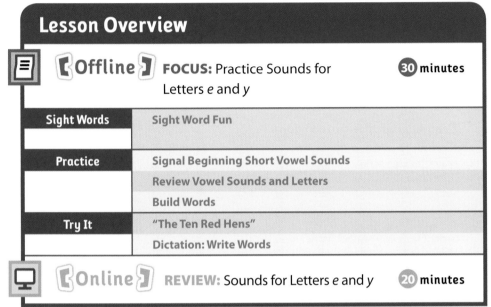

Lesson Overview

Offline	**FOCUS:** Practice Sounds for Letters *e* and *y*	**30** minutes

Sight Words	Sight Word Fun

Practice	Signal Beginning Short Vowel Sounds
	Review Vowel Sounds and Letters
	Build Words
Try It	"The Ten Red Hens"
	Dictation: Write Words

Online	**REVIEW:** Sounds for Letters *e* and *y*	**20** minutes

Materials

Supplied

- *K¹² PhonicsWorks Readers Basic 4*, pp. 1–6
- whiteboard, Learning Coach
- whiteboard, student
- Tile Kit

Also Needed

- sight words box
- dictation notebook

[Offline] 30 minutes

FOCUS: Practice Sounds for Letters *e* and *y*

Work **together** with students to complete offline Sight Words, Practice, and Try It activities.

Sight Words

Sight Word Fun

Help students learn the sight words *that*, *of*, and *put*, and up to two additional sight words they have yet to master.

1. Gather the sight word cards *that*, *of*, and *put*, and up to two additional sight word cards.

2. Choose one sight word card to begin.

   Say: Look at this word and take a picture of it in your mind. When you think you can spell the word yourself, turn the card over and use your letter tiles to spell the word.

3. After students spell the word, have them check the card to see if they spelled the word correctly.

   Say: Read aloud the word you spelled with the letter tiles.

4. Repeat the activity with the remaining sight words.

TIP Sight words can be very difficult for some students. Let them work at their own pace and really master these words.

Objectives
- Read sight words.
- Spell sight words.

Practice •

Signal Beginning Short Vowel Sounds

Use a special signal to help students identify **beginning short vowel sounds** in words.

1. **Say:** I'm going to tell you a special sound, and then I'll say some words. Repeat each word I say and make a special signal to tell me where the special sound is. If the special sound is at the beginning of the word, touch your nose. If the special sound is **not** at the beginning of the word, just smile at me. For example,

   ▸ If I ask you to listen for the sound /ă/ and I say the word *apple*, you'll repeat the word *apple* and touch your nose because *apple* has the sound /ă/ at the beginning.

   ▸ If I say the word *odd*, you'll repeat the word *odd* and smile at me because *odd* has the sound /ŏ/, not /ă/, at the beginning.

2. Say each sound and group of words. Have students make the special signal to identify the beginning sound.

   ▸ /ĭ/: *up, illness, and, Indian, inside* touch nose: *illness, Indian, inside*
   ▸ /ĕ/: *echo, edge, opposite, after, ever* touch nose: *echo, edge, ever*
   ▸ /ŏ/: *Oscar, everywhere, under, otter, on* touch nose: *Oscar, otter, on*
   ▸ /ă/: *Abby, accent, uncle, in, after* touch nose: *Abby, accent, after*
   ▸ /ŭ/: *Ollie, unkind, ugly, apple, under* touch nose: *unkind, ugly, under*

TIP If students can't identify the beginning sound of each word, say the word again and emphasize the beginning sound by repeating it three times (for example, /t/ /t/ /t/, *taste*). You can also draw out the beginning sound when you say the word (for example, *mmmommy*). If necessary, have students look at your mouth while you repeat the sounds.

Review Vowel Sounds and Letters

Help students review vowel sounds and letters.

1. Place the following letter tiles on students' whiteboard: *a, e, i, o,* and *u,* plus any letters that are confusing for them.

2. **Say:** I am going to point to each letter. Tell me a sound for that letter.

3. **Say:** I am going to say a sound. Repeat the sound and touch its letter.

4. Point to some letters two or three times, so students don't think that once they have named a sound they are finished with it.

5. Redirect students if they name the letter and not its sound.

   Say: You are right that the name of the letter is [letter]. We want the sound for this letter. What is the sound?

6. Redirect students if they name the sound incorrectly.

   Say: That is the sound of another letter.

Objectives
- Identify beginning sounds in words.
- Identify and use vowels and vowel sounds.
- Identify and use the sound /ă/.
- Identify and use the sound /ĕ/.
- Identify and use the sound /ĭ/.
- Identify and use the sound /ŏ/.
- Identify and use the sound /ŭ/.
- Identify the letter, given the sound /ĕ/.
- Identify the sound, given the letter *e.*
- Identify the letter, given the sound /y/.
- Identify the sound, given the letter *y.*
- Blend sounds to create words.

7. Provide additional guidance if students touch the wrong letter during the review.

   Say: That is the letter for the sound [sound for incorrect letter]. We are looking for the letter for the sound [target sound].

8. If students touch the wrong letter again, point to the correct letter.

   Say: This is the letter for the sound [target sound]. Touch this letter and say its sound.

Build Words

Help students use letters and sounds to build words.

1. Place the following letter tiles at the top of students' whiteboard: *e, g, h, m, o, p, s, t,* and *y.*

2. Draw three horizontal lines across the middle of students' whiteboard to represent the sounds in a word.

3. **Say:** Let's use letters and sounds to build the word *met.*

4. Have students finger stretch the sounds in *met.*

5. Have students

   ▸ Identify the first, next, and last sounds in *met.*
   ▸ Choose the corresponding letter for each of the sounds.
   ▸ Move the letters to the correct lines on their whiteboard.

6. Guide students with these questions:

   ▸ What is the first sound in *met*? /m/
     Which line does the letter for that sound go on? the first one
   ▸ What is the next sound in *met*? /ĕ/
     Which line does the letter for that sound go on? the second one
   ▸ What's the last sound in *met*? /t/
     Which line does the letter for that sound go on? the last one

7. Have students touch and say the word.

8. Redirect students if they select the incorrect letter.

   Say: That sound is in the word [word], and it is the [first, second, third] sound. We want the sound [target sound].

   Continue until students select the correct letter.

9. Repeat the activity to build the following words:

   ▸ *hog* /h/ /ŏ/ /g/
   ▸ *pet* /p/ /ĕ/ /t/
   ▸ *yes* /y/ /ĕ/ /s/

Try It

"The Ten Red Hens"

Have students read "The Ten Red Hens" on page 1 of *K¹² PhonicsWorks Readers Basic 4*.

Students should read the story silently once or twice before reading the story aloud. When students miss a word that can be sounded out, point to it and give them three to six seconds to try the word again. If students still miss the word, tell them the word so the flow of the story isn't interrupted.

After reading the story, make a list of all the words students missed, and go over those words with them. You may use tiles to show students how to read the words.

Dictation: Write Words

Have students practice identifying sounds and writing words.

1. Gather a pencil and the dictation notebook. Say the word *let*. Then give these directions to students:

    ▸ Repeat the word.
    ▸ Write the word in your notebook.
    ▸ Read the word aloud.

2. When students have finished, write the following word on your whiteboard: *let*.

3. Have them compare their answer to your correct version.

4. Repeat this procedure with the words *hen*, *peg*, and *yet*.

    ▸ If students make an error and don't see it, help them correct their mistake by having them finger stretch the sounds in the word they missed.
    ▸ If students are having difficulty selecting the correct letters or sounds, review those letters or sounds that are confusing them.
    ▸ If students have difficulty with first, middle, and last sounds, have them finger stretch the sounds in words.

Objectives

- Read aloud grade-level text with appropriate automaticity, prosody, accuracy, and rate.
- Decode words by applying grade-level word analysis skills.
- Track text from left to right.
- Turn pages sequentially.
- Write words by applying grade-level phonics knowledge.
- Follow three-step directions.
- Identify and use the sound /ĕ/.
- Identify and use the sound /y/.

 **20 minutes**

REVIEW: **Sounds for Letters *e* and *y***

Students will work online independently to

▸ Practice the sounds /ĕ/ and /y/ made by the letters *e* and *y*.

Help students locate the online activities and provide support as needed.

Offline Alternative

No computer access? Have students name the letters that make the sounds /ĕ/ and /y/. Vice versa, have students name the sounds made by the letters *e* and *y*. You might also ask students to spell simple words that contain the sounds /ĕ/ and /y/ made by the letters *e* and *y* and other letters students have learned, such as *set, men, yen,* and *yes*.

Objectives

- Identify the letter, given the sound /ĕ/.
- Identify the sound, given the letter *e*.
- Identify the letter, given the sound /y/.
- Identify the sound, given the letter *y*.
- Identify individual sounds in words.

Unit Checkpoint

Lesson Overview

 【Online】 **REVIEW:** Sounds for Letters *e* and *y* · **20** minutes

【Offline】 **UNIT CHECKPOINT:** Sounds for Letters *e* and *y* · **30** minutes

【Materials】

Supplied
- *K¹² PhonicsWorks Basic Assessments,* pp. PH 91–96

Objectives
- Identify the letter, given the sound /ĕ/.
- Identify the sound, given the letter *e*.
- Identify the letter, given the sound /y/.
- Identify the sound, given the letter *y*.
- Identify individual sounds in words.
- Given the letter, identify the most common sound.
- Given the sound, identify the most common letter or letters.
- Read sight words.
- Read instructional-level text with 90% accuracy.
- Read aloud grade-level text with appropriate automaticity, prosody, accuracy, and rate.
- Write words by applying grade-level phonics knowledge.

 **【Online】** **20** minutes

REVIEW: **Sounds for Letters *e* and *y***

Students will review sounds for the letters *e* and *y* to prepare for the Unit Checkpoint. Help students locate the online activities and provide support as needed.

 **30 minutes**

UNIT CHECKPOINT: Sounds for Letters *e* and *y*

Explain that students are going to show what they have learned about letters, sounds, and words.

1. Give students the Unit Checkpoint pages for the Sounds for Letters *e* and *y* unit and print the Unit Checkpoint Answer Key, if you'd like.

2. Use the instructions below to help administer the Checkpoint to students. On the Answer Key or another sheet of paper, note student answers to oral response questions to help with scoring the Checkpoint later.

3. Use the Answer Key to score the Checkpoint, and then enter the results online.

Part 1. Say Sounds Have students read across the rows from left to right and say a sound that each letter or letters make. Note any sounds they say incorrectly.

Part 2. Word Dissection For each word, say the sound students should identify. Have them read the word aloud and circle the letter or group of letters that spells the requested sound.

19. *middle sound*

20. *ending sound*

21. *beginning sound*

22. *ending sound*

23. *middle sound*

Part 3. Finger Stretching Say each word to students. Have them say each word and finger stretch the sounds. Note any words they finger stretch incorrectly.

24. *yet*   26. *rid*

25. *men*   27. *wet*

Part 4. Dictation Say each word to students. Have them repeat and write the word.

28. *yes*   30. *bed*

29. *get*   31. *ten*

Part 5. Read Aloud Listen to students read the sentences aloud. Count and note the number of words they read correctly.

Part 6. Say Letters Say each sound. Have students say the letter or letters that make that sound. Note any incorrect responses.

33. /ĕ/

34. /ă/

35. /ŏ/

36. /y/

37. /ks/

38. /ĕ/

39. /ĭ/

40. /kw/

41. /ŭ/

42. /ă/

43. /ĕ/

44. /ĭ/

45. /ŭ/

46. /y/

47. /ŏ/

48. /w/

49. /z/

50. /ĕ/

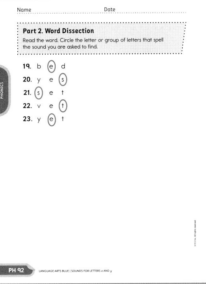

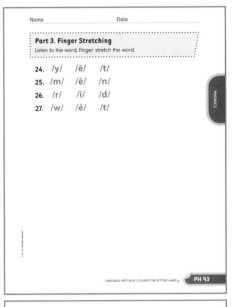

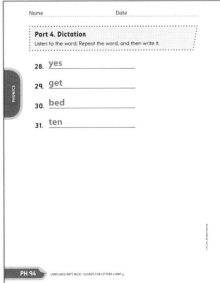

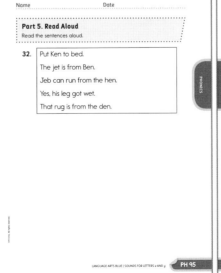

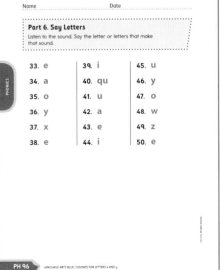

Getting Stronger: Sounds /ă/, /ĕ/, /ĭ/, /ŏ/, and /ŭ/ (A)

Unit Overview

In this unit, students will
- ▸ Review sight words.
- ▸ Identify the letters and sounds in the alphabet.
- ▸ Practice the sounds /ă/, /ĕ/, /ĭ/, /ŏ/, and /ŭ/.
- ▸ Identify beginning and ending sounds in words.
- ▸ Build words.

[Materials]

Supplied
- K¹² PhonicsWorks Basic Activity Book, p. PH 51
- whiteboard, student
- Tile Kit

Also Needed
- sight words box

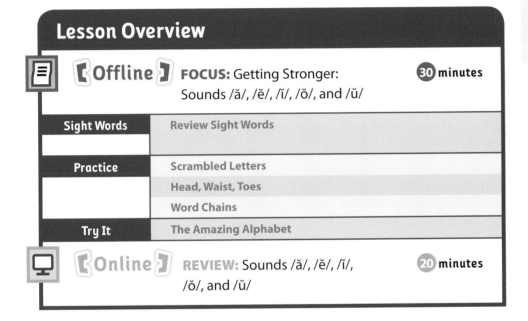

Lesson Overview

▤	[Offline] FOCUS: Getting Stronger: Sounds /ă/, /ĕ/, /ĭ/, /ŏ/, and /ŭ/	**30** minutes

Sight Words	Review Sight Words
Practice	Scrambled Letters
	Head, Waist, Toes
	Word Chains
Try It	The Amazing Alphabet

🖥	[Online] REVIEW: Sounds /ă/, /ĕ/, /ĭ/, /ŏ/, and /ŭ/	**20** minutes

 **Offline** 🕒 **30** minutes

FOCUS: Getting Stronger: Sounds /ă/, /ĕ/, /ĭ/, /ŏ/, and /ŭ/

Work **together** with students to complete offline Sight Words, Practice, and Try It activities.

Sight Words

Review Sight Words

Help students learn to recognize sight words.

1. Gather all the sight word cards students have yet to master from their sight words box. Stack the cards on the table face down.

2. Have students pick up a word and read it to you.

3. If they read it quickly and correctly, put the card in one stack. If they hesitate or do not read the word correctly, put it in another stack. The second stack should have words that they will review again.

4. Take the stack of words that students read correctly and dictate each word to them. They may choose to either write the word or spell it aloud.

5. If students spell the word correctly, they have mastered the word. If they misspell the word, add it to the stack of cards to review again.

6. Chart students' progress on the back of each card.

   ▸ Divide the back of the card into two columns.
   ▸ Label the first column "Read" and the second column "Spell."
   ▸ Record the dates that students read or spell the word correctly. When students can read and spell the word correctly three times in a row, they have mastered the word. You may want to put a star or sticker on their card when they have mastered that word.

TIP Even if students can read and spell all the words correctly, it is still beneficial for them to review sight words. Choose as many additional words as you would like for each subsequent activity.

> **Objectives**
> - Read sight words.
> - Spell sight words.
> - Write sight words.

Practice

Scrambled Letters

To help students master the alphabet, have them practice identifying and naming letters.

1. Place the following letter tiles in random order on students' whiteboard: *a, b, c, e, g, o, p, r, u,* and *w.*

2. Have students arrange the letters in alphabetical order.

(TIP) Students may find this activity easier if they slowly sing "The Alphabet Song" to themselves as they work.

Head, Waist, Toes

Help students practice identifying the sounds in words.

1. **Say:** Let's identify sounds in words by touching parts of our body as we say each sound. For example, I'll say *ant,* which has three sounds, and you'll repeat the word. Do these steps with me:

   ▸ The first sound in *ant* is /ă/, so I touch my head as I say /ă/.
   ▸ The middle sound is /n/, so I touch my waist as I say /n/.
   ▸ The last sound is /t/, so I touch my toes as I say /t/.

2. Say the words below. Have students repeat each word and then touch their head, waist, and toes as they say each sound in the word. After they say the sounds in each word, ask them the question for that word.

   ▸ nut /n/ /ŭ/ /t/   What is the first sound? /n/
   ▸ six /s/ /ĭ/ /ks/   What is the middle sound? /ĭ/
   ▸ fan /f/ /ă/ /n/   What is the first sound? /f/
   ▸ get /g/ /ĕ/ /t/   What is the last sound? /t/
   ▸ fin /f/ /ĭ/ /n/   What is the first sound? /f/
   ▸ bun /b/ /ŭ/ /n/   What is the middle sound? /ŭ/

(TIP) If students have difficulty with this activity, be sure they can identify beginning, middle, and ending. If they still have difficulty with this activity, try finger stretching the words instead.

Objectives

- Identify letters of the alphabet.
- Identify short vowel sounds.
- Identify and use the sound /ă/.
- Identify and use the sound /ĕ/.
- Identify and use the sound /ĭ/.
- Identify and use the sound /ŏ/.
- Identify and use the sound /ŭ/.
- Identify individual sounds in words.
- Identify the new word when one sound is changed in a word.

Word Chains

Have students build words by adding and changing letters to help them recognize and use individual sounds in words.

1. Place the following letters at the top of students' whiteboard: *b, e, d, g, i,* and *p.*

2. **Say:** I am going to build the first word in a chain. The word is *bed.*

   ▶ I will pull down the letters for the sounds /b/, /ĕ/, and /d/ to spell the word *bed.*

   ▶ Next I will touch and say *bed.* To change *bed* to *beg,* I will think about what sound is changed from the word *bed* to *beg.* We will need to change the letter *d* to the letter *g* at the end of the word to make the word *beg.*

   ▶ Touch and say the word *beg.* Now it's your turn to change *beg* to *peg.* You can spell *peg* by making only one change. Touch and say the new word.

3. Redirect students if they select the incorrect letter for any sound.

   Say: That letter is for the sound [incorrect sound]. We want the letter for the sound [target sound]. What letter makes that sound? Answers will vary.

4. Redirect students if they name the sound incorrectly.

   Say: To change the word [first word] to [target word], we need the letter for the sound [target sound].

   Show students how to make the change. Have them touch and say the new word after they move the letters.

5. Follow this procedure to make the following words: *pig* and *big.*

6. For every new word, have students add, replace, or remove only one letter.

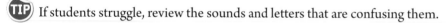 **TIP** If students struggle, review the sounds and letters that are confusing them.

Try It

The Amazing Alphabet

Have students complete page PH 51 in *K[12] PhonicsWorks Basic Activity Book* for more practice with the sounds /ă/, /ĕ/, /ĭ/, /ŏ/, and /ŭ/. Have students circle the letter that makes the vowel sound in the name of the picture and write the letter. Have them read the word aloud.

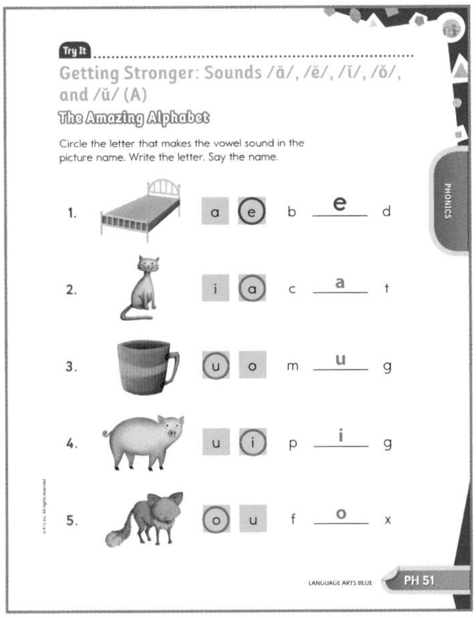
Try It

Getting Stronger: Sounds /ă/, /ĕ/, /ĭ/, /ŏ/, and /ŭ/ (A)

The Amazing Alphabet

Circle the letter that makes the vowel sound in the picture name. Write the letter. Say the name.

1. a (e) b _e_ d
2. i (a) c _a_ t
3. (u) o m _u_ g
4. u (i) p _i_ g
5. (o) u f _o_ x

PHONICS

LANGUAGE ARTS BLUE PH 51

> **Objectives**
> - Read aloud grade-level text with appropriate automaticity, prosody, accuracy, and rate.
> - Write words by applying grade-level phonics knowledge.
> - Identify and use the sound /ă/.
> - Identify and use the sound /ĕ/.
> - Identify and use the sound /ĭ/.
> - Identify and use the sound /ŏ/.
> - Identify and use the sound /ŭ/.

Online 20 minutes

REVIEW: Sounds /ă/, /ĕ/, /ĭ/, /ŏ/, and /ŭ/

Students will work online independently to

- Practice the sounds /ă/, /ĕ/, /ĭ/, /ŏ/, and /ŭ/ made by the letters *a*, *e*, *i*, *o*, and *u*.
- Practice decoding text by reading sentences.

Help students locate the online activities and provide support as needed.

Offline Alternative

No computer access? Have students point out and name things or words that contain the short vowel sounds /ă/, /ĕ/, /ĭ/, /ŏ/, and /ŭ/, such as *act*, *elbow*, *itch*, *fog*, and *ugly*. You might also ask students to spell simple words that contain the sounds /ă/, /ĕ/, /ĭ/, /ŏ/, and /ŭ/ made by the letters *a*, *e*, *i*, *o*, and *u* and other letters students have learned.

> **Objectives**
> - Identify and use the sound /ă/.
> - Identify and use the sound /ĕ/.
> - Identify and use the sound /ĭ/.
> - Identify and use the sound /ŏ/.
> - Identify and use the sound /ŭ/.
> - Identify individual sounds in words.
> - Read aloud grade-level text with appropriate automaticity, prosody, accuracy, and rate.
> - Decode words by applying grade-level word analysis skills.

Getting Stronger: Sounds /ă/, /ě/, /ĭ/, /ŏ/, and /ŭ/ (B)

Lesson Overview

[Offline] **FOCUS:** Getting Stronger: Sounds /ă/, /ě/, /ĭ/, /ŏ/, and /ŭ/   **30** minutes

Sight Words	Use Words in Sentences
Practice	Listen for Short Vowel Sounds
	Review Vowel Sounds and Letters
	Word Walk
Try It	"Ted"

[Online] **REVIEW:** Sounds /ă/, /ě/, /ĭ/, /ŏ/, and /ŭ/   **20** minutes

[Materials]

Supplied
- *K¹² PhonicsWorks Readers Basic 4*, pp. 7–12
- whiteboard, student
- Tile Kit

Also Needed
- sight words box

 **[Offline]** **30** minutes

FOCUS: Getting Stronger: Sounds /ă/, /ĕ/, /ĭ/, /ŏ/, and /ŭ/

Work **together** with students to complete offline Sight Words, Practice, and
Try It activities.

Sight Words ••

Use Words in Sentences
Help students use sight words in sentences.

1. Gather all the sight word cards students have yet to master from their sight
   words box. Spread the sight word cards on the table.

2. **Say:** Let's use sight words in sentences.

3. Have students

   ▸ Touch each card and read the word on it.
   ▸ Make up a sentence using the word.
   ▸ Put the card in a pile after using the word in a sentence.
   ▸ Go through the pile of cards and read each sight word again.
   ▸ Spell each word.

(TIP) If students have difficulty with any of the sight words, place those cards in a pile
to review again.

> **Objectives**
> ● Read sight words.
> ● Spell sight words.

Practice ••

Listen for Short Vowel Sounds
Say words with the sounds /ă/, /ĕ/, /ĭ/, /ŏ/, and /ŭ/ to help students identify the
difference between short vowel sounds.

1. **Say:** I'm going to say a word. You'll listen for the **vowel sounds /ă/, /ĕ/, /ĭ/,
   /ŏ/, or /ŭ/** in the word. Tell me the vowel sound that you hear. For example, if
   I say *mop*, you'll say /ŏ/ because the vowel sound you hear in *mop* is /ŏ/.

2. Say each word. Have students identify the vowel sound in the word.

   ▸ *lip* /ĭ/   ▸ *fin* /ĭ/
   ▸ *lap* /ă/   ▸ *fun* /ŭ/
   ▸ *sad* /ă/   ▸ *cog* /ŏ/
   ▸ *not* /ŏ/   ▸ *jet* /ĕ/
   ▸ *let* /ĕ/   ▸ *nut* /ŭ/

3. Guide students with these questions if they have difficulty identifying the
   vowel sound:

   ▸ What is the sound you hear in the middle of the word? Answers will vary.
   ▸ Do you hear the sound [target sound] in the word? Listen to the word
     again [target word].
   ▸ Can you think of another word that has the sound [target sound]? Answers
     will vary.

> **Objectives**
> ● Identify short vowel sounds.
> ● Identify and use the sound /ă/.
> ● Identify and use the sound /ĕ/.
> ● Identify and use the sound /ĭ/.
> ● Identify and use the sound /ŏ/.
> ● Identify and use the sound /ŭ/.
> ● Identify and use vowels and vowel sounds.
> ● Write words by applying grade-level phonics knowledge.
> ● Decode words by applying grade-level word analysis skills.

Review Vowel Sounds and Letters

Help students review vowel sounds and letters.

1. Place the following letter tiles on students' whiteboard: *a, e, i, o,* and *u,* plus any letters that are confusing for them.

2. **Say:** I am going to point to each letter. Tell me a sound for that letter.

3. **Say:** I am going to say a sound. Repeat the sound and touch its letter.

4. Point to some letters two or three times, so students don't think that once they have named a sound they are finished with it.

5. Redirect students if they name the letter and not its sound.

   Say: You are right that the name of the letter is [letter]. We want the sound for this letter. What is the sound?

6. Redirect students if they name the sound incorrectly.

   Say: That is the sound of another letter.

7. Provide additional guidance if students touch the wrong letter during the review.

   Say: That is the letter for the sound [sound for incorrect letter]. We are looking for the letter for the sound [target sound].

8. If students touch the wrong letter again, point to the correct letter.

   Say: This is the letter for the sound [target sound]. Touch this letter and say its sound.

Word Walk

Help students recognize words for things that are found outdoors.

1. **Say:** We're going to take a walk outside to see what we can find. You will help me write a list of things that we may find.

2. Help students write things they might see outdoors.

   Say: If you think we will see something, write it on your list. Remember, when we take our walk, check off each thing you see.

TIP If the weather is bad, create a list of words that the student is likely to see indoors, and add those words to the list before you do a word walk inside.

Try It ··

"Ted"

Have students read "Ted" on page 7 of *K¹² PhonicsWorks Readers Basic 4.*

 Students should read the story silently once or twice before reading the story aloud. When students miss a word that can be sounded out, point to it and give them three to six seconds to try the word again. If students still miss the word, tell them the word so the flow of the story isn't interrupted.

 After reading the story, make a list of all the words students missed, and go over those words with them. You may use tiles to show students how to read the words.

Objectives
- Read aloud grade-level text with appropriate automaticity, prosody, accuracy, and rate.
- Decode words by applying grade-level word analysis skills.
- Track text from left to right.
- Turn pages sequentially.

 **20 minutes**

REVIEW: Sounds /ă/, /ĕ/, /ĭ/, /ŏ/, and /ŭ/

Students will work online independently to

▶ Practice the sounds /ă/, /ĕ/, /ĭ/, /ŏ/, and /ŭ/ made by the letters *a, e, i, o,* and *u.*

Help students locate the online activities and provide support as needed.

Offline Alternative

No computer access? Have students point out and name things or words that contain the short vowel sounds /ă/, /ĕ/, /ĭ/, /ŏ/, and /ŭ/, such as *hat, red, pit, job,* and *rug.* You might also ask students to spell simple words that contain the sounds /ă/, /ĕ/, /ĭ/, /ŏ/, and /ŭ/ made by the letters *a, e, i, o,* and *u* and other letters students have learned.

Objectives
- Identify and use the sound /ă/.
- Identify and use the sound /ĕ/.
- Identify and use the sound /ĭ/.
- Identify and use the sound /ŏ/.
- Identify and use the sound /ŭ/.
- Identify individual sounds in words.

Getting Stronger: Sounds /ă/, /ĕ/, /ĭ/, /ŏ/, and /ŭ/ (C)

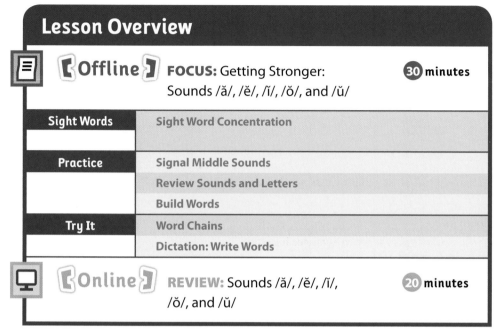

Lesson Overview

Offline	**FOCUS:** Getting Stronger: Sounds /ă/, /ĕ/, /ĭ/, /ŏ/, and /ŭ/	**30** minutes

Sight Words	Sight Word Concentration
Practice	Signal Middle Sounds
	Review Sounds and Letters
	Build Words
Try It	Word Chains
	Dictation: Write Words

Online	**REVIEW:** Sounds /ă/, /ĕ/, /ĭ/, /ŏ/, and /ŭ/	**20** minutes

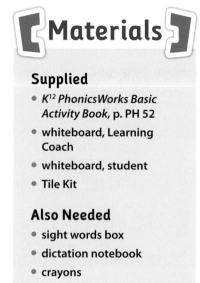

[Materials]

Supplied
- *K¹² PhonicsWorks Basic Activity Book*, p. PH 52
- whiteboard, Learning Coach
- whiteboard, student
- Tile Kit

Also Needed
- sight words box
- dictation notebook
- crayons

Advance Preparation

Gather two sets of all the sight word cards you have used to date.

 **30 minutes**

FOCUS: Getting Stronger: Sounds /ă/, /ĕ/, /ĭ/, /ŏ/, and /ŭ/

Work **together** with students to complete offline Sight Words, Practice, and Try It activities.

Sight Words ··

Sight Word Concentration
Help students review sight words.

1. Gather the two sets of sight word cards.

2. Scramble both sets of sight word cards and place them face down on the table or floor.

3. Turn over two cards at a time; take turns with students. If the cards match, the person turning over the matching cards reads the word and uses it in a sentence. If the cards don't match, the person turns them back over.

4. Remove and save the matching cards.

5. Continue the activity until all the cards are paired.

6. Have students read all the words.

7. Take the stack of words that students read correctly and dictate each word to them.

8. Have students write each word or spell it aloud.

TIP If students have difficulty with any of the sight words, let them work at their own pace to really master these words.

 Objectives
- Read sight words.
- Spell sight words.
- Write sight words.

Practice ●

Signal Middle Sounds

Use a special signal to help students identify **middle sounds** in words.

1. **Say:** I'm going to tell you a special sound, and then I'll say some words. Repeat each word I say and make a special signal to tell me where the sound is. If the special sound is at the middle of the word, pat your cheek. If the special sound is **not** at the middle of the word, just smile at me. For example,

   ▸ If I ask you to listen for the sound /ă/ and I say the word *mat*, you'll repeat the word *mat* and pat your cheek because *mat* has the sound /ă/ in the middle.

   ▸ If I say the word *pop*, you'll repeat the word *pop* and smile at me because *pop* has the sound /ŏ/, not /ă/, in the middle.

2. Say each sound and group of words. Have students make the special signal to identify the middle sound.

   ▸ /ă/: *cat, ten, tip, tap, fan* pat cheek: *cat, tap, fan*
   ▸ /ĕ/: *fat, fed, sod, met, set* pat cheek: *fed, met, set*
   ▸ /ĭ/: *pit, fin, pod, gut, six* pat cheek: *pit, fin, six*
   ▸ /ŏ/: *got, sag, gap, pot, cob* pat cheek: *got, pot, cob*
   ▸ /ŭ/: *hog, tug, Gus, top, shut* pat cheek: *tug, Gus, shut*

3. Guide students with these questions if they have difficulty identifying the vowel sound:

   ▸ What is the sound you hear in the middle of the word? Answers will vary.
   ▸ Do you hear the sound [target sound] in the word? Listen to the word again [target word].
   ▸ Can you think of another word that has the sound [target sound]? Answers will vary.

TIP If students can't identify the middle sound of each word, say the word again and emphasize the middle sound by stretching it out (for example, *reeeeed*). If necessary, have them look at your mouth while you stretch the sounds.

Objectives

- Identify short vowel sounds.
- Identify and use the sound /ă/.
- Identify and use the sound /ĕ/.
- Identify and use the sound /ĭ/.
- Identify and use the sound /ŏ/.
- Identify and use the sound /ŭ/.
- Identify and use vowels and vowel sounds.
- Given the letter, identify the most common sound.
- Given the sound, identify the most common letter or letters.
- Blend sounds to create words.

Review Sounds and Letters

Help students review sounds for the letters *d, g, i, n, o, qu, s,* and *w*, plus any letters that are confusing for them.

1. Place the following letter tiles in random order on students' whiteboard: *d, g, i, n, o, qu, s,* and *w*, plus any letters that are confusing.

2. **Say:** Let's go over some letters and sounds.

3. Point to each letter tile and have students say a sound that letter or letters make.

   ▸ *d* /d/   ▸ *o* /ŏ/
   ▸ *w* /w/   ▸ *i* /ĭ/
   ▸ *qu* /kw/   ▸ *s* /s/
   ▸ *n* /n/   ▸ *g* /g/

4. Say each of the following sounds. Have students repeat the sound and touch the corresponding letter tile.

- ▸ /d/ *d*
- ▸ /w/ *w*
- ▸ /kw/ *qu*
- ▸ /n/ *n*

- ▸ /ŏ/ *o*
- ▸ /ĭ/ *i*
- ▸ /s/ *s*
- ▸ /g/ *g*

5. As you do the activity, point to some letter tiles two or three times so that students don't think they are finished with a sound after they have named it.

6. Redirect students if they say an incorrect sound when you point to a letter tile.

   Say: That's the sound of another letter. What is the sound for this letter?

7. Help students if they touch the wrong letter tile after they repeat a sound.

   Say: That letter goes with the sound [sound for incorrect letter tile]. We're looking for the letter that goes with the sound [target sound].

Build Words
Help students use letters and sounds to build words.

1. Place the following letter tiles at the top of students' whiteboard: *a, b, c, e, g, i, l, o, p, t, u,* and *y.*

2. Draw three horizontal lines across the middle of students' whiteboard to represent the sounds in a word.

3. **Say:** Let's use letters and sounds to build the word *leg.*

4. Have students finger stretch the sounds in *leg.*

5. Have students

   - ▸ Identify the first, next, and last sounds in *leg.*
   - ▸ Choose the corresponding letter for each of the sounds.
   - ▸ Move the letters to the correct lines on their whiteboard.

6. Guide students with these questions:

   - ▸ What is the first sound in *leg*? /l/
     Which line does the letter for that sound go on? the first one
   - ▸ What is the next sound in *leg*? /ĕ/
     Which line does the letter for that sound go on? the second one
   - ▸ What's the last sound in *leg*? /g/
     Which line does the letter for that sound go on? the last one

7. Have students touch and say the word.

8. Redirect students if they select the incorrect letter.

   Say: That sound is in the word [word], and it is the [first, second, third] sound. We want the sound [target sound].

   Continue until students select the correct letter.

9. Repeat the activity to build the following words:

   ► *cap* /k/ /ă/ /p/
   ► *bug* /b/ /ŭ/ /g/
   ► *yip* /y/ /ĭ/ /p/
   ► *top* /t/ /ŏ/ /p/

Try It

Word Chains

Have students complete page PH 52 in *K¹² PhonicsWorks Basic Activity Book* for more practice with the sounds /ă/, /ĕ/, /ĭ/, /ŏ/, and /ŭ/. Have students read each word and color the box that has the changed letter.

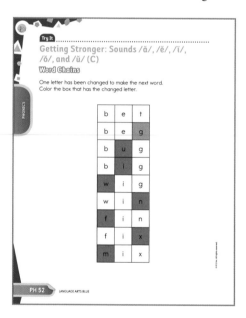

Objectives
- Identify the new word when one sound is changed in a word.
- Identify individual sounds in words.
- Write words by applying grade-level phonics knowledge.
- Follow three-step directions.

Dictation: Write Words

Have students practice identifying sounds and writing words.

1. Gather a pencil and the dictation notebook. Say the word *tug*. Then give these directions to students:

   ▸ Repeat the word.
   ▸ Write the word in your notebook.
   ▸ Read the word aloud.

2. When students have finished, write the following word on your whiteboard: *tug*.

3. Have them compare their answer to your correct version.

4. Repeat this procedure with the words *met* and *pod*.

   ▸ If students make an error and don't see it, help them correct their mistake by having them finger stretch the sounds in the word they missed.
   ▸ If students are having difficulty selecting the correct letters or sounds, review those letters or sounds that are confusing them.
   ▸ If students have difficulty with first, middle, and last sounds, have them finger stretch the sounds in words.

 **20 minutes**

REVIEW: **Sounds /ă/, /ĕ/, /ĭ/, /ŏ/, and /ŭ/**

Students will work online independently to

▸ Practice the sounds /ă/, /ĕ/, /ĭ/, /ŏ/, and /ŭ/ made by the letters *a, e, i, o,* and *u*.
▸ Practice decoding text by reading a story.

Help students locate the online activities and provide support as needed.

Offline Alternative

No computer access? Have students point out and name things or words that contain the short vowel sounds /ă/, /ĕ/, /ĭ/, /ŏ/, and /ŭ/, such as *ant, bed, fin, pot,* and *cup*. You might also ask students to spell simple words that contain the sounds /ă/, /ĕ/, /ĭ/, /ŏ/, and /ŭ/ made by the letters *a, e, i, o,* and *u* and other letters students have learned.

 Objectives

- Identify and use the sound /ă/.
- Identify and use the sound /ĕ/.
- Identify and use the sound /ĭ/.
- Identify and use the sound /ŏ/.
- Identify and use the sound /ŭ/.
- Identify individual sounds in words.
- Read aloud grade-level text with appropriate automaticity, prosody, accuracy, and rate.
- Decode words by applying grade-level word analysis skills.

Getting Stronger: Sounds /ă/, /ĕ/, /ĭ/, /ŏ/, and /ŭ/ (D)

Lesson Overview

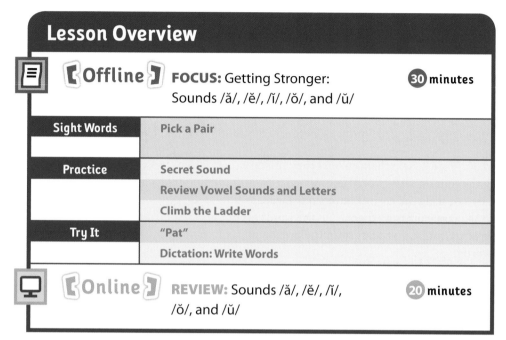

	Offline FOCUS: Getting Stronger: Sounds /ă/, /ĕ/, /ĭ/, /ŏ/, and /ŭ/	**30** minutes
Sight Words	Pick a Pair	
Practice	Secret Sound	
	Review Vowel Sounds and Letters	
	Climb the Ladder	
Try It	"Pat"	
	Dictation: Write Words	
	Online REVIEW: Sounds /ă/, /ĕ/, /ĭ/, /ŏ/, and /ŭ/	**20** minutes

Materials

Supplied

- *K¹² PhonicsWorks Readers Basic 4*, pp. 13–18
- whiteboard, Learning Coach
- whiteboard, student
- Tile Kit

Also Needed

- sight words box
- dictation notebook

 **30 minutes**

FOCUS: Getting Stronger: Sounds /ă/, /ĕ/, /ĭ/, /ŏ/, and /ŭ/

Work **together** with students to complete offline Sight Words, Practice, and
Try It activities.

Sight Words ....

Pick a Pair

Play a card game with students for more practice with sight words.

1. Gather the sight word cards that students are reviewing. Choose two words
   and place the cards on the table.

2. Ask questions to help students identify each word. For example, if the words
   are *or* and *one*, you could ask, "Which word names a number?" If the words are
   on and *but*, you could ask, "Which word is the opposite of *off*?"

3. Continue the activity until students identify all the words.

4. Take the stack of words that students read correctly and dictate each word
   to them.

5. Have students write each word or spell it aloud.

 Objectives
- Read sight words.
- Spell sight words.
- Write sight words.

Practice ....

Secret Sound

Say groups of words to help students recognize **middle sounds** in words.

1. **Say:** I am going to say some groups of words. Listen for a secret sound in the
   middle of each word. Then tell me what sound you hear in the middle of each
   group of words.

2. Say each of the following groups of words. Have students identify the secret
   sound in each group.

   - *fed, step, let, met* /ĕ/
   - *tub, cub, fun, lug* /ŭ/
   - *gap, fan, mat, hat* /ă/
   - *hog, top, got, dog* /ŏ/
   - *fit, pit, zip, nip* /ĭ/

    TIP If students can't identify the secret sound, have them listen while you say each
   word again and then have them repeat each word. Have them say what sound they
   hear in the middle of each word.

Objectives
- Identify middle sounds in words.
- Identify short vowel sounds.
- Identify and use the sound /ă/.
- Identify and use the sound /ĕ/.
- Identify and use the sound /ĭ/.
- Identify and use the sound /ŏ/.
- Identify and use the sound /ŭ/.
- Identify and use vowels and vowel sounds.
- Identify individual sounds in words.

Review Vowel Sounds and Letters

Help students review vowel sounds and letters.

1. Place the following letter tiles on students' whiteboard: *a, e, i, o,* and *u,* plus any letters that are confusing for them.

2. **Say:** I am going to point to each letter. Tell me a sound for that letter.

3. **Say:** I am going to say a sound. Repeat the sound and touch its letter.

4. Point to some letters two or three times, so students don't think that once they have named a sound they are finished with it.

5. Redirect students if they name the letter and not its sound.

   Say: You are right that the name of the letter is [letter]. We want the sound for this letter. What is the sound?

6. Redirect students if they name the sound incorrectly.

   Say: That is the sound of another letter.

7. Provide additional guidance if students touch the wrong letter during the review.

   Say: That is the letter for the sound [sound for incorrect letter]. We are looking for the letter for the sound [target sound].

8. If students touch the wrong letter again, point to the correct letter.

   Say: This is the letter for the sound [target sound]. Touch this letter and say its sound.

Climb the Ladder

Help students use letters to build words.

1. On students' whiteboard or a sheet of paper, draw a ladder with five or more rungs.

2. Write the word *cup* on the bottom rung.

3. Point to the word *cup*.

   Say: I can make the word *pup* by changing one letter in this word.

4. Write the word *pup* on the second rung of the ladder.

   Say: Think of a word that you can make by changing only one letter in *pup*. Tell me the word and write it on the next step on the ladder.

5. If students struggle, coach them to change the first letter in each word.

   Say: Read the word on the bottom rung. What sound do you hear at the beginning of the word? What letter has that sound?

   Say: Name a word that rhymes with the word at the bottom. What sound do you hear at the beginning of the rhyming word? What letter has that sound? Make a new word by using the new letter. Read the new word.

6. Continue the process until students reach the top of the ladder. Remind students that they may change only one sound: the beginning, middle, or last sound.

7. Redirect students if they select a word that changes more than one letter.

   Say: How many letters changed from the last word to your new word? Try to think of a word that has only one letter change.

8. Redirect students if they spell a word incorrectly but the sounds they spell are correct (such as *ruf* for *rough*).

   Say: You have the sounds and letters right, but that word doesn't follow our spelling rules. We will learn how to spell it later. Try another word.

(TIP) If students have difficulty thinking of real words, have them use nonsense words.

Try It

"Pat"

Have students read "Pat" on page 13 of *K¹² PhonicsWorks Readers Basic 4*.

Students should read the story silently once or twice before reading the story aloud. When students miss a word that can be sounded out, point to it and give them three to six seconds to try the word again. If students still miss the word, tell them the word so the flow of the story isn't interrupted.

After reading the story, make a list of all the words students missed, and go over those words with them. You may use tiles to show students how to read the words.

Dictation: Write Words

Have students practice identifying sounds and writing words.

1. Gather a pencil and the dictation notebook. Say the word *sun*. Then give these directions to students:

   ▶ Repeat the word.
   ▶ Write the word in your notebook.
   ▶ Read the word aloud.

2. When students have finished, write the following word on your whiteboard: *sun*.

3. Have them compare their answer to your correct version.

4. Repeat this procedure with the words *tin* and *yet*.

   ▶ If students make an error and don't see it, help them correct their mistake by having them finger stretch the sounds in the word they missed.
   ▶ If students are having difficulty selecting the correct letters or sounds, review those letters or sounds that are confusing them.
   ▶ If students have difficulty with first, middle, and last sounds, have them finger stretch the sounds in words.

Objectives

- Read aloud grade-level text with appropriate automaticity, prosody, accuracy, and rate.
- Decode words by applying grade-level word analysis skills.
- Track text from left to right.
- Turn pages sequentially.
- Write words by applying grade-level phonics knowledge.
- Follow three-step directions.
- Identify and use vowels and vowel sounds.

 **20 minutes**

REVIEW: Sounds /ă/, /ĕ/, /ĭ/, /ŏ/, and /ŭ/

Students will work online independently to

▶ Practice the sounds /ă/, /ĕ/, /ĭ/, /ŏ/, and /ŭ/ made by the letters *a*, *e*, *i*, *o*, and *u*.

Help students locate the online activities and provide support as needed.

Offline Alternative

No computer access? Have students point out and name things or words that contain the short vowel sounds /ă/, /ĕ/, /ĭ/, /ŏ/, and /ŭ/, such as *cat*, *pet*, *quit*, *on*, and *hum*. You might also ask students to spell simple words that contain the sounds /ă/, /ĕ/, /ĭ/, /ŏ/, and /ŭ/ made by the letters *a*, *e*, *i*, *o*, and *u* and other letters they have learned.

Objectives

- Identify and use the sound /ă/.
- Identify and use the sound /ĕ/.
- Identify and use the sound /ĭ/.
- Identify and use the sound /ŏ/.
- Identify and use the sound /ŭ/.
- Identify individual sounds in words.

Unit Checkpoint

Lesson Overview

 【Online】 REVIEW: Sounds /ă/, /ĕ/, /ĭ/, /ŏ/, and /ŭ/ — **20** minutes

【Offline】 UNIT CHECKPOINT: Getting Stronger: Sounds /ă/, /ĕ/, /ĭ/, /ŏ/, and /ŭ/ — **30** minutes

【Materials】

Supplied
- *K¹² PhonicsWorks Basic Assessments,* pp. PH 97–102

Objectives
- Identify and use the sound /ă/.
- Identify and use the sound /ĕ/.
- Identify and use the sound /ĭ/.
- Identify and use the sound /ŏ/.
- Identify and use the sound /ŭ/
- Identify individual sounds in words.
- Given the letter, identify the most common sound.
- Given the sound, identify the most common letter or letters.

- Read sight words.
- Read instructional-level text with 90% accuracy.
- Read aloud grade-level text with appropriate automaticity, prosody, accuracy, and rate.
- Write words by applying grade-level phonics knowledge.

 **【Online】** **20** minutes

REVIEW: **Sounds /ă/, /ĕ/, /ĭ/, /ŏ/, and /ŭ/**

Students will review the sounds /ă/, /ĕ/, /ĭ/, /ŏ/, and /ŭ/ to prepare for the Unit Checkpoint. Help students locate the online activities and provide support as needed.

 **30 minutes**

UNIT CHECKPOINT: Getting Stronger: Sounds /ă/, /ĕ/, /ĭ/, /ŏ/, and /ŭ/

Explain that students are going to show what they have learned about letters, sounds, and words.

1. Give students the Unit Checkpoint pages for the Getting Stronger: Sounds /ă/, /ĕ/, /ĭ/, /ŏ/, and /ŭ/ unit and print the Unit Checkpoint Answer Key, if you'd like.

2. Use the instructions below to help administer the Checkpoint to students. On the Answer Key or another sheet of paper, note student answers to oral response questions to help with scoring the Checkpoint later.

3. Use the Answer Key to score the Checkpoint, and then enter the results online.

Part 1. Say Sounds Have students read across the rows from left to right and say a sound that each letter makes. Note any sounds they say incorrectly.

Part 2. Word Dissection For each word, say the sound students should identify. Have them read the word aloud and circle the letter or group of letters that spells the requested sound.

19. *middle sound*

20. *ending sound*

21. *beginning sound*

22. *ending sound*

23. *middle sound*

Part 3. Finger Stretching Say each word to students. Have them say each word and finger stretch the sounds. Note any words they finger stretch incorrectly.

24. *fox*   27. *tab*

25. *yes*   28. *run*

26. *win*

Part 4. Dictation Say each word to students. Have them repeat and write the word.

29. *red*   31. *cup*

30. *bat*   32. *tin*

Part 5. Read Aloud Listen to students read the sentences aloud. Count and note the number of words they read correctly.

Part 6. Say Letters Say each sound. Have students say the letter or letters that make that sound. Note any incorrect responses.

34. /w/	**43.** /ă/
35. /ă/	**44.** /m/
36. /ŏ/	**45.** /ŏ/
37. /y/	**46.** /p/
38. /ks/	**47.** /f/
39. /ĕ/	**48.** /b/
40. /g/	**49.** /kw/
41. /k/	**50.** /z/
42. /v/	**51.** /d/

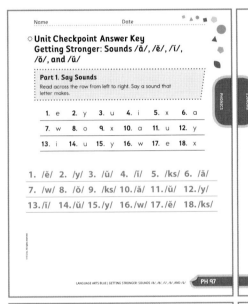

Name _____ Date _____

Unit Checkpoint Answer Key
Getting Stronger: Sounds /ă/, /ĕ/, /ĭ/, /ŏ/, and /ŭ/

Part 1. Say Sounds
Read across the row from left to right. Say a sound that letter makes.

1. e 2. y 3. u 4. i 5. x 6. a
7. w 8. o 9. x 10. a 11. u 12. y
13. i 14. u 15. y 16. w 17. e 18. x

1. /ĕ/ 2. /y/ 3. /ŭ/ 4. /ĭ/ 5. /ks/ 6. /ă/
7. /w/ 8. /ŏ/ 9. /ks/ 10. /ă/ 11. /ŭ/ 12. /y/
13. /ĭ/ 14. /ŭ/ 15. /y/ 16. /w/ 17. /ĕ/ 18. /ks/

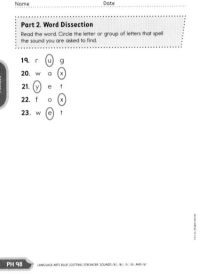

Name _____ Date _____

Part 2. Word Dissection
Read the word. Circle the letter or group of letters that spell the sound you are asked to find.

19. r (u) g
20. w a (x)
21. (y) e t
22. f o (x)
23. w (e) t

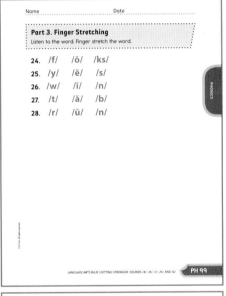

Name _____ Date _____

Part 3. Finger Stretching
Listen to the word. Finger stretch the word.

24. /f/ /ŏ/ /ks/
25. /y/ /ĕ/ /s/
26. /w/ /ĭ/ /n/
27. /t/ /ă/ /b/
28. /r/ /ŭ/ /n/

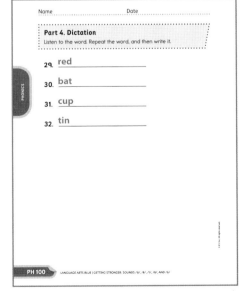

Name _____ Date _____

Part 4. Dictation
Listen to the word. Repeat the word, and then write it.

29. red
30. bat
31. cup
32. tin

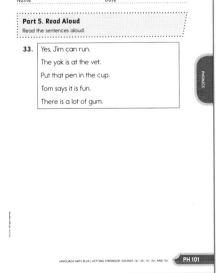

Name _____ Date _____

Part 5. Read Aloud
Read the sentences aloud.

33.
Yes, Jim can run.
The yak is at the vet.
Put that pen in the cup.
Tom says it is fun.
There is a lot of gum.

Name _____ Date _____

Part 6. Say Letters
Listen to the sound. Say the letter or letters that make that sound.

34. w	40. g	46. p
35. a	41. k or c	47. f
36. o	42. v	48. b
37. y	43. a	49. qu
38. x	44. m	50. z
39. e	45. o	51. d

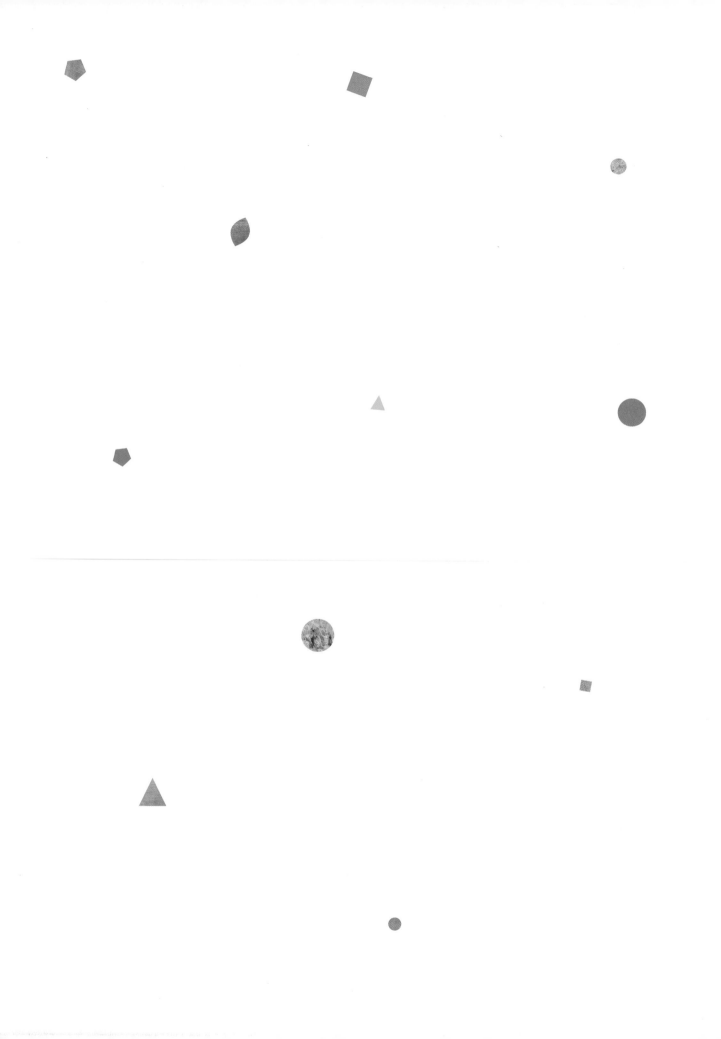